By the same author

MUCH DEPENDS ON DINNER

MARGARET VISSER

THE
RITUALS *of* DINNER

The Origins, Evolution, Eccentricities, and
Meaning of Table Manners

VIKING

VIKING

Published by the Penguin Group
Penguin Books Ltd, 27 Wrights Lane, London W8 5TZ, England
Penguin Books USA Inc., 375 Hudson Street, New York, New York 10014, USA
Penguin Books Australia Ltd, Ringwood, Victoria, Australia
Penguin Books Canada Ltd, 10 Alcorn Avenue, Toronto, Ontario, Canada M4V 3B2
Penguin Books (NZ) Ltd, 182–190 Wairau Road, Auckland 10, New Zealand

Penguin Books Ltd, Registered Offices: Harmondsworth, Middlesex, England

First published in Canada by HarperCollins Publishers Ltd 1991
First published in Great Britain by Viking 1992
1 3 5 7 9 10 8 6 4 2

Printed in England by Clays Ltd, St Ives plc

A CIP catalogue record for this book is available from the British Library

ISBN 0–670–84701–1

For Emily and Alexander

Acknowledgements

My thanks are first of all to Colin, who helped me to realize, before I finished my last book, what this one would need to be about. His support and guidance throughout have, as always, been of inestimable value to me. My children taught me most about the subject, in the course of their "learning to behave." Among the many friends who have given me ideas, suggested avenues of research, and often made me change my mind, I must especially thank the following, who read the manuscript and helped reduce the number of errors in it: my daughter Emily, Emmet Robbins, Barbara Moon, Jacqueline d'Amboise, and Pat Kennedy. Casey Rock was an ingenious research assistant in the early phases. In France, my work was greatly facilitated by the advice and practical help of the Reverend Louis Bareille and of Mme. Françoise Merlet. Most of the reading was done at Cambridge University and in the Robarts Library at the University of Toronto, with its excellent Inter-Library Loans Service. The staff of the Robarts Library in particular have been unfailingly helpful; I could never have completed the research without them. I would like to thank my editors, Walt Bode, Barbara Berson, and Ann Adelman; and my agents, Susan Petersiel and Ursula Bollini of M.G.A. I am especially grateful to Nancy Colbert of HarperCollins, who nursed the project along with patience and enthusiasm from the beginning.

Contents

Introduction

This book is a commentary on the manifold meanings of the rituals of dinner; it is about how we eat, and why we eat as we do. Human beings work hard to supply themselves with food: first we have to find it, cultivate it, hunt it, make long-term plans to transport and store it, and keep struggling to secure regular supplies of it. Next we buy it, carry it home, and keep it until we are ready. Then we prepare it, clean it, skin, chop, cook, and dish it up. Now comes the climax of all our efforts, the easiest part: eating it. And immediately we start to cloak the proceedings with a system of rules. We insist on special places and times for eating, on specific equipment, on stylized decoration, on predictable sequence among the foods eaten, on limitation of movement, and on bodily propriety. In other words, we turn the consumption of food, a biological necessity, into a carefully cultured phenomenon. We use eating as a medium for social relationships: satisfaction of the most individual of needs becomes a means of creating community.

Table manners have a history, ancient and complex: each society has gradually evolved its system, altering its ways sometimes to suit circumstance, but also vigilantly maintaining its customs in order to support its ideals and its aesthetic style, and to buttress its identity. Our own society has made choices in order to arrive at the table manners we now observe. Other people, in other parts of the world today, have rules that are different from ours, and it is important to try to comprehend the reasoning that lies behind what they do if we are to understand what we do and why.

For in spite of the differences, table manners, all things considered, are remarkably similar both historically and the world over. There is a very strong tendency everywhere to prefer cleanliness or consideration for others or the solidarity of the dining group. Ritual emphases on such matters are occasionally highly idiosyncratic. But most rituals with these meanings have a good deal in common, and when people do things differently they usually do them for reasons that are easy to understand and appreciate. Sometimes, for example, festive diners are expected to eat a lot. Feasts are exceptional occasions, and a great deal of work has gone into them: the least a guest can do is show enjoyment. Fasting beforehand may very well be necessary, and exclaiming with pleasure, smacking one's lips, and so on might be thought both polite and benevolent. Other cultures prefer to stress that food is not everything, and guzzling is disgusting: restraint before the plenty offered is admired, and signifying enjoyment by word or deed is frowned upon. Sometimes it is correct to be silent while eating: food deserves respect and concentration. In other cases one must at all costs talk: we have met not merely to feed, but to commune with fellow human beings. Even though we come down on one side or the other, we can sympathize with the concerns that lie behind the alternative choice of action.

The book is organized neither chronologically nor by culture and geography. I have elected rather to "travel," both in space and in time—to choose examples of behaviour from other places and periods of history wherever they throw light, whether by similarity or by difference, upon our own attitudes, traditions, and peculiarities of behaviour. My aim has been to enrich anyone's experience of a meal in the European and American tradition, to heighten our awareness and interest on the occasions when we might be invited to share meals in other cultures, and to give the reader some idea of the great range of tradition, significance, and social sophistication which is inherent in the actions performed during the simplest dinner eaten with family or friends.

The two opening chapters deal with basic principles. The first of these considers why it is that every human society without exception obeys eating rules; what ritual is and why we need it at dinner (cannibalism, for instance, is found to conform to strict laws and controls); and the meaning of feasting and sacrifice. The second chapter is about how people the world over teach children table manners, and how our own culture evolved its dinner-time etiquette. We have insisted more and more strictly on bodily control; and we have often used table manners to serve class systems and snobbery.

Chapter Three starts to take us through a meal eaten in company with others: the etiquette of invitations, the laws governing hosts and guests, behaviour on arriving at somebody's house for dinner, and the seating arrangements. The dinner we are about to share is a sit-down meal with friends, some of them intimate and some only slight acquaintances; the party takes place in the host's house. Such a meal invariably includes comfort, risk, and significance, complexity, plotting, setting, and dramatic structure enough to supply ample material for a book-length commentary. We necessarily leave out not only the specific menu of our meal, but also the characters and stories of individual guests, their preferences, conversation, and idiosyncrasies—everything that makes each dinner party different from every other. In this book we shall be concerned merely with conventions, where they come from, and what they signify.

"Dinner Is Served" in the course of the long central Chapter Four. We watch each other eat a meal, from first bite to leaving the table and then the house for home. In order to understand our manners, we must consider what they might have been and are not. Sitting on chairs round a table to eat is not necessarily "the way it's done"—why then did we decide to do it? How do people behave who do without chairs? When and why did we stop eating with our hands, what does that decision tell us about our attitude to food, and what difference has it made to our eating behaviour? How do we account for tablecloths, candles, serving spoons, wineglasses, and for ceremonials such as saying grace or toasting? Even though many people may eat formal sit-down dinners rarely or not at all, the fully deployed formal meal remains the paradigm from which other food events borrow their symbols, sequences, and categories. Picnics, air-line dinners, cocktail parties, and fast-food breaks are among such variants discussed in the book. They reveal, in the very changes rung or in their choice of quotations from the original, many of our atti-tudes towards food rituals.

Restaurant meals are an immensely complex subject that I have had, regretfully, to treat only tangentially. For the most part, eating in a restaurant requires the same table manners as those expected at a fairly formal dinner at home. (Readers interested in pursuing the social issues raised by the topic might start with the books by J. Finkelstein, and G. Mars and M. Nicod, listed in the Bibliography.)

The reason why I chose to describe a formal meal is its fullness—it covers the broadest range of activities—and its intricacy. Informality, as the word tells us, presupposes at least some concept of a formal model, and informal behaviour is to be understood in the first place by considering the rules that it disregards, and then seeing what rules it invariably retains.

Chapter Five is a detailed treatment of bodily propriety when eating: control above all of the mouth, but of the rest of the body as well. It is at this point that pollution avoidances during meals are briefly discussed. The final postscript addresses itself to the so-called falling off of manners and ritual in modern Western society; it considers why we are so determined to be casual, and whether we are in fact ruder than we used to be.

The themes of violence and repression necessarily recur in the narrative. Table manners are social agreements; they are devised precisely because violence could so easily erupt at dinner. Eating is aggressive by nature, and the implements required for it could quickly become weapons; table manners are, most basically, a system of taboos designed to ensure that violence remains out of the question. But intimations of greed and rage keep breaking in: many mealtime superstitions, for example, point to the imminent death of one of the guests. Eating is performed by the individual, in his or her most personal interest; eating in company, however, necessarily places the individual face to face with the group. It is the group that insists on table manners; "they" will not accept a refusal to conform. The individual's "personal interest" lies therefore not only in ensuring his or her bodily survival, but also in pleasing, placating, and not frightening or disgusting the other diners. Edward Lear was extremely sensitive to the relationship between the eccentric individual and "them," the unnamed others:

There was an Old Person of Buda
Whose conduct grew ruder and ruder;
Till at last, with a hammer,
They silenced his clamour,
By smashing that Person of Buda.

He was, "they" will claim later, asking for it. The limerick, light-hearted as it is and hilarious in its finality, nevertheless delivers a sinister warning that is impossible to miss. Manners, and table manners in particular, are no laughing matter. Good manners help make our own lives easier because they set other people at ease. What other people consider to be bad manners—and politeness has everything to do with the perceptions of other people—never escape punishment, sooner or later, from "them."

1

Behaving

Table manners are as old as human society itself, the reason being that no human society can exist without them. The active sharing of food—not consuming all of the food we find on the spot, but carrying some back home and then doling it systematically out—is believed, even nowadays, to lie at the root of what makes us different from animals. Birds, dogs, and hyenas carry home food for their young until they are ready to find food for themselves, and chimpanzees may even demand and receive morsels of meat from other adults in their pack. (Chimpanzees apparently exhibit this behaviour only on the occasions when they consume meat; their main, vegetable diet they almost invariably eat where they find it, without sharing.) Only people actively, regularly, and continuously work on the portioning out of their food.

This activity presupposes and probably helped give rise to many basic human characteristics, such as kinship systems (who belongs with whom; which people eat together), language (for discussing food past, present, and future, for planning the acquisition of food, and deciding how to divide it out while preventing fights), technology (how to kill, cut, keep, and carry), and morality (what is a just slice?). The basic need of our stomachs for food continues to supply a good deal of the driving force behind all of human enterprise: we have to hunt for food, fight for it, find it, or sow it and wait for it to be ready; we then have to transport it, and distribute it before it goes rotten. It is in addition easier for us to ingest food chopped, ground, cooked, or left to soften. Civilization itself cannot begin until a food supply is assured. And where food is concerned we can never let up; appetite keeps us at it.

The active sharing out of what we are going to eat is only the beginning. We are ineradicably choosy about our food: preference enters into every mouthful we consume. We play with food, show off with it, revere and disdain it. The main rules about eating are simple: If you do not eat you die; and no matter how large your dinner, you will soon be hungry again. Precisely because we must both eat and keep on eating, human beings have poured enormous effort into making food more than itself, so that it bears manifold meanings beyond its primary purpose of physical nutrition. It becomes an immensely versatile mythic prototype (modern economists, for example, love to assure us that our longing to "consume" goods in general, like our need to eat, is insatiable), an art form, a medium for commercial exchange and social interaction, the source for an intricate panoply of distinguishing marks of class and nationhood. We have to keep eating, so we make eating the occasion for insisting on other things as well—concepts and feelings which are vital for our well-being, but many of them complex, difficult to analyse or understand, and definitely not so easy to concentrate on as food is when we are hungry. Even where actual eating is concerned, bread alone is not enough.

"Bread," in western European languages, often means food in general; in our tradition, bread is basic. This is true even in our own day, when people eat far less bread than they used to, and when bread often comes to us from a factory, bleached, squishy, ready-cut (so much for "breaking bread"), wrapped in plastic or cellophane. Yet we still expect to have bread on hand at every meal, as background, as completion, as dependable comforter and recompense for any stress or disappointment the rest of the meal might occasion. Bread is for us a kind of successor to the motherly breast, and it has been over the centuries responsible for billions of sighs of satisfaction.

Because we are human and because, as we shall see, "cultural" behaviour appears in us to be a "biological" necessity, bread became in addition, and has remained, a deeply significant symbol, a substance honoured and sacred. We still remember that breaking bread and sharing it with friends "means" friendship itself, and also trust, pleasure, and gratitude in the sharing. Bread as a particular symbol, and food in general, becomes, in its sharing, the actual bond which unites us. The Latin word *companion* means literally "a person with whom we share bread"; so that every *company*, from actors' guild to Multinational Steel, shares in the significance evoked in breaking bread.

Food can be shared, abstained from, used as a weapon or a proof of prestige, stolen, or given away; it is therefore a test of moral values as well. Everyone understands exactly what going without food will mean: food is the great necessity to which we all submit. We also share a similarity in stomach size—no matter how much money you have, there is only so much you can eat. So, food metaphors are numerous and powerful in moral and aesthetic discourse; we speak of "greed," "taste," and "thirst" in contexts that seem to have little to do with eating and drinking. Women have always been another symbol, used for the knitting together of families and tribes; they too are "given away" in marriage, shared, stolen, used to enhance status, or abstained from. But food, as the anthropologist Raymond Firth pointed out, has the enormous advantage, as a symbol, of divisibility. "Women can be shared but they cannot be divided, whereas food can be almost infinitely portioned out without loss of quality." The remark is amusing because it is, so to speak, "close to the bone." Somewhere at the back of our minds, carefully walled off from ordinary consideration and discourse, lies the idea of cannibalism—that human beings might *become* food, and eaters of each other. Violence, after all, is necessary if any organism is to ingest another. Animals are murdered to produce meat; vegetables are torn up, peeled, and chopped; most of what we eat is treated with fire;

and chewing is designed remorselessly to finish what killing and cooking began. People naturally prefer that none of this should happen to them. Behind every rule of table etiquette lurks the determination of each person present to be a diner, not a dish. It is one of the chief roles of etiquette to keep the lid on the violence which the meal being eaten presupposes.

We shall begin, therefore, with a brief look at cannibalism, its nature as a taboo and as a myth, its main varieties, and a few representative contexts in which it has been found. Cannibalism (which we are schooled to think of as unthinkable and therefore barbarous behaviour) is never in fact meaningless, automatic, or free from etiquette. Indeed, it has no doubt usually been hedged about with more solemnity and consciousness than have everyday meals: eating other people can seldom, perhaps never, have been ordinary. It evokes care and clarity, and gives rise to categorizations and limits, at all times. In other words, a cannibal repast, being a social custom, is no more lacking in table manners than is any other kind of meal. It is one of the suppositions underlying this book that no society exists without manners, and specifically without rules that govern eating behaviour. Table manners are politeness where food is concerned. They comprise the ritual movements which each culture chooses as those most appropriate to handle the mightiest of necessities, the most potent of symbols, the medium through which we repeatedly express our relationships with each other. Culture has to impose itself upon natural instinct and inclination—but it invariably sets out to do so. It is the nature of human beings not to be able to leave nature alone.

• The Artificial Cannibal •

While Christopher Columbus was temporarily shipwrecked off the island called by the Spanish Hispaniola (now divided into Haiti and the Dominican Republic) in December 1492, he was regaled by the Arawaks living on the island with stories about the terrible Caribs. These were natives originally of Brazil, who had left their home for the Guianas, then set out from there in their long canoes, each hollowed from the trunk of a single tree and carrying a hundred men, to conquer the islands which are now called Caribbean, after them. By about one hundred years before Columbus arrived, the Caribs had conquered the inhabitants in all the eastern Caribbean islands and dominated the entire region.

An Arawak chief on Hispaniola invited Columbus to a feast of cassava and sweet potatoes (which the Arawaks called *batatas*: it is the origin of our word "potatoes"). They gave him in addition "some masks with eyes and large ears of gold and other beautiful objects which they wore around their necks. [The chief] then complained about the Caribs, who captured his people and took them away to be eaten, but he was greatly cheered when the Admiral comforted him by showing him our weapons and promising to defend him with them." The fear of the Arawaks impressed Columbus, and what he subsequently found out about the Caribs— whether or not he accurately interpreted what he was told—did nothing to mollify him. In Cuba he heard the dialect form of the word "Carib" as *Caniba*, and in Spanish the adjective *canibal* was derived from this. The word *anthropophagi* (Greek for "man-eaters") was now mostly withdrawn from circulation and replaced by *cannibals* in the languages of Europe.

When Shakespeare created Caliban in *The Tempest* (1611), he made him the embodiment of the bestial aspects of humankind. Begotten of the devil upon the Algerian witch Sycorax, yet worshipping a Patagonian god, Caliban is also humanity in its primitive, "uncultured" state. (Not being European, he could roam from North Africa to South America without changing the main point that he was from "out there," beyond the boundaries of "the civilized.") Shakespeare's monster does not eat human flesh, but the idea of cannibalism attaches to him nevertheless, for the poet has given him a name derived from "cannibal," another deformation of the word "Carib": Caliban. Being a "thing of darkness," Caliban poetically and appropriately has cannibalism imputed to him through his name.

The very idea of people eating each other is so abhorrent to us that we usually prefer not to think about it. Cannibalism is to us massively taboo, and forbidden with far greater success than is incest. Freud pointed out, as Montaigne had before him, that it is curious we should feel so badly about eating people, when we frequently kill them and often sense only gratification for having done so. The reason derives from the way in which most human beings have categorized their experience. If you can classify people as enemies you may feel you can kill them with justice; but people are not food, and let us keep that straight. Anthropologists interested in the purely utilitarian aspects of human behaviour have also pointed out that human flesh is simply not very economical as a source of protein: human beings are the most dangerous animals a hunter could face, and in any case eating one another has to have limits or the social group would necessarily dwindle. No, other people are better taken as allies, or even as necessary evils, than as nutrients.

Just because cannibalism has been so very successfully rendered taboo, it has always been one of the major "effects" a writer can rely on when he or she reaches for some fully fledged enormity, an atrocity to make our skins crawl. For thousands of years cannibalism has seemed to us to be everything that civilization is not—which is why Homer's hero Odysseus, in search of home, city, order, and seemliness, must meet and vanquish such creatures as the cannibal Cyclops. Cannibalism is a symbol in our culture of total confusion: a lack of morality, law, and structure; it stands for what is brutish, utterly inhuman. The idea is that, unlike cannibals, we are upright, orderly, enlightened, and generally superior. But what we might use for symbolic purposes as an embodiment of structureless confusion has nevertheless a basis in clear cold fact: cannibal societies have existed since time immemorial. As social beings, however, cannibals must inevitably have manners. Whatever we might think to the contrary, rules and regulations always govern cannibal society and cannibal behaviour.

It was suggested by W. Arens in 1979 that there never has been any such thing as deliberate cannibalism, unprovoked by a threat of starvation; that cannibalism is merely a literary device and a libel against races we wish to cast as "other" than ourselves. The Spanish, according to this theory, made up the man-eating of the Aztec; Hans Staden, who was kept by a South American tribe as a possible future cannibal victim during the sixteenth century, and who lived to describe what he had seen, was accused of simply fabricating the entire horrific story; other reports of cannibalistic behaviour were similarly disbelieved. The theory caused a useful flurry of research, examination, discovery, and controversy. The result has been to make it clear that the sources we have cannot be discounted. This rather attractive idea—that people have never really eaten each other—has had to be abandoned. We can be sure that cannibalism has been practised in Africa south of the Sahara, in Oceania, America North, Central, and South, in northern Europe, and in the ancient Mediterranean region.

Specialists in Neolithic archaeology have on a number of occasions claimed that the broken bones and cracked skulls discovered at several sites prove that our Stone Age ancestors relished human brains and sucked bone marrow when they could get at it. If they did this, they may well have eaten human flesh also. A recent find has rendered some of the best-preserved and most meticulously gathered data in support of the argument for early cannibalism so far: at a six-thousand-year-old site at Fontbrégoua, near Nice, there were bones from many butchered animals, including sheep, goats, boar, and deer. All had been routinely slaughtered, the finders say, and the bones broken to extract marrow, then unceremoniously discarded. Human bones were found among the animal ones; they had been treated in exactly the same fashion as the others. Three human adults, two children, and one person of undetermined age had almost certainly been eaten. The remaining seven or eight other human skeletons showed less certain signs of having been gnawed by other people.

We are all aware, of course, that in times of desperate hunger people are sometimes driven to eat dead companions in order to save their own lives. If there has been no actual killing of one member of the party in order to provide food for the others, and if the eating has been done with reverence for the solemnity and dire necessity of the action, then even modern people find such an emergency measure understandable and forgivable. Indeed, we emphasize the singularity of these occurrences with such fervour that we are probably underscoring for ourselves a fundamental law for our culture: that such acts could never become normal. Eating human flesh under extreme duress and treating it as an act which would never otherwise be countenanced is not what I mean here by "cannibalism." True cannibalism is publicly approved by the society which practises it, and is at least potentially a repeated, and usually a ritual, act.

What little we know of the ideas and attitudes of cannibals suggests that they might have done shocking things according to our system of rules, but they did *not* behave with merely random brutish greed. Hunger was doubtless often a driving force behind the practice; excellent arguments have been made that cannibalism can arise as a society's response to a lack of protein. But descriptions of cannibals usually insist that they surrounded the eating of human flesh with carefully prescribed ritual. The great Aztec state, for example, fought wars to provide itself with prisoners, who were eventually eaten. Estimates of the number of victims put to death and consumed annually when the Spanish arrived in Mexico in the sixteenth century (estimates made from Spanish sources, but also inferred from archaeological remains such as skull-racks) range from 15,000 to 250,000; the figures are highly uncertain, but everyone agrees that the numbers were huge. All these thousands of prisoners of war were taken, it is suggested, in order to feast the Aztec elite and also to reward soldiers who distinguished themselves in capturing human "meat."

The argument is that, because the Aztec had never managed to domesticate large animals which they could eat, they hungered for meat, and the desire of some of them was met by killing enemies for food. (The only large animals the Aztec had domesticated—they had killed off all the wild game except that to be found at the edges of their empire—were turkeys and dogs. They bred dogs whose flesh was not too muscular and therefore edible, but these required fattening on meat themselves; and turkeys had to be fed with precious grain.) Other, smaller societies have consumed much less spectacularly large numbers of people—whether the latter were their enemies or their own kind—for similar "biological" reasons. Where food is concerned, hunger must always play its role. But we should not be so carried away by our modern pride in practicality and in our demythologizing skills that we deliberately ignore what accounts we have of actual Aztec behaviour. We can still see the magnificent stepped pyramids they built for the performance of human sacrifices to the Sun, patron of warriors. The Sun God demanded human hearts to feed him; without these, he would pale and die, darkness would cover the earth, and chaos and death would rule as they had before time began.

In 1521, sixty-two Spanish soldiers, captured in war by the Aztec, were led in procession to one of the temple-pyramids of the capital, Tenochtitlán, now Mexico City. As Aztec prisoners of war, they were to be violently killed and their beating hearts offered to the god. Bernal Díaz del Castillo, a soldier in the army of Cortés, describes the scene: "Again there was sounded the dismal drum of Huichilobos and many other shells and horns and things like trumpets and the sound of them all was terrifying, and we all looked towards the lofty Cue [temple-pyramid] where they were being sounded, and saw that our comrades whom they had captured when they defeated Cortés were being carried by force up the steps, and they were taking them to be sacrificed. When they got them up to a small square in front of the oratory, where their accursed idols are kept, we saw them place plumes on the heads of many of them and with things like fans in their hands they forced them to dance before Huichilobos, and after they had danced they immediately placed them on their backs on some rather narrow stones which had been prepared as places for sacrifice, and with stone knives they sawed open their chests and drew out their palpitating hearts and offered them to the idols that were there, and they kicked the bodies down the steps, and Indian butchers who were waiting below cut off the arms and feet and flayed the skin off the faces, and prepared it afterwards like glove leather with the beards on, and kept those for the festivals when they celebrated drunken orgies, and the flesh they ate in *chilmole*."

Fray Bernardino de Sahagun described another sacrifice as follows: "One at a time they stretched them out on the sacrificial stone. Then they delivered them into the hands of six offering priests; they stretched them out upon their backs; they cut open their breasts with a wide-bladed flint knife. And they named the hearts of the captives 'precious eagle-cactus fruit.' They raised them in dedication to the sun, Xippilli, Quauhtleuanitl. They offered it to him; they nourished him. . . ."

Each heart was "dehusked" from its enveloping body like a corn cob from its sheath; it was then pressed to the stone statue of the god and dropped into a temple vessel. Cutting out the heart by severing the vena cava and the aorta would produce an enormous outpouring of blood; into this one of the officiating priests inserted a straw, sucked some of it up, and ritually splashed it over the victim's body. The heart fed the Sun, conceived as eagle energy and as voracious jaguar; the blood quenched the thirst of the earth and produced fertility. The body was then heaved *gently* (the adverb recurs in the different descriptions) over the edge of the pyramid's top and fell down the steep steps to men waiting below. The falling blood red bodies of sacrificed victims were said to imitate the sun setting in the west. But to the watching Spanish the scene partook of nightmare: "Afterwards they rolled them over; they bounced them down. They came breaking to pieces; they came head over heels; they each came headfirst, they came turning over. Thus they reached the terrace at the base of the pyramid."

The head of each was cut from the body and taken to a rack, to be displayed in another part of the temple complex, which to Spanish eyes was a "plaza." There in serried rows the heads rotted in the heat, the stench, and the flies, till only skulls were left. "I remember that in the plaza where some of their oratories stood there were piles of human skulls so regularly arranged that one could count them, and I estimated them at more than a hundred thousand. I repeat again that there were more than one hundred thousand of them. And in another part of the plaza there were so many piles of dead men's thigh bones that one could not count them; there was also a large number of skulls strung between beams of wood, and three priests who had charge of these bones and skulls were guarding them. We had occasion to see many such things later on as we penetrated into the country, for the same custom was observed in all the towns. . . ."

What exactly happened in the end to the bodies we do not know, except that the limbs and some other portions were shared out among the rulers (one thigh from each corpse was offered to Moctezuma himself), their elite entourage, and the actual captors of the prisoners. The flesh was cooked with peppers and tomatoes, and served up upon bowls of maize, the universal sacred staple of the Aztec. Mexican archaeologists have found, elsewhere in Mexico City, many headless human rib-cages. A different group of people had presumably eaten the rest of the bodies—minus the hearts, of course.

The Aztec cared intensely *how* they ate people and also whom they ate, when, and where. Every gesture of the sacrifice was laid down as ritual: architecture, costumes, sacred weapons, and utensils were carefully prescribed and prepared. People were allowed to eat only the portions of meat assigned to them by their status. In fact the Aztec were terrified by the idea of human sacrifice carried out in chaotic disorder; it could only mean darkness (the failure of the power of the Sun), and destruction: the gods would become violent and brutish themselves, descend to earth, and eat people just as indiscriminately and with as little regard for protocol and etiquette as people had shown earlier. There were a thousand meanings and emotions associated with the sacrifice, besides the wish to eat and enjoy. Eating people was hedged about with ceremony and elaborate care; what they saw as neatness and propriety governed every gesture.

The same can be said of many other cannibal societies, even though we cannot forget that we have never been able fully to interrogate and learn from a real ritual cannibal about what he or she actually felt and knew of the gestures and meanings employed. The Aztec case is unique in its scope and intricacy, and also because this was the only imperialist state we know of, with a large population, fully to institutionalize cannibalism. Being so complex, Aztec practice included many attitudes that are found only in part in much smaller cannibal groups.

There are two main types of simple cannibal society: those who eat their own people, especially their relatives; and those who eat only enemies, foreign to their tribe. These two broad categories cover a great variety of behaviour and belief—even given the fact that we know about very few cannibal societies compared with the many that must have existed in the past. "Endo"-cannibals (who eat their own) have been described as "cemeteries for their dead." They may believe, for instance, that a sort of life essence inhabits every human body, that this essence flows via most social activities, including those to do with sex and food, through the community. Members of a tribe can, and indeed must, "take in" the life essence of a dead fellow tribesman by eating him after he has died a natural death. Failure to eat a dead parent might mean poor health, or barrenness, or weak children, since the life essence has not been "topped up" properly by the living members of the tribe. This kind of cannibalism is felt directly to influence plant and animal fertility as well.

Flesh is often not consumed in endo-cannibalism; people prefer to grind up bones or burn the body to ashes, then eat the powder mixed in a drink, or with, say, mashed banana. (Such practices show that eating people is not always for their protein content.) There might also be a taste—culturally induced, we are relieved to remind ourselves, in this particular social constellation—for half-rotted corpse carefully dug up and consumed, or for festering flesh from wounds. The action of eating one's relatives is often sad, solemn, and loving: it can be a form of mourning ritual. It is also possible, however, for people in these societies to appear quite matter-of-fact, to eat up cheerfully and feel no apparent awe during the process.

Exo-cannibalism was more common than endo-cannibalism, more violent and destructive—and easier for us to understand. Here people hate the people they consume, but eating their flesh is a joy. They pursue their victims (who must be foreigners) and eat them for vengeance. Captives were often tortured before being killed, or made to do battle against hopeless odds; it was hoped that, in the process, they would show considerable courage. They would then be eaten with special appreciation, the bravery they had been proven to possess passing into the bodies of their killers.

At the Aztec "gladiatorial" sacrifice, for instance, the captive was tied by the waist to a sort of umbilical cord attached to the centre of the sacrificial stone. He was given weapons, and then attacked by warriors one by one until he fell. When he was seen to be about to die, he was seized, stretched on the stone, and slaughtered. The man who had captured him in battle would take his captive's blood in "a green bowl with a feathered rim. . . . On the lips of the stone images, on each one, he placed the blood of his captive. He made them taste it with the hollow cane." The body was flayed so that its skin could be used later as a cloak, and the flesh carved up and eaten.

The captor of this man was proud of his victim's prowess, and identified himself with him and his courage. He would therefore refuse to eat him. "He is my son," he would say. "Shall I perchance eat my very self?"

It was quite often the case that the person who did the actual slaying of the victim was not allowed to eat him. He would have to fast for days or change his name or hide in the forest for weeks before returning to the group. In these cases, it was important that eating should be dissociated from killing; the killer was seen to be merely doing his duty, or acting for the good of other people and not himself. In the account of Hans Staden, the German naval gunner who was captured by the cannibal Tupinamba of Brazil in 1554, "Then the slayer seizes [the club] and thus addresses the victim: 'I am he that will kill you, since you and yours have slain and eaten many of my friends.' To which the prisoner replies: 'When I am dead I shall still have many to avenge my death.'" Then the slayer strikes from behind and beats out his brains. "The women seize the body at once and carry it to the fire where they scrape off the skin, making the flesh quite white, and stopping up the fundament with a piece of wood so that nothing may be lost. Then a man cuts up the body, removing the legs above the knee and the arms at the trunk, whereupon the four women seize the four limbs and run with them around the huts, making a joyful cry. After this they divide the trunk among themselves and devour everything that can be eaten. When this is finished they all depart, each one carrying a piece with him. The slayer takes a fresh name. . . . He must lie all that day in his hammock, but they give him a small bow and arrow so that he can amuse himself by shooting into wax, lest his arm should become feeble from the shock of the death blow. I was present and have seen all this with my own eyes."

Cannibals themselves often regard the eating of human flesh in general with awe and horror; it is ritually marked off from regular eating. The ancient Fijians, for example, ate everyday meals with their hands; when it came to eating human flesh, and only then, they used a special wooden fork. Cannibals often deny that they started the practice of eating people. The gods may have demanded it; we have no choice. Bloodthirsty enemies beyond our boundaries think of nothing but how to kill and eat us; we must meet force with force, and assure them that they will not eat us without paying exactly the equivalent price. The relationship of a cannibal with his victim may involve an elaborate metaphorical construct: the one to be tortured, killed, and eaten might represent darkness, primitive bestiality, the animal. (This is rather like our own imaginary monsters, who often turn out to be cannibalistic.) Or the victim is a monster, to be devoured—with care and propriety—by the enlightened, in order that the power he represents may be destroyed and civilization triumph. This power might be recognized and revered as useful energy, which is required by the good cannibal society that eats him and will thus channel his force to useful purposes. To eat one's enemy is to "take in" his power, to one's own increase.

An exo-cannibal society, preying on its enemies, *needed* those enemies. There was a weird sort of interdependence between the two warring groups, each of whom wanted "others" to feed their wrath. Moctezuma explained that his people could not seek "reconciliation" with the Tlaxcalans, whom the Aztec loved to sally forth and capture for the feeding of hearts to the Sun: if the Aztec made friends with the Tlaxcalans, where would the victims come from, to propitiate the gods? Endo-cannibalism may look inward-turning, and for that reason sick (by our no doubt ethnocentric standards); exo-cannibalism however represented another kind of symbiosis, this time with enemies. The "biological" advantage of exo-cannibalism was that it insisted that people who were eaten should be taken in war; they were healthy specimens, and unlikely to be infected by disease.

Techniques, in exo-cannibalism, of showing contempt for vanquished enemies were many and dramatic. The ancient Maoris of New Zealand were "an exceedingly good-tempered and sociable people . . . courteous and polite . . . it was considered a mark of inferior breeding to be rude in either speech or bearing." Men ruled; women were profane, defiling—and never allowed to eat human victims. Food was also profane and impure, especially if it was cooked; so much so that everything associated with trapping and cooking food became profane, like the women who prepared and cooked it. All houses were *tapu* or the opposite of profane (the Maori word *tapu* is the origin of our "taboo"), and therefore food had to be eaten

out of doors. Even touching cooked food was a defilement to the
highest-ranking men; the Maori accordingly invented a kind of fork,
a pointed stick called a *tiirou*, with which an exceptionally pure man
could convey food to his mouth; in some cases this had to be done
for him by another pure, *tapu* person. The pure one ate well away
from women, and usually alone. If the food being consumed had
first been offered to the gods, and there was no sufficiently *tapu*
friend present to feed the loftily pure one, he had to eat it with his
mouth from the ground, not touching it with his hands.

Now it followed that food, being so low in the scale of purity, was
not something with which you could compare a man; there was no
more certain way to insult someone than to say, "I will use your
head as a cooking pot," or to refer to a man or a part of him as
"cooked," or to give some dish the man's name. It will quickly be
seen that the ultimate degradation one could inflict was to make
metaphor a fact and actually eat the person: turn him into food.
Most Maori cannibalism took place on the battlefield, where the
enemy dead would be butchered on the spot and cooked in steam
ovens swiftly constructed for the purpose by the victors. The bones
would be collected afterwards and turned into profane domestic
implements, especially those used in catching and cooking food. So,
hands and fingers were used as hooks for holding food-baskets; fish
hooks, pins, whistles, spear-points, needles, flutes, and rings for the
legs of captive parrots could all be made of bits of enemies. A skull
could be debased and mocked for decades by being used to carry
water for household purposes. Knowledge that the deceased man's
bones had been quarried for everyday, profane use and were being
contemned in this constant and ingenious manner would humiliate
and exasperate his relatives and fuel in them the determination to
avenge the enormity with an outrage if possible more satisfying still.

Cannibalism, whatever form it took and for whatever reason, was
never, in real life, a disorderly activity within the culture that practised it. The fact that it was allowed, sanctioned, or institutionalized
made it a practice that was regulated, even if the rules were occasionally simple—on the face of it, and as far as we can tell with our
scrappy information—and even if rules were commonly broken, as
reporters from some societies say they were. Even when violent

aggression reigned, there were social preferences, tastes, and traditions; something almost amounting to a cuisine.

Many were the methods of preparing a man as a meal. The anthropologist Paul Shankman, in the course of examining cannibal cooking practices as a test of Lévi-Strauss's claims that roasting is high in prestige, boiling low, and so on, collected ways of cooking people culled from reports on cannibal societies. The resulting collection was a "veritable smorgasbord" of methods. People have indeed been boiled in pots, and roasted by spit, rack, or exposure to an open fire. They have also been steam-baked, cooked on preheated rocks and in earth ovens, smoked, decomposed first, dried, powdered, preserved, stuffed into bamboo tubes and placed in the embers, their bones burned to ashes and stirred into many kinds of sauces, juices, and mashes. A body could be buried, then exhumed and eaten in its rotten state. Here is an account, by Ronald Berndt, of one such meal: "On the afternoon of the sixth day following his death his corpse was exhumed. The maggots were scraped off and placed on banana leaves. The body was then cut up, the meat and bones being cooked in one oven, and the maggots, tied up in small leaf bundles, in another; these are regarded as a delicacy." The attention to detail, the neatness, and the decisiveness about what one wanted and how to achieve the necessary effect give this description a weird but unmistakably technological air like that of a careful culinary article from a magazine for gourmets.

There were various tortures where people were prepared for cooking while still alive. People were eaten raw at times—but this was quite seldom, and even then there were rules. There was always the matter of who got which piece, and how much of it. Sometimes women did all the cannibalism ("materialist" anthropologists point out that this would have been because the men ate nearly all the animal meat themselves, leaving the women little protein), and sometimes it was the men, exulting over their prisoners of war by eating them. There were rules, among endo-cannibals, about which relatives one must not, or which one must at all costs, eat. A dying endo-cannibal might catalogue in detail which parts of him or her were later to be eaten by whom: a last will and testament of admirably generous detachment. Then there were the rituals during cannibal meals.

These ranged from matters of simple order—whether or
should collect the grease falling from cooking limbs, for exam
who had the right to eat it and how—to the extreme formal
richness of Aztec breast-cutting and heart-snatching ceremoni
their blood-blackened pyramid shrines. Indications are that more ritual usually governed the eating of people than was found necessary at
ordinary meals. But every dinner eaten with others requires rules, and
these soon become elaborated into a system of table manners, which
are ritual where eating is concerned.

• *Ritual* •

A North American father, presumably initiating his son, aged fifteen, into the world of adult business affairs, took him out to what
the boy described as "a big dinner meeting." When the company
was served spaghetti, the boy ate it with his hands. "I would slurp it
up and put it in my mouth," he admitted. "My dad took some grief
about it." The October 1985 newspaper article does not describe the
response of the rest of the company. The son was sent to a boarding
school to learn how to behave. "When we have spaghetti," he
announced later, "you roll it up real tightly on your fork and put it
in your mouth with the fork."

What he described, after having learned it, is a dinner-table ritual—as automatic and unquestioned by every participant in it, as
impossible to gainsay, as the artificial rules and preferences which
every cannibal society has upheld. Practical reasons can be found for
it, most of them having to do with neatness, cleanliness, and noise-
lessness. Because these three general principles are so warmly
encouraged in our culture, having been arrived at, as ideals to be
striven for, after centuries of struggle and constraint, we simply
never doubt that everyone who is right-minded will find a spaghetti-
eating companion disgusting and impossible to eat with where even
one of them is lacking. Yet we know from paintings and early photographs of spaghetti-eaters in nineteenth-century Naples (where
the modern version of spaghetti comes from) that their way of eating pasta was with their hands—not that the dish was likely to
appear at a formal dinner. You had to raise the strings in your right

hand, throw back your head, then lower the strings, dexterously, with dispatch, and *without slurping* (there are invariably "polite" and "rude" ways of eating), into your open mouth. The spaghetti in the pictures does not seem to have sauce on it.

Today, spaghetti-eating manners demand forks, and fistfuls of wet pasta are simply not acceptable at any "civilized" occasion. The son's ignorance cast a dark reflection upon his father: he had not been doing his duty, had not given his child a proper "upbringing." Even if the boy had not seen spaghetti before, he subsequently admitted that what he ought to have done was to look about him, watch how other people were eating this awkward food, and imitate them. In any case, the options were clear after this demonstration of ineptitude: either the boy learned his table manners, or he would not be asked to a "big dinner meeting" again, by anyone who had heard of his unfinished education.

He had offended not only against modern proprieties that limit the use of hands while eating, but also against ritual: he had done something *unexpected*. Ritual is action frequently repeated, in a form largely laid down in advance; it aims to get those actions right. Everyone present knows what should happen, and notices when it does not. Dinner too is habitual, and aims at order and communication, at satisfying both the appetite of the diners and their expectations as to how everybody present should behave. In this sense, a meal can be thought of as a ritual and a work of art, with limits laid down, desires aroused and fulfilled, enticements, variety, patterning, and plot. As in a work of art, not only the overall form but also the details matter intensely.

This pernicketiness has some of its basis in biology. Human beings, like animals, are extremely sensitive to small signs, to tiny noises in the night, to small discrepancies in the customary layout of their environment, for these may be the only warnings received before a hidden danger strikes. Alertness and sensitivity are normally essential for survival, especially in the wild. But being human, and depending as we do on knowing our way round our complex and perilous social world, it is entirely necessary to us that we should also react instinctively to very small signs given by other people in social contexts. No one in the group might even be conscious that such a sign has been given. But those of us with the best-attuned social sense will instantly and instinctively "know" what is afoot. Every person must be careful—or rather, drilled from an early age until automatically disposed—not only to notice signs, but also to *provide* them, as a reassurance that this person is what other members of the group hope he or she is; that this individual wishes to join in, play the game, and be civil.

It is equally understandable that mixing with people whose rituals differ from our own can be very trying. Innumerable travellers' tales involve the visiting hero being offered some horrendous "delicacy" which he has either to eat, or risk offending his host. But we can be put out just because some foreigner raises his eyebrows to mean yes, or asks us how much money we make, or stalks off in a rage because we folded our arms or failed to take our hands out of our pockets. The really dramatic "ethnic" behaviour we consciously apprehend at once, and so can "make allowances" for; everyone has heard of the chances of having to eat an eyeball, or smash glasses after the toast. But the smaller, less noticeable signs can catch us off our guard and rob us more insidiously of our sense of security. Most of the picturesque details that strike travellers as weird have to do with table manners. Tourists quite commonly visit marvels as mighty as the Pyramids of Egypt, but come home really jolted by, and unable to forget, the Egyptian manner of pouring tea into a glass until it slops into the saucer. When eating and drinking we are particularly sensitive and vigilant, and immediately react to the slightest deviation from what we have learned to regard as the proprieties.

Ritual, being both expected behaviour and correct, is a series of actions constantly repeated. Repetitiveness serves the meaning being expressed, for if the pattern is at least generally constant we can concentrate on the message embodied in the performance. (We do not have to think how to handle our knife and fork every time we are served, but can set to and enjoy the steak, while demonstrating effortless restraint and competence, and showing our desire to be communicative, sharing companions.) We also notice the slight *intentional* variations which always occur in ritual, and are therefore thrown into relief. (What fun, and how formally informal, to be served artichokes and be allowed to use our hands.) But this does not entirely account for our need constantly to repeat actions ritually. The repetition soothes us, apparently, in and by itself—inducing what James Joyce called "those here-we-are-again gaieties." Rituals survive because people want them to do so; they "work." Culture, not instinct, determines a good deal of what we do. Human beings rejoice in the action of patterning, in itself.

There is no etymological connection whatever between the words "man" (or "wo*man*" or "hu*man*") and "manners," but speakers of English have nonetheless found the presence of that common syllable fascinating. "Meat feeds, cloth cleeds, but manners make the man," went a sixteenth-century jingle: what you eat and what you wear are less important than how you do both. In our own time, Mae West assures us:

It's not what I share but the way that I share it—
That's all, brother, that's all.

The problem is: how much of the way we are *is* culture, and how much is not ours to control?

Ever since humankind began thinking (the word or syllable "man" very possibly comes from a root word meaning "think"), at any rate since the age of the earliest cave paintings, we have speculated and worried about the difference between ourselves and animals. It has always been intensely important for us to grasp this difference as far as we are able to do so, especially since we cannot help noticing how much like animals we are. For animals have no culture in the human sense; animals are therefore not, as human beings are, free from some of the tyranny of natural law. Nothing could be more revealing about twentieth-century preoccupations and anxieties than the latest way of posing this forty-thousand-year-old problem. We now tend to ask not "How are people different from animals?" but "In what ways are we the same?" We are so terrified of our own power, our own clear *difference* from animals, that we desperately seek ways to assure ourselves of our affiliation with the rest of creation. We are trying to remind ourselves, among other things, how much we belong; and struggling to restrain our greed and control our power, which we now see as threatening the earth and everything living on it. We are especially fascinated to find correspondences in animals, not only with our physical nature and biological needs, but with our social behaviour as well.

It was with considerable excitement, therefore, that a longing to repeat a successful scenario was reputedly found among monkeys living on Koshima Islet in Japan. One day in 1953 a year-and-a-half-old female ape called Imo appears to have deeply impressed her fellows (and the watching Japanese scientists) by washing her sweet potato in water before she ate it. She repeated this action whenever she subsequently ate. She would hold the potato under the water with one hand and brush it, presumably trying to get the mud off, with the other. Other monkeys imitated her. The fashion spread, mainly among her kin and playmates. Within four or five years, potato-washing before eating had become *de rigueur* among most monkeys aged two to seven, and among some adults as well. All monkeys over five who took up washing potatoes were females.

Starting in 1958, a tradition had begun, as these females passed on potato-washing by example to their children. The salt taste on potatoes dipped in sea water seems to have resulted in a variant: some monkeys began dipping their potatoes in salt water in between bites; others kept on simply washing them first. It certainly is tempting to detect here not only an ability in a group of monkeys to adopt improvements once they have been discovered by a particularly gifted member, but also an obsessive delight in drama that "works," and a love of sticking to "the way it's done," even without the conscious perception of material benefits. We are reminded of human rituals, and the satisfactions we find in the constant re-enactment of routines, experiencing them as not merely useful but pleasantly repeatable.

Another of the reasons for "manners" is precisely that they pressure people to behave in a predictable fashion. When we all "know what to do" on a given occasion—say at a wedding, or a death—we are all enabled by convention to interrelate, to play our often preordained roles, just where having to make choices and think up scenarios would be most difficult and exhausting. This is why rules of politeness tend to cluster round moments of transition, of meeting others, making decisions, conferring, parting, commemorating.

Rituals are there to make difficult passages easier. They include the gestures—waving, nodding, smiling, speaking set phrases—which daily smooth our meetings with other people; the attitudes and postures we adopt when standing or sitting in the presence of others, especially when we are talking to them; the muttering of "excuse me" when interrupting others or squeezing past them. Full-dress celebrations of coming together, of marking transitions and recollections, almost always require food, with all the ritual politeness implied in dining—the proof that we all know how eating should be managed. We eat whenever life becomes dramatic: at weddings, birthdays, funerals, at parting and at welcoming home, or at any moment which a group decides is worthy of remark. Festivals and feasts are solemn or holy days; they are so regularly celebrated by people meeting for meals that "having a feast" has actually come to mean "eating a lot."

Families meet for meals, too; the custom goes back 2 million years, to the daily return of protohominid hunters and foragers to divide food up with their fellows—whom they have usually, but by no means always, decided they would *not* eat. The extent to which we demand meals at regular times, mostly giving them specific names each with their own connotations (breakfast, lunch, supper), is as arbitrary as it can be solemnly binding. We even develop physical demands for food when food is "due"; the stomach contractions we experience at midday or in the evening, often quite painful ones, which signal mealtimes and which we call "hunger," are strictly speaking nothing of the kind. They are the result of habit and bodily rhythms only, and they result from a culturally induced custom of eating regular meals. It is often part of a society's manners code never to eat between meals, so that not only the meals but also the spaces between them are controlled. This turns every shared family dinner into a mini-feast or festival, so that it can, like a feast, celebrate both the interconnectedness and the self-control of the group's members. Family dinners are rituals too, even though the typical "plot" of a family meal might include the device of lowering the level of formality as compared with other ritual occasions.

The predictability of manners (if *this* is happening, then we must all do *that*) makes us interlock with each other, all act in concert. We connect, in addition, with events, dates, shared emotions, kinship and group ties, the life cycle, the world in general. Conventions, as the word suggests, are attitudes and patterns of behaviour we have in common: we "come together" (as in a business or political "convention") in accepting them, or at least in knowing what they are, as everybody else does—everybody, that is, with whom we are accustomed to associate. It is an extremely complex and time-consuming business, making all these customary links and celebrating all this understanding. But if we stop celebrating, we also soon cease to understand; the price for not taking the time and the trouble is loss of communication. And conversely, the moment communication is lost, "manners" drop away. *Li Chi*, the Chinese *Book of Rites*, compiled in the first century B.C., warns that "the ruin of states, the destruction of families, and the perishing of individuals are always preceded by their abandonment of the rules of propriety."

Today, whatever we eat is enormously controlled and limited by rules—we demand that it be so—and the conditions under which we live make food supplies necessarily impossible without artifice. We also, even when alone, keep rules of bodily propriety that are as strict as they are largely unconscious; other people are present to us in that they have formed our habits. And few of us willingly eat always alone. Food is still our ritual relaxation (a "break" in the working day), our chance to choose companions and talk to them, the excuse to recreate our humanity as well as our strength, and to renew our relationships.

Ritual is an expression of solidarity. Our own society is not one homogeneous mass: individuals in it belong not only to it and to their families, but often, in addition, to groups of people chosen for various reasons; one person may belong to many such groups. Each of these groups must "define" itself (literally, "place a boundary round" itself), or cease to exist as a group; it must declare itself to be *both* a single entity *and* marked off from the rest. Definitional enactment of togetherness and difference may include clothing style, bodily markings such as shaven heads or wild locks, and "in" language; nothing is as powerful, however, as ritual performance. People get together and enact what they hold in common. They might speak their agreement as part of the occasion, but more satisfactory still is the doing of an action together. The actual taking part establishes identity. It is obvious why the action of eating together—of *partaking* in a meal—suggests itself so immediately. An action comprises not only what is done, but how: the two are indissociable in the course of the action's performance. In ritual behaviour, the "how" as well as the "what" of the matter have been laid down in advance. The individual performs, but the group's conventions have decided the sequence, the spatial layout, and the manner. Table manners are rituals because they are the way in which it is commonly agreed that eating *should* be performed.

There is another kind of solidarity expressed by ritual, and this it shares with language. Language is a cultural construct inherited from the past. If we wish to speak and be understood, we have no choice but to learn the linguistic system. This necessity forces us to enter into relationship—whether we like it or not—with the past: we need, and willingly accept, the constraints of pre-ordained rules. Language is not only for communication with people our own age; it is something we have in common with people older than us, who may have spoken our language before we were born. (Writing and reading have been invented to permit the extension of this continuity into the past and the future.) When we are young, older people occupy the field; they are in charge and in power. We must learn their language in order to meet and communicate with them, and if we want one day to occupy their place. We must, similarly, learn their manners if we want to be asked to dinner by them.

The group which decides the "how" of ritual is composed not only of the present participants but also of the dead, insofar as we are prepared to entertain the ideas of people no longer living. Ritual is about *lasting* (which is one reason why ritual occasions are constantly repeated). Because it is pre-ordained, it always expresses order, and it predicts endurance; it links the present with the past, and it hopes also to link the present with the future. Ritual can be used, in its "continuity" function, to keep things going when energy flags and the members in a group cannot maintain their experience at the pitch they would like. People often say that "going through the motions" can help to remind them of past, more successful, experiences. It is possible to look about and see other people apparently rising to the occasion—so perhaps those less inspired might manage, too. Ritual can not only raise the emotional tone of the proceedings, but also lower it if necessary: for instance, ritual politeness can prevent rage from boiling over into action.

But what about ritual that is merely empty form? Animals can "pretend," as a puppy does when playing with a ball instead of pursuing prey; but animals can never match the human capacity for performing a ritual without intending what it says. Ritual becomes meaningless to us, and finally destructive, if it is used for deception. Jesus participated in many social and religious rituals and objected to bad manners. He nevertheless condemned the false pretences to purity of soul which were expressed, for example, by pre-dinner ablutions, and pointed to Isaiah's insight that God detests "lip-service" that covers up the truth. Self-aggrandizing ritual was to be replaced by actions expressing real love and humility: where rituals impede us, they must be changed.

In our own time, cataclysmic social revolutions have made large numbers of rules and conventions redundant, and many of them have not yet been replaced with new signs and voluntary constraints that are broadly recognized and accepted. This is a time of transition, when old manners are dying and new ones are still being forged. A good many of our uncertainties, discomforts, and disagreements stem from this state of flux. Sometimes we hold the terrifying conviction that the social fabric is breaking up altogether, and that human life is becoming brutish and ugly because of a general backsliding from previous social agreements that everyone should habitually behave with consideration for others. At other times a reaction against the social rituals of our own recent past leads us to lump all manners together as empty forms, to be rejected on principle. There is a shying away from elaboration, a preference for the bare bones of everything. We often seem, for instance, to prefer listening to incoherent speakers than to articulate ones, feeling that incoherence is "straight from the heart" while fluency must be a trick, or at least a method of hiding something. Apologies have almost gone out of style because they are hard to make, and being required by others to make them easily convinces us that they are merely insincere.

We do cling to the (largely unexamined) ideal that we should strive to be "natural." Spontaneity seems to be annihilated by anything resembling ritual: how can you be "natural" and still behave in predictable, because pre-ordained, patterns? (People rarely think of animal rituals, which are natural yet invariable, in this context.) We are also deceived, by our desire to reject ritual, into thinking that we are "freely choosing," from within each individual self, to act in ways that are often in fact decided in advance by cultural forces, or by unrecognized but nevertheless real social structures. Such structures, indeed, often govern us precisely insofar as we are unconscious of their existence.

The conventional prejudice against ritual assumes that rituals never change, and that individuals can have no influence upon ritual forms. In fact, individuals are just as important to ritual performance as the group and the rules are. It is only the individual who can personally *mean* what is going on. Each participant uses that ritual, plays with it, rings changes on it, subtly brings it into line with his or her present needs. Ritual is a process; it guides, but it also serves, and is guided. People do influence ritual—and they do so just because human rituals are not "natural." We made them, so we can adapt them to our present requirement. We can also bend the rules if necessary: ritual codes that last always make allowance for circumstance.

The fact is that our personalities are necessarily both individual and social, "natural" and "cultural": these aspects of us can be discussed separately, but they cannot exist alone. The life of the social and cultural "parts" of us is communication with others, and this is achieved and enhanced by means of shared patterns, routines, systems of signals, in a word the performance—whether conscious or not—of rituals. (Even a hermit is a socially conditioned being. Hermits react to society by deliberately leaving it. They normally live alone, and act differently, in ways their societies can "read" and understand.)

It might well seem to us at times, when we are disheartened by spectacles of human error and iniquity, that "culture" is a thoroughly bad thing; that we should stick with plain sex and nutrients and try to get over the rest. But as long as we live in society, purely physical and individual needs and desires must be mediated by rituals and manners.

Social forms become part of the environment; society cannot exist without them. None of us would want to live "by bread alone," even if it were possible. We are forced to create culture just because we are ourselves the building blocks of society. But that very condition makes society a human construct: if its manners deteriorate or become inappropriate, they can conceivably be changed, just because we ourselves collectively make and live by them. Therein lies our freedom.

• Feasting and Sacrifice •

When the American anthropologist Hortense Powdermaker visited Melanesian New Ireland for ten months in the 1930s, she participated in eighty-five feasts. She was invited to parties for births, marriages, deaths, circumcisions, first teeth ("eating for tooth"), before war ("feast to bring fight"), and to make peace ("finish"). You could not name an infant, go on a long journey, receive help from neighbours, finish your house, or recover from an illness without throwing a party for between twenty and five hundred people. She was sure that other, minor feasts occurred without her knowledge. Only one of those she attended was held "just for sociability"; getting together was neither rare nor in need of intentional encouragement.

Feasts the world over are given as celebrations of relationship among the diners, and also as expressions of order, knowledge, competence, sympathy, and consensus at least about important aspects of the value system that supports the group. Feasts display the fruits of human labour and good fortune. (One of those Powdermaker enumerates was held simply because there was plenty to eat: "food much," it was called.) Feasts can also become boasts of the riches of the giver, enhancements of status, demands for attention, and even straight propaganda, urging certain courses of political action and condemning others. Olivier de La Marche described a banquet entertainment designed to rouse Europe into starting a new crusade against the infidel, in 1453. Charles the Bold hosted many "political" meals, crammed full with entertainments and what we would now call advertising; one such dinner placed before the guests thirty large pies bedecked with painted cloth to resemble blue and gold castles, each of them named, and symbolic of a walled town ruled by Charles.

In sixteenth-century France Catherine de Médicis staged spectacular *fêtes*, which she called "magnificences," to promote political unity; they included ballets, music, costume, and always dinner. Guests were once floated down a river to the banqueting house set up on an island, past elaborately staged allegorical happenings: an attack on a whale signifying war; a marine tortoise with musicians dressed as tritons on its back, singing about the king; Neptune in a car drawn by sea-horses, imposing order over savagery. In order to raise the patriotism of the French and prevent the breaking up of her kingdom, she undertook a "progress" that lasted two years, during which she travelled round the country with her fourteen-year-old son Charles IX, presenting him to the people. There were royal meals in castles, in inns, and in farmhouses; palace chefs in her retinue collaborated with local professionals to produce the kind of meals to which Catherine was accustomed. People ate with her, watched her eat, and marvelled at her Italian refinement. Catherine's dinners inspired, impressed, drew people together—and incidentally helped to spread the "advanced" cooking techniques and the new table manners of the ultra-modern Italians.

Extravagance can be the essence of a feast: quantity and richness of food, and enough alcohol to break down inhibitions. Rabelaisian dinners are expressions of human triumph over the riches of the earth. In *A Christmas Carol*, Dickens piles up a gargantuan feast for his Ghost of Christmas Present to sit upon; it is the expression of generous plenty, hot, fruity, meaty and bright, and specific to this particular season: "Heaped up on the floor, to form a kind of throne, were turkeys, geese, game, poultry, brawn, great joints of meat, sucking-pigs, long wreaths of sausages, mince-pies, plum-puddings, barrels of oysters, red-hot chestnuts, cherry-cheeked apples, juicy oranges, luscious pears, immense twelfth-cakes, and seething bowls of punch that made the chamber dim with their delicious steam." A seventeenth-century plea for enjoying seasonal cheer had shown fat, florid Christmas being arraigned by his Scrooge-like opposition—twelve dreary jurymen most significantly named: Starve-mouse, All-pride, Keep-all, Love-none, Eat-alone, Give-little, Hoard-corn, Grudge-meat, Knit-gut, Serve-time, Hate-good, and Cold-kitchen.

Festal lavishness is often used to redistribute wealth. Where beer plays a great part in social intercourse, being what the anthropologist R. Netting calls "both the symbol and the essence of a good life," among the Kofyar of Nigeria, for example, or the Jívaro Indians of the Amazon, or the Bemba of Zambia, having a large stock of nourishing and convivial drink on hand constitutes riches. But beer parties have to be given regularly, or the standing and reputation—and with them a good deal of the power—of the rich man is lost; the enormous prestige that accrues to being able to invite many guests is "bought" with, and depends upon, the pleasure of other people. Food and drink cannot be hoarded like money; they must be consumed and the surplus shared, so that where they constitute wealth they act partly as society levellers, even though party giving is productive of power and influence.

Food is tradition, largely because a taste acquired is rarely lost; and tastes and smells which we have known in the past recall for us, as nothing else can, the memories associated with them. Marcel Proust made *Remembrance of Things Past*, one of the longest novels ever written, arise out of a bit of cake which one day he soaked in tea, just as had been the custom in his childhood. A shudder ran through him, and an exquisite pleasure he could not at first fathom. And then he understood: "Taste and smell alone, more fragile but more enduring, more unsubstantial, more persistent, more faithful, remain poised a long time, like souls, remembering, waiting, hoping, amid the ruins of all the rest . . . so in that moment all the flowers in our garden and in M. Swann's park, and the water-lilies on the Vivonne and the good folk of the village and their little dwellings and the parish church and the whole of Combray and its surroundings, taking shape and solidity, sprang into being, town and gardens alike, from my cup of tea."

Feasts, by means of structure and ritual, deliberately use the powerful connotations of food to recall origins and earlier times. They also attempt to be events in themselves unforgettable, in order to furnish recollections for the future. The food served at festivals is, therefore, not only richer and more splendid than what we usually eat, but also traditional, inherited from the past and intended to be experienced as ancient custom; the recipes and the lore associated with it are to be handed on by us for use again in ritual celebrations. Festive food is both out of the ordinary, and (if the festival is a recurring one) always the same. English Christmas pudding and brandy-soaked Christmas cake is heavy, sweet, and rich: it is eaten in the depth of winter when we can permit ourselves dense food that "sticks to our ribs." Even then, in the context of the season's feasting, a tiny bit suffices: once we have recovered from Christmas, we are quite happy to wait a year before trying the cake and pudding again. Dried fruit mixes require long hard work in the making and "maturing" of them: time taken in the preparation of festival foods is part of the value attributed to them, and focuses attention upon that value. There is a tendency, also, to associate very dark food, such as coffee, chocolate, truffles, caviar, and *cèpes*, as well as plum cake, with excitement and luxury. We feel obscurely that such strange dark stuff must be meaningful and ancient. (Fruit puddings and cakes do have very old roots, but the modern forms of them are quite recent ritual adaptations.) We are eating cultural history and value as well as family memories.

Weddings are initiations into a new way of life; they are usually celebrated with festive food and drink, which includes, in our own case, wedding cake and champagne. Modern wedding cakes in the Anglo-Saxon tradition are huge and gorgeous creations which rise in tiers, cake upon cake. The English version belongs to the same category as Christmas puddings and cakes, being rich, dark, fruity, long-lasting, labour-intensive, costly, and heavy. The top cake is often kept long enough to be served forth at the first child's christening party (the littlest tier is of course appropriate for this function), or at the couple's first anniversary. At the wedding the bride shares her luck by tossing the bouquet to be caught by a fortunate guest, and by giving out bits of her cake; girls used to take these home and sleep with them under their pillows to induce dreams of future husbands. American wedding cakes, on the other hand, are sponges, even cheese-cakes: light but larger than iced fruit cakes, resolutely ephemeral, and not meant to be slept on.

Since the early twentieth century in Britain, the tiers of cake have been lifted on pillars (upturned champagne glasses are now a popular variant). Americans prefer cakes that maintain the older ziggurat form because soft cake cannot support pillars; upper layers of soft cake rest upon a system of wooden dowels and cardboard plateaux disguised with piped icing or ribbon. A mounted, usually white-iced wedding cake may be piped with scrolls, scattered with icing flowers, studded with pearls and silver balls, beribboned, caged in a shiny sugar filigree, and topped with a nosegay of fresh flowers or porcelain figures of the bride and her groom. There is no wedding without photographs of the couple together, cutting this extraordinary cake. The ritual took hold in the 1930s, when dense British cakes were encased in extra-hard white icing, to hold up the pillared layers. The groom "helped" the bride to cut the cake with a beribboned knife or sword. Now the pair perform as a team. The cake stands tall, white, archaic, and decorated, pyramidal like the veiled bride herself, and dominating the proceedings; it is a version of the bride, and the piercing of it dramatizes her rite of passage.

It has been rare in the history of humankind for people to eat as much meat as we do. Killing an animal has not been always an automatic or an everyday affair: it has tended to be done on solemn occasions, and for a special treat. Feasting meant meat, a meal unusually rich in protein, for as many as shared in it. But a dead animal can no longer give milk or breed young; its loss had to be calculated and deemed worthwhile. Festivals and celebrations helped force owners of animals to stop saving and enjoy; and since meat could not be kept long, other people would necessarily be called in to help finish the meal, with all the social side effects which must result.

Such extravagance was, however, supposed to be occasional and therefore exciting and meaningful. It might be so different from the normal diet that feasts could be a trial as well as a pleasure. As late as the mid-1950s in Hong Kong, meat was a luxury, eaten *only* at banquets; older villagers still remember being so unaccustomed to meat that they used to become ill after banquets, especially after the annual division of pork, which was sponsored by their lineage ancestral halls. They loved the luxury, but could tolerate only a very little pork. Now there is more meat available, and more tolerance of it. On the other hand, Xenophon made Hieron the tyrant say that feasts are unusual, and that is why they give pleasure; people who can eat whatever they like every single day quickly become jaded, stuffed, and unable to enjoy holiday junketing.

We need to eat in order to live; yet even eating vegetables means cutting and killing first. When the meal includes meat and especially if the animal is domestic and therefore "known" to us, death can be dramatic. In order to affect people, such a death must be witnessed by them, and not suffered out of sight as we now arrange matters; attention is deliberately drawn, by means of ritual and ceremony, to the performance of killing. This is what is meant by "sacrifice," literally, the "making sacred" of an animal consumed for dinner. It is a practice still common in many societies. Yet sacrifice, because it dwells on the death, is a concept often shocking to the secular modern Western mind—to people who calmly organize daily hecatombs of beasts, and who are among the most death-dealing carnivores the world has ever seen.

Sacrificing an animal means consciously participating in cosmic movement, from life through death to life. The dead creature is eaten in the context of sharing, both with other people and with unseen supernatural forces, part of the meat being set aside to be offered up to the gods; sometimes the whole animal is destroyed and not eaten by its sacrificers, so that the gods receive all of it as a gift. ("To sacrifice" in English means "to give something up" in consequence.) Sacrificial animals are usually males, which makes sense in the context of animal husbandry, where females produce both the milk and the young. Emphasis is placed in addition on the unblemished state of the animal chosen, because generosity and not merely economics enters into the offering and eating of the sacrifice.

The "change" brought about in the animal—its death—is used to suggest endings of various kinds: the end of hostility, of impurity, of an earlier state of being. The subsequent eating then performs the function of moving forward, by incorporating the change into the life of the group. Sacrifices are used for initiation ceremonies, to mark the "death" inherent in every new start. The dead creature mediates and reconciles: it is a kind of hyphen, separating but uniting one side and another. Sacrifice was used to celebrate one of the world's great religious ideas: that of the covenant between the Jews and their God. As a linking device, sacrificial offering was a perfect expression of the tremendous and irreversible connection. The Hebrew prophets railed repeatedly against sacrifice—but only whenever the connection between sacrifice and the covenant was forgotten; for sacrifice could be abused, as any ritual can be subverted when it is performed for debased ends, or as a hypocritical facade.

Myths about sacrifice often tell us that the animal killed and eaten takes the place of the original sacrificial offering, a human being. Time and again the point is made that in the past, or elsewhere—or even now if we are not very careful about it—the group on hand at this violent death might have murdered, or wanted to kill and even eat, a human victim. Animals, according to this apprehension, are surrogates, substitutions for members of our own species whom we once joined in killing. Nothing so unites us as gathering with one mind to murder someone we hate, unless it is coming together to share in a meal.

Many of the rituals of sacrificially slaughtering an animal for dinner include gestures of identity with the victim (putting a hand on it, for example, before striking the blow), the expression of admiration and gratitude (treating it gently, dressing it with wreaths, gilding its horns), and the eliciting of signs that the animal does not mind dying to feed us (the creature might be made to lower its head in agreement, or be required to walk calmly to its fate). There are often ritual cries of sorrow when it dies. For *gratitude* is the result of sacrifice: thankfulness for dinner, for contact with God and conscious participation in the cycle of the cosmos, for the social well-being which sharing in a meal inspires, and to the victim for bringing us together. Animals killed sacrificially can also induce a fearful awareness of the human capacity for violence. In sacrifice, violence is noted and regretted, and attempts are made to transcend it. (The modern institution of mechanical slaughterhouses and butchering behind the scenes, on the other hand, is designed to preclude any experience of what must invariably happen before we select our supermarket slice of steak, spread out on its cardboard tray under a chaste stretch of plastic film.)

The ancient Greeks used sacrifice to express contact with—but also their difference from—the gods, who were not only immortal but capable of dining on whiffs of the smoke of burned animal bones and fat. Every meat meal began with a sacrifice; Homer used a word meaning "to make holy" (like the word "sacrifice") for slaughtering an animal for dinner meat. The way in which sacrifice was performed was extremely important, being sacred ritual: the rules were like a solemnized code of table manners. If anything went wrong, the whole ceremony became fraught with danger. Homer's epics provide many descriptions of sacrifice carefully performed in preparation for dinner. One such narrative, from the *Odyssey*, describes a ritual that was pious yet primarily secular in the sense that it required no temple and no priest; it was not festive behaviour. On this occasion a boar was selected, and some of its bristles burned as a preliminary offering to the gods. This was like the offering of "first fruits" at a harvest of vegetable crops, the first small consecration to the gods before anything can begin. (The Jewish rite of circumcision is a sacrificial offering in this category, as well as an initiation and a celebration of belonging.) The boar was struck on the head and stunned, then slaughtered and cut in large pieces. From each of these another "sacrifice" was made, of a small slice which was covered with fat, sprinkled with barley groats, and thrown into the fire.

These pieces-of-pieces were consumed by the gods, who delighted in fat and smoke; they shared the dinner with the people eating together. Behind this practice lay the story of Prometheus, the humanity-loving god who tricked Zeus into letting human beings sacrifice the way they do, sharing with the gods yet eating the meat themselves, using fire, and learning technology and all that it entails. Prometheus was to be crucified for his pains, bound and nailed to a rock for thousands of years, until he was rescued by a man, Heracles, who was to become immortal and go to live with the gods. It was in honour of the binding of Prometheus that every Greek banqueter wore a wreath tied round his head. Sacrifice, which deals death, was always an institutionalized bridge linking—but separating—mortality and immortality. The barley groats sprinkled on the gods' portions were agricultural offerings; in Latin they were known as *mola*, ground grain, a word related to "mill" and "meal," and the root of the word "immolation."

As the feast of Eumaeus in the *Odyssey* continued, the remaining lumps of pork were sliced, skewered, and grilled. From the cooked meat yet other "first fruits" were offered up: seven portions were laid aside, in this case for Hermes and the Nymphs; they were thought of as invited to the meal as invisible guests. When the mortals present finally came to be served, Odysseus, disguised as a stranger-guest, was given the choicest portion of meat, "long slices from the chine," which he deserved both as guest of honour and because he was, in reality, the master of the feast. When everyone was served, each diner took another offering from his portion, and gave it up to the gods. There followed the sharing out of wine. But first a little of it was splashed on the ground: again "first fruits," this time poured out, as a libation. Only after all this piety could the diners settle down to eat their meal.

The Jewish feast of Passover is a ritual meal which used to begin with a sacrifice, wedding the products of the nomadic pastoral life (in the slain lambs eaten) and of agricultural settlements (in bread). The bread contained no leaven and no flour from the previous harvest because Passover initiates the new year, being held on the night of the full moon of the vernal equinox. It stresses cleansing, formerly through selection of the victims and through their carefully separated blood poured out for God, and today through rejection of leaven as impurity. It celebrates the unbreakable covenant between God and the Jews; and it commemorates their liberation from Egypt after the last of the seven plagues, which struck the first-born children of the Egyptians but "passed over" those of the Jews. It includes first fruits of both animal husbandry and agriculture, provides initiation, commemorates and reseals connection with God, and strengthens the community of the group celebrating: all of these intentions were present within ancient Greek sacrifice, in its own context.

During Passover, past events such as the Exodus from Egypt become present truths by the ritual repetition of them; people relive and incorporate the past which has formed them. The killing of sacrificial victims ended in Judaism with the destruction of the Temple in Jerusalem in A.D. 70. The commemoration continues as the annual Seder celebration, a ritual dinner (*Seder* means "order") that remembers and makes present the Jewish past, the story of which is retold by the partakers in both meal and history. Yearly repetition makes it a cyclical feast, but it relives initiatory historical events: it knows time as both linear and circular at once. It is about the creation of the world, its preservation, and the cleansing of old imperfections so that new life can begin and continue.

The Christian Eucharist (*Eucharist* means "thanksgiving") was born directly from the Jewish Passover sacrifices. In it, animals are not killed because one message of the Eucharist is that, for believers, it re-enacts the conclusive sacrifice; neither human beings nor animals need ever be immolated again, because the thing has been done. Sacrifice is not abolished but *included*, in something larger than itself, which is done but not over. One way in which Christians can relive the uniting of the great oppositions articulated in their religion is in the celebration of what Catholics call "the Mass," literally, "the sending" of the congregation out into the world after they have experienced what is undoubtedly the most significance-charged dinner ritual ever devised.

In this ritual, Christ, who is for believers both God and human, enters not only into the minds but into the bodies of the congregation; the people present at the table eat God. No animal and no new death is needed, no bridges required: God enters directly. The Eucharist is the ritual perpetuation of the incarnational relationship with humankind which God initiated through Christ (the word "incarnation" means "becoming flesh"). The death of Christ—injustice, torture, murder, and sacrilege—is experienced as transformed by him, and his acceptance and forgiveness of it, into grace and salvation; an ending and an initiation into new life. And then the ultimate taboo is reverently broken as the people share out and consume his body and blood, the proofs of his love. They become "one body," as they say, "through him, with him, and in him."

The ceremony uses every psychological device defined by scholars of ritual. These include notions such as entrainment, formalization, synchronization, tuning, and cognitive structuring, as well as spatial organization and focusing, and perfected ordinary action. Distances both temporal and spatial are collapsed, as ritual contact is made with past, present, and future at once, and as "this place" is united with "everywhere else," including the realm of the supernatural. When the bread and wine are consecrated, the profane becomes sacred, the sacred insists on annihilating the difference between it and the profane. One past death ritually repeated leaves no excuse for any further violence or scapegoating. All the boundaries are crossed: between individual and group; death and life; spirit and body; meaning and fact; beginning, lasting, and ending; old and new; here and elsewhere; eternal and temporal; linear and cyclical time; host and guest; God and humankind. As a meal, the Mass spans all of the meanings of eating at once—from cannibalism to vegetarianism, from complete fusion of the group to utterly individual satisfaction, from the breaking of the most fearful of taboos to the gentlest and most comforting restoration. All this and more is contained, expressed and controlled by ritual: dramatic movement and structure, song, costume, poetry, incense, gesture, and interaction; every one of the five senses is employed in the service of mystical experience. There are also tablecloths and napkins, candles, cups, plates, jugs, and wash basins. The Eucharistic celebration is a dinner, at which table manners are entirely necessary; for nothing like it—no ritual celebration whatever, not even the most ordinary lunch at a fast-food restaurant—can begin to be imagined unless the people participating in it commit themselves, both now and in future, to behaving.

2

Learning to Behave

*P*olite behaviour is ritual performed for the sake of other people, and for the sake of our relationship with other people. Its purpose is to please and soothe them, especially where a rough passage is to be feared; to recognize and supply their need for esteem and comfort; to get one's way with them without arousing resentment. "Arousal" and "roughness" are avoided; smoothness and lubrication are what is sought. A polite person is *polished* (from the French *poli*; words to do with etiquette tend to derive from French).

> Men are polished, through act and speech,
> Each by each,
> As pebbles are smoothed on the rolling beach.

Being made "smoother" by others' insistence, by "rubbing up against each other," we become easier to deal with and better able to handle other people. By an odd coincidence, "politeness" sounds like "politics," which comes from the Greek word for a city (*polis*), just as "civilized" and "civil" come from Latin *civis*, a dweller in cities. It is often the assumption that "polished," "civil" people are to be found where many other people live: they are probably in an urban environment, which renders them "urbane."

Politeness forces us to pause, to take extra time, to behave in pre-set, pre-structured ways, to "fall in" with society's expectations. It is therefore the object of education, both by our parents when we are small and by society later. Other people inevitably make demands on us and inhibit us, partly in order to make room for themselves; we learn that it is in our best interests to play the game, because we also require the freedom which other people's restraint allows to us. But nothing about being polite is simple: the "polish" intended to help people interact with one another can be used to prevent real contact from occurring at all. It can also become itself a barrier, keeping the "unpolished" beyond the pale.

Mark Twain spoke of the cauliflower as "nothing but cabbage with a college education." We immediately see what he means: cabbages are simple, round, and lowly; but cauliflowers erupt into a sort of solid flower, elaborate, white, delicate, and somehow "refined." "Training is everything," Twain concludes—although, in the very metaphor he uses, he draws attention to cauliflower's original cabbagy "background," which the vegetable can never entirely transcend, no matter how much success its college degree might signify. But the cauliflower has complicated itself; it has put on embellishment. And in doing so it has prepared itself to move in "the best circles."

· Bringing Children Up ·

It is not enough that a child must grow up; he or she must "be brought" up as well. The verb is passive—the bringing is done to the child—and the implication is that the road travelled leads to a higher level.

Babies cannot be treated as though they were adults. They are utterly dependent on adults for their survival; they cannot walk or talk or eat or control their bowels. People have often thought of babies as not quite human—feeding off their mothers like little cannibals, impossible to discuss things with or explain things to, unruly, messy, demanding, "untamed," and rowdy. The ancient Romans believed that baby bears were born not only helpless but shapeless as well: mother bears (who had presumably been seen from a distance cleaning their newborns with their tongues) were thought actually to lick their offspring into the shape of little bears after their birth. We think of human children as needing, culturally speaking, to be "licked into shape"; fitted to be "one of us."

The process begins as soon as possible, with nursing. Mothers can be indulgent nursers, or let their babies cry to be fed; the infant soon experiences the degree to which it, or its mother, determines the feeding schedule. The mother's attitude in this regard, as in so much else, tends to be culturally induced. In most of the societies anthropologists have studied, mothers show enormous indulgence in feeding their babies, tending on the whole to feed them as soon as they show the slightest sign of wanting to be fed. In many cases women are not allowed any sexual relations while nursing. Sooner or later—very often because her husband demands it—the mother must wean her child. Renewed sex is desired, a new sibling has arrived, the woman's labour and unremitting attention are required in other fields. The baby, like its mother, has no choice but to fit in with these claims, suddenly laid by other people.

Every human being without exception must pass through this rite of passage, being forbidden the motherly breast or the bottle and taught to eat solid food. The child must learn for most of its meal-times to give up sucking, the skill with which it was born. The area inside the cheeks of small children is well provided with tastebuds, which adults' cheeks are not; babies taste not only with their tongues but with their cheeks. This is thought to be why they like packing their mouths with food. They must be made to take less at a time. Chewing itself has to be learned, by trial and error. Hunger— direct, physical, and individually experienced, the natural necessity to which every one of us submits—now truly enters the social domain. It will continue to be teased, delayed, diverted, interpreted, and manipulated by other people until the day we die.

The growing child is educated in, and becomes accustomed to, the food of its culture (the English word "wean" originally meant "to accustom," as in one's "wont"). If adults commonly eat powerful substances like chili peppers or fermented fish, the child will have become accustomed even before it is weaned to the smells of these, and even to their taste, through its mother's milk. Foods like these are usually culture-specific; they may function as distinguishing marks of the society that learns from childhood to eat them. Other people, who have not been taught as children to like them, find the consuming of them incomprehensible. They might mock the chili-eaters and the swallowers of smelly fish by jeering at their weird tastes—but even in so doing they are forced to recognize the identity of the group. So the Germans are nick-named "Krauts," the French "Frogs," and the Inuit "Eskimo" (from an Indian word meaning "those who eat meat raw"). It is well attested that people continue to enjoy as adults the food they learned to like as children. They grow up loving, say, curries and chutneys, or pasta and tomatoes, olives, sharp cheeses, and bitter herbs, and this food seems normal to them. Other people seem to them to eat very poorly indeed by comparison. The language one first learns to speak, and the food one is accustomed to eat in childhood, are two of the most fundamental preservers of an adult's social and racial identity.

Many adults are extremely conservative about what they eat. This attitude, which is known as *neophobia*, "the fear of the new," has the important biological function of guarding us from eating unknown, possibly poisonous substances: people all have a tendency to be fussy about what they put into their mouths. Children who are first learning to eat solid foods will try (or resign themselves to) almost anything; solidity itself is enough of a problem to get on with. But this is a temporary phase; they soon "lock in" to a set of expectations about what to eat and what to refuse. These are derived from a combination of their own personal experiences with food and the prevailing cultural pattern. They become extremely finicky as they learn to differentiate, deciding what to choose and what to reject from the vast numbers of possibilities in the world, which have been made available to them by the weaning process itself.

There is another, totally different attitude towards food, which is *neophilia*, "the love of the new." Human beings are capable of seeking for variety, almost in itself. They will try new ways of cooking, new ingredients, new combinations of tastes. They hunt through books describing the food of cultures very different from their own, searching for new things to eat, new flavours and textures to try. Such people have usually had occasion to conquer and break out of their "fear of the new" through contact with other cultures and the availability to them of a wide assortment of "strange" foods. We admire and envy such people, and feel we should try to imitate them, thinking how sophisticated, knowledgeable, and broad-minded they are. Yet neophilia, in fact, is a typical human reaction to eating. Our own culture is experiencing at the moment a strong bias, or perhaps more specifically a pull exerted by the trend-setting "upwardly mobile" classes, towards neophilia.

Human beings are omnivorous, which means far more than being able to live on flesh, or vegetables, or both. They can survive either on a very monotonous diet (if only a few things happen to be on hand) or, if that small but satisfying range of foods becomes scarce, they can leave for new pastures and search for other things to eat. This physical capability, and the openness to experimentation which it allows, was as important for our successful evolution as was neophobia. Both tendencies inhabit all of us. The philosopher Wittgenstein hated being confronted with a change in his diet: he regarded the effort involved in adapting to it a waste of his energy. He once made it clear to some friends with whom he was staying that it did not much matter to him *what* he ate, so long as it was always the *same*. He settled during those months for an almost unvarying diet of Swiss cheese and rye bread.

Fast-food manufacturers and other mass producers of foodstuffs love and encourage the neophobia in us: the acceptance of, even preference for, hamburgers or pizza day in, day out, served always in the same way, in similar surroundings, and with always the same small range of trimmings; the eternal steak or lobster because these are the "best," the "most unadorned," the "most expensive"; the constant comforting presence on the table of the same brand-name sauce to lend a predictable taste to everything. A place in our lives for the monotonous is assured in any case, because people under stress always settle for eating what they are used to. We reject, for instance, anything fancy for breakfast, feeling fragile and unadventurous just after the little daily trauma of getting out of bed. Similarly, sick people are not usually tempted by strong-tasting, constantly changing, or "inventive" food.

Nowadays there is tremendous encouragement to develop the neophiliac tendency in ourselves. In parts of the world where people already have plenty to eat, "more" can only mean "more expensive" and "more various." Adventurousness has become an aspect of consumerism; it is in addition a cultural expression of one of the cardinal principles of modern ideology, which is mobility. It is a response to the increasing pluralism of modern society, and the unavoidable contact into which we are flung, with new ideas and different tastes. "Love of the new" has come to seem a hallmark of experience and awareness, a sign of competence and a willingness to accept cultural enrichment—part, in short, of the modern middle-class image. "Ethnic" food was once regarded as a sort of obstinate hangover from the past, clung to by simple folk who ought to have learned how to eat better. Nowadays, smart restaurants set out to tempt smart mobile people with the richly various products of *all* the traditions. We are exhorted to try not only French and Italian ideas about food, but also Thai and Japanese—or Afghan, Ethiopian, or Sri Lankan.

Neophilia receives strong backing from the health craze. Dieticians tell us to eat a wide variety of foods, plenty of vegetables, fish, meat, cheese, fruit. Parents are convinced for many reasons that what their children need is variety. And so the battle begins, as children, having only just learned to be neophobic, confront tremendous parental and cultural pressures to "eat well," that is, variously. Parents are trying to do what they are convinced is best; children often resist. They learn quickly that refusing food is a sure way of gaining attention, of upsetting the person who has bought and worked to prepare a meal according to the best modern advice.

It is impossible for us, given our whole background, to let children do without their food; if they refuse to eat, we feel acutely unhappy. Preventing children from eating (sending them to bed without any supper or without any dessert) was a common punishment for bad behaviour until only very recently. Adults themselves used regularly to fast or abstain from luxury foods, for reasons having to do with autonomy in its original sense, "self-control." The idea of fasting for most Western people has undergone a mysterious change: self-control where food is concerned now means control of one's shape, in conformity with the convention that people should look narrow rather than wide. Children (who must get bigger) cannot be "on a diet" except for strictly medical reasons; children, unlike adults, must obviously *eat*. If they (often like adults themselves) refuse to eat much, or want to eat only certain things, adults must try to change their ways.

In France, parents traditionally insist that it is good manners for children to "try a little of everything." The rule prepares small French people to accept the variety that is offered by French cuisine; it is one reason why the French have withstood the modern onslaughts of sugar as well as they have. North American parents impose no such rule of manners; their insistence has to do entirely with health. Food manufacturers infinitely prefer "health" to "manners" as a guide to behaviour. Manners are matters of self-control and a semi-moral guide; they cause people to make up their minds before commercial interests have a chance to assert themselves. "Health" is vaguer, more scientific and less human, and far less attainable as an ideal. Into the breach between this abstract goal and our hesitations about how to achieve it leap the purveyors of foods and of technology.

They love giving advice to parents on how to persuade children to eat a healthy diet. The promoters of microwave ovens, for instance, put out a whole line of "microwavable" foods which come to us in small, crumb-coated pieces. The advertising of such products suggests that children be allowed to eat these crumbed, "bite-sized" pieces with their fingers, "because this might persuade the child to try different foods." Microwave ovens happen to manage small pieces best, and in addition the manufacturers capitalize on the "neat, clean, separate" symbolism so precious in our culture generally. Ready-yellowed coatings are designed to look appetizing even as they cover awkward food colours and shapes, and disguise the raw look which customers are said to object to, even if the food *is* raw. The promoters also strengthen and "package" their contents for easier transport and longer shelf life. If you buy your broccoli bits crumbed (that is, disguised) and then microwave them, you will make your life a lot easier; and your child just might be seduced by the novelty, and by not having to use knives and forks, into eating, for once, "something green."

It is very common for the difference between adults and children to be underlined by food distinctions. Many societies decide that there are foods children must not eat. Often the reasons given are half-physical, half-moral ones. Chaga children were told, "Don't eat the mouthparts of any animal, especially its tongue: it causes you to quarrel"; "Don't eat the animal's head—it makes you stubborn." So adults attempt to assure children that bad moral behaviour can be "turned down" as an option, just as food can be relegated to the "not eaten" category. In our own culture, where taboos are underpinned less by moral than by health rules, children are prevented from eating and drinking what is "bad for them"—but all right for adults. It is our way of finding some respite from our demanding offspring: while we are drinking our unhealthy tea or coffee, children cannot be admitted to the party. They must go away and play together, or drink something "safe"—like soft drinks. Finally being admitted to coffee- and tea-drinking, then, is a minor initiation rite: you are old enough to "take it," and by that time you are also likely to know how to "behave."

We also provide "children's food," which we ourselves rarely eat; children may be allowed to eat substances like peanut butter (now almost forbidden to adults for slimming reasons) whenever they feel like it. In precisely the same way, an African tribe, otherwise quite fierce in matters of child discipline, decided that adults do not much like ripe bananas. Bunches of them would be kept under the eaves of the houses, so that children could help themselves whenever they felt like it. The tactic reminds us of the way in which milk has in most human societies been always for children, and not "grown-ups'" food.

Children take years and years to train; for a long time they simply cannot be expected to "behave" like adults. The Indian anthropologist Arjun Appadurai has remarked that children in his culture are treated "like gods"—in that they cannot be expected to follow human rules; they have, like beasts, gods, and prophets, "no manners." They, like the gods, eat before everybody else does. Serious attention has to be paid to their tastes. The food they leave on their plates is not degraded or polluted as left-overs generally are in Hindu religion: like the food which is offered to the gods but "left over" by them and distributed to the worshippers, children's left-over food is edible, especially by their mothers.

Until children can "behave," they may have to eat away from the adults, who have learned not to be able to bear watching someone spill food down their front, splash in their drink, or suddenly yell with delight. It is in our society still a common punishment for bad behaviour to be sent away from the table, to eat alone elsewhere. Mothers, whose job it mostly remains to teach children their manners, often feed the children early in the evening—children "need" to eat early—and have them in bed and out of the way so that parents can eat together later, in peace. Parties, in upper-class western European and North American practice, are now either for children only, or they are wholly adults' night-time affairs, at which alcoholic drinks are served, and spicy, "original" food which is officially unsuitable for children. Other people, for example, the English working class, give parties which are largely for the family, and the children are welcome. The sociologists N. Charles and M. Kerr speculate that this may be because non-professional people are less likely to move away from home because of their jobs. They keep in much closer contact with family and old friends while they are having their children, and in any case their dinner parties tend to be given more for family than for friends. Food is served which is not exotic, not "too strong," "too spicy," or "indigestible." Everybody, without regard to "generation gaps," can come to the party. What is being celebrated here is the clan, which includes the children; whereas the "Young Urban Professional" kind of party strongly accentuates the difference between adults and children.

It is very often rude to take food without asking first. The anthropologist Bambi Schieffelin tells us that this rule is especially carefully instilled among Kaluli children in Papua New Guinea, in a society with a strong cultural preference for explicit verbal communication. If people stare at food, it means they want some—and very small Kaluli children are taught not to annoy others by "asking with the eyes." A right to the food requires that one ask for it; if one has no right, one does not look. Staring at somebody else's plate during dinner is very effectively discouraged in our own culture; for us it forms part of our insistence on spatial boundaries, which are observed at every meal as they are in many other areas of our lives.

African children at dinner must watch their elders serve themselves first; important adults might take whole spoonfuls of relish from the central dish, while the children themselves are only allowed a little—perhaps merely to dip their porridge (the staple of the meal) into the pot. From medieval times in Europe, children have been warned, "Ask not for any thing, but tarry till it be offered thee." "Not asking" might be part of a further rule, enjoining silence upon children: even if social rules permit adult conversation at dinner, all good children should be "seen and not heard." These are, of course, children old enough to "behave," and therefore old enough to be silenced: license might be given to the youngest child ("as to a god") to talk, run around, or ask for food from adults' plates. But it is important that children, though "not heard," should nevertheless be "seen": they must be scrutinized by grown-ups as they learn to behave. Surveillance and control is part of the reason for their admittance to the group of their elders. "Every meal," goes a proverb popular with the Victorians, "is a lesson learned." Reaching adulthood often means a relaxation of regulations, rather than a tightening, and old people may be allowed special privileges at dinner.

It is clear from European paintings of family meals, and from injunctions such as the following, that children often stood to eat their food when at the table with adults.

Look thou be courteous standing at meat
And that men giveth thee, take and eat,
And look thou neither cry nor crave,
Saying, "That and that would I have!"
But stand thou still before the board
And look thou speak no loud word.

This was partly a function of their size—a standing child could reach the top of the table more easily, and not everyone possessed small chairs or high ones for the use of children only. (Children in seventeenth-century Britain seem sometimes to have sat apart from the table for meals, using stools for tables and footstools for seats.) But standing, in the language of European etiquette, also quite certainly signified lower status. There may also have been a "health" reason invoked. It was believed that eating food while upright facilitated digestion: to this day Scots like eating their porridge standing up. In other cultures, children have been expected to remain outside the circle of adults, either sitting on the floor or standing behind the seated group; they would then either wait to be fed until the adults were finished, or be passed food as and when their parents felt it was appropriate.

Rules of this sort (there are many variations), ancient and still common as they are, sound strange to many in our own culture today. In a tiny modern family it seems absurd to expect any members of the group to keep quiet. Children, especially those from middle- and upper-class backgrounds, are deliberately encouraged to talk at table, to ask questions—even to ask why they should follow any of the rules of etiquette. Parents who are so busy that they are coming to wonder whether they should go on "staging" family meals at all often continue the tradition almost entirely because they feel that children need these meals: they must learn how to converse. Our cultural tradition expects us to bring up children to ask why; and where people's lives are lived so separately, dinner-table conversation becomes a unique opportunity for the family to find out what all its members are thinking and doing.

Many of the rules of etiquette which children absorb at mealtimes will be important throughout their lives, and in spheres beyond that of the dinner table. In European culture, saying "thank you" is one of the first lessons children learn. British English provides a special word ("ta") to serve as both "please" and "thank you," because the lesson is expected to be learned as children first find out about giving and taking—that is, when they are just beginning to learn to talk, and before they can even pronounce "thank you." Thanking people properly is still one of the most important rules of etiquette; in the English study by Charles and Kerr, in which mothers were asked to rate the importance of what children learn at table, saying "please" and "thank you" was at the top of the list. Following it came the correct use of utensils, not bringing books and toys to table, not making a noise while at table, and asking permission before leaving.

An African child may have to become accustomed to using both hands when receiving anything. What more appropriate place to learn this essential gesture than when sharing a family meal, with all the solemn "serving" that goes on? In many cultures, accepting in both hands means appreciation of the generosity of the donor: the idea is that one hand would not be sufficient to hold the symbolic value of the gift. Stretching out only one hand to receive shows lack of gratitude, and might be interpreted as contemptuous behaviour. (A Malawian riddle gives us an idea of the shock experienced when white people would accept proffered objects in one hand. Question: "Even the European respects this. What is it?" Answer: "A peanut: even they always hold it in both hands"—that is, in order to shell or peel it.) If food is given to a child by a relative, however, the giver may not expect to be thanked: thanking in its fullest, or its verbal, expression may be regarded as due only in transactions with strangers, people who have no obligations to each other. The anthropologist Audrey Richards reports the explanation given her of a child's apparently ungrateful behaviour: "He doesn't thank because they are his own people. If it had been an outsider, he would have said, 'Thank you, Sir,' because it would have been from pity they gave to him. To one's own people one does not thank, not at all!"

Children learn when eating with their elders all the status and kinship patterns of their family as they watch how adults treat each other and discover their own "place." An Indian child, for instance, soon knows as many as twenty-four castes, in their correct hierarchical patterns, and how they relate to each other— through food rules, and watching who can eat what from the hand of whom. An African boy, asked who the "fathers" were in the complex kinship structure of his tribe, could reply, "The men I kneel to when I bring them water to drink." Traditional families in Europe and America which sat down to a dining-room table with Father at the head, and Mother, who had prepared everything to his liking, seated at a "lower" place at table to signify her subordination, soon taught the children who, officially at least, wielded the real power in the group.

Every society has its store of traditional exhortations, cries of warning, proverbs, verses, and sing-song phrases which are produced whenever children's manners threaten to lapse; indeed, eating and its vital interest for the child is an important locus for language learning. Tiny babies hear words of comfort and encouragement when being urged to "bubble up" after nursing (later they will have to relearn: belching becomes taboo once solid food is normally eaten). Messy eaters soon discover the culture's sounds of disgust and disapproval. A "distinctive pharyngeo-velar friction," linguists such as John Widdowson tell us, is extremely common—and effectively memorable for the child. Praise and smiling greets the child who shows it is eating with appetite. Downing a meal is encouraged by pretending the food is a wasp and the child's mouth a cave, or the spoon an aeroplane zooming in to land; and when the plate is empty, triumphant cries like "All gone!" are given "the typical intonation of a sign-off, greatly exaggerated in pitch pattern."

In cultures rich in proverbs, riddles, and oral mnemonics, the child may be taught simultaneously its manners and how to interpret and apply quite complicated parables. In Malawi, for example, according to Margaret Read, a proverb might suddenly, in the middle of dinner, be dropped "like a stone into a pond"—"I hear the guns of the Tyandla people booming." Conversation ceases; everyone stops eating and looks at the child who has been slurping his food. The child begins "to wonder to himself: 'Can that be for me? No? Yes? It *is* me. I am ashamed.'" Nothing further is said, but the lesson is learned—presumably unforgettably. The child is taught as well to interpret his culture's way of uttering veiled rebukes, how to understand and accept their application to him- or herself, and also exactly how, and how much, to suffer social pressure.

Our own elders are ready with a whole litany of traditional reproaches and commands to choose from and apply to rude children. "Waste not want not!" "Hunger is the best sauce!" "All uncooked joints off the table!" "Whose eyes are bigger than their stomach?" "Think of the starving children [elsewhere]!" "Eat it—it'll make your hair curl! [if you are a girl]," or, "it'll put hair on your chest! [if you are a boy]." There are also monsters and dire warnings, such as those popularized in Hoffmann's horrific *Struwwelpeter* (1876): the "great, long, red-legged Scissor Man" who cuts off your thumbs if (having been early weaned) you won't stop seeking comfort in sucking them; the dreadful fate of Augustus, who refused to have any soup:

> He's like a little bit of thread,
> And, on the fifth day, he was—dead!

and the mortification of Fidgety Philip, who falls back on the chair he *will not* stop balancing, and drags the tablecloth and everything on it on top of himself.

Children are often taught when tiny not to waste food, and always to share it with others. All of a society's manners might be summed up in the exquisitely difficult rule: Have a small appetite. The rule need not exist wholly because food is scarce. Even where there is plenty to eat, the principle of respect for food is commonly upheld; wasting it shows lack of respect for God, the earth, and each other. Children who waste food are punished, and may find their dinners given away to someone else. In a Malayan village, where children liked the expensive fish but not the inexpensive vegetables (children very quickly know which foods are prized by the community), they were firmly served very limited amounts of fish by their mothers. When they were older they could serve themselves, the reason being that "they were now of an age" to know how to hold themselves back from the expensive dishes.

European and North American anthropologists describe with astonishment the way tiny African children learn to divide any tempting morsel, such as a single piece of fruit, with everybody present; a small Malawian child "was made to unclench his fist in which he was hiding three ground-nuts and give two of them to his fellows." Mothers who are otherwise indulgent towards their children are, in such cultures, extremely exigent in this: sharing with others, and the giving of hospitality to strangers, are both at the top of the list of rules of good behaviour. In our own culture, special attention is paid to making the strong share with the weak: "Give some to baby!" This principle, even where there is great value given to "the rights of the elder," always operates to some extent. Where a whole family shares its dinner by taking it piecemeal from a single pot, very sophisticated timing might be going on as the dinner progresses, with rules that the bigger ones finish sooner, so that the slower ones, including the children, are left enough to satisfy them.

A Chaga mother who had prepared the family meal would be the only person present at dinner without a plate. She ate straight from the pot, and when there was little food would take nothing at all. Each child had then to leave a handful of food on his or her plate for the mother. To a child who did not do this, the mother would say, "Look, you haven't given me any food. Don't be astonished if I do the same to you next time!" Sharing is the foundation of civilized behaviour; it is what links individuals, families, villages, and tribes together. People should know how to share even when they are hungry: hard times may come for you, too, and you may then look with some rightful expectancy to another's generosity.

A sociological study by R. Dyson-Hudson and R. Van Dusen of middle-class North American schoolchildren in 1972 found that a whole food-sharing "culture" existed among them. It was not just that some food items were preferred, and owners of them profited from the power they achieved by sharing some with certain others. Children were seen exchanging lunchbags without looking at the contents first, and swapping identical cookies. Food linked these particular children, but in a manner which separated the *meaning* of the food very firmly from its objective self. The children were discovered to insist at home on being given cookies, fruit, and candy to share with others at school; they became furious if they found none of these in their lunchboxes. Mothers who gave these useful items were helping their children to hold their own in a complex, ruthless schoolyard world, much as African mothers in the Chaga tribe would secretly send food out, via a younger sibling, to boys who had just begun their lives as herdsmen with the other males, where they were supposed officially to start finding their own food by their wits alone. It was noticed in the American study that children never shared the "central" part of their meals—their sandwiches and milk—as adults share the entree or the roast. It was always the "extras" and "luxuries"—gum, pretzels, raisins—that could be used symbolically to create or cement friendships and alliances.

The battle waged by parents in order to teach their children manners is often itself a largely symbolic power struggle. Parents soon find out, however, that children are capable of behaving perfectly well when strangers are visiting, or when they are invited out. And this is one of the reasons why children must be taught at all costs how to behave: they soon "represent" their families to other people, especially when they are out alone; and they are capable of giving their relatives, even in our own society, a good or a bad reputation.

In societies more family-conscious than our own, a great deal of trouble is taken to make children "behave" when away from home. One of the family secrets is liable to be how much food it has access to, or holds in store (it is rather like the amount Mom and Dad earn, in our own case). Households are very anxious that other people should not think they are doing badly, or going short. Very small children are therefore deceived about the family's food stores, just in case they prattle. They may be discouraged from visiting other houses at mealtimes, where hospitality demands that they be fed: what might the neighbours think—that we haven't enough at home? Children in traditional societies might be expected never to demand to eat while neighbours are visiting, or to gulp down their food when they are served; they must never pick up food in other houses and eat it. Indeed, one of the signs that a child is ready to appear at dinner parties when guests are present is its proven ability to conceal what is known. A well-behaved child never tells what it has found out about the family business; it has learned that family loyalty is prior even to commensal togetherness. (No doubt part of the reason for our own law of children's silence before guests at the dinner table was the danger that a child might suddenly embarrass the family with its revelations.)

In our own culture, children are taught how to eat at an exceedingly culture-specific *table*. The dining table is not only the setting they will surely encounter, and need to have mastered, in life away from home; it is also a constraining and controlling device, a place where children eat under the surveillance of adults. In families which are too poor, or who live in a space too confined, to possess a table where everyone can sit down together, mothers complain that it is impossible to control their children during meals. A typical scenario, reported by Charles and Kerr, is Mother battling to keep the children eating "properly" in the kitchen, while Father is watching TV next door. Where everyone's eating is done before the television set—that is, side by side and with the scrutiny of grown-ups concentrated elsewhere—children might never learn how to cut and chew neatly, how to notice what it is that other people need or are saying, or any of the other marks of being "well brought up." English people can be surprisingly adamant about "Sunday lunch," deliberately staging weekly, full-dress "proper" meals, with courses and tablecloths, where children can learn how to behave when out. One of the hallmarks of a "proper" meal has come to be "having the radio and TV turned off."

People commonly complain—with some justification—that it is difficult to teach children any manners in the fragmented, frenetic modern world with its overworked parents, its rudimentary skills in group behaviour, and its apparent devotion to doing away with the formalities. But we do in fact have standards, which are invisible to us most of the time, but which become more obvious when we hear how people behave who have different ideas, and expectations other than our own. In the mid-nineteenth century, Osgood Mackenzie and his mother visited Harris in the Outer Hebrides, off the northwest coast of Scotland. Mackenzie described, in *A Hundred Years in the Highlands*, his reception at a low, damp Harris house with walls six feet thick. His hostess, he begins by saying, "had most charming manners," like all Harris people. "She was busy preparing the breakfast, and bade us sit down on little low stools at the fire, and wait till she could milk the cow." The cattle in the Harris long house lived under the same roof as the family. "The wife took an armful of . . . heather, and deposited it at the feet of the nearest cow, which was tied up within two or three yards of the fire, to form a drainer. Then, lifting the pot off the fire, she emptied it on the heather; the hot water disappeared and ran away among the cow's legs, but the contents, consisting of potatoes and fish, remained on top of the heather. Then, from a very black-looking bed, three stark-naked boys arose, one by one, aged, I should say, from six to ten years, and made for the fish and potatoes, each youngster carrying off as much as both his hands could contain. Back they went to their bed, and started devouring their breakfast with apparently great appetite under the blankets."

• *Inhibitions* •

Because table manners are drummed into us so early and so insistently, the rules upon which they are based rarely need to be remembered once we have grown up; we have made them part of the way in which we habitually act and expect the world to operate. But for this very reason, we love hearing about people who are other than ourselves—who often seem to have no idea how to "behave" at all. Their actions remind us that manners are not nature but—at most—*second* nature; we are forced to wonder whether, if we lived elsewhere, in different conditions, our presuppositions and therefore our behaviour might have been different.

This ancient pleasure, in contemplating other people's odd behaviour (nearly always, it should be noted, with at least some contempt and complacency), is gradually being withdrawn from us. The world, for many complex reasons but chiefly because of increased communications and machine-driven standardization, is becoming more and more homogeneous. We have to look hard for manners that will shock us these days, not only because we have seen or heard of most of them already, but because there are fewer and fewer varieties to view. Those so disposed are prepared, however, to derive shock value from details, and stare in disbelief if a foreign group leaves teaspoons standing up in cups or enthusiastically toasts the hostess before eating.

But there is one direction in which we can always turn to find deliciously "other" behaviour—and that is to the past. It is not so much travellers these days as historians who can satisfy our thirst for revelations of oddity and difference. The danger with travellers' tales was always ethnocentricity, and perhaps the condescension which can easily arise from a mixture of ignorance and racial prejudice. The same kind of risk occurs when the enterprise is historical research. History answers only the questions we put to it, and the past has even less chance than a modern foreign tribe has of ensuring that we have sufficient data to make informed judgements, of not falling victim to the time-bound prejudices of the researcher, or of answering back. There is always a possibility that what we see of the past could merely be a reflection of our own beliefs and fears. If the past ever becomes our only "other," we shall be in dangerous straits indeed.

It is common knowledge (and a flattering social myth for us) that our own ancestors used to have very different—and much cruder—table manners from those we practise today. We have "come on," in other words; we have "progressed." The simplest historical novel or movie can make an exotic effect by presenting a scene in which dinner guests gnaw meat straight off bones gripped in their greasy fists, then hurl the remains into the corners of the room. These, the audience accepts without difficulty, were the manners of the past, before we became modern and civilized. (This sense of superiority does not prevent us from feeling proud, at the same time, of modern simplicity and lack of pomp. We are as capable of despising our ancestors for their tradition-bound complexity as for their rudimentary standards of propriety.)

Manners have indeed changed. They were not invented on the spot, but developed into the system to which we now conform. Since manners are rituals and therefore conservative—part of their purpose is always conservation—they change slowly if at all, and usually in the face of long and widespread unwillingness. Even when a new way of doing things has been adopted by a powerful elite group—using forks instead of fingers, for example—it may take decades, even centuries, for people generally to decide to follow suit. Forks had not only to be seen in use and their advantages successfully argued; they had also to be made and sold, then produced in versions which more and more people could afford, as they slowly ceased being merely unnecessary and became the mark of civilized behaviour. After the eleventh-century date of the first extant document describing (with wonder) the sight of someone using one, the fork took eight centuries to become a utensil employed universally in the West.

Naturally enough, historians interest themselves in why such a change—from eating with our hands to using a metal mediating instrument instead—took place at all. In our more thoughtful moments, we no longer allow ourselves to feel, simply and happily, that what has happened is "progress," that the eight centuries were an apprenticeship, a preparation for the attainment of our present enlightened state. Forks have placed us in a singularly distant relationship *vis-à-vis* our food, and, more importantly, they both express and influence our self-enclosed, fastidious attitude towards the people with whom we eat. The universalizing of the use of forks is among other things a sign of the spreading of a social attitude.

Our own culture, as it happens, provides us with a means of tracing this development, through the survival of books on etiquette that have appeared through the ages. These humble, mostly dully written little pamphlets can be studied and compared, so as to document shifts in table manners and etiquette in general. Manners books have supplied the sociologist Norbert Elias with data upon which he has built a coherent theory of the development of Western inhibitions since the Renaissance. Elias claims that at that point—specifically from 1530, the date at which Erasmus published his short treatise on manners, which he called *de civilitate morum puerilium* (On the Civility of the Behaviour of Boys)—momentous changes began in our history. The medieval concept of manners, called "courtesy" because it was practised by noblemen at court, begins to be called "civility," a term for a wholly new system of bodily propriety, which is henceforth applicable to all citizens, not merely the elite. "Civility" governs far more behaviour than table manners. The seven chapters of Erasmus's treatise concern body posture and facial expression, dress, behaviour in church, table manners, conversation, and comportment at play and in the bedroom.

From this point onwards, Elias claims, bodily functions came to be displayed in public less and less. People began to refrain in company from belching, farting, excretion, and spitting. Eventually, even speaking and writing about these things (Erasmus had been quite unembarrassed about mentioning them) was to be banned in polite society. As Elias puts it, "walls" of restraint and embarrassment grew up between people; where once dinner was *handled* by the whole group, and cutlery, dishes, and goblets passed about for all to use, now each person had his or her own implements. As time went on it was insisted that no one touch even his own food with his hands except in certain specific cases, and postures were devised which would make even brushing against another person at table as unlikely as possible.

The most interesting part of all this was that people increasingly obeyed these rules (there were fluctuations and differences among groups, and the changes came about in the course of three centuries), not primarily because they were conscious of constraint, but because they were genuinely convinced that no other ways of eating would "do." *Civilized* people behaved like this: those guilty of infractions were merely showing how uncivilized they were. The new standards, which began to be introduced in the Renaissance, became gradually internalized, which means that, once learned in childhood, people took the rules for granted; they never thought about them—unless they were suddenly confronted with an action that was "unmannerly." Then their reaction was likely to be one of disgust and revulsion, shock or laughter.

During the seventeenth century, in France, manners became a political issue. King Louis XIV and his predecessors, in collecting together the nobility of France to live with the sovereign at Versailles, instituted a sort of school of manners. At the palace, the courtiers lived under the despotic surveillance of the king, and upon their good behaviour, their deference, and their observance of etiquette their whole careers depended. If you displeased Louis, he would simply *not see you* the following day; his gaze would pass over you as he surveyed the people before him. And not being "seen" by the king was tantamount to ceasing to count, at Versailles. A whole timetable of ceremonies was followed, much of it revolving round the king's own person. Intimacy with Louis meant power, and power was symbolically expressed in attending to certain of the king's most private and physical needs: handing him his stockings to put on in the morning, being present as he used his *chaise percée*, rushing when the signal sounded to be present as he got ready for bed. It mattered desperately what closeness the king allowed you—whether he spoke to you, in front of whom, and for how long.

The point about Versailles was that there was no escape: the courtiers had to "make it" where they were. The stage was Louis's, and the roles that could be played were designed by him. It was up to each courtier to fit him- or herself into one of the slots provided. The leaders of all the other towns and villages of France were made, largely through the use of etiquette, and more specifically through rudenesses and judicious slighting by the tax-collecting intendants, to feel their subordination, their distance from the court. Once, the nobility had relied on strength, swagger, and vigour, even violence, personally to make their mark and uphold their honour; at Versailles, the way to success became discretion, observation, cunning, and the dissembling of one's aims and passions. At Versailles—and at the courts all over Europe which imitated it—everything was done to make it very clear who was superior to whom; and of course, each time anyone was polite, he or she was simultaneously acknowledging rank and demonstrating who stood where.

The new manners—both the formal rules of protocol and precedence and the unspoken, more profoundly enculturated rules like table manners—were seen increasingly, according to Elias, as ways in which one did not offend *other people*. You were controlling yourself, so as to prevent other people from being disgusted or "shocked." People lived very closely together at Versailles; everyone was watched by everyone else, and actual physical proximity helped raise some of the new sensitivity to other people's real or imagined susceptibilities. Men were expected on the whole to give up physical force as a means of getting their way, and—as always when "the graces" are preferred over brute strength—women began to count for more. Within the aristocratic court circle, people became, in spite of the obsession with rank, far more equal. Secure in the knowledge that just being at court was the pinnacle of prestige, from which most of society was shut out, courtiers could permit themselves to respect each other.

As the bourgeoisie became richer and more indispensable even at court, they demanded—and were given, by self-appointed experts who wrote manuals for them—instruction in how to behave as people did in "the best circles." In 1672, Antoine de Courtin produced *Nouveau traité de la civilité qui se pratique en France parmi les honnestes gens* (The New Treatise of the Civility Which Is Practised in France Among Honest People). ("Honest"—*honnête*—kept its original association with honour and the opposite-but-supporting notion, shame.) De Courtin writes about manners for both hosts and guests, and advises his bourgeois readers on how they should address the nobility. The Church in France also produced handbooks of manners and taught their precepts in schools. Gradually gentility spread down from the court to the bourgeoisie, and finally trickled further down to the rest of the population.

The bourgeoisie were even stricter about standards of civility than the nobility were; having no ever-present king to enforce the rules, they imposed restraints on themselves. Being more anxious to rise, they had more to lose by making slips and gaffes; so their self-inhibiting mechanisms had to be deeper rooted, less obviously the donning of an external persona than the nobility could permit themselves. The policing of emotions became internal, and finally invisible even to themselves: they were able to think that they acted, not in obedience to power and self-interest, but for purely moral reasons.

In the meantime, according to Elias, another momentous change was taking place: "childhood" was invented, in the course of the centuries following the sixteenth. The small, eventually "nuclear" family was engendered by the need for families to become consuming, as opposed to producing, units. Children had to learn the new "civilizing" rules, and in order to do so and to build up the necessary "walls of shame" required by the new individualism and the manners that protected it, they were turned into a whole new social category, different from that of adults. They were held, as no children had been before, for a protracted period in ignorance of the private world of adults.

Twentieth-century children now have, Elias claims, "in the space of a few years to attain the advanced level of shame and revulsion that has developed over many centuries." Today, our apparent freedom and unconcern about bodily and verbal proprieties is possible only because inhibitions are everywhere, and self-imposed. What we know is "relaxation within the framework of an already established standard." And the table manners we teach our children at a very early age are those which in the Middle Ages adults had still to be taught.

But drawing a line separating the sixteenth century off from everything that preceded it can give a false impression, as can limiting one's perspective to that of a single culture. As we have seen, people everywhere teach manners to their children by means of precepts, riddles, and traditional proverbs, and they seem to have done so for millennia. "At the abundant dinner of the gods, do not sever with bright steel the withered from the quick upon that which has five branches," advised Hesiod about 2,700 years ago. What he meant was, "Fingernails are not to be cut at table." Didactic poetry has existed since at least the time of Ptah-Hotep's *Instructions*, written apparently to his son, which date to about 2000 B.C. but were almost certainly copied from another book five hundred years older. Eating behaviour has also been described ethnographically and used as a fictional device since ancient times. Aristotle wrote a treatise, which has unfortunately not survived, on the behaviour of diners at the famous Spartan communal feasts called *sussitia*, and Roman literature includes stories of boorish behaviour, part of the intention of which was to confirm readers in their preference for their own good taste. We would reject today the excesses of people like Petronius' vulgar boor Trimalchio, and for very much the same reasons as the ancient Romans had for doing so.

Medieval manners books—at first in Latin, and later in Italian, French, German, and other vernacular tongues—had been jingles and rhyming verses, written to be easily memorized. (Books were scarce before the advent of the printing press.) An early English version was *The Babees' Book*, composed in the fifteenth century not for what we now call "babies," but for young pages and maids-in-waiting. The English nobility educated their children by exchanging them, after the age of about eight, with the children of other aristocratic households, so that they could be disciplined outside their own homes; it was an early version of the later British institution of boarding schools. The boys would learn, among other things, how to bow, pose, carve, and wait at table; girls would be schooled in decorative feminine movements, and in serving in the women's apartments. One English manners book for pages was called *stans puer ad mensam*, The Boy Standing at the Table (about 1430).

Treatises written to instruct novices in monasteries, like that of Hugh of St. Victor in the twelfth century, included directions on manners. Since monks came from every social class and all had to live together for life, the learning of a common standard of manners must have been an important part of the preliminary training. There is a long tradition of ecclesiastical manners books, designed to teach priests, who often came from the lowest classes, how to behave when they suddenly found themselves dining at the local château, or having to advise and chasten their bourgeois parishioners. A late example of the genre is that by Louis Branchereau (1885).

None of the medieval books on etiquette which have come down to us offer brilliant or inspired writing; the genre neither aimed for literary excellence nor attracted gifted writers to it. People were not interested in manners that were "original." They wanted to perform well the customs that were time-honoured, and welcomed traditional, well-worn statements of what was "the done thing," and more especially (and more simply) what was to be avoided. It is therefore not entirely correct to think of medieval (or any other) manners as being always horrendous (which in this context means breaking the rules) because the etiquette books constantly repeat the old precepts. It seems likely that people did not always "fall upon the dishes like swine while eating, snorting disgustingly and smacking their lips," as the poet Tannhäuser complained in the thirteenth century, even though manners books disapprove, century in, century out, of their doing so. We should note the constant likening of rude people to animals, and remember that a universal purpose of good behaviour is to demonstrate how *un*like beasts we mannerly people are. And etiquette manuals have often been addressed not only to people ignorant of "the proprieties," but also to those who consult them for esoteric details, together with satisfying reminders of what dreadful behaviour they would witness, if they were ever to associate with the sort who lack "breeding."

It seems questionable to me also that care for other people's opinions, ability to see ourselves as others must see us, and fear that gaffes and lapses in physical propriety might disgust or revolt them, only began to develop in the sixteenth century. It is true that standards of cleanliness, for instance, have risen—but other levels of the "proper" have fallen in our own living memory. Such standards rise and sink, and vary still according to class, country, and circumstance. But what remains constant is the universal—even primordial—terror of offending "them," of not measuring up to what society expects of competence, awareness, and the desire not to offend.

Where cutlery, dishes, and seating arrangements are concerned, manners in the West have changed in significant respects—although only very slowly, as in the case of the adoption of the fork. But the old ways, of eating with the fingers and sharing the drinking vessel, involved manners, too—manners particular to those ways of eating and drinking. The careful rules governing those old ways became obsolete as the new implements took over and demanded (as well as being created for) new ways of behaving. The counsel that people should not scratch themselves at table, for instance, becomes less common as access to soap and hot water reduces the discomfort at the root of the habit. In other words technological change, brought about in part by demands for increased physical protection and isolation from other people, in turn forces up the barriers and standards that structure our most intimately personal choices.

The early manners books, unless they are outlining a specifically ceremonial sequence of action, rarely tell their readers what to do: laws tend to define what is to be refrained from. Given the human propensity to laugh at the breaking of personal and physical taboos like those governed by table manners, a whole list of such rules, providing examples of the rudest behaviour imaginable, must have made hilarious reading even in medieval times. In Germany during the sixteenth century a whole genre of comic manners books began to appear, which traded on the humour that can be derived from gross behaviour. The joke was to recommend outrageous manners, solemnly and in high-blown phrases, claiming for instance that if you want to improve your health, increase your standing in the community, and do yourself justice, you really must grab what you want off the table. As Elias points out, this kind of merriment about greed and the uncouth was heartily bourgeois, and had nothing to do with the court.

Grobianus is the patron saint of the Grobe Narren or Boors in Sebastian Brandt's *Narrenschiff* or Ship of Fools (1494). Friedrich

Dedekind made him the hero of his verse satire, *Grobianus* (1549); he later added a female boor, Grobiana. The text derives very clearly from the table rules of Erasmus, which it gleefully inverts. Roger Bull published an English translation in 1739; two intervening centuries and a very different audience do not seem to have changed the humour, and therefore the relevance, of the "advice" offered. Bull dedicated the work to Swift, who "first Introduc'd into these Kingdoms, of Great Britain and Ireland, an Ironical Manner of Writing To the Discouragement of Vice, Ill-manners, and Folly." (In 1745, Swift was to write *Directions to Servants*, in which he advised the cook never to use a spoon for fear of wearing out the master's silver; he should in all things use his hands. And it was Swift whose "Modest Proposal" it had been in 1729 to deal with the problem of the poverty-stricken Irish by encouraging them to raise their children as delicacies to be consumed at table.) Bull's version of Dedekind is written in a mock-heroic style:

> But do not (if to laugh be worth your while)
> Instead of Laughter substitute a Smile.
> No, no; be sure your Merriment be loud,
> Heard in the Street by all the passing Crowd.
> Extend the Gulph your Mouth, from Ear to Ear;
> Let ev'ry Tooth in sable Pomp appear:
> Those Fangs, bespeckled like some Leopard's Skin,
> The Heart of each admiring Maiden win.

You must yell for your food, fight your way to the dishes, seize the best pieces, lick the fat off your fingers, belch, come to blows with the other guests—and never worry if your nose runs:

> If with your Elbow you wipe off the Snivel
> No Man alive shall be esteem'd more civil.

Long scenes of prandial disaster are described, in the tradition of Horace or Petronius—or of the nineteenth-century *Struwwelpeter*. Readers are assumed to be aware of the "manners code" such stories subvert—but they are not reading for instruction, nor even because they are in the habit of breaking the rules. The grotesque unseemliness, even during the "refined" eighteenth century, is sufficient attraction—that, and the eternal secret underpull in all of us: the suspicion that for two pins we might let the whole thing slide and "become like animals" too.

Erasmus's little treatise, *de civilitate* (1530), stands out from all the doggerel verses that preceded and followed his contribution to the genre. For once, manners are treated by a man of genius who had travelled widely and seen much. Erasmus, who was nearing the end of his life, decided that although external decorum was the *crassissima pars* (the "crassest part") of philosophy, and only the last on his list of four aspects of a youth's training (the first being religion, the second study, the third duty), he would set out what he thought about manners, because they were important in winning good will and in "commending" the better parts of philosophy "to the eyes of men." Manners were external signs of what ought to be real virtue.

Erasmus thinks *all* boys, not only noble ones, should learn these manners. The nobility have a duty to live up to the position they have inherited, but others have to "strive all the more keenly to compensate for the malignity of fate with the elegance of good manners. No one can choose his own parents or nationality, but each man can mould his own talents and character for himself." Our approval of Erasmus's charity and broad-mindedness is immediate; but we should not be too easily convinced that his attitude is new or revolutionary. True, the earlier manners books were written for young aristocrats, but that does not mean that no one outside the nobility wished, before Erasmus, to learn good manners, or had any idea of how to "behave."

Experience and confidence permitted Erasmus to decry manners he disapproved of, even if they were the habits of certain noblemen. For instance, it is not polite, he says, "to be repeatedly pursing the lips as if making a clucking sound, although that gesture is excusable in grown-ups of high rank as they pass through the midst of a throng; for in the case of such people all things are becoming, while we are concerned with moulding a boy." A statement like this is surely addressed not so much to the boy as to adults reading the text: it is a magnificently unassailable rebuke. Literary works—and this goes for many of the medieval and later manners books—often aim "over the heads" of the audience they are supposed, by convention, to be addressing. Again, "Grasping the bread in the palm of the hand and breaking it with the fingertips is an affected practice which should be left to certain courtiers. You should cut it properly with your knife. . . ." The courtiers' affectation was to win out in the long run and become the way we are supposed to eat dinner rolls today. But, as Elias pointed out, it is Erasmus's independence, and his preparedness to criticize even the great if they disagree with him or the tradition to which he adheres, which make his work different from most other prescriptions of civility.

The style, stature, and humanity of Erasmus, as well as the lucidity and usefulness of his observations, made his book so famous that a sixteenth-century French typeface, an imitation of handwriting, was called *civilité* after it, and manners books were set in this particular type until the nineteenth century—by which time it had become so old-fashioned as to be almost illegible. Educators for centuries killed two birds with one stone by teaching children how to read Latin through construing Erasmus on manners. The book was rewritten in dialogue and in catechism form, and done over in verse to assist in memorizing it. Gradually, examples like these of Erasmus's frankness were censored: "Withdraw when you are going to vomit; vomiting is not shameful, but to have vomited through gluttony is disgusting," and "Fidgeting in one's seat, shifting from side to side, gives the appearance of repeatedly farting, or of trying to do so." Probably schoolmasters were finding such specificity a danger to discipline in the classroom. But also discussing, even mentioning, such loss of control over the bodily orifices had become simply and generally impolite. Erasmus's *de civilitate* continued to be printed, pillaged, quoted, set on school courses, imitated, and adapted until the nineteenth century; and for the most part Erasmus on manners is as pertinent today as he was in 1530.

His treatise ends with the most important advice of all, where manners are concerned: "The essence of good manners consists in freely pardoning the shortcomings of others although nowhere falling short yourself: in holding a companion no less dear because his standards are less exacting. For there are some who compensate with other gifts for their roughness of manner. Nor should what I have said be taken to imply that no one can be a good person without good manners. But if a companion makes a mistake through ignorance in a matter which seems of some consequence, then the polite thing to do is to advise him courteously of it in private." Erasmus would have been the first to disclaim any originality for his ideal.

It is difficult to know whether *de civilitate* was popular because there was a new need for manners books, or whether the recent availability of the printed word made the book affordable to people who, had they lived before this period in history, might also have liked to have access to this kind of written treatment of the subject. The fact that printed books have played such an important role in the culture of the West has given us a tool for historical research which is denied to many other cultures. Because we have a richness of documentation in this area—partial, occasional, and in need of careful interpretation though it is—we should not imagine that other cultures have not developed and elaborated their table manners just as assiduously through time. China's three great books of ceremonial, *Tcheou-Li*, *I Li*, and *Li Chi*, were compiled between the second century B.C. and the first century A.D., all from much older sources. The *Li Chi* especially has important sections on table manners. Since then, there have been no Chinese Emily Posts, or books *de civilitate*, although books have been written on Chinese manners as guides to Westerners. Yet Chinese table manners have been for thousands of years, and remain, strict and distinctive. No doubt these manners too have changed—and also conserved themselves— over the past two thousand years; a lack of historical documents in no way signifies a lack of history.

There is no reason to believe, either, that our society has a particular claim to shame. Other societies are not more "spontaneous" or "free"—or less "civilized"—than ours in the domain of table or any other manners. Where eating dinner is concerned, human beings all over the world call upon systems and codes which are designed to control appetite and maintain social awareness of others' needs. They have done so ever since we became human. Inhibition in every case is culturally induced, by precept, example, and social conditioning.

• *Aspirations* •

An anonymous Victorian manners manual (1879) calls etiquette "the barrier which society draws around itself, a shield against the intrusion of the impertinent, the improper, and the vulgar." So much for the civility of Erasmus. "Society," in this statement, means a tiny part of society, those who are distinguished from everyone else because of their manners; this group is extremely anxious—anxious enough to put on armour and enclose itself behind a barrier—because it knows that people who are not "society" are trying to break in.

Part of the reason for good manners has always been a notion of safety: standards of behaviour are imposed in order to protect us from other people's roughness and greed, and from the consequences of pandering to our own lower instincts. Restraint is required from all of us precisely because we all mix and interact. A very different principle underlies the picture of politeness, not as protecting everyone in order to facilitate encounters each with each, but as a rampart enclosing a group. This principle has probably always existed, in some degree, in all but the simplest and most egalitarian societies. In rigidly hierarchical societies, "top" people protect themselves by ensuring that it takes extraordinary will and talent to cross the barriers. But the pressure of the principle is also powerfully felt in societies like our own, where walls exist between groups, but people are encouraged to believe there are none, or that they can cross them with ease.

Even before Louis XIV contained the nobility of France at court, groups of French aristocrats had performed an important experiment in manners. They were following in the tradition of Italian Renaissance treatises on behaviour, such as *Il Libro del Cortegiano* (The Book of the Courtier) by Baldassare Castiglione (published two years before Erasmus's *de civilitate*), the *Galateo* of Giovanni della Casa (the word for "etiquette" in Italian is still *il galateo*) (1558), and *La Civil Conversazione* by Stefano Guazzo (1574). These works—more philosophical, ethical, and political than regular manners books had set out to be—were addressed to aristocrats only, although like Erasmus's treatise, they soon became much more widely read, translated, adapted, copied, and discussed.

They emphasized the uniqueness, the grace, the innate good taste of the ideal courtier. You do not *learn* these graces, you just have them, and you know them when you see them; you recognize them in yourself and in the people you choose to associate with. People who do not possess them are pitiable perhaps, but most probably irredeemable. You try your best to keep them out of your life.

An essential part of the charm of those with taste is its effortlessness: you must, says Castiglione, show *sprezzatura*, a word meaning slightly contemptuous indifference. You are not *trying* to be charming—to try is to ruin the entire effect, for you become thereby pretentious. To "reach" in this manner is by definition to pretend to a level you have not attained. Indeed, the very fact that you are pretentious means you can never achieve it. Pretentious people sweat and struggle in their attempt to be what they are not—whereas the elect, the born "powerful because best" (which is the original meaning of the Greek term *aristocrat*), must achieve *nonchalance*, literally, the state of "not being heated." Apart from the quality of being cool (that is, relaxed and unpretentious), it was very difficult to say in what, exactly, such charm consisted. One was forced to fall back on admitting that it could not be explained. The person in question just had a *je ne sais quoi*, an "I don't know what."

The little groups of aristocrats, the "chosen few," who met in noble Parisian houses and most notably at the Hôtel de Rambouillet beginning in the 1620s and 1630s, despised the court with its pomp and hierarchy. Before Louis clamped down on them, they had time to rejoice in an ideal which was to have a long history, and is with us still: that of being an elite group of people who, having chosen one another's company, recognize their affinities and reject all boors and charmless *parvenus*. They loved simplicity, an ineffable *je ne sçais quoi* (as they spelled it then), a cool manner, and good taste. The concept of "good taste," French historians tell us, was invented in the early seventeenth century. John Dryden is said to have been the first to introduce the term to English. Aristocrats "of taste" met not in public (they abhorred the court's theatrical pomp and general exteriority) but at home. Since they preferred intimacy and small numbers, they were often invited together by a hostess, for women played a powerful role in this informal, exclusive world.

The new chic image was born in an age when the bourgeois class was quickly becoming richer, more competent, and more powerful. It was increasingly difficult for the nobility to use wealth to mark the difference between themselves and the *arrivistes* or *parvenus* (literally, those "who had finally—and only just—arrived"). They held one advantage, however, which was impregnable: unlike the *parvenus*, they were already in possession of the territory, and had been for some time. And this is where "good taste" and manners come in: taste (that great culinary metaphor) implies *experience*, direct acquaintance and familiarity with what is desirable—whether this be food or pictures or music or clothes. Manners are how things ought to be done: being polite in French is being *comme il faut*, "as you *must be*"; in English you do what you "are supposed"—by other people—to do. Manners of a kind deemed exquisite, like manners of every sort, require education from childhood.

We should notice that there was total agreement among aristocrats and *parvenus* about what it was that those at the top of the pyramid wanted: there was one goal, just as at Versailles there was only one stage on which to perform. Both at Versailles and among the tight circles of upper-class intimates, those who were "in"— those around whom that barrier was raised—knew and even decided what was what, and how to behave. The bourgeois with his undeniable wealth longed to be accepted, to crown his achievement with the "finishing touches," the aristocratic *je ne sais quoi*.

It is clear why manners should have become so mystifying, so ineffable. It was essential that those outside the pale should not be able simply to *learn* the social skills required to be "accepted." It could not be that for the steadily decreasing price of a book on manners you could make your way into "the best circles." If you could, you would in any case no longer want to be let in, for the whole point about prestige is that it is possessed by few—what is available to the multitudes is devalued by the very fact of being "common." Manners, and most especially "manner" or "air," which includes speech, bearing, and gesture, require to be learned at one's mother's knee. One has to be born in the right place and brought up there; one has to be "well bred." Manners of the "ineffable" kind are learned, above all, by living with people to whom the style is "second nature."

Not to know how to behave—and nowhere is this more the case than at the sensitive and essential dinner table—is never to be invited in the first place. If you "arrive" at the table of the great, and there disgrace yourself, you will never be invited again. Mere breaches of manners are not immoral; but partly for that very reason they are, in "society," unpardonable: forgiveness, where adroitness rules, is an inappropriate response to incompetence. Never being invited means never becoming intimate with those who count: dinner invitations have always constituted vitally important rungs on the ladder to worldly success. Not knowing how to behave, you are never in the company of those who do know, and therefore you will never have a chance to learn the only way it is possible to learn, by their example.

It is also clear why simplicity, informality, and intimacy were so useful to aristocratic mores under the threat of being "arrived" at. It was ingenious to outlaw and ridicule expense and bombast, because these came increasingly within the reach of the *nouveau riches*; profuseness, if you have riches, is easy to copy. The rules of protocol, of ritual, everything that can be known by precepts beginning "Do not . . ."—all these can be written down and learned. They are wares which the etiquette books can offer; they are vulgarly available. But when a pinnacle of prestige is created, where an exclusive few have it in their power to decide who will "do" and who will not, then, with the aid of ineffable charm, indescribable simplicity, and exquisite taste, a fortress is created which is almost unassailable.

Furthermore, this particular "fortress" (and here begins a dance we feverishly perform to this day) need never stand still. Whenever the anxious intruders, the "impertinent, the improper, the vulgar," draw close enough to achieve the object which will grant to them, too, the honour of being inside the charmed circle, the elite simply moves on; it changes the fashion. As soon as too many have whatever it is (holidays on the Riviera, shoes the right shape, the latest turn of phrase), the prestige of the thing is automatically disqualified. The aristocrats, the trend-setters, have already fled elsewhere. *Timing* is the trick. Mobility, the freedom conferred by money, appears to offer even to the hordes of the excluded a chance to "get there" in time. In fact, the race dooms them to failure in terms of the very metaphor of races; those not to the manner born begin way behind the starting line. They will suffer continuing disappointment because they will never be in the right place *at the right time*. The "right time" of course, in this particular game, usually means "first." And whoever tries really hard to catch up is condemned from the start as "pretentious."

No sign must appear of all the training involved in the production of "polish." As Castiglione put it when speaking of noble prowess at tennis, "Never let it appear that the Courtier devotes much effort or time to it, even though he may do it ever so well." Correct manners at table must make the politeness surrounding food—the tight control over appetite, the elevation of conversation and "things of the mind" over the merely physical love of eating, the consideration not for self but for neighbours—seem the most natural behaviour in the world. No effort, no hesitation, no clumsiness of movement must intrude, in spite of the fact that table manners, which constitute proof positive that the people employing them are not "like beasts," have always set out to make eating not easier but (until the techniques are mastered) more difficult. You must sit straight, no elbows on the table, no slouching or fidgeting—all the while, of course, contriving to look relaxed and "natural." There are particular ways of handling knives, forks, and spoons, and rigid rules for what can and cannot be used with what: take olives with a spoon but never a fork, take walnuts with fingers, serve cheese with a knife, always take milk products with a spoon even if they are firm enough for a fork, use a spoon to eat curry, and know which way to sweep your spoon when eating soup (one never *drinks* soup). "The expert," we are informed by the Chinese writer B. Y. Chao in 1956, "removes the bones from his mouth with his chopsticks." We must talk as we eat—it is rude not to—but never open our mouths if food is in them. "Nothing indicates a well-bred man more than a proper mode of eating his dinner," wrote "Agogos" in 1834. "A man may pass muster by *dressing well*, and may sustain himself tolerably in conversation; but if he is not perfectly 'au fait,' *dinner* will betray him."

In republican and egalitarian North America, it was soon not enough to get rich; you had next to learn "the graces," and polish the roughness which might well have aided your rise to power in the first place. But Americans were much harder to persuade that they should wait before bounding over the barriers. "I have seen it gravely stated by some writer on manners, that 'it takes three generations to make a gentleman,'" wrote an American expert on how to behave in 1837. "This is too slow a process in these days of accelerated movement." And she stoutly encouraged her readers to work and study hard, in order to fit themselves "for intercourse, on equal terms, with the best society in our land."

Americans were not suspicious of handbooks. As another great leap forward took place in printing technology and book distribution, etiquette manuals poured off the presses of the United States during the nineteenth century. They offered advice on how to become "refined." The models were English and French—but there was a determination, too, to search for new American ways. The etiquette of blatant deference to superiors was ignored, as members of the middle classes increasingly demanded ritual expressions of mutual respect from one another. There was a tendency from the beginning to counsel against stiffness, pomp, and over-refinement: both eighteenth-century aristocratic ideals of simplicity and revolutionary American egalitarianism are tightly intertwined at the roots of the modern craving for the casual. Another tradition which Americans inherited was a British distrust of overdone manners, of foppishness, affectedness, and other "Continental" exaggerations; the island British had their own line in snobbish contempt for foreigners in fancy clothes, with food smothered in sauces and no respect for "genuine" simplicity. American opposition to theatrical manners was further reinforced by a "radical Protestant antipathy toward social and religious ritual."

American etiquette books explained all the ancient precepts of table manners, simply and clearly. There was little embarrassment about being basic or cut-and-dried; people who knew very little about the niceties were anxious to learn, and the manual-writers— many of them claiming to be high-born themselves and therefore assumed by everybody to be "in the know"—enjoyed spreading the word. They were much less afraid, to begin with, than their European counterparts of seeing their ramparts stormed: they felt it was far more urgent to raise the general level of correct behaviour. Their desire to improve the manners of the working classes is now viewed with suspicion. "Their enterprise," says John Kasson, a historian of nineteenth-century American civility, "must be viewed within the larger concern of how to establish order and authority in a restless, highly mobile, rapidly urbanizing and industrializing democracy. Seeking to avoid overt conflict, they turned issues of class and social grievance back upon the individual" by redefining such problems as questions of propriety and "good taste." Nevertheless, European visitors to America, such as the petulant Mrs. Trollope, complained about the roughness of manners among the Americans, and stung some of them into redoubling their efforts at improvement.

By the end of the nineteenth century, the great shift from the countryside to the huge modern cities was under way. City people could live rushed but anonymous lives: no one need know who you were or where you had come from, provided you looked like everybody else and gave no clues. It was usually politic to behave as everyone "was supposed to." One manners manual, typically forthright, explained that chances for success in the city were better if "a person going from one place to the other [that is, from the country to town] should be utterly undistinguishable from those about him." Having good manners (but nothing too refined or overdone) had become a way of avoiding remark. And it had always been the case that showing *bad* manners was truly unforgettable behaviour. As Erving Goffman has put it, "Infractions make news."

A whole new generation of etiquette manuals began to appear in the twentieth century. The doyenne of the new breed of experts was Emily Post, who produced *Etiquette in Society, in Business, in Politics and at Home* in 1922. Her text was enhanced with examples figuring characters many of whose names expressed the snobbery of "polished" society: the Smartlingtons, the Oldnames, Mr. Stocksan Bonds, the Bobo Gildings, and even the Onceweres. But Post was careful to remind her readers of the greater tradition of civility: "Best Society is not a fellowship of the wealthy, nor does it seek to exclude those who are not of exalted birth"; but she adds, with at least one ear cocked in the other direction, "it is an association of gentlefolk, of which good form in speech, charm of manner, knowledge of the social amenities, and instinctive consideration for the feelings of others, are credentials by which society the world over recognizes its chosen members." Her rules are utterly categorical. If one's table-cloth is made of lace, on no account should a coloured undercloth be laid so that it will show through; and "To eat extra entrées, Roman Punch, or hot dessert is to be in the dining-room of a parvenu." According to Post's grand-daughter-in-law and recent editor, Elizabeth Post, "When [the book] was first written, Emily Post thought it would be bought by the upper class, but that wasn't true—they didn't need it."

Emily Post had thought of herself as writing a book that was to be a bastion against a tide of new ways of which she could not approve. The people who did read the book—people who longed for advice in a world where conditions were indeed quickly changing, and they wanted to know how to cope "correctly"—wrote thousands of letters which convinced Post that her attitude should change. The next and succeeding editions of her book began to include advice on how to remain cool and polite when faced with new social facts. She admitted that women now smoked, and could not be frowned upon for doing so: the frowner, not the smoker, was now "out of place." She virtuously allowed that "No rule of etiquette is of less importance than which fork we use" (1929). From now on, writers on politeness were going to have to see one of their duties as keeping their readers up to date; they remain defenders of what the French call "the usages," but must extend their repertoire of rules if they wish to keep their readership. The latest *Emily Post's Etiquette* (1984) has new material on single parents and unmarried couples living together, and answers doubts about whether French fries may be eaten with the fingers (use a fork—unless they are served with sandwiches, when fingers become permissible).

As early as 1924, the etiquette manuals recognized the trend towards simpler and simpler manners; the Great War had played havoc with custom. But Americans could see the new attitude as in fact a return to the past—to the homespun values and the spontaneity of the American tradition, and to freedom from pomp, pernick-etiness, and repression. They could choose to have their cake and eat it, however, through also insisting on the ineffable primacy of taste. "This liberty of behaviour," wrote Emily Post, "requires more real *breeding* than ever. You must have an *innate* sense of the fitness of things, and sure *feeling* for the correct time and place" [my italics].

The most popular of the new arbiters of elegance on the North American scene is Judith Martin, "Miss Manners." She keeps thoroughly in touch with the preoccupations of her readers by listening, as Emily Post learned to do, to their questions. Miss Manners is a syndicated columnist. Her persona is crisply rigid, as her role requires, and she always sticks to the wonderfully formal third person, for instance as she remains firm where even Emily Post had caved in: "If Miss Manners hears any more contemptuous descriptions of etiquette as being a matter of 'knowing which fork to use,' she will run amok. . . . Forks are not that difficult . . . we will now take a minute to learn everything there is to know about Which Fork to Use." She injects common sense and asperity into her rulings: "There is no such thing as instant intimacy" . . . "Nothing is more ingratiating than asking a foreigner for instruction in his code of manners."

She also maintains the humorous tradition in picturing disastrous mistakes, especially those involving food. "At the party, a lady in a low-cut gown tripped, stumbled, lurched across a table, falling face first into a bowl of guacamole dip, and in the process 'popped out' of her top." You really have to permit yourself to laugh on such an occasion, Miss Manners replies to the reader's question about the right response. After wondering briefly whether a mere avocado dip would have been less demanding of mirth than guacamole, she goes on to point out that not to laugh would be to suggest "that the lady did it all the time and her friends have gotten used to it."

Miss Manners supplies for her readers a system of etiquette that is demanding, unbending, and precise. Her constant charge is "You must not be rude," but the point is that you can win much more roundly through maintaining the civilities. People read her avidly, partly because she is so much fun to read, and partly on account of the prevailing fear that a total demise of "good behaviour" might be just round the corner. People appear to have tried—and, worse, experienced—careless spontaneity, and wonder what the other possibilities might be.

A whole new branch of the genre of etiquette manuals is the lucrative list of books on manners for people "in business." People making money know that good impressions can facilitate the making of more of it, whereas an image wanting in the proprieties can actually get in the way. Where aspiration has definite chances of leading to success, decorum and inhibition lose their connotations of repression and pretentiousness, and take on suggestions of honing, competence, confidence, and speed. "Even polished brass," Lord Chesterfield wrote to his son in 1777, "will pass upon more people than rough gold."

3

The Pleasure of Your Company

The Latin word for a hearth or fireplace is *focus*. The meaning which that word now has in English has developed directly out of the role which fireplaces have played for thousands of years in western European households, and indeed in most dwellings on earth: where the fire in the house is kept, there is the household's focus. Since before the dawn of history, we have cooked on that fire, made our beds near it, sat round it as a family "circle," and eaten with the sound and sight of the fire as a comforting background to our meals.

Fireplaces have always tended to be placed physically and psychologically in the centre of the house. We have now pushed ours to one side of our living rooms (families are only semi-circles these days); both the cooking and the eating are done elsewhere. What is called, interestingly enough, "central" heating is all over the house, and not solely at the "focus." But in modern houses too, if they include the luxury of a hearth which can contain a real fire, or even an electric one disguised as glowing coals, the fireplace remains the spot where family and friends meet. We sit and face the fire to talk or read; near it we watch television, a new and rival focus of attention; we decorate the mantelpiece with family photographs, a mirror, a clock, vases of flowers, and annual Christmas cards. Clichés like "hearth and home" are still comprehensible to us, and we hope when we are away that the family will "keep the home fires burning." The French word for a household is a *foyer*, literally, a "hearth." (Our theatres have foyers because they once offered their patrons a fire in the vestibule, so that people could warm themselves on arrival.)

The cooking that went on over the hearth fire, and the daily meals consumed nearby, expressed the relationship of members of the family to each other, their kinship and their unconditional, continuing loyalty. One definition of a family—a definition with different degrees of significance in different cultures—is "those who eat together." In Africa as a general rule, according to L-V. Thomas, people traditionally eat daily meals together because they are consanguineous, and the fact of doing so proves kinship. Marriage means, for a man, being cooked for by a woman, and for a woman, feeding a man: eating together and sleeping together are two sides of the same coin.

In some societies it is considered shameful to be seen eating by outsiders, even guests; people may sit in a corner or facing the wall to eat in some cases, or delicately hide their mouths when masticating. Visitors must be offered food in most cases, so that unexpectedly visiting others at dinner-time is always tactless behaviour. The Wamirans of Papua New Guinea, for example, feel they must share their food out equally with as many people as have set eyes on it; visitors are thought to be slighted if not fed. Food might be hidden away if people visit and there is not enough to give them, or if unprepared hosts do not feel like sharing: the family will fast until the coast is clear. People may (perhaps as a result of this caution before visitors) count eating with defecation and sex, as behaviour intensely private and hedged about with taboo.

What we call a couple's "living together" can be expressed as much by food as by sex and common shelter. Here for example are some lines of a love song from Papua New Guinea:

You told me, "I'll cook your food in my oven,"
You told me, "I'll cook your food on my fire."
But I haven't eaten
Any of this food yet.
I'm in my men's house, far away.
Girl Wakle, up in the place of Mbiltik
With skin like that of a ripe banana,
Let me take you off to Kendipi Rapu.

It follows in such cases that if a woman decides to stop cooking for
her man, or if he refuses to be fed by her or insists on cooking for
himself, the breakdown is an outward signal of a serious failure in
their relationship; such an action is often the beginning of a divorce.
In Assam, south of Tibet, if a family member is furious enough to
refrain from eating with the household for a whole twenty-four
hours, the dissension is extremely grave. If he then decides to cook
separately, he is taking an irreversible step; it must be followed by
his building a new house and by a splitting up of lands and property.
There is a terrible rite of rejection called "the throwing away of the
cooking pots," which is so deadly and final that, though it is often
threatened in the heat of anger, it is rarely actually carried out. It
constitutes the symbolic death, as far as the household is concerned,
of the offending member of the family.

It is a pattern widely found in Africa that adult men and women
almost never eat together, even in the family living quarters. A
woman cooks the food and brings it to her husband or to the men
eating apart as a group, then leaves to join the other women and the
children. In polygamous African families, the children of any one
mother often eat with her, in a separate group from others fathered
by the same man. The African anthropologist L. C. Okere describes
dinner-time among the Igbo of Nigeria: "The division of the fufuu
meal or porridge each evening is an impressive sight. . . . In front of
the hearth, children start to bring around some small earthenware
and enamel plates. From the steaming pot on the fire, the women
scoop out soup and lump after lump of porridge into the eating containers. A ring of younger girls and children watch the spoon intently

as it hovers a moment above each receptacle." When all are served, the three or four children of each mother go and sit with her and eat from a single soup dish and from the same plate of fufuu or from one gourd-shell. This communal habit expresses a particular closeness of kinship; it produces solidarity for life. Father himself eats alone; it is a sign of prestige, the respect due to him. He may request the company of one of his children—typically the youngest toddler. In some African societies, he may expect to receive a dish of food from each wife—and how much he eats is an important index of his sentiments about the provider, and of his opinion of her prowess in that essential female skill, cooking. His avoiding the food in any particular wife's dish is a deep insult, ritually suggesting that he suspects her of trying to poison him.

In our own society the dining-room table, in houses and apartments large and affluent enough to have one, traditionally stands in a room separate from both the kitchen and the fireplace. It has for centuries been the locus of the typical household's daily meals, and represents, as no other piece of furniture can, the family as a whole. If any member of the family should be absent, the empty place at table is a mute reminder of the missing person; when the children have all grown up and left home, the parents, left behind, face each other across the expanse of table, which after twenty years and more (and even if several tables have succeeded each other over the years) is haunted by memories of the dramas that have certainly taken place round this symbol of the family itself.

A traditional dining-room table is often heavy, dark, and assiduously polished, as befits the embodiment not only of togetherness but of continuity and solid worth. Even modern dining-room tables, created out of light woods in order to reduce costs, are often stained or provided with veneers in dark colours, and weighted and glossed to produce a solid, heavy, "long-lasting" image. But many families now eat in the kitchen—where the table need not even pretend to be made of precious wood. Where a special dining room exists, it takes on a new and important role as a space set aside for large dinners and special occasions. In such a dining room stands the sideboard or dresser, containing china and silver brought out only for guests.

The move towards having everyday meals in the kitchen began as a labour-saving measure, as servants disappeared and women went out to work. In large old apartments in Paris (these are often the most desirable and most expensive lodgings) the kitchen has been carefully placed a long way from the living and dining rooms. When these apartments were built, cooking smells were thought to be suggestive both of food in its purely nutritive function and of the intimate background workings of the household; the smell of food was therefore considered to be an imposition upon the guests. ("The one thing every hostess tries to avoid is the risk of the smell of cooking," wrote Emily Post as late as 1950; the meal she is describing is centred on steak and broccoli.) Servants were also to be contained in their own separate quarters until they issued forth to serve. Nowadays, a long passage from kitchen to dining room is merely a nuisance for the toiling hostess. And now that good home cooking has taken on the allure, and the costliness in terms of time and skill, of couture clothing as compared with something bought off the hook, guests are delighted to be greeted on arrival by delicious smells of food being prepared, by their hosts in person, especially for them.

Being asked to eat in the kitchen was for a long time, in houses and apartments large enough to possess dining rooms, the ultimate gesture of intimacy, extended in principle only to close family. It has become entirely normal these days to hold dinner parties in the kitchen. Most European kitchens, in this still transitional period, remain functional, non-celebratory rooms. The Scandinavians, however, have for some time been leading the way in turning the kitchen into a large and splendid room, gleaming with technology but also comfortable, attractive, and hospitable. The dining table has been moved, and has in many instances changed its size, its weight, and its colour. But it is still the same table that gave us the word "commensality," meaning "togetherness arising out of the fact that we eat at one table." Eating round a table is an ethnocentric way for us to express a bonding mechanism which is common to every human society: that of mealtime sharing.

• *Company* •

"Dinner-parties rank first among all entertainments," wrote an anonymous "Member of the Aristocracy" in an English manners book dated 1879. An invitation to dinner, he or she goes on, "conveys a greater mark of esteem" than being asked to any other gathering could do; and most importantly, "It is also a civility that can be readily interchanged, which in itself gives it an advantage over *all* other invitations." Just because everybody must eat every day, offering dinner to people outside the family circle, eating with them in their houses, or in designated places for socializing over meals, becomes an essential means of binding families to one another and knitting society in general together. Food is not normally too expensive to share, even if you are quite poor; the fact that it does not last encourages reciprocation and repetition of the act of sharing. Food is also immensely malleable, so that there are endless possibilities for ringing the changes on the single theme of dinner. The necessity of eating, terrible as it is when there is not enough to feed us, also provides, in times of peace and plenty, the certainty of appetites reviving in time for every dinner engagement.

Reciprocation is an essential part of this social system. Accepting a dinner invitation usually means promising to ask your hosts to a meal sometime later; eating together with members of a group proves loyalty to that group, and signifies a willingness to serve its interests in future. Every society pressures guests to become hosts in their turn. Resistance may result in unpopularity, ostracism, even withdrawal of aid when times become hard. "Hospitality begets hospitality" is an Igbo proverb. A popular modern Igbo song goes, *Erigbuo ya konye ozo erigbuo*—"Eat it up, because it's someone else's!"—and a traditional song asks pointedly,

(Oh) drinker of other people's liquor,
When shall we drink yours?

Group meals often involve the contribution of food by the guests themselves: the banqueters are in these cases both hosts and guests. The phrase "pot luck" was originally used when inviting someone to a very informal family dinner, on the spur of the moment. The visitor was to expect nothing specially prepared, but only what the family would have eaten in any case that day. The guest's "luck" lay in what day he or she happened to arrive, and what meal had been prepared for the family. The phrase has changed its meaning with the increasing popularity of meals or parties where the guests come with contributions of food: the "luck" now lies in the uncertainty about what everyone will bring. The host can suggest what might be needed, but cannot control the quality of the offering.

"Pot luck" dinners in this sense have an ancient history, and exist in some form in most societies on earth. They usually celebrate the intimacy of the guests, or at least the hope that they have a great deal in common. The host's authority is considerably reduced by means of the arrangement, but the fact remains that the party has to be held somewhere, and the host or hosts remain responsible for the venue, the guest list, even for the possibility of gate-crashers. The success or failure of the party still depends mostly on the "givers" of it. Being expected both to sustain loss of authority, and to retain responsibility, is a peculiarly modern predicament. But the informality gained is so important to us that we are prepared to pay the price; and enough honour still attaches to having the premises, being able to pay for a party (even if the guests help and must accept the blame for the food provided), and to knowing the "right" people to ask, that hosts continue to shoulder the burden and the risk of inviting people for "pot luck."

Many societies have knitted themselves together by throwing city, town, or tribal feasts; here those responsible are the inhabitants of the town or the whole host group, and the honour risked is the reputation of the collectivity. Regular attendance at city feasts could be part of one's obligations as a citizen in ancient Greece. A city, tribe, or club holding a feast might often of course be stating not only its internal solidarity but also its distinctiveness from other such groups. The Wamirans of Papua New Guinea hold two main kinds of feast: "incorporation," communal dinners, where no meat is eaten; and "transaction," distributions of raw pork as well as taro, where the food is cooked and eaten in separate groups or taken home to be consumed. The first type stresses solidarity, the second difference and potential conflict.

In south-western France, there has been a recent resurgence of annual village banqueting. Everyone in town ought to go and eat at the long trestle-tables which are set out every year on the town's patronal saint's day, in the main square, which becomes the hosts' "premises." Absentees are noted with displeasure. People from other towns attend as well, and everybody compares notes: it matters a good deal who gave the best feast this year. The dinners are called *moungetades*, after the traditional white beans with pork and sausage which are the climax of the meal. These beans were in recent memory the staple food of everybody in this area of France. Today, they have become "fancy" food, a regional *spécialité* in restaurants, or nostalgia-producing festal food, expressive of tradition, solidarity, and a hard but valued past.

Coming together once a year "to eat the beans" is, for the local inhabitants, an act of pride in their own home town; it is consciously intended to create community, where modern threats to group loyalty and personal contact are felt as a real danger. Everybody contributes something: food-provisioning and cooking expertise, time, organization, singing in the church choir in the morning, skill at playing *boules* and other traditional games in the afternoon, while the feast is tended by the designated cooks in huge vats over fires in the middle of an open field. All pay an equal fee for the dinner, and all participate in the lusty singing and the raucous jokes as course after course is served under strings of fairy lights in the open air; dancing goes on in the square, to deafening amplified music, till dawn. *Moungetades* have appeared in south-western France, apparently quite spontaneously, within the past fifteen years or so; the new "tradition" has grown to the point that any village that cannot "get it together" to mount one every year scarcely counts as a living community at all.

Eating together helps people get over fights. Since friends and families share food, the action of eating together can ritually express what is held, shared, and enjoyed, after all, in common; it therefore signifies the dropping of hostilities. The Gogo of Tanzania reconcile people after a bitter quarrel, as when a father curses and disowns his son, by first slaughtering a goat and removing its liver. Each of the parties bites on the goat's liver; the priest then cuts it in two. When each has eaten his half of the meat, peace is officially restored. Only food—all-necessary, visible, divisible, an external object which becomes internal, and which then turns into the very substance of the eater—could give rise to such a clear yet mysterious and effective ritual.

Eating when we are hungry is a relief; eating with others is also fun, and conducive to eating more. Modern would-be slimmers are commonly and coldly advised that the quickest way of cutting down on food is to avoid seeing friends for meals: leave out the social element, and it will quickly become easier to cut down on eating as well. Chinese meals are, on the other hand, an example of how eating in common can be encouraged by making it advantageous in terms of the actual food served: the larger the commensal number, the greater the variety of dishes which all can share. A single person or a mere couple in a Chinese restaurant suffers the melancholy fate of having to make a meal of only one or two foods, whereas a crowd ensures variety. Visitors and annual food "events" are everywhere an excuse to eat a lot. When guests visit, even if they have not been expected, they must usually be fed on their arrival. The food given them is shared: it would be an insult to guests to let them eat alone, just because eating together expresses friendship—even if what is offered is just "a nice cup of tea," or a drink with a dish of salted pieces to take with the fingers.

In many cultures, two people do not feel they can talk in a friendly way with each other unless they have first eaten together: it is an equivalent of being "properly introduced." A corresponding attitude is that which makes it impossible for a desert Arab who has once eaten salt with a man ever to treat him thereafter as an enemy. It is as though reconciliation must never be needed, because it has taken place already; enmity has been overcome in advance. The personal "guest-friendship" of Homeric Greece meant that, because a man had once been entertained in the house of another, not only the host and the guest but their descendants for generations remained joined by bonds resembling those of kinship. Two "paternal guest-friends" could meet for the first time on the battlefield, on opposite sides of the combat, and refuse to fight each other.

Such kinship through hospitality is achieved in imitation of marriage, the social mechanism by which women, "given away" to families other than their own, bind their "natal" and their "procreative" families together. Marriage ceremonies the world over include the sharing of food and drink among the two families and their friends; often the bride's and groom's consuming of food and drink together *is* the wedding itself, as ours is the slipping on of binding rings and the saying of vows. A fairly recent addition to North American wedding festivities (it is an ancient idea which has resurfaced, probably through the agency of various immigrant groups) is the sharing of the first slice of the wedding cake by the bride and groom.

One society, the Tibetan Buddhist Sherpas of the Himalayas, is described as imposing on every one of its members an extremely individualistic, self-sufficient attitude. There is a religious bias towards "anti-relationalism": sanctity often requires some kind of isolation, at least from time to time. This is temporarily achieved in rituals which include fasting (not sharing food) and silence (no conversation). There is a strong secular preference for the family to maintain itself and need no help from outsiders. People dislike lending, or even selling, anything; their goal in life is to be as autonomous as possible. Yet they regularly attend large parties. A host is good enough to supply the occasion, and the people who come are filled with exhilaration if the party succeeds. Sherry Ortner believes that the "host" is only a nominal figure at these celebrations: the real host is the group itself. She explains that the Sherpas know that they *need* these parties, to break down their own normal resistances to giving and receiving. People agree to "lose the struggle" now and then, and become, for a ritually organized and limited time, a close-knit community.

"We invite each other not to eat and drink, but to eat and drink *together*," Plutarch remarked. The point is that the people at the party are more important than the food; but the secondary meaning is that eating together implies selectivity. Hosts of parties, especially if they are large and "pot luck," cannot impose strict control over the number and identity of the guests; and if people pay a fee to come, anybody who behaves must be welcome. But only a certain number of people can sit down to dinner together; it is one of the necessities imposed—and advantages gained—by seating diners at a table. The host chooses the guests, and takes care that they already have a good deal in common.

One of the uses to which extremely rich people can put their money is giving frequent parties, and especially dinner parties. Being a famous host or hostess is a gruelling enterprise: the rich who attempt to achieve the honour are people for whom money is not enough. They need to know "everybody who is anybody"; they have what the Germans call *Geltungsbedürfnis*, a need to acquire value through association with the acknowledged great. They also revel in the power derived from being able, through their money and their connections, to bring "everybody" together. Like food in itself, money in itself cannot create a good evening's entertainment. "To make those eat who lack appetite, to make the wit of the witty sparkle, to help the would-be witty to find some witty saying, these are the supreme achievements of the gastronomer as host," wrote the great-nephew of Brillat-Savarin, Lucien Tendret, in the late nineteenth century. A good host or hostess must bring together wit, talent, and variety, so as to achieve the correct "mix," the right atmosphere, the indefinable feeling in the air that *this* dinner is where all the really "interesting" people have gathered, that this is "where it's at." To be included in the list of the invited at such an event is to have reached the pinnacle of social ambition. The "happy few" are happy just because they are few, and have been chosen. The happy host is elated to have done the choosing, to have created a memorable event, and to have placed these powerful or promising people in his or her debt.

A person we like, we find "sympathetic," *sympathique* or *sympa* in French; this is a person we can literally "feel with." The ancient Greeks had another term which is more precisely used of dinner guests: one we get on with at such an event is *sympotikos*, a person with whom we can enjoy a symposium, or dinner followed by a drinking party. A dinner party held in somebody's own home, with table, courses, drinks, and conversation in common, is always a closely "hosted" event. It requires effort, time spent, and at least some expense; it must therefore be worth the while of hosts and guests alike. If it is not, then rancour will inevitably result.

• Hosts and Guests •

Don't hit the person across from you with bits of toast,
And don't, when dinner is nearly through, say "Who's the host?"
  It isn't done.
                                        — Cole Porter

The etiquette books reiterate that dinner parties are extremely difficult to carry off. Giving one is "not for the novice." If you are the host, your house is on view; your food (offered as the result of your best efforts) is open to judgement; your taste, your social connections, your ability to manage are all potentially "on the line." Things can go dreadfully wrong. Emily Post, in 1922, gave a description of the horrors of trying to give a dinner party without prior experience and without her advice.

The servants, insufficiently instructed and trained, are most likely to let you down, and a servant's clumsiness is her mistress's fault. Sigrid the maid, "instead of bowing slightly and saying in a low tone of voice, 'Dinner is served,' stands stiff as a block of wood, and fairly shouts, 'Dinner's all ready!'" She clashes the plates, she piles them up (you *never* pile plates, says Post in edition after edition; the most that may be carried on any one journey to or from the kitchen is two, one in each hand, even if the plates have not been used). Sigrid even goes so far as to *deal the plates out*. The fire smokes, the soup is brown rather than amber, there is too much food on the serving dishes. Disaster follows disaster until you feel "Mrs. Worldly looking with almost hypnotized fascination—as her attention might be drawn to a street accident, against her will." Later on, "You notice that none of your guests eats anything. They can't." Mr. Kindhart offers sympathy: "'Cheer up, little girl, it doesn't really matter!' And then you know to the full how terrible the situation is. . . . Your husband, remembering the trenches, tries to tell you it was not so bad!"

Post makes it very clear that it is the woman, and she alone, who bears the brunt of any horror that might occur at a dinner party; her husband is never mentioned except when he is imagined condoling. "You know that it will be long—if ever—before any of [the guests] will be willing to risk an evening in your house again." They will also ruin your reputation in speaking to other people: "Whatever you do," they will advise, "don't dine with the Newweds unless you eat your dinner before you go, and wear black glasses so no sight can offend you." But hosts continue to give parties in spite of the suspense and the risk, and guests accept invitations even though the evening might turn into a disaster, and often if they do not especially want to go. The benefits to be gained from being either a host or a guest are very real, otherwise dinner parties would not be given.

Confusing as it seems to us at first sight, the words "host" and "guest" originally meant the same thing. They both derive from Indo-European *ghostis*, "stranger." This is the origin of the Latin *hostis*, which meant "stranger" and therefore "enemy"; from it English derives the word "hostile." In Old French, *hoste* used to mean both "host" and "guest," as *hôte* still does (though the French increasingly call the guest an *invité*). What this single term refers to is not so much the individual people, the host and the guest, as the bond that unites them. (The origin of the word "hospitality" gives us some idea of the web of interchangeable and alternating identities and obligations that are interwoven in this complex notion. It seems to have referred to the power of a citizen "host" [*hospes*] who was benevolent enough to represent before Roman institutions someone who was not a Roman citizen. The *hospes* was thought of as impersonating—the full meaning of our term "representing"—the foreigner on those occasions. He "was the stranger himself.")

One role cannot exist without the other: host and guest participate in one action, and together they submit to the laws of hospitality and their jurisdiction over the offering, and the accepting, of food and shelter between "strangers." Those laws in turn are based on ambivalence, in the full sense of "power on both sides." Hostility might always lurk in the background, either existing before the event or arising out of it. To receive a guest or to accept an invitation into someone's house is to be ritually bound for a time to another person or group. Both sides accept, for the sake of peace, order, and the benefit of the whole community, to be constrained by intricate sets of obligations.

One way of understanding table manners is to recognize that they are a system of civilized taboos which come into operation in a situation fraught with potential danger. They are designed to reduce tension and protect people from one another. Listen, in Homer's *Odyssey*, to Agamemnon, a resentful ghost in the Underworld, describing how his life ended:

> It was Aegisthus who designed my death,
> he and my heartless wife, and killed me, after
> feeding me, like an ox felled at the trough.
> That was my miserable end—and with me
> my friends butchered, like so many swine
> killed for some troop, or feast, or wedding banquet.
> . . . .
> but these were murders you would catch your breath at:
> think of us fallen, all our throats cut, winebowl
> brimming, tables laden on every side,
> while blood ran smoking over the whole floor.

Murder at dinner is especially horrendous, "worse than death in war," just because it is so easy to achieve, and *therefore* so unexpected: it is "not done." Everybody present is armed, with knives. Their teeth—formidable human weapons—can scarcely remain invisible, in spite of every effort, as they chew. (Table manners commonly forbid what we call belly-laughs, partly because uproarious mirth is expressed by the baring of teeth. Erasmus advises that "If something so funny should occur that it produces uncontrolled laughter . . . the face should be covered with a napkin or with the hand.") Agamemnon and his men were invited guests; he trusted his hosts, who included—another horror—his own wife. She had taken Aegisthus for her lover while Agamemnon was away at the war, so betrayal is heaped upon betrayal.

The ancient Greek myth of Agamemnon's death is told in two distinct versions. In one he is butchered at table; in the other his wife offers him a bath, as wives were expected to do for homecoming warriors. Having reduced her man to nakedness in his tub, she flings a net over him, rendering him utterly defenceless; she then hacks him to death with an axe. The story of Agamemnon's death in his bath does not contradict the version in which he died at dinner: the two stories are mythic equivalents, and in that sense the same thing. The essential points are the betrayal of trust and the horrific pollution. In the story of the bath, water—the symbol of purity—is stained with the blood of the helpless victim, as in the appalling murder scene in the shower in Hitchcock's movie *Psycho*. The dinner table, too, is polluted; the blood flowing; the table, which has been laid in orderly and civilized fashion for the fellowship expressed in the dinner, desecrated by the blood of the guests—including the guest of honour, the king himself.

For this is the theme that underlies all table manners: we may be slicing and chewing; we may have killed or sacrificed to supply our feast; we may be attending to the most "animal" of our needs; but we do so with control, order, and regularity, and with a clear understanding of who is who and what is what. We are neither beasts nor monsters with no manners, but men and women of culture. We do not treat people as though they were the swine or the oxen slaughtered for the feast: *we do not get the guests mixed up with the dishes*. For the point is that we so easily could. At table we are both armed and vulnerable; we are at such very close quarters.

The laws of hospitality deal firstly with strangers—how to manage their entry into our inner sanctum, how to protect them from our own automatic reaction, which is to fear and exclude the unknown, how to prevent them from attacking and desecrating what we hold dear, or from otherwise behaving in a strange and unpredictably dangerous manner. We remember that we too might one day need a stranger's help. So we behave in the prescribed civilized manner, *hostis* to *hostis*. Abusing a defenceless stranger is disgraceful. Strangers are especially protected by the gods in many cultures; in ancient Greece, Zeus himself is called Xenios, Protector of Hospitality. Many are the cautionary tales where the unknown beggar or the needy traveller turns out to be a god in disguise, testing the level of morality in the host. Generosity in this circumstance is proof of greatness, as was the unhesitating hospitality given the three strangers by Abraham at Mamre, or the gift of everything they had by the poverty-stricken couple Philemon and Baucis in Ovid's

Metamorphoses. The punishment for failure to help strangers who throw themselves on your mercy or to treat guests with the proper hospitality is severe; it was administered in ancient Greece by the Furies, demonic fiends who were capable of pursuing then sucking the blood of offenders, until they were as hard and dry as mummies. In Christianity the law has a much broader application: not only the guest—invited or not—but *everybody* is God in disguise, and what you do to others you do to Christ.

Hosts and guests, even in our own most casual gatherings, play very different roles: the host is at home, and giving; the guest is away, receiving. A decided imbalance is set up and deliberately maintained, the purpose being that the reciprocity or equalization which is forbidden at present will have to be achieved later—there will be a return invitation. It follows that being a host can be a bid for power, a way of placing people under an obligation, very possibly unwanted. If the host, for example, gives a party which is so lavish that it cannot be returned by the guest, then the debt will have to be paid in other ways. The host will decide what he or she wants in return, when the time comes to collect his or her due.

A primitive form of prayer is the setting up of God as the recipient of a gift which must receive recompense later: *do ut des*, "I give so that you might give in return." One form of this ritual demand is to invite the gods to dinner. The ancient Greek version of this kind of transaction was called *theoxenia*, "hospitality for the gods": couches would be set up on which the gods were invited to recline, with food provided for them. The Roman version of the ritual was *lectisternium*, "lying on couches." Statues of the gods were crowned with wreaths and laid out, with cushions for their comfort; food was then served to them as at a dinner. These feasts took place at times of national crisis—or, alternatively, as thanksgiving for favours received. The gods, having accepted this hospitality, were expected to provide the help so much hoped for, or to accept thanks and continue to be benevolent.

In cultures where the dead are especially honoured, they might be invited regularly to meals. The celebration of Halloween is a staged propitiation of the ghosts—a precaution against their mischief-making—by giving food to impersonators of them at the point of entry to our houses. Because sharing food is so essential to human fellowship, bonds are felt to be created with the other world by offering its denizens food. We hope they will be satisfied for the time being, and possibly also nagged by their knowledge that the "done thing" is to respond, to "discharge," as we put it, the obligation placed upon them.

The myth of Amphitryon was one where not the guests but the host turned out to be a god. Zeus took Amphitryon's shape in order to sleep with the latter's wife, Alcmena, and—according to a medieval addition to the Greek myth—gave a banquet in her honour. When the real Amphitryon got home, Zeus's trick was discovered, but not before the god had engendered Heracles. Amphitryon retrieved his wife, but everyone agreed that the host of the feast had been not the head of the house, but he who, in spite of being an impostor, had invited the guests and presided over the feast: Zeus himself, as "Amphitryon." As Molière put it in his play *Amphitryon* (1668), "The real Amphitryon is the Amphitryon with whom one dines." The food and the expense are less important than is the actual presence of everyone at the feast. The French still call a host an "amphitryon"—partly to relieve the confusion arising from the word *hôte* meaning both "host" and "guest."

The guest, at the opposite end of the bond of hospitality, also has power. Who of us are such dutiful housekeepers that we can afford not to look at our living arrangements with a sharp eye, and adjust and improve them before guests arrive? The sharp eye is that of the imagined guests: we are putting ourselves in their place and seeing ourselves from their point of view. So we rush about, dusting formerly forgotten surfaces, organizing the visible reading matter so as to give a better impression of our taste, polishing the glasses as we would never polish them for ourselves. Guests must be satisfied; if they are not, they will become demanding, irritable, discontented. They will look with less charity than ever upon us and our houses, and after they have gone home they will talk, ruining our reputation. Guests are invited because we want their friendship and cooperation; we may even crave their approval. An angry or contemptuous guest is the very opposite of what the dinner party sets out to achieve.

It is the host who is bestowing generosity by having people to visit, and yet any well-mannered host treats guests as if *they* are honouring the host by their presence. This could well be true as well as polite, since the number and quality of the guests add honour to the host. Honour is part of the hospitality bond, and honour is in this case, as in so many others, a force moving in two directions at once. Guests are given precedence, fed first, their wishes constantly ascertained and if possible granted. Any visiting strangers must become guests by ritual means; the transformation means that instead of being treated with guardedness or disdain, they must receive the opposite treatment, being cosseted, helped, and honoured. But the host, in spite of every protestation to the contrary, is normally, and from a ritual point of view, more powerful than the guests. In our own culture, for example, a guest is placed close to the host if he or she is being especially honoured. We should note however that the rule is: the smaller the distance *from the host*, the greater the honour.

Guests have no real say in how their host will treat them: while they are in another's house they have to become ceremonially passive, and accept what is offered. For a person cannot be called a "guest" in a place where he or she has any responsibilities; no obligations, other than respect for the host, can be laid upon a guest while he or she is under the host's roof. "Respect" for the host includes not fighting with the other guests (they were the host's choice, and now are temporary dependents), and perhaps living up to an expected role: being witty if invited because of one's entertainment value, telling the story of one's adventures if invited so that other people can hear what happened. Guests are not allowed to usurp the host's role. They cannot, for example, take what they have not been offered, give orders to the host's children, or demand different food, except where there is danger of violating a taboo. Since health is regarded with awe in our society, and protected by unconditional sanctions against anything which might even conceivably endanger it, we are permitted to ask for alternatives to be served us because of something like an allergy—but only if we make our request with all the elaboration and the deference that politeness demands.

Ancient Greek myths make the ultimate crime of a host the murder of his guest: a person invited is vulnerable, trusting, and dependent;

the host's role is that of protector of whoever is under his roof. (A wife, in traditional Mediterranean societies, is in some respects like a permanent guest, who comes as a "stranger" from another family, and is supposed to be "looked after" and "respected" by her husband—and to play a subordinate role.) A guest's archetypical crime against a host is adultery: making off with his wife (or her husband). The Trojan War was caused by Paris running off with his host's wife, Helen; the crime was always called not so much adultery as a crime against *hospitality*—Paris had dreadfully insulted his host, Menelaos. A host "lays himself open" to a guest by letting him into his house and permitting him contact with his wife; this advantage is freely given, and must never be abused. Several societies are on record as permitting a host to offer his wife, for a prescribed period of time of course, to a visitor whom he wished especially to honour. The guest would have been very rude to refuse; it would have been thought impolite to ask in the first place, and ruder still to do what Paris did and take without asking. (Zeus, who impersonated Amphitryon, took his wife, and hosted his dinner, had broken all the main rules of hospitality for guests, but ancient Greek gods were allowed liberties denied to human beings; they could for example marry their sisters. They did these things, of course, partly to remind mere mortals of what lay out of bounds.) Our own typical example of impropriety in a guest is trivial partly because we mean to express our contempt, but it shows the same fear of theft: a bad guest is "the sort of person you would not trust with the teaspoons."

Normally what the guest is offered is food, the symbol of fellowship with the host. To refuse food is to reject the fellowship, and also to prevent the host from playing the hostly role, which is to confer honour. So important was the rule among the Franks that guests must accept what is proffered, that a guest who refused food was in duty bound to accept a drink. When the wicked Fredegonda was blamed for having murdered Praetextatus, archbishop of Rouen, she asked her accuser to dinner. He refused to eat, but she was ready with the obligatory drink. He accepted it, knowing his danger, and died poisoned.

Researchers into the dynamics of family relationships assure us that most quarrels in the home take place at table. But so successful is the conviction among us that physical fights must not break out during dinner, that we almost never imagine that they might. We do make rules about the handling of utensils, and especially the knives. Knives must be set at the diners' places with blades facing in, towards the plate; they should never be held upright, or in the fist: one's grip on a knife at table must suggest concentration upon small, delicate, specific, and entirely necessary operations within the confines of the plate. When the meal is finished, once again the blade should be set towards the middle of the plate, and not facing neighbours. When great banquets used to begin with processions into the hall, all knives had to be sheathed until carving began. The points of formal dinner-table knives in the West became rounded during the seventeenth century, apparently beginning in France. We have learned to use forks instead of knives for introducing food into our mouths, partly in order to spare our companions the faintest suggestion of the consequences which could result from that knife-point approaching our faces. You never point at anybody else with a knife, of course—neither do you do so with a fork or spoon.

In the past, people were often far more amenable to the violence which knives and meat could arouse in them, and to the heady combination of hosts, guests, warmth, and plenty of liquor. Athenaeus tells us that the ancient Celts whetted their appetites by watching bloody gladiatorial combat during dinner, and that Roman orgies could include the same kind of entertainment. The motif of the severed head being brought to the table on a dish is not confined to the martyrdom of John the Baptist; Alexander the Great, for instance, was urged to receive a delegation bearing the heads of his enemies during dinner.

People have always longed to fling food at each other, and to smash the crockery. Louis XIV (he who ruled over the etiquette of Versailles) is said to have baited his brother, the august Monsieur, by splashing soup at his wig until Monsieur lost his temper and flung his bowl of boiled beef at the king. The ancient Greeks were capable of hurling cups of wine at each other if sufficiently annoyed. The favourite game at Greek symposia was *kottabos*; it involved the guests taking turns to swing a great flat wine-cup, twirling one handle of it round the index finger, so that the wine left in the cup shot across the room and struck (if the turn was successful) a small pan balanced on a pole, so that it fell onto a bronze disk. The word *kottabos* probably referred to the reverberating clang signalling a winning strike.

The hilarity occasioned by custard cream pies flung in faces must be part of the same complex of emotions. In the Baroque period in Europe, when food was spectacularly arranged—it often took kitchen staff days to sculpt and decorate pyramids, *pièces montées*, and architectural fantasies for a banquet—and a royal feast was like an opera, with gorgeously dressed players at the table and spectators standing round about to view the eating, it was common for the inner circle of noble guests to retire after dinner, leaving the onlookers to move in for the kill. They would rush the table and demolish all the exquisite culinary edifices, with a pleasure perhaps like that of children knocking down sandcastles or towers of building blocks. They would eat some of the food, and throw the rest at each other. John Evelyn, describing a great dinner for the Garter Knights in the Banqueting House in Whitehall on April 23, 1667, says the feast ended with the "banqueting-stuff" being "flung around the room profusely." When eastern Europeans traditionally toast each other and then smash their glasses, they are declaring the intensity and the permanence of the sentiments expressed: "Never again [after this dramatic pronouncement] shall this glass hold wine." But surely there is a simple thrill in extravagantly and publicly smashing one's glass to smithereens.

· *Invitations* ·

Anyone giving a dinner party must begin by rounding up guests. The people on the list may include close friends asked repeatedly for the sheer pleasure of seeing them, and those who "ought" to be entertained because contact with them is rare and the relationship could fail because of it, or because there was an obligation set up at a previous occasion where this evening's host was that evening's guest. There are useful or otherwise important people, people the host would like to know better, those invited out of concern that they might never otherwise be asked out, and some invited only to please

other guests or to add lustre to the gathering because of their repu-
tations. Since dinner parties permit unrelated people to meet on
intimate terms, they are also one of the primary methods of advanc-
ing social ambition. "Markby, Markby, and Markby?" notes Oscar
Wilde's Lady Bracknell with approval, in *The Importance of Being
Earnest*. "A firm of the very highest position in their profession.
Indeed I am told that one of the Mr. Markby's is occasionally to be
seen at dinner parties."

In the modern world, where openly stratified hierarchy is an
affront to the egalitarian myth, people are rarely permitted to display naked social ambition; snobbery must go decently disguised as
creativity, free choice, good taste, and so forth. There must be
enough money to pay for such social feats as carrying off dinner parties to which the Right People would agree to come. A currently
fashionable term for some of the guests required in such enterprises
is "the glitterati." It perceptively combines, in what Lewis Carroll
would have called a portmanteau word, two necessary ingredients
for success in some of the top echelons: celebrity (for whatever reason) in the art world, plus money displayed upon the person.

To be successful in such a milieu, a host must have not only
money but also the social power which is needed to attract more
power, in the shape of guests who are "in demand," yet amenable to
accepting *this* invitation and turning down the others being offered.
At the same time, hosts should know how to evade whatever and
whoever might cost prestige. They must be in a position above all to
persuade other people to remain a part of their "scene," attaching to
their coterie even those who are expected to play subordinate roles.
Indispensable as this last achievement is to social success, it is especially difficult to maintain in a world where mobility and fluidity
continually provide avenues of escape. To be able to control the
stage upon which the social spectacle is enacted is to experience
massive power. A dinner table is one such stage; presiding over it, a
host can be a conductor, a director, an impresario—and occasionally
also a star performer. He or she has to engage the right cast, or
expect the production to fail.

Invitations are tricky, because people on the host's list might
either want too much to come, or try to get out of accepting the

invitation and thereby ruin the whole projected configuration. This kind of problem is avoided in many small traditional societies, where community is of an unconditional nature. People know each other, and everybody's business, so well that someone's desire to give a party may be common knowledge long before inviting begins. Everyone knows who is eligible to go, and who cannot absent himself without insulting not only the host but the entire community.

The Javanese *slametan* described by Clifford Geertz is a gathering which is called together for the achievement of *slamet*, or bodily and mental equanimity. Guests are needed to show support, renew neighbourly bonds, and help the host reach accommodation with the supernatural. Some of the reasons why a host would call a *slametan* include a birth in his family, marriage, sorcery, death, bad dreams, house moving, or opening a factory. Guests come because they live nearby; they are the appropriate people for the event, and they know their friend, relative, or neighbour so well that the call to a *slametan* comes as no surprise.

Accordingly a messenger, often the host's child, is sent to call the guests, *after* the special ritual food has been set out. (The women, who are never allowed to attend a *slametan*, have worked hard preparing the food—a fact of which the neighbours are probably aware.) No more than five to ten minutes' notice are given, and everyone must drop what he was doing and come. The guests sit in a ring on the floor as the house slowly fills with the smoke of burning incense, and listen to a speech given by their host, explaining why he has called them together, and sometimes pointing out the symbolic meaning of the food they are to be given. They respond politely, helping him to achieve *slamet*. Chanted prayer follows, and then everybody eats quickly and silently, being served not by the host but by one or two of the guests. After a ritual five minutes' eating, the guests go home, carrying the rest of their food with them to eat with their wives and children.

When a Sherpa host wants to give a dinner party, it is made extremely difficult for a guest, unless he or she is willing to insult the host, to refuse an invitation. For example, he sends a small child as a messenger to call the guests. This is a matter of convenience, certainly, but it is often also an ingenious pressure tactic; the child is not told the time or occasion for the party, so that guests have no information to manipulate in sidestepping acceptance of the invitation. In any case, the child is too young to be entrusted with carrying back correctly phrased explanations—complex and subtle as unreal excuses always are—for non-appearance at the party. All must come. Where parties are large and important, of course, Sherry Ortner says that guests are "more likely to feel offended at not being invited than put upon when the invitation comes." They are entertained, and (if the event is successful) they are pleased; bonds of future obligation and continued interrelationship have been tied.

Modern Western society works extremely hard to prevent human relationships of any kind from lasting; claims to anything like unconditional loyalty are experienced by many of us as a fearful imposition. Our invitation techniques are accordingly different from those in small, close-knit, honour-bound groups. There is rarely the sort of tribal duty or social pressure to attend functions that the Sherpas and the Javanese understand and cultivate in their own interests. The closest equivalent for us is a family reunion, where invitations are scarcely necessary and obligations are the stronger for it. So great is the duty to entertain relatives among the Tanga of Melanesia that if a distant kinsman fails to be included in the celebration, he can appear at the feast and make his claim known to the host. If the claim is upheld, the kinsman is allowed to take the first bite from the best pig on the menu. Louis XIV, on the other hand, is said to have solemnly invited his brother, every day of his life, to eat with him. Monsieur had daily to accept. Ceremonial invitations are for strangers, not family: the result would have done a great deal to distance the brothers, and so balance the familiarity and the fractiousness which had once permitted them to fling food at each other at table.

We, however, are accustomed to choosing not only our guests but the parties we wish to attend; family reunions and similar obligations are few and far between. One problem for us is how to get out of an unwelcome invitation. A refusal immediately suggests that one is saying no out of a simple preference for going elsewhere that night, or even for not going anywhere. Because we are all so well supplied with transport and mostly so unencumbered with responsibilities for other people, all we can do, often, is claim that we have a previous engagement. We hope we can persuade the hostess not only to believe this, but to think that we would have chosen her party if she had invited us earlier. The hostess in turn owes it to her honour, and to any hope for a future relationship with the recalcitrant guest, to ensure that the excuse has a chance of being as plausible as possible. Invitations must not, for this reason, be sent or telephoned too early, because that deprives the recipient of a chance to refuse politely by claiming a prior appointment, and removes the possibility that the would-be hostess might convincingly believe the excuse.

Telephoning an invitation, which most of us almost invariably do, is always slightly rude because it forces a quick decision, which might be regretted later. A preferable invitation might, for example, be expected but not have materialized yet. We all know masters of the adroit and graceful sidestep, but most of us are slower and less convincing than we need to be to get out of a date when suddenly importuned on the telephone. On the other hand, a guest must not be asked too close to the date, because that looks as though he or she is really being asked to fill in for a preferred guest who has dropped out. Friends need to be very close and compliant if they are to be asked on short notice to fill a gap.

Among the Min Chia of Yunnan in China during the thirties, guests had to receive a written list of all the other people invited; they were then given several days in which to weigh up whether they wished to go or not. This must have been nerve-wracking for the host, but at least it placed a good deal of the burden of responsibility on the other guests if somebody refused to attend. The use of the telephone makes this kind of delicacy all but impossible to achieve, even though most of us would like to know who else is coming before we accept an invitation. Also in China, guests would once have been affronted to find themselves among people of a status lower than their own; a host could ruin his reputation by subjecting guests to such insensitivity. The Baronne Staffe, the doyenne of late nineteenth-century French etiquette, warns would-be hosts never to invite people richer than themselves. For one thing, such guests would have to be offered food, cutlery, plates, and wines of the level to which they are accustomed. Even if you could pull it off, you would not only impoverish yourself, but you would commit the social gaffe of pretentiousness. The nineteenth-century rich, like the aristocratic class earlier, had to protect themselves because hosts are, at least ritually and temporarily, more powerful than guests.

It is polite in many Eastern societies, for example among the Yao of northern Thailand, not to hear an invitation clearly, and certainly not to accept it, until it has been made three times. In this way the host has time to reconsider his project of extending hospitality, or alternatively a host with no food to offer may still invite, and so show benevolent feelings: when the third invitation is not stated, guests sensitive to the social complexities will understand. The guest who is asked three times before responding, on the other hand, makes it clear that he or she is not hanging about dying to be asked. In New Testament times, invitations were issued in two stages: a first, formal request was always refused with thanks (which added ritual stature to the guest). There followed—if the host really wanted to pursue the matter—a much more urgent and personal badgering; eventually the guest might allow his or her resistance to crumble. An example is the hospitality offered Paul and his friends by Lydia, the dealer in purple textiles, in the Acts of the Apostles. She first asked them, then "constrained" them, or, as we still say, "prevailed upon" them.

The word "invite" appears to come from the Sanskrit *in* ("towards") and *vitas* ("pleasant"). But there is a possibility (appropriately reflecting the ambiguity) that "invite" is related to Latin *invitus*, meaning "unwilling"; *in-* is more frequently a negative than a positive prefix. Inviting guests is always a delicate operation; the unwillingness of the guest at being laid under an obligation, and at being made into what we might call an "honour object," is therefore allowed expression. Behind the etiquette, the guest might also shelter from suspicions that he or she was ever anxious to be invited.

The host, meanwhile, must try to set up a well-balanced grouping of guests. He would be wise to include a guest of honour, somebody witty, someone relatively unknown to him or to the group, someone in need of kindness; it would be useful to discharge some of his own obligations at the same time. This conventional set of suggestions roughly corresponds to what were once very clear, set roles for dinner guests.

A Roman banquet would include parasites. The word designating these people literally means "bread with," like the root of the term "companion." Parasites were clients or retainers, fed at the table of a rich man. (A "parasite" now means, in English, a person who lives off others or a creature that feeds on another animal, known as its "host.") Parasites, in ancient Greece and Rome, lived under a permanent obligation to their benefactor: they were guests who could never turn into hosts, and who therefore had to render other—doubtless more useful—services instead. Parasites were often placed in a demeaning position at dinner. They might sit on a stool, for example, instead of reclining on a couch; they could be served last, or not given any of the delicacies. They were made the butt of jokes, and were expected to fawn, flatter, and be ridiculed for it. The emperor Augustus had an Etruscan parasite called Gabba, whose wife was as welcome at dinner as he, for Maecenas, the emperor's powerful friend and patron of the arts, was fascinated by her. Gabba would keep his eyes closed while Maecenas ogled his wife. One day when a slave attempted to filch his wine, he remarked, "I am asleep only as far as Maecenas is concerned."

There were guests designated, sometimes officially, as jesters and buffoons. (Often a parasite at a Greek or Roman party was given this role.) Jesters were part of the entertainment at medieval banquets. Henry II of England gave a serjeanty to a man named Roland "le Pettour" or "le Fartere" and to his heirs, provided they could be counted on to perform at his annual Christmas Day banquet *saltum, siffletum et pettum* or *bumbulum* ("a leap, a whistle, and a fart"); and a minstrel in *Piers Plowman* (ca. 1380) complains that he lacks the skill to "fart in tune at feasts."

I have myself seen a self-appointed jester perform a less specific role at one of the French *moungetades* described earlier. He was known as *Fil de fer* ("Wire"), and was a migrant labourer, not a native of the village. He stood throughout the meal, remaining physically apart from the seated diners. Striding about, he harangued the crowd in patois, picking on certain well-known characters present and abusing them till the other diners wept with laughter at his raillery. He was not expected to pay like the other guests for the food he was given. Athenaeus tells us of various comic parasites in the ancient world who were expected to mimic their hosts' disabilities. The point of this was perhaps to draw the sting of the guests' critical glances, or simply to make the host's blindness or his lameness less singular, his power to command more obvious.

A Roman guest of honour, or an especially powerful man, was allowed to bring one or more people with him. These were called *umbrae*, "shades" or "ghosts." They helped to make the VIP feel comfortable, and enabled him to poach on the host's power, since he had himself invited some of the guests. The *umbrae* were also a sort of bodyguard or extension of him as "more than other men." Powerful modern guests, visiting film directors perhaps, or famous art collectors, often arrive at social gatherings flanked by minions, with a very similar effect. Ancient Athenian men out on the town might move from party to party; it was apparently to be expected that uninvited guests would burst in on a symposium, often bringing with them a revival of the party spirit among those already installed.

The ideal number of guests at a dinner party has always been a matter for strong opinions in Western traditions, where meals have been organized for a set number and planned, typically, round a meat course. In many other parts of the world, dinners are mostly vegetarian and divided in advance into small morsels; they lend themselves to the serving of quite elastic numbers of guests. Varro said that diners should number no fewer than the Graces (three) and no more than the Muses (nine)—the latter figure being the number which could be comfortably accommodated in a Roman *triclinium* or dining room. (The mad emperor Heliogabalus enjoyed choosing guests for their physical peculiarities: eight bald men, eight one-eyed men, eight fat men, and so forth—he himself being always the ninth.) Thirteen people sitting down to dinner is considered unlucky—and not only because either Judas or Jesus was the thirteenth man at the Last Supper. The superstition is also found in pre-Christian Greece (where there were, for instance, twelve Olympian gods, so who could be the thirteenth?), and in many other cultures as well. The Greeks and Romans disliked even numbers in any case because two meant conflict; also, "one" was male, but "two" was female and therefore malign. They tried hard not to allow an even number of guests to eat together, believing that it produced sinister silences in the conversation, which would result in danger for somebody present.

It has been the rule until recently in our own culture, and it still is the tendency, to ask an equal number of men and women. (The convention itself is fairly recent, because respectable women have tended not to be invited to men's dinner parties during most of human history.) Hosts have had to keep lists on hand of unattached people who could be invited to fill a gap where somebody, and especially a woman, lacked a "partner." The problem was compounded, of course, if a party of fourteen lost a guest: it was imperative that someone be found, to keep thirteen from sitting down to table. An institution called the *quatorzièmes* ("fourteenths") existed in nineteenth-century Paris. These were men who waited at home between 5:00 and 9:00 p.m. every night, all dressed up and ready to step into the breach where any dinner party threatened suddenly to number thirteen. You could hire a presentable, experienced "fourteenth" whenever you needed one.

Since invitations, and especially dinner invitations, can be fraught with hope and danger, and dinner parties are dramatic events at which decisions can be made and important relationships initiated, tested, or broken, the act of inviting is often surrounded with care and regulation. How invitations are written can be a matter of strict etiquette. They should still, ideally, be handwritten, and until quite recently it was not "done" in high society to send them in the mail: they were supposed to be delivered by hand. For socialites, invitation cards, like Christmas cards, are physical expressions of how much honour one can muster. The outlay—of time, effort, honour, and care—by people who take hosting seriously can be considerable. Lady Sybil Colefax, a London hostess famous in the 1920s and 1930s, was capable of writing hundreds of dinner invitations in a month. She wrote them at home, in trains, at every spare moment, just as a different kind of woman would never waste time while she could be knitting. Colefax invitations would pour in to people whose company was greatly in demand. "Resistance was futile," Brian Masters writes. " . . . She simply issued another, and another, she would mount up scores of them if necessary, until the prey eventually succumbed, like a fox pursued by hounds, through sheer weariness." Her nearly illegible handwriting was famous. People used to puzzle over their invitations for days, trying to make out when they were supposed to appear for dinner, and who the other guests would be. "One usually placed the card on a mantelpiece and glanced at it from time to time, hoping that its secrets would suddenly be revealed; or threw it on the floor in the hope that the odd angle would make all clear."

But very soon they would have to reply. The guest's obligation is in the very first place to reply, as soon as possible. Hosts should be told within days—the Victorians made that twenty-four hours—whether guests will be coming or not, so that substitute invitations can be issued to similarly dazzling people. Once an invitation has been accepted, it must at all costs be honoured. "Nothing," wrote Emily Post, "but serious illness or death or an utterly unavoidable accident can excuse the breaking of a dinner engagement." The flatness and clarity of this ruling rests on a guest's knowledge of what goes into a full-dress dinner party, or even a much simpler but carefully home-cooked meal: of the hard work, the cost, the skill and attention to detail which every good host expends on guests. It would be unthinkable for polite people to neglect playing their part, and risk ruining the host's evening and that of the guests who do go.

The obligation is underlined by myth: the issuing of an invitation to dinner is so solemn, the agreement to arrive so binding, that even a guest who is no longer wanted (so the stories have it) will insist on keeping the appointment. A host who murders an invited dinner guest really should consider cancelling the projected party, because such guests are likely to turn up anyway and ruin the evening. Supernatural beings are fairly accustomed to sitting down to dinner with the living. Many are the stories of dead men who arrive to appal the host and terrify the other guests. Sometimes they are invisibly present, sometimes not.

An ancient Greek ghost attends a wedding feast, dripping with mud from his grave or from the Underworld:

Lame, branded, wizened with age, like a wandering stranger he came,
Begging for a lump of fat, when Meles celebrated his wedding.
Uninvited, he demanded soup. In the midst of them he stood,
A ghost, risen from the mire.

Macbeth murders his invited guest, then dares to provoke criticism of him for not coming to the feast. Suddenly the dead man occupies the stool reserved by the other guests for Macbeth. With his gory locks, marrowless bones, and glaring eyes, the ghost of Banquo drives Macbeth mad with fear and forces his hostess to end the meal and dismiss the guests, throwing etiquette to the winds: "Stand not upon the order of your going, / But go at once." Don Giovanni's impudent dinner invitation to the statue of the man he had killed is heard, accepted—and fate must be fulfilled. The Commendatore arrives at the appointed hour, to pound at his host's door with his stone fist. Since banqueting tables unite large groups of chosen guests, interventions by ghosts can make a most theatrical effect. In the legend of the Singing Bone, a murdered prince's bone, found in the forest and carved into a flute, announces to the entire banquet-hall as the bard innocently plays it that the king, their host, has murdered his brother and usurped his place.

An empty chair, with its empty place at the table, easily becomes an eerie, uncomfortable sight: it insistently calls to mind the person who ought to be sitting there. Children used regularly to be expected to leave the table before the end of dinner; it was a sixteenth-century rule of etiquette that they should take their place setting and the chair with them. At a Jewish Seder, a goblet of wine is set out ready for the prophet Elijah, who is invited to the feast and expected to attend. It is still a custom that, if an expected guest does not arrive, his or her place may be laid, with the glass or goblet turned upside down; during World War II this tradition was followed when a pilot's plane failed to return from its mission. In Rembrandt's painting of the *Supper at Emmaus* in the Louvre, a glass upside down is on the table, signifying the despair of the disciples at Jesus's death. The moment portrayed in the picture is that of the bread being broken, to reveal that the unknown guest is really he.

• Coming Right In •

The metaphor of crossing a threshold is used for rites of passage, initiations, and psychological turning points all over the world. The humble, ordinary act of stepping over the boundary which demarcates the inside of the house from outside is used to dramatize some of the great oppositions upon which social and physical categories are based; it differentiates for example such concepts as public and private, light (sunshine) and dark (shade), male (working away from home) and female (whose "place is in the home"), profane (in front of, *pro*, the temple, *fanum*) and sacred (inside the temple walls).

Moving from one of these categories into its opposite is always, ritually speaking, a momentous act. The acceptance of an outsider into one's house can also be thought of as potentially dangerous; a guest, even somebody well known, is in many cultures a temporary "pollution," which chiefly means something out of place. (The modern concept of physical pollution is curiously and strikingly analogous with this social attitude. Oil in a lake pollutes it, and socks in the soup would be disgusting: both oil and socks have places assigned to them; they pollute places where they do not belong.)

A "polluting" stranger in one's house needs to be incorporated and, as we say, "made to feel at home." The status of a guest lies somewhere between that of a hostile foreigner and that of a family member. "Guesthood" is an artificially created ritual role, participating in both extremes; hence its ambiguity and the need for care in its regulation. Guests must do everything to reassure their hosts that they bear nothing but good will, and a determination to subordinate themselves to them while they are under their roof. There are various ritual ways in which entry to a house is noted and "managed."

In Japan or in the Middle East, one takes off one's shoes. Outside the house is dirt, and leaving shoes at the door not only respects cleanliness, but also ritually recognizes the sacrality of "inside." In the past, when people usually walked to where they were going even if the distance was great, guests had their feet washed by the host or the host's servant on arrival. Water, the great purificatory symbol, brings about not only physical but also ceremonial cleanliness. In hot countries a drink of water, or of a staple liquid such as beer, is offered on arrival, and immediately the guest has entered into a pact of obligation. The entry of a guest begins the whole complicated drama which the roles of host and guest impose. The guest, who is penetrating into the host's most vulnerable and intimate space, often makes motions of ritual deference. A man used to leave his hat and stick (vestiges of helmet and sword) with the maid on entering a house; or he would be required to leave his stick at the door, take his hat off, and go into the drawing room holding it. Baring one's head or "uncovering," like the bowing that used to accompany it, shows deference, a ritual lowering of oneself before another. The taking off of shoes is a very practical gesture, but it also means to a Middle Eastern guest that he is disarming himself, showing respect, and making himself similar to the host, who himself is shoeless. A milder version of this takes place when guests arrive at our houses and wipe their shoes on a mat with "Welcome" printed on it. After having rung the bell and been let into the house with ritual handshakes, cries, and kisses, in snowy weather they take off their boots and put on "indoor" shoes, or in the presence of intimate friends remain shoeless, then remove hats, gloves, and coats, and hand them over to be put away in the host's closet. All this having taken place in the hallway—a semi-public, neutral area of transition—the next step is reached in the guests' progress, the introduction into the living room.

Dinner guests often bring gifts, typically flowers, wine, or chocolates, which they give to the host on arrival. This is a part-payment for the hospitality about to be given, and for this reason it is possible for such a gift to be thought lacking in civility: a gift already bestowed might mean less pressure to return the invitation. But the custom has spread in recent years, even to previously immune Anglo-Saxon countries. Dinner gifts, it should be noted, ought still to consist of food or flowers because these things do not last. A durable and inappropriately valuable gift would upset the delicate imbalance created by a dinner invitation.

Many and various are the rules about what gifts one may present to one's host. Flowers are particularly laden with symbolic meanings which might trap a foreign guest into committing a faux pas. Roses, in eastern Germany, mean you have romantic intentions; yellow flowers mean hatred in Bulgaria, and in Norway carnations and white flowers generally refer to funerals and death. Chrysanthemums are usually inappropriate gifts in Europe because they are commonly placed on graves, chrysanthemums being at their best at the time of the Feast of the Dead. Offering wine is an insult in Portugal, Spain, or Italy, because it looks as though you think your host might not be prepared to supply enough of this basic commodity. (All these rules are modified, of course, by the principle of politeness, which enjoins people on their own home ground to make allowances for the ignorance of foreigners.)

The way hosts accept gifts also varies. In Turkey, the hostess would not dream of opening a gift you have presented because she would be taking her attention off you, the guest, and that would make you feel unwanted. In other countries, a gift might be ceremonially ignored so that the host will not look greedy, or it might be opened at once with cries of delight, together with reproaches for the giver's generosity. In North America, gifts tend to be opened immediately. Flowers are displayed so that everyone can enjoy them, whereas in other cultures it might be thought rude for the hostess to absent herself in order to find and fill a vase; a gift of wine should if possible be served during the meal, and chocolates handed out after dinner, so that the hosts do not appear to be gleefully hoarding gifts for themselves, and so as to display the gift-giver's generosity to the other guests. In France, a gift bottle of wine might not be served at dinner because a host is supposed to have complex and subtle reasons for having chosen specific wines as a function of the dishes to be served, or to have chosen the dishes to complement the wines.

On a Middle Eastern guest's arrival at a traditional house, he or she must give a formalized greeting and then sit down at the place designated, on the floor. This immediate lowering of the body is a ritual act of deference to the host and his household. Not to do it, say the people of the United Arab Emirates, "would be sitting on the head of the host." For the rest of the visit, guests must take care not to rise while the host is sitting. The aim is never to stand higher than the host; if somebody leaves, they bend while exiting, demonstrating a desire to stay lower: physical demeanour is an outward sign of one's will and intent. Great care must be taken when sitting not to let legs straggle over the floor, taking up too much room. (Our dining chairs automatically prevent people from appropriating extra space; but we do request that their occupants refrain from extending their legs out as far as possible. The correct position of the seat and spine in an upright dining chair helps keep shins decorously vertical.) People who sit on the floor to dine must keep their naked feet in their proper place, tucked decently away from the eating space and from the other people present. Feet, like shoes, are "low" and potentially polluting: one never knows what they have trodden on. They are also extremely intimate parts of the body, and to feel free to present them to another person at an occasion like a dinner party is likely to be interpreted either as a deliberate insult or as a sign of great pride.

The Arab hostess, giving an all-female party, now pours coffee, which in this culture is an opening ritual as well as a closing one. Then she provides food, eats it with her guests, pours coffee again, and finally offers perfumes and incense: guests will return home bearing the perfumes of the house they have visited. All these rites are performed by the host personally. A guest shows honour and deference by placing herself entirely in the hands of her hostess; indeed, she has no say, as long as she is in the hostess's house, about how she is to be treated. Resentment for any incivility may be expressed, and revenge exacted—but normally only later, when the guest has left the house and tells everyone else what happened. The perfumes and incense are intended to purify the pollution represented by the outsider's presence, in addition to lavishing attention and respect. In ancient times Arabs and Jews would pour perfumed oil over the heads of arriving visitors. Jesus rebuked Simon the Pharisee at a dinner party when criticized for letting a prostitute approach him and then wash his bare feet with her tears. Simon had not welcomed him as a truly caring host should, had not kissed him when he came in, had not provided water for his feet, had not anointed his head with oil.

A guest must appear at the host's door—especially when the occasion is dinner—looking as clean and respectable as possible. A dirty guest, unscented and unkempt, shows great dishonour to the host in the United Arab Emirates. Her hostess might show her understanding of the slight by neglecting to offer food and perfumes in turn; she can count only on coffee, the least a host can offer. Guests are expected to bath carefully, to put on cosmetics and perfumes (if women), and come in their best clothes. Again the expectation has not changed in traditional society for two thousand years: in the New Testament, a man who comes to a wedding "without a wedding garment" enrages the king because it shows a lack of preparedness, an uncaring attitude, and even calculated disrespect. (This parable is inserted, in Matthew's text but not in Luke's, directly after the wedding feast is offered to people who have been hurriedly gathered in from the streets because the original guests had turned their host's invitation down. The story of the guest who had not bothered to dress for the occasion clearly belongs in a different place in the text.) Plato has Socrates, who normally went barefooted, appear at a friend's house for dinner noticeably having bathed, and wearing sandals.

At dinner parties the public and the private realms intersect; this meeting of two separate categories is one reason for the social and ritual importance of inviting guests for a meal. But even family meals are turned into mini-"feasts" if they are held at set times, if all the family is expected to attend, and if eating between meals is regulated. This is why festive dressing for dinner—even for family dinners—has been a common response to an eating event the world over. Cleanliness and purity always accompany the idea of eating, so clothes must be clean—and not sullied during the meal. Wearing clothes is a social act, and (except for protection and warmth, neither of which is usually very necessary at dinner) has nothing to do with "nature" or common sense. Clothes are an overlaying of the physical, like table manners themselves. They bow to social agreements (for example, in following fashion); they adorn their wearers and enhance their appearance, just as laying a table or decorating a dish helps make the meal aesthetically pleasing.

In many cultures there are clothes designed only for eating, just as we have special outfits to sleep in. Like nightdresses, dinner garments, in societies which allow their members this comfort, must always be loose. (Our "dinner jacket" is dressy, but not made especially roomy because of the occasions on which it is worn.) The Japanese Tea Ceremony often includes a time when guests are left alone to admire the beauty of the host's arrangement of the room; during this interval he changes into a special tea-drinking robe, and reappears to give the guests a new view of their host. In ancient Rome, guests changed into a tunic and shawl for dinner. These were colourful and becoming garments, either thin in summer or woollen in winter. In imperial times the outfit, called a *synthesis* or "combination," was considered rather effeminate because it had once been female apparel only. It was never worn out of doors, except during the Saturnalia, when as much behaviour as possible was deliberately reversed. The emperor Nero once caused a scandal by being seen outside with only half a *synthesis* on, and a silly-looking handkerchief tied round his neck.

Roman guests were given thin slippers to put on in their host's house, but these too were removed by the slaves before the meal proper began. If a guest "called for his slippers," it was a sign that he wanted to leave the dining room, change into his street clothes, and then go home. It was considered very chic to come with several changes of *synthesis* to wear during one meal. Martial describes a fop who changed eleven times, complaining of heat and perspiration. The poet sourly remarks that owning only one *synthesis* seems to prevent sweat.

In ancient China, the togetherness signified by a banquet was sometimes underlined by all the diners appearing in the same colour, rather as members of a choir must all dress alike or at least in matching colours. We sometimes hand out similar decorations to all the diners, for the sake of hilarity or to promote a sense of community and occasion, as when the men all wear red carnations and the women corsages, or when everyone puts on a paper party hat. But normally it was the servants (now it is the waiters in expensive restaurants) who have been dressed alike in our culture. They often wore white gloves so that their fingers could not come in contact with the food; in addition, any touching of the sauce would immediately show, and could not be licked away.

In the nineteenth and early twentieth centuries, women had to bare their shoulders in order to eat at formal dinners. They also had to put on long gloves, only to remove them before the meal began. Buttoned, elbow-length gloves could be so hard to get off that one could buy a pair with hands that rolled back. The etiquette manuals were never very sure whether they approved of this labour-saving device; Emily Post pronounced it "hideous." Gloves, once removed, had to join evening bag, fan, and large damask napkin, all precariously balanced on a slippery, possibly satin-sheathed, lap. Emily Post suggested rather daringly ("this ought not to be put into a book of etiquette, which should say you must do nothing of the kind") that one might cover all these objects with the napkin placed cornerwise across the knees "and tuck the two side corners under like a lap robe, with the gloves and the fan tied in place, as it were." She went further, since one could no longer count on receiving a very large napkin, and promoted the carrying of paper clips, by gentlemen as well as ladies, to hold the napkin in place. All this assumes that a civilized diner would never require any dabbing at the lips with a napkin during dinner.

Until quite recently women kept their hats on in restaurants and when invited to a formal lunch. Liselotte, a French arbiter of etiquette, says in 1915 that women may keep their hats on even if the lunch is not very ceremonious "so as not to derange the edifice of their hair," and so that they can leave after the meal without having to recreate their *toilette*. But a hostess, who had not had to go out, could remain hatless, even at formal functions. It has usually been the case that hosts, because they are at home and also because they are ritually more powerful, could wear less formal clothes than guests. A hostess never wore gloves or a face veil in her own home, "unless," Emily Post added jocularly but rather brutally in 1922, "there is something the matter with her face." Guests wearing face veils were allowed to fasten the lower edge "up over their noses." Women in the United Arab Emirates, eating with their hands, delicately lift their black masks (which they wear even at all-female dinner parties) with one finger each time they take a mouthful. When Western women wore huge fruit-laden hats, the table decorations greatly resembled the headgear; old photographs of turn-of-the-century lunches remind us that the ensemble must have been impressive.

In ancient Greece and Rome, a banquet was simply no banquet unless everybody present wore a wreath. The purpose of crowns was partly like that of paper party hats: they signified festivity. The scent of the plaited flowers and vegetation was said to prevent drunkenness too early in the symposium. Another meaning was erotic, since dinner wreaths denoted passionate excitement. The religious significance was deeply solemn. Wearing the wreath symbolized completeness and integrity (a broken wreath, from an erotic point of view, signified a personality enthralled by *eros*, his inviolability broken). Fate in the ancient world was thought of as a bond, and the wreath bound round the head meant human limitation in general: the necessity which all of us share, and which includes the need to eat. The crown was a pledge that one would observe the cardinal rule of table manners, not to be guilty of appropriating the food due to other people; stealing, and ignoring the rights of others, was a form of *hybris* or disregard for limitation.

Wreaths went with perfumed oils. Both were put on at the same time, at the beginning of the feast (this would be the second perfuming, if the host had anointed the guest's head on arrival), or before the second "table" or course, and after the meal before the symposium. Roman cities had wreath and perfume shops, at which prospective hosts could get supplies ready-made, or where party-goers could buy their headgear and perfumes on their way to the host's house. Modern Western people have largely replaced the arts of perfumery with constant washing and a determination to do away with all bodily odours. A modern rule at gourmet dinners is that anyone who wears perfume on such an occasion has no idea how to behave—perfume fights the bouquet of the wine. But for much of history, scent was thought essential to festivity (partly but by no means entirely because crowds of people quickly smell rank), and incense and perfume were especially appreciated at dinner. Ancient Egyptian frescoes show us dinner guests with large cones of scented fat fixed to the tops of their heads; these were designed to melt during the feast, and drizzle deliciously down over the diners' faces and bodies.

When the guests arrive, the hosts must be ready, impeccably dressed and calmly waiting, all preparatory struggles over. A host is responsible for a guest within the boundary of his or her domain. For this reason, if the boundary of the house is felt to be the gate to the whole property, the host may await the guests there and conduct them across the grounds and into the house; he will similarly "see them off" at the end of the visit, as far as the front door or to the property's gates, and might even travel part of the way home with a guest of honour.

Guests must know when to arrive—exactly at the time mentioned when they were invited, or later. (Hosts rarely welcome guests who arrive earlier than the stated time.) Punctuality is extremely culture-specific; the correct time of arrival for dinner is partly a function of the type and temperature of the food served. Western European cuisine demands to be eaten hot, and many of the dishes require to be what the French call *à point*, cooked to a certain point, no more and no less. We rarely chop food in advance, as the Chinese do, and stir-fry it moments before serving. Our etiquette books accordingly used to insist that hosts should not wait longer than a quarter of an hour at the most, after the first course is ready, for tardy arrivals; guests were warned of the fury they could cause by coming late for dinner. Other cultures have other ideas. Traditional Japanese expected guests to come one hour late; modern Greeks (who dislike very hot food) would be shocked if you arrived less than half an hour after the stated time. Respect for and submission to the host's expectations is common to both systems: a polite guest should adapt either to the nature of the meal and the trouble that has been taken with it, by coming on time, or to the host's privacy and a culture's general distaste for hurrying, by coming late.

Punctuality has a lot to do with another cultural particularity: the nature and length of pre-dinner socializing. We ourselves expect guests to contain their appetites for some time before dinner is ready; we keep them busy with tidbits, conversation, and pre-dinner "drinks." No matter how slow the hosts are about giving us something solid to eat, we as guests must never ever complain, or even look as though we are aware of the delay. In some northern European societies, as most of us used to do in the past, guests arrive and everyone sits down at once to dinner, so it is essential to be on time. In many non-European cultures socializing takes place first, but talking is kept to a strict minimum while eating, and people might be expected to leave straight after the meal, so that it would be extremely rude to arrive just before dinner, skipping all the conversation beforehand. It would look as though you were breaking a fundamental rule of all dinner-time politeness, which decrees that guests will not come for the food alone.

There might be a ceremony that takes place before the meal begins, establishing in advance the companionship which is essential for eating together. One example is the almost sacramental sharing of a cola nut in Nigeria. The cola (which provides the name for a type of Western pop drink, the formula for which might or might not contain a minute quantity of cola) is a large nut with several bitter-tasting cotelydons, full of the stimulants caffeine, theobromine (as in chocolate), and kolanine. An Igbo host, after greeting his guests, must share with them a cola nut; on even the most informal occasions he will apologize profusely if he is caught without one to offer. After a prayer, one nut is split by the oldest or most honoured person at the gathering, and tiny pieces are eaten by all present. "During the sharing," writes O. Nzekwu, "a religious feeling pervades the atmosphere. All talking stops." The Yoruba tribe makes cola part of the ritual of ending, rather than opening, a meal: cola nuts are presented to departing guests. To be given an odd number of nuts is an insult and lets you know that, although careful manners may have prevailed during dinner, the host is angry with you for some reason. An even number of nuts is offered to signify the desire of the host for a closer relationship with his guest, and the larger the (even) number of nuts the greater his esteem.

In France, guests are often expected to meet for an *apéritif* before dinner. This institution grows out of the nineteenth-century French custom of a *coup d'avant* or "shot before," a small glass of vermouth given before dinner, at first only to the men. The French word *vermouth* is related to English "wormwood" (a corruption of German *Wermut*), an ingredient of absinthe. *Wermut* meant "man courage": the substance is thought to be a powerful aphrodisiac. Vermouth, made by mixing white wine with "Turin bitters," derived from plants like artemisia and bitter oranges, was invented by the Italian Alessio during the eighteenth century and put on sale commercially in Turin in 1786. The French met vermouth on Napoleon's forays into Italy. They joined in the gradual change from an ancient taste for spiced and honeyed wines before dinner to a new love for bitters. New drinks often become popular because people persuade themselves that they are somehow good for the health. The noun *apéritif* ("opener") appears only in 1888; the adjective had been used previously in a medical sense, referring to the opening of pores, veins, and blocked passages. The word suggested that these increasingly popular drinks were entirely benign, being used as they were to stimulate the appetite for the enormous meals which people expected in nineteenth-century France. What in the body was being "opened" was left unclear.

Now the *apéritif* has become a sharing ritual in France, a preparation for the companionship of dinner itself; it includes food offered as accompaniment. Whiskey is the favoured drink, especially for French men, whereas women are likely to prefer port, Cinzano, or even mineral water; in rich and fashionable circles one is served champagne. The word denotes two periods every day (*"apéritif* time"), before lunch and supper. The "opening" now has to do, in most people's minds, with the beginning of the meal; the drink called the *digestif*, which complements it, also has a comforting sound and reputation, and marks the meal's end.

Drinks before dinner are often much stronger than those which accompany the meal. Beer and wine may, if drunk in moderation and "in their place," be thought inoffensive, even nutritious—they can be drunk both before and during meals. But the higher the alcohol level, the less the drink is equated or associated with food; gin and whiskey are never consumed at the dinner table, but given a different role entirely. In North America, where alcohol has long been the object of passionate condemnation, having a drink with colleagues after work is of necessity a sharper, more decisive act than is taking the comfortable French *apéritif*. An evening drink can be used to mark the transition, for a North American, between worlds which the social system divides so brutally that the walls erected need resolute crossing: from work to relaxation, from constraint to freedom, from productivity and money-earning to its opposite, from hierarchy and role-maintaining to equality and camaraderie. There is danger in the "crossing over" and in the release of inhibitions, and even a degree of defiance. But this is contained by the limited, definite time slot allowed for the ritual (drinking must never become an "anytime" activity), by the specially allocated places in which it occurs, and by the general agreement that this should be a *social* performance.

When people get home from work they might use an evening drink as a rite of passage not only from work to "play" but also from public to private—yet another of the great oppositions which form the framework of the modern industrial system. Drinks before dinner can perform all these transitions at once. If the dinner is one to which guests have been invited, drinking together will serve in addition as a "rite of passage" from each person's own house into that of the host, and as both symbol and creator of solidarity among the artificially created gathering as they prepare to sit down together at table.

• Taking Our Places •

"Hsiang Yu invited Liu Pang to stay for a banquet. Hsiang Yu and his uncle Hsiang Po sat facing east, the patriarch Fan Tseng faced south, Liu Pang faced north, and Chang Liang, who was in attendance upon him, faced west." These are the opening remarks in an early Han account (second century B.C.) of a banquet during which Hsiang Yu intended to have Liu Pang murdered. But Hsiang Yu, in spite of henchmen ready with swords, and hatred in the hearts of many, could not bring himself to make a move against his guest. His uncle, Hsiang Po, even joined in a sword dance, a dinner entertainment which was supposed to climax with the assassination, and shielded Liu with his body as the dance continued. When another killer appeared, with bristling hair and eyes "nearly starting from his head," he was merely invited by the host to eat and drink. The text gives us no reason for this sudden protection for an enemy, but the seating arrangements, for those who can read them, tell the whole story. Sitting facing the east was to have the seat of honour. When Liu Pang sat down facing north, he was accepting Hsiang Yu (who was therefore able to sit with his uncle facing east) as his superior; it was enough to save his life, at least while they all sat at the feast.

Eating together is a sign of friendship and equality, and yet people have always used the positioning of the "companions" as an expression of the power of each in relationship to the others. Hierarchical seating arrangements make up one of the most intricate aspects of protocol, for placing guests at table is a deeply political act. Where diners are *not* ranked, a political, or social and religious, statement is just as surely being made. A great and deliberate distinction is always created between meals that are formal and carefully structured, and those that are casual and relaxed. Intimacy can be fostered by "breaking the rules" (though one of the apparent paradoxes of social communication is that some level of formality must be maintained or relationship among dinner companions will be forfeited). Seating arrangements are made to be rigidly adhered to, kept only in part, or rejected; in every case they are important.

Hierarchy at dinner is usually enforced when a group comes from a mixture of social backgrounds. We hear a good deal about what seems to us the outrageously discriminatory practices at medieval banquets. (One source of frustration for the scholars who research the history of medieval food is that the texts of the period—and the Middle Ages are not unique in this—seldom describe the food served at a banquet in any detail; but they do make clear everything to do with precedence in the seating arrangements. This is because food was regarded as beneath literary consideration, whereas the seating was fascinating enough to be recorded.) Special guests and the hosts of the banquet sat at the raised "high table," upon which stood a huge silver salt cellar, marking the place of the host or of an outstandingly important guest; the other people sat therefore "below the salt," and the further away from it the lower. The high-ups were deliberately given better food, and more of it.

Seventeenth- and-eighteenth century aristocrats in Europe, on the other hand, increasingly ate together in small groups, and would not hear of hierarchical seating; their hosts decided who would be a compatible group to invite, and guests sat down near the people they preferred. Tables were often quite small and, significantly, round. What had in fact happened at these "intimate suppers" was that the people who sat "below the salt" had simply been banished from the party. During the course of two centuries, the lord of the manor had gradually removed himself, during dinner, from the sight of his retainers, to eat with chosen companions in a room set apart from his great hall. It is easy—and so very modern—to be egalitarian once the lower orders have been placed in a totally different sphere, out of sight and out of mind, and certainly not invited to one's table.

The presidents of the revolutionary United States began by insisting, on diplomatic occasions, that all foreign envoys be treated equally on American soil. Thomas Jefferson's *Rules of Etiquette* (1803) removed all precedence from visiting dignitaries, and the resulting rage and confusion they felt must have been deeply satisfying.

George Washington had insisted that as head of the nation he could never be anyone's guest; his reasons were deeply moral, but he probably also understood very well the ritually subordinate role of guests. After 1815, when, as we shall see, diplomatic protocol was redefined by the international community, the American presidency restored precedence as a device for ordering ceremonial proceedings. But the tradition of amazing foreigners with American informality has remained. Casual manners can be delightfully warm and direct. Yet snobbery is apparently inescapable, for it is chic nowadays to be relaxed, and it can look old-fashioned and ridiculous to be formal. It is also an ancient status-enhancing device for those whom everyone knows to be the most powerful to waive pernickety rules and treat their inferiors with familiarity.

A space is often made where people can meet on equal terms, freed for a time from social structures and at least partly relieved of power struggles. Modern large cities are socially viable perhaps only insofar as they provide such places, where people can appear, unknown and unasked, with no past unless they feel like revealing it; no one they meet (provided they are careful with their manners, dress, and speech habits) should be able to "place" them. Image becomes everything—consciously projected, instantaneously perceived, and either corresponding to reality or not. Close-knit, stable community having been sacrificed, its alternative, anonymous separateness and mobility, must be provided. The birth of cafés in the late seventeenth century in Europe was one of the prerequisites for the growth of modern city life. Almost at once, anti-hierarchy and the shrugging off of social roles not only made economic sense for the café owner, widening the clientele as it did, but it provided an important service. *The Rules and Orders of the Coffee-House* (London, 1674) begin with the following:

First, Gentry, Tradesmen, all are welcome hither,
And may without Affront sit down Together:
Pre-eminence of Place, none here should Mind,
But take the next fit Seat that he can find;
Nor need any, if Finer Persons come,
Rise up for to assigne to them his Room.

A deliberate contrast is being made in these verses with the customers' experience of formal dinner parties, where guests are first selected by their hosts, and then carefully seated with regard for rank, etiquette, and protocol.

The word "etiquette" is said to come from the idea of labels or stickers attached to things (and now people) proclaiming what they are and where they belong. "Protocol" comes from the Greek *protokollon* (*proto*, first, and *kollan*, to glue), a sheet glued to a manuscript case, giving some idea of its contents. Places at a formal dinner are designated by a card set at every cover, with the diner's name on it. It was once *de rigueur* to give each male guest an envelope addressed to him, with the name inside of the woman to whom he should give his arm for the procession into the dining room, and who would be his dinner partner. The hostess may dispense with cards, but she must have the seating planned, and be able to direct her guests to their places. For in our society it is the hostess (or the host) who decides (unless he or she formally renounces this right) where guests shall sit, and this order determines that in which diners will be served their food.

Precedence at table was rehearsed, as it were, by performance of the procession into the dining room. In the nineteenth century, house guests at a mansion would gather, sometimes in the ground-floor hall, descending the great staircase to do so, wearing the formal *toilette* they had changed into for dinner, before the gaze of the others assembling. The butler announced that the meal was ready: "Dinner is served." "*Madame est servie*" was the ritual French phrase: Proust describes a manservant intoning it so mournfully that it sounded as though Madam was dead. Then the previously instructed guests would line up, the host leading the way with the senior woman guest holding his arm. (Women attaching themselves to an arm of their partnering males became usual during the eighteenth century; earlier guides took their charges, as men took women, by the hand.) The guests followed in the order of the women's precedence, with the partners preordained for them by their hosts. The hostess (who in English-speaking countries sat at the foot of the table facing her husband at the head) went in last, with the senior male guest accompanying her.

Guests are allowed, in some cultures, to demand the "honours" they consider their due at table; the host remains responsible, however, for justice overall, and must ask an over-ambitious guest to move over if someone more distinguished than he would more fitly occupy that seat. Relying on the host's competence in this matter, a more intelligent guest can seize the initiative, even if only temporarily. He can do more than accept his host's decision (as he finally must if he is to remain polite), by seating himself in a *lower* place than he deserves. "After you is manners," a sixteenth-century English proverb has it: begging someone to precede oneself indicates attention being paid and a desire to respect others. Deliberately taking a lower place shows contempt for rank, and since rank is mere "culture," an artificial facade, it is always admirable to demonstrate an underlying indifference to it. Taking a lower seat will also constrain any host worth his salt to close the gap between appearance and social reality by inviting the guest to "come up higher."

The New Testament is full of dinner parties and stories about feasts. Humility, which is for Christians an aspect of wisdom, is presented in a parable about a guest who lowers himself instead of competing for the best place at dinner—but is rewarded with higher consideration. It typically expresses spiritual values in terms familiar to participants in the worldly rat race. Dinner, because of the exigencies of table manners, was one of the rare contexts where competitive and powerful people were likely to have witnessed adjustments being made, where the low were asked to move higher and those at the top embarrassed by being demoted to a more fitting place. (There is a culturally specific aspect to the parable's setting, however. Today, it might be considered quite rude to take a seat other than the one to which the host motions you. In our society the host has to make the decisions and the guests must obey. Branchereau's book on manners for priests [late nineteenth century] says that seating is very difficult to get right. It would be false humility, therefore, and only cause trouble, to upset the host's seating arrangements.)

The role of the host or guest who begs to defer to others, only to be overridden after a lengthy struggle the outcome of which everybody knows in advance, is fairly common. An Arab guest murmurs

"*Tafaddal*" ("Be so good") to the host, trying to get him to go first to the eating area, but the guest eventually yields because going in first is his role; he has precedence. This procedure is called "wrestling for the merit" of giving way; the struggle itself is an expression of polite good will, even though etiquette has already decided who will win. Chinese and Japanese etiquette is perhaps the most full-blown example. Dinner in China begins, B. Y. Chao tells us, with a fight over yielding precedence on entering the dining room: "Among familiar friends, it may come to actual pushing, though never to blows." An elder guest, after the ritual time has been allowed for a struggle to occur, may take it upon him- or herself to permit entry at last to be effected by pronouncing *Góng jìng búrù cóng-mìng*, a saying which means roughly "Better obedience than deference."

Another fight follows, this time over seating precedence—a subject which Chao says is far too complex to explain to Westerners. "Sometimes we seem to be actually quarrelling and fighting when we are really each trying to be more polite than everybody else." One ingenious way in which "culture" defeats "nature" is by keeping the aggression but changing its goal. This is an example, where competition is recast as a battle to *lower* oneself, and thereby to win a reputation for politeness. A struggle, furthermore, inevitably implies contact between the fighters; the playful quarrel over the lowest seat forces people to relate with each other as they perform their manoeuvres.

Arjun Appadurai, describing how food can be used to express conflict in a Tamil Brahman household, shows how the women responsible for cooking and serving food in a large family can "abbreviate" the meal to express any grievances they might be harbouring. They can also direct members of the family to inappropriate places—for example, a teenager being seated with the children, or a senior member of the family next to a "poor cousin"; or they might serve the food in an order calculated to insult someone who has offended them. Relatives or guests who are in disfavour can be "put down," as we say, in what amounts to revenge by seating and serving order.

Invited guests who are affronted by the host's estimate of their rank can do nothing about it, unless they are prepared to break up the entire proceedings by walking out. A rather clever compromise was once possible within the boundaries of diplomatic etiquette, whereby a guest who thought himself misplaced could turn his plate over to indicate silent displeasure: he was preventing the drama of serving food and eating it from continuing, until such time as his host could redress his slighted honour, or at least notice his protest. The action did not count as an insult to the host, with all the consequences that would necessarily ensue.

Examples of the sort of hard feeling which could be aroused by seating offences may be taken from *The Court of civill Courtesie*, translated from the Italian in 1591. The "young gentleman" for whom the tract is written is given a whole list of ploys, complaints, and repartee which he should learn and have ready in case of such a slight. If for instance the host is shameless enough to make no redress for an error made in seating him, "The young Gentleman should be furnished with some guirding speeches or els some pleasaunt scoffes, to countenance out the matter, with those that sit by him, that the rest may see he chose the place in scorne of the other. As thus: . . . Beware friends, pride will have a fall: Speake not so loud, your betters be in place." It is very clear that not receiving his due situation at dinner is "an abasement not to be suffered." And yet, a civil man cannot start a fight. He should confine himself to saying things like "If it were not for troubling this company, I would be your carver with a peece of my Dagger: but doubt not but I shall find a time for you."

In many societies the host has normally no need of telling guests where to go: each person knows his or her place. (An American manners book of 1855 explains that the reason why seating poses such difficulty is "because distinctions are not so explicit now.") Usually, though not always, guests must position themselves with reference to the host, the guest of honour being at his right, or at his left, or diagonally across from him as in Japan. The other guests find their rank, by juxtaposition and distance, without a word needing to be said. Everybody must play the game, however: even one change can wreck the whole picture. Louis XIV was so incensed when a woman once sat higher than her place at table that he could scarcely speak, and almost left the table altogether; he said later that only his consideration for her husband restrained him. He was just as angry with the woman whose seat was taken, for not remonstrating, and he let it be known that he took this dislocation of table ranking as an insult to himself. Once again we notice how hosts and guests rely upon each other. In Louis's view, his dinner companions were supposed to know their rank, and accept it without question; he was the hub of the whole system, with reference to whom all took their different places.

Diplomatic protocol is supposed to prevent rather than provoke arguments among guests. Diplomats are not merely themselves: they represent, and exist to make known, the wishes of their governments, and the ability of the people they represent to get what they want. A diplomat needs to be as sensitive to punctilios (on behalf of his country, of course) as a Spanish grandee. Hence the endless wrangling about the shapes of conference tables, the insistence on the use of correct titles and forms of address, and the order of the "receiving line" where hosts formally welcome guests at the top of the carpeted stairs. Fights and struggles over diplomatic precedence used to be savage; we hear for example of eighteenth-century horses and carriages galloping across town so guests could arrive early enough to ensure that they got their "due" seats.

Finally, in 1815 at the Congress of Vienna, the nations present made an ingenious choice, to keep protocol but remove from it any reason whatsoever, so that conflict would become pointless. They submitted ranking to chance. Ambassadors have been ranked ever since by the date and hour of their accreditation. For example, an ambassador who presented his letters in February is placed at a higher place at table than one whose credentials were submitted in March, even if the representative of a more powerful nation completed his ritual later. Any doubt about two diplomatic rivals is often ended by resort to the alphabet: the nearer the first letter of a name is to "A," the nearer the name's owner is to first place. Choice being removed, protocol is demoted to being a tidying device whose very meaninglessness helps prevent resentment.

At the opposite extreme, perhaps, from using fate to decide precedence is the "casual" modern manner of allowing guests to sit wherever they like (which in fact presupposes a fairly high level of internalized good manners among the guests themselves), or of the hostess seating guests as she believes they would like to be seated. She thinks she knows, and her guests can only hope she does. There are guidelines, of course: never seat business rivals side by side, or people of opposing ideologies, or heavy thinkers with frivolous fun-lovers. But the hostess must take risks, too, or her party could be dull. In the end, freedom to choose where to put her guests makes her task so complex—far more so than even the dizzying intricacies of ancient Chinese protocol—that no one can give her advice; every single dinner party is a totally new enterprise.

A modern move back as it were towards the fatal attitude is the spreading custom of making guests move during the meal. The men (supposing that, as the modern tendency still is, men and women alternate, which already restricts seating freedom) all rise after each course and seat themselves two "male places" down, so that every-one speaks to someone new—even if they do not want to. It is in effect a variant of a custom called "the turning of the table," which is said still to be employed at extremely formal dinners: at the merest turn of the hostess's head, from the guest on her left to the guest on her right, every couple has to interrupt their conversation. The women take the responsibility of turning in the direction the hostess has initiated; the gentlemen, turned from and turned to, merely sub-mit. It would of course be exceedingly rude, not only to the host but to everyone present, to become so engrossed in conversation that you failed to notice the command, or refused to change partners; chorus-line precision is required, or else at least two people would be left "staring alone at their plates." The hostess, Emily Post says, should in such a case cry out, "Sally, you cannot talk to Professor Bugge any longer! Mr. Smith has been trying his best to attract your attention." The device certainly ensures that no one is ignored in dinner-time conversation.

It has always been a rule of politeness that people in groups should show no favouritism. There must be no whispering in cor-ners, no sharing of private jokes or blatant preference for particular company; attention should be given to everyone present, as equally as possible. This is the reason why it is customary to separate engaged and married couples at table. Etiquette manuals remind us that dinner parties are for opening out towards other people; pairs or groups who do not want to do this should stay at home.

The dining-room table round which people in the Western world sit on separate chairs to eat not only raises food waist-high—which is necessary because of the chairs—and provides a sort of stage upon which the dishes can make entrances and exits; it also pins everyone down to specific places and both unites and separates everyone seated round it. All the diners are spread out and on view; nobody can escape, because it is forbidden to leave the table before everyone has finished eating and all agree to rise. Dining-room tables are usually oblong, to fit our oblong rooms; the shape provides four sides, at two of which only one person can ordinarily sit. That one person is distinguished thereby from people sitting at the table's long sides. (A round table, or everybody sitting on the floor in a circle round the food, does not give rise to the same hierarchical distinctions; substituting a round table for an oblong one is often resorted to when wrangling cannot be stopped.)

The "top" people at dinner, in Anglo-Saxon custom, are those most plainly in everyone's view; which is why the advantage of an oblong table's "short ends" is repeated at large banquets or in college dining halls, where there is a "high" table, one literally raised from the level of the rest, set along one short side of the room, often at right angles to the other tables running lengthwise. This layout survives from medieval usage; at that period long tables set perpendicular to the high table and along the side walls of the hall were called "sideboards." In France, and in several other Latin countries, the hosts are traditionally placed not at a short end but in the middle of the long sides of the table, host and hostess facing each other, and the guests of honour on each side of them; the ends of the table are therefore distinguished as being *low*, not being "in the centre of things." In the past, where great banquets were themselves theatrical events with a crowd of spectators watching and processions of servants bearing dishes, seating was on one side of the tables only; the metaphor of tables as stages was even stronger. At the high table, which was designed to be on view to the whole gathering, the most important people sat in the middle, honour radiating from their persons and diminishing with distance towards the table's ends, as in the traditional French system, and in the arrangement of the modern high table still. In several countries in Latin America, the host's desire to honour his guest results in the guest of honour being placed at the head of the table (one of the short ends) with the host on his or her right.

Where women are allowed to be present at all, they may sit in a separate group, or take their seats all together observing precedence among themselves. Alternatively the women may sit together without any seating order: the men's having to rank themselves then becomes a sign of the political status of males, and of the extent to which they count. Among the Sherpa, rank among men is not fixed, but renegotiated at every party. There are no formal seating positions, but the men all work together on moving the more honourable higher, the less honourable lower, with everybody present looking on; it is the way society dramatizes its shifting power structure.

In our own culture, women were once commonly relegated to the spectators' gallery. Then they were permitted at table, but all together at one end—the lower end, of course—while the men sat at "the top." Fierce ranking sorted out the women as it did the men. Very important men at large banquets were once permitted to demand that the women who attracted them most sit at their table, or at a nearby table at which they might easily be viewed. Eventually (the change came gradually, sporadically, and with regional variations and occasional reversions to former practice) men and women sat alternating at the table. A lady never sat at her companion gentleman's left because, as Emily Post put it, "a lady 'on the left' was *not* a lady"—and the custom survives that a woman's place is at the right hand of her male partner.

Formal table precedence—even in our own culture, where the rules in this matter seem crude, even coarsely rustic in their simplicity, to some foreigners—is not only rigid but a study in complexity. "The lady of highest rank," says Emily Post, "is on the host's right. The lady of next highest rank is on his left. The third lady sits on right of man of highest rank. The fourth lady on left of man of the second rank. . . ." (Notice that the definite article begins to be left out, as is the practice when writing recipes.) At dinners where guests are multiples of four, the hostess relinquishes her place and the host keeps his; this will avoid either two males or two females being at the table's two ends.

With a dinner for twelve, seating problems are massive. The hostess takes the seat *on what would have been her left*; she does not move to the right as in other multiples of four, or else she might occupy the seat of the person who is always served first, and that would never do. The host will be served second, an unfortunate circumstance which is thought preferable to its alternative, which involves breaking the sequence of serving moves by skipping him and returning to him later. It is almost impossible, says Emily Post, to seat twelve in the house of a widow. She is advised to solve the conundrum by appointing a male guest to take the place of the host; otherwise she might find herself having to commit the rudeness of serving herself from an untouched dish. Then the lady of honour must be seated at the right of the gentleman of honour, who sits at the right of the hostess. The choreography of serving moves is even more intricate than the seating plan.

Very important diners, at medieval banquets for example, used to be distinguished by having a canopy erected over their seats, rather as an Eastern potentate or a West African chief has been marked out in a throng by an umbrella being held over him. (People used to have such canopies over their beds as well; a "canopy" was originally a mosquito net, from the Greek *konops*, a mosquito.) In the East—in Korea, for example—honour was given by the placing of a screen behind a distinguished back.

Separate chairs encourage separateness, and also status: it is hard to distinguish oneself as one of a row on a bench. It could matter desperately what *kind* of chair you sat on—an armchair, an armless chair with a back, or a mere stool. There was a lower level still: you could be expected to stand. (As we saw earlier, children frequently stood at table.) At Versailles the supreme dignity, the chairs with backs and arms, was reserved for the king and queen. Their family sat on three-legged stools, known as *tabourets*. The royal family—and only they—could use armless chairs with backs, but only when the king was not present. Being permitted a *tabouret* was a great honour, allowed only to certain women among the non-royal nobility; even their husbands had to stand. A woman with the privilege of sitting was herself called a *tabouret*, or a *femme assise*, a seated woman; the husband's rank was raised by his spouse's being allowed to be seated, so that courtiers would fight tooth and nail to obtain for their wives the *tabouret*. At Louis XIV's ceremonial suppers he would "give his hand" to a guest of honour, that is, seat the person on his right. *Tabourets* sat, and everyone else stood. Standing, in our culture, has the opposite meaning from that among the Arabs whom we saw earlier striving not to raise themselves higher than their host. We still stand to show respect, for example, at an ovation, or when someone important enters a room, or when men are in the presence of women who are standing.

Distinction can go no further than refusal to consort with any-body at all. In many African cultures, the father of the family is so important that he often eats separately from everybody else; his food is taken to him. The polygamous male may choose the family of one of his wives as dinner companions. However, eating being so impor-tant to marriage, he is usually obliged at every meal at least to taste food cooked and sent to him by his other wives as well. He may be offered all the best morsels—and eat them, as his due, and perhaps also as his duty. He may be served by one of his children, kneeling so as not to tower above him, and reserve the right to demand the company of one of them, often the youngest son, for the duration of his otherwise solitary meal. A paterfamilias among the Tallensi would politely taste each of the dishes sent him by his wives (it was an insult to the cook if one of them was not tried), eat what his first wife had provided, then call in the children and share the rest out among them.

Men rarely cook the food, but at dinner they often share out the most prestigious dishes, as when our own paterfamilias carves the roast. He sits at "the head" of the table, with his wife at "the foot," or perhaps at his right. He is traditionally expected to rule over the meal (which is chosen with his preferences very much in mind), to control the conversation even if he does not say much, and to demand correct behaviour from his offspring. In many European societies he is served first. Far more egalitarianism reigns at meal-times in societies where men eat together, separately from the women and children. Men and women quite often eat together in the home, but women in most places and times have been forbidden to attend public feasts, although they cook and often serve the food. Equality in human society usually turns out to mean equality *among peers*. The tautology is similar to that which upholds honour: people are honoured because they are honourable, and they become honourable by being honoured.

The role of host as provider for his guests may make it the custom for him never to eat any of the meal. In Iran, for example, a host's job was to circulate among his guests and ensure that they had what they wanted to eat and drink. Our own version of this expression of the host's role is our rule that the host should be served last. He ceremonially "backs off" from the power he wields in his own house, in order to produce a flourish both of grand detachment and of polite deference to his guests. The guest served first is further honoured by being offered fresh and untouched dishes, with unused serving utensils; everyone else takes his or her "left-overs."

A different rule appears to have obtained in some circles in the United States, however, in the first half of this century: the hostess would serve herself *first*, even when other women were seated at the table. Emily Post was horrified by this. She called it "the Great American Rudeness," and was forced to wonder what on earth it could mean. She thought it derived from earlier (*much* earlier) obsessions with the food being poisoned: the hostess was showing her guests that the food was safe to eat. Perhaps the idea had been revived because a host tastes the wine before he will let his guests drink it, in case it is a dud bottle or not sufficiently *chambré*—but only this sip is served first: the host's glass is in fact filled last.

Was it so that the hostess could add a last-minute *coup de main* to a dish, patting it and arranging it on the plate because kitchen help at frontier towns was formerly so lamentable? Was it so that the hostess could show her guests how to approach the food and the correct way to eat it? (Towering food edifices and heavily decorated dishes could be a problem for timid nineteenth-century diners; even Henry James remarked upon an "inscrutable entrée.") An old-fashioned deference to age, Post goes on—Grandmother being seated in "a high-backed cushioned armchair" at the head of the table—might have been transferred by Americans to hosts. (In the nineteenth century, the higher ritual rank of host and hostess was underlined by their sitting, at the table's roomy head and foot, on large stuffed easy chairs, the "stately appearance" of which "would be peculiarly appropriate," according to an article written in 1897.) Perhaps, Post speculates, Americans confusedly remembered that royalty was served first. Or maybe staff have been so badly trained that they serve their employer (who is more important to them) before the guests, and "one whose early life has been spent in simple servantless surroundings" hesitates to criticize the butler. Or—and here Emily Post hardly dares contemplate the abyss—perhaps all that was taking place was "an epidemic of discourteous behaviour." She is not surprised, she says, that "Europeans smile."

Her analysis is a marvellous illustration of hostly anxiety, and of the ways in which hosts wield the power but ought not to let it show. She does not mention another custom (which she advises against following, but which is in fact time-honoured) that might have contributed to "the Great American Rudeness": if it is polite to wait until everybody has been served before all begin to eat together, then the first person served may wait until her food is cold. A hostess who takes this disadvantage upon herself would be showing that she effortlessly controls her appetite for food, and in fact is deferring handsomely to her guests. But polite customs have to interlock correctly: it must be admitted that if a hostess serves herself first and does *not* wait for everyone else to begin, the spirit of dinner-table conduct is threatened. Hosts should defer to guests precisely because they need not; guests always resent infractions of this rule.

John Russell's *Boke of Nurture* (1460, but deriving from sources more than a century older) speaks of the "cunning, curious and commendable" art of the usher or marshal, whose job it was to seat guests according to precedence. In his day the four different estates—royalty and high ecclesiastics, what we would call professionals, semi-professionals, and businessmen—should each "sit at meat by itself, not seeing the others, at meal-time or in the field or in the town; and each must sit alone in the chamber or in the pavilion." Within the first group, he goes on, priority was to be given to birth over wealth: "The substance of livelihood is not so digne as royal blood." For this reason the parents of a pope or cardinal have no status at all because of their relationship to their son; the parents and children of the king are another matter.

The principle that "blood" ranks higher than one's profession continued, and was applied to the aristocracy with greater and greater precision as wealth provided the bourgeoisie with increasing numbers of points of entry into the circles of the nobility. As time went on it became obvious that precedence, reflecting "blood," was really all that the nobility possessed: as it frequently happens, the artificiality of culture was unmasked largely owing to the fact that the tradition which upheld it was already almost dead. In the eighteenth century, Henry Fielding could still advise that hosts and ushers should give the honours to nobility, but only because everyone knew that the real power lay with money: "for though purse-pride is forward enough to exalt itself, it bears a degradation with more secret comfort and ease than [pride of birth], as being more inwardly satisfied with itself, and less apprehensive of neglect or contempt."

The word "inwardly" is important. Outward show, the obligation to display magnificence and express power through giving, was passing away. As wealth became synonymous with power, rich people became less and less visible to the multitudes. Today, great wealth is almost never on view, except possibly from outside the pale of the owners' grounds, as the amount of space occupied. The very richest people remove themselves from the public gaze so that they need suffer neither envy from others nor obligation towards them. They leave it to the *nouveau riches*, the flashy upstarts and trend-setters, to flaunt their money. Sharing they do only with each other; privacy in them achieves its apotheosis and becomes total exclusivity. Such people might find an insistence upon precedence at table to be an unnecessary affectation; but no doubt they manage to establish inequality among themselves.

4

Dinner Is Served

A banquet, which includes the pleasure of eating, the room in which dinner is served, the tables and chairs (or the mats and the trays), the lights, the dishes, the decorations, and the companions themselves, is a common image for the cosmos, for life, or for Paradise. The Roman emperor Nero had dining rooms with ceilings made of ivory panels, which could swivel and shower down flowers; they were also fitted with pipes for sprinkling the guests with perfumes. His main banqueting hall was circular and "constantly revolved day and night, like the world." The dome above it apparently also moved, displaying the heavenly bodies wheeling in order—a conceit which reminds us of the modern love of restaurants slowly revolving high above a city skyline with stars overhead at night, and city lights stretching to the horizon. The table, cloth, or tray, the circle of guests, and the duration of the meal represent the earth and humanity as a whole, and the story of their existence.

Death is remembered at feasts, just because food is life, and such a concrete, certain, but temporary joy. We have seen how bloody death could come to mind at dinner-time as a natural association of ideas, and how the dead may be thought of as joining the living at dinner. Banqueting ceremonies have often included entertainments reminding diners that life is short, that we should seize the occasion to "eat, drink and be merry." Ancient Greeks, who dined on couches, were laid out on couches for the funeral ceremony—perhaps on the very beds they had used for dinner when alive. At the end of an ancient Egyptian meal, a man carried round among the guests a skeleton or a wooden image of a corpse in a coffin, reminding them, before they started drinking, that they were all mortal. The Greek custom of wearing wreaths also had something of this connotation.

Homer imagined a sort of vacation-land for the gods, where they could go to visit the "Shiny-Faced People" (which is the meaning of the originally Greek word *Ethiopians*), so named because they lived near the house of the Sun. There the gods would be invited to dine, for weeks at a time, from splendid tables automatically replenished for ever. The Persian Paradise was a land of banquets where the water of life was handed carefully round, as water was passed at Persian dinners on earth, to be sipped by every guest in turn from a ladle. Roman and early Christian funeral monuments commonly showed the dead feasting with friends in the hereafter. Christian poetry also makes Paradise a banquet, specifically a wedding dinner (the sexual imagery is direct), with death a solemn but triumphant procession into the dining hall, beyond the threshold of which lies bliss for the soul as bride of the Beloved.

• *The First Bite* •

Once the meal is ready there is usually, on earth at least, a wait before eating begins. Dinner, in ordinary households, in monasteries, or in the halls of great medieval lords, in large Victorian mansions and hotels, or in disciplined modern resorts such as the Club Méditerranée, has always been announced by a call to the diners to assemble. The dinner bell in a monastery would declare what time it was not only to the monks but to the people outside the monastery walls. The prayer bells and dinner bells, the town curfew bells and tocsins, were sounded by the person whose job it was to keep watch from the church steeple and ring the bells in warning of danger, or simply to mark the time; he was called "the watch," a name we now give to the timepiece we wear on our individual wrists. The Victorians opted for the butler and his gong. "Beneath the master touch," wrote Arnold Palmer at the beginning of *Moveable Feasts*, "of one of those butlers whose glance, like Medusa's, one never dreamed of meeting, it could murmur, hum, and finally mount to a reverberating crescendo that made ears sing, temples throb, that drowned speech and thought and almost consciousness itself . . . and how, at its accents, those gastric juices flowed!"

We ourselves are supposed to have washed our hands before approaching the table. But often, especially if people eat with their hands, careful hand-washing will take place in front of the assembled diners, the purpose being not only to safeguard the hygiene of each washer, but to initiate everyone into the sacred ceremony of dining together, and also to pay attention to the peace of mind of everybody who will share the meal. It may be good manners therefore to wash ostentatiously, even if *you* know your hands are clean. In medieval France the nobility, and they alone, were allowed a trumpet blast to announce dinner; this action was called *corner l'eau*, "to sound the horn for water"—the water being that used for washing hands in preparation for the meal. People would line up to wash their hands at a side table, or pages would approach the dining tables and proceed to pour scented water over all the guests' hands and hold out napkins for drying, in the sight of everybody.

European medieval ceremony required that in a noble house hand-washing should be followed by an elaborate, often extraordinarily lengthy tasting ritual, where the food for the lord or his high table was "assayed" by officers whose job it was to die if the food should turn out to be poisoned. Tasting was called "credence," because of the belief or confidence which the ritual was meant to instil; side tables at feasts were known as "credence" tables. (The term is still in use for the table standing near the altar in a church; and an Italian sideboard is known today as a *credenza*.) Tasters were trained to perform their task with grace, deliberation, and an air of the utmost unconcern. Assaying could be done by touching the food with substances reputed to change colour or bleed if poison should be present. There were serpents' tongues which specialized in testing salt (these are now said to have been in reality sharks' teeth), narwhal ("unicorn") horns, rhinoceros horns, pieces of rock crystal, agate, or serpentine, and jewels said to have been found in toads' heads. The fear of being poisoned appears to have haunted the medieval imagination, and indeed unintentional food poisoning, ergotism, and germ-infested water were a constant danger. Yet tainted as opposed to deliberately poisoned food was never obviously enough the cause of sickness for the efficacy of magical objects to be discredited.

Dinners at seventeenth-century Versailles were brought to the royal table under armed guard, to forestall thefts and tampering, from the main kitchens and from *l'office de la bouche* (the office of the mouth), a kitchen used only for the preparation of desserts. The dishes had to travel an enormous distance—nearly a quarter of a mile—to their destination; as the formidable procession passed by, courtiers would take off their hats and bow, murmuring *"C'est la viande du Roi"* ("It is the King's meat"). The food was covered for its journey, to prevent the loss of some of its heat; modern historians speculate nevertheless that Louis XIV must rarely have eaten food that was more than slightly warm. The coverings, which were removed just before the food was tested by the assayers, were also intended to foil would-be poisoners en route; they, and the napkins wrapped round the chief diner's spoon and knife, are the origin of the term "covers" for place settings. (We have only to think of the hysterical wrappings which enclose modern fast foods to realize that coverings still provide people with the impression that their safety is being taken care of.) Only the most important people had their food tested for poison; the ceremony conferred enormous prestige. It was flattering to be considered so great as to be a likely candidate for assassination, and flattering to watch such elaborate care being taken to prevent any harm to one's person—while other people looked on, waited, and were not given the same regard.

Tasting for poison is still etiquette in some modern societies. In Papua New Guinea, it is good manners for a host to sip water before offering it to a guest; in several African societies, food is ritually tasted by the host before guests receive it. The person who splits and shares the cola nut in Nigeria must kiss it first, reputedly to reassure everyone present that poison is out of the question. There is normally no real anxiety among the guests; the act is initiatory and honorific, a polite flourish like publicly washing one's hands even if they are clean. Our custom of having the host taste the wine before approving it for his guests seems merely practical and entirely in the interests of the palate, but it is often at the same time a purely ceremonial expression of concern for the well-being of the guests.

It was only in January 1989 that the new emperor of Japan announced that for the first time in history there would be no requirement of food-tastings before every royal meal. His father, the emperor Hirohito, had updated the tasting ceremony by employing scientists to go over the food beforehand, chemically analyzing every morsel before it was served on sterilized dinnerware and then formally tasted; the royal faeces and urine were also scientifically inspected before bedtime. The emperor's cook, Tadao Tanaka, committed ritually prescribed suicide when his master died. The prestige value of tasting everything for poison could, and in occasional modern instances still can, be turned into a rather unsubtle insult. When the Communist dictator of Romania, Nicolae Ceausescu, and his wife visited Buckingham Palace as guests of the queen in 1978, they brought with them in their entourage a food-taster. He was to ensure that "the lay God, the heart of the Party and the Romanian nation, the heir of Caesar, Alexander the Great and Napoleon" would not fall victim to an untrustworthy British queen.

Another initiatory rite before dinner is prayer, a blessing on the food and a thanksgiving (which is the meaning of the word "grace") for sustenance, life, and the health implied by being able to eat and enjoy. Grace may be said by the host, or a child in a family setting, or a guest might be honoured by being asked to say it. An ancient Christian custom accompanying grace was the host's marking with a cross the round bread-loaf that was about to be shared. Prayer may end the meal, as it commonly does in Jewish practice. There may be two prayers, strictly speaking a *benedicite* ("blessing") at the beginning and grace, a thanking, at the end. The custom in Europe and America has been to stand for grace at formal banquets, and men's hats, when it was correct for men to wear them during dinner, were removed for the prayer. Each diner at an Arab meal rolls back his right sleeve with the prayer "*Bismil'lah!*" ("In God's name!") before beginning to eat, and says "*Hamdallah!*" ("Praise be to God!") at the end. An Abbasid text (ninth century) warns, understandably, that it is very rude to say "*Hamdallah*" in the middle of the meal: one might be interpreted as expressing a wish that the meal were over. In our own culture grace is not, of course, said by people who do not believe in God. Religious people themselves may not say it in case they might embarrass non-believers, or because they find it quaintly demonstrative as a ritual. We should note that where grace is said, the occasion is usually a full-scale or "proper" meal, especially when there are many people present; grace includes a recognition of community. At breakfast, an intimate family affair where there is relatively little emphasis on centralizing the meal or on sharing, and to which people often come and go as they please, grace is almost never said, even by people who retain the custom.

The prototypical beginning of every feast is, as we have seen, a sacrifice. Many people to this day perform a mini-"sacrifice" before beginning every meal; often the food or drink thus expended is thought of as feeding the dead, remembering them at the most life-giving moments of the day. Among the Igbo of Nigeria, one of the diners may first rotate a pinch of fufuu above his or her head, then throw it outside before the meal begins. American Indians have many different rituals whereby a little food is taken from the feast before anyone may eat, and burned in the fire with a prayer. One of the most important uses for tobacco was as a pre-prandial burnt offering to the gods, its smoke ascending to them as prayers were said. The Ainus of Japan, who take pride in their long hair, moustaches, and full beards, use beautifully carved wooden moustache-lifters to prevent any mess as they drink during dinner. Before the meal begins, the men ceremonially dip their moustache-lifters into their saké or their soup, and sprinkle some drops on the floor as they make their prayer. Ancient Greeks and Romans would fill a special flat bowl full of wine and sing together as they poured some out as a libation to the gods.

The host, as convenor of the feast, is often expected to display leadership, and continue to do so as the meal progresses. No one should sit down before the host has made the first move. At a modern Western meal, the host usually gives some sign that everyone may sit down at their "proper" places. Very polite men may still pull out chairs for women and slide them back under them as they sit down. The host then unfolds his napkin and lays it over his lap; the guests do the same. As this happens a second, secular "grace" is often said—words like "*Bon appétit!*" in Czech or Hungarian or Dutch, from diners to their neighbours, wishing them lots of room to fill and much benefit from the meal.

The English, who, unusually among the nations of the earth, commonly make no response to expressions of thanks, also omit this ritual effusion. Germans say, "*Gesegnete Mahlzeit!*" ("Blessed dinner-time!") just before eating; or they say, "*Guten Appetit! Prost Mahlzeit!*" ("May dinner-time prove beneficial!"), or simply "*Mahlzeit,*" before or after the meal. In Hispanic cultures, people are traditionally constrained when dining in public to invite any stranger in their vicinity to share their meal. Strangers, as Julian Pitt-Rivers explains, must be changed into guests before eating in their presence can be thought proper. The custom today is found mostly in the "lower" classes: a Spanish peasant, travelling for instance in a train, will offer his sandwiches to his fellow travellers; they thank him and politely refuse. In simple Portuguese restaurants, a new arrival, friend or stranger, walking past someone's table, will be asked, "*E servido?*" ("Have you been served?"), meaning "Will you have some?" The passer-by must reply, "*Não, muito obrigado. Bom proveito*" ("No, thank you very much. May it profit you"). In Hugh Rhodes's sixteenth-century *Boke of Nurture* we hear that the English themselves once wished their neighbours well after the meal:

When ye perceive to rise, say to your fellows all,
"Much good do it you," gently, then gentle, men will you call.

A man hosting a communal feast has often been expected to give a speech (still before anyone begins eating!), explaining the reason for the gathering and thanking everyone who has helped prepare it. A relic of such a custom is to be found in Portugal (which is often singled out as one of the politest countries in Europe), where the host at a formal dinner frequently says a few words to the guests just before the meat course is served; the Portuguese do allow guests to take the edge off their hunger first. The host of a feast in Melanesian New Ireland, having made his speech, supervises the "waiters" who serve the guests with equal portions of food on their banana-leaf plates; then he and his fellow host walk down the centre of the enclosure round the walls of which the banqueters are sitting. They each hold a small pig's bone. Everyone falls silent. When they throw their bones away, the guests fall to. In this culture, as in many others, hosts do not partake of the meal; they are givers, and throw this role into relief by not themselves taking. In societies where it is bad form for a host to eat at his own feast, he must walk around and talk to his guests; or he may be expected to sing or play the flute to them while they silently eat.

The Russian emperor, wrote Richard Chancellor of his meeting with Ivan the Terrible in 1553, "before the comming in of the meate . . . according to an ancient custome of the kings of Muscovy, doth first bestow a peece of bread upon every one of his ghests with a loud pronunciation of his title, and honour . . . whereupon all the ghests rise up, and by and by sit downe again." This fatherly role, where the host takes it upon himself to express both hierarchy and sharing in common, is given to the host in many societies. Ever since the days of the *Li Chi*, the Chinese host has been expected to lead his guests every inch of the way; their part is to accept his lead as passively and obediently as possible. The beginning of a modern Chinese banquet, as described by B. Y. Chao, goes like this: The guests arrive to find either four or eight small cold dishes ready for them on the table. When all are comfortable, the host lifts his wine-cup as a signal for his guests to thank him. They say, "*Duō xiè, duō xiè!*" ("A thousand thanks, a thousand thanks!"), lift their cups, and drink. The host raises his chopsticks and holds them poised over the dishes; the guests do the same. He moves his rice bowl off the plate to the side; the guests follow suit. The last person to touch the food is the politest. When at last the cold food has been tasted, the hot dishes can arrive, and the banquet proper begins.

All these complicated manoeuvres have been devised by their various cultures in order to make the person who is about to eat conscious of what he or she is doing, and to force the members of the group to take notice of one another. An ascetic practice common to many religious traditions requires the adept always to think about the first bite while making it: the first bite is acknowledged as being different from every other bite. Always remembering to detach oneself by consciously consuming the first bite is extremely difficult, because nothing could be easier to forget to do than to recollect oneself before the simple action of eating, when one is hungry and the food is ready and waiting. Table manners everywhere insist on the rituals of starting: they impose rules which delay the beginning of eating and override the natural impulse simply to get stuck in. They represent, both practically and symbolically, an option not to be satisfied with merely assuaging our bodily hunger, but to overlay and control "nature" in order to enjoy it more. The idea is also that other attitudes can then find expression—ideals such as mindfulness, gratitude, and willing awareness of people other than ourselves.

Our own culture has to deal with a dilemma in that we are served, or serve ourselves, with portions; we do not take pieces from a common heap of food and eat each mouthful as we take it, nor do we pick bits from different central dishes whenever we like, as the Chinese and Japanese do with their chopsticks. We have to decide whether to eat as soon as we are served, or to wait till everyone has received his dinner before starting. The old way was for everyone to wait till all have been served before beginning; this is still the rule in Portugal, for instance, where everyone awaits everyone else before eating, at each course that is served. The new custom is to start eating at once, "or it'll get cold." We now like eating food hot, and we do not have the aid of servants to supply everyone with portions very quickly. It is still ritually correct for the hostess to invite guests to start immediately, making it clear that she thinks they were capable of having waited, letting the gravy congeal on their plates, for politeness' sake. Emily Post says the guest of honour should wait until one more guest has been served after herself, and then begin, so she will not find herself the only person eating and no one else will be tempted to wait for her. It is still strict etiquette in many countries to wait until all drinks are served before picking up one's glass. There is no problem or excuse about the temperature of drinks; and looking as though one were dying for a drink is even more to be avoided than is obviously longing for food.

An anonymous nineteenth-century American manners book (1855) warns the hostess never to send her plate away until everyone has finished, because that could be interpreted as a wish that everyone would stop eating. Queen Victoria, who as royalty had always to be served first and who would start eating as soon as the food was set before her, is said to have been unaware that as soon as she had finished and put her knife and fork down, the plates of everybody at the table had to be removed at once. Dinners with her must have been extremely anxiety-ridden, until a desperate and courageous guest once called the footman and asked him to bring back his plate. Queen Victoria (luckily) noticed, enquired into the custom, and put a stop to it.

• Taking Note of Our Surroundings •

A princely house, in early Greece or at the beginning of the European Middle Ages, used typically to have as its centre a spacious hall where retainers ate dinner under the eye of their lord. He was enthroned alone or with a few highly favoured or important people at his high table, or at a similarly prominent place in the room. As time passed, the lord gradually withdrew from his hall and dined in private, with his chosen companions. He needed the assistance less and less of assiduously feasted followers to help him fight his battles and to express his power by the allegiance he was able to muster. In ancient Greece, the aristocrats formed themselves into coteries; in fourteenth-, fifteenth-, and sixteenth-century Europe the inner circle tended increasingly to eat in a chamber away from the lower orders.

In modern houses the ancient hall has dwindled into a little space just inside the front door; in North American English, a corridor is called a "hallway"—an important artery in a house, but utterly subservient to the rooms which open off it. Rooms specifically for dining began to be built into middle-class houses only in the seventeenth century; they are unnecessary luxuries, and modern apartments, and houses too, often do without them altogether. The dining-room table in North America now tends to occupy one end of the living room—an arrangement which returns somewhat to the ancient concept of the hall, especially since living rooms are where the fireplace (if any) is to be found. As we have seen, the hearth or *focus* once provided the site for meals, as it provided the heat source for cooking them. We do not cook at the fireplace, of course: we have kept to the distinction between kitchen and "hall" which began with the trend towards separating out the functions of the house into specialized rooms.

The "chamber" into which the medieval lord withdrew from his hall to eat was a more recent forerunner of our "living," "sitting," or "[with]drawing" room. It originally contained a bed and fireplace; often the women would eat there while the men dined in the hall. But by 1450, the privacy offered by this chamber was increasingly being claimed by the most important of the men. It held only a few people, and exclusivity is ever the promoter of chic. John Russell explains in his *Boke of Nurture* (1460):

The pope, an emperor, king, cardinal, prince with a golden royal
    rod, archbishop in his pall—
All these for their dignity ought not to dine in the hall.

The withdrawing chamber, later called a "parlour" or "conversation-room" (from French *parler*, "to talk"), eventually split in two. The table, which it now normally contained, moved into a room of its own, which was known first in English as the "eating-room," and then the "dining-room," a word which is first found in 1601, and which attained common usage during the eighteenth century, as dining rooms in bourgeois houses became the norm. At the table in this private room, the diners could sit facing each other, not ranged along one side only, as they were when "on display" in the hall.

In the sixteenth century, after dinner in the hall or the chamber, the head of the house and his chosen companions might withdraw for dessert to what was called a "banqueting house." This was either a separate building, like the famous Banqueting House of Whitehall Palace, London, or, if a house was situated in the country, a room at the top, ideally one with a splendid view. A "banquet" was a collation of fruit, cakes, sweets, and wine; it could be a separate meal, rather as we serve afternoon tea. An alternative word for a banquet was a "voydee," from a French term for the withdrawal from or "voiding" of the hall for the chamber; a voydee could also be a final collation of wine and spices, just before the departure of the guests. The word "banquet," which derives from the same root as "bench," often denoted only a part of a meal; it has now come exclusively to mean a costly feast of the highest status. The banquet and voydee became what we now call dessert, which was often eaten in the drawing room after everyone had left the table. Eighteenth-century diners would sometimes stand or stroll about to eat and drink dessert, in the manner of a cocktail party, but held after the dinner. The tradition of moving somewhere else for the end of the meal is still maintained at such places as traditional men's clubs, Oxford and Cambridge colleges, and the British Inns of Court.

A special dining room contains a special table—solemn, solid, perhaps extensible but otherwise immovable. Kitchen tables, at which the peasantry continued to eat near the fire, were all-purpose but not meant to be moved about. (It is this ancient custom to which we are returning as more and more of us find it cosy as well as handy to eat in the kitchen.) In the Middle Ages and later, tables called *dormantes*, "sleeping" because they were heavy and seldom moved, were often placed before a bench with its back to a fire for warmth in middle-class houses. The practice among the nobility in their châteaux was different: tables were boards laid on trestles, set up for dinner and removed afterwards. (When the earliest specifically dining-room tables were made for the rich, their makers were apparently unable to imagine them totally stationary and provided them with a "break" in the middle so they could be removed. The normal run of seventeenth-century Parisian apartments, short as they were on space, also required folding tables; "to lay the table" in French is *dresser* ["set up"] *la table*.) For a long time after the introduction of permanent eating tables, the aristocracy often maintained their boards and trestles; they decided that tradition in this matter lent them a distinction which recent, upstart bourgeois arrangements could not match. Trestles and boards were always very simple and definitely not created to be seen; they were invariably covered, first with an undercloth or sheet of leather or carpeting, then with various, often magnificent, draperies.

At formal medieval, Renaissance, and Baroque dinners, an edifice of shelves known as a "buffet" was erected to one side of the dining hall; upon it the family silver—which was often far too valuable to be subjected to the hazards of use—was proudly displayed. Later the food was displayed there as well, so that guests could have a preview of what they would be eating, rather as modern restaurants often exhibit dishes of food to tempt their customers. Later still, yet another little room led from the dining room, where guests could visit the "buffet." These shelves for display, like the tables, had often been boards set up (*dressées* in French) for special occasions; they are the origin of our "dressers" and "cup boards." The number of shelves a medieval cup board could boast was sometimes regulated: five shelves for a high-ranking duke, four for a lower duke, three for a nobleman, two for a knight, and one for a mere gentleman.

Beginning apparently in the nineteenth century, a "buffet" meal used to be laid out, not on the dining-room table but on the dresser or sideboard. (This solid, very permanent piece of furniture still plays the role of the ancient buffet in that it often displays the family china.) People would help themselves at the sideboard, and then carry their food to the table to eat it. This is still a customary way of presenting a copious British breakfast, and it is commonly used in modern hotels. A "buffet dinner" now refers mainly to the action of helping oneself to the food and then carrying it away to eat it elsewhere; guests often stand to eat, or sit down with their loaded plates on their laps.

The idea, which we take for granted, that everyone usually sits round a table to eat is in fact very specific to our own culture. Many people sit on the floor to dine, round a tray or trays of food. Another widely followed custom is for each diner to have his or her own table, like the small tables we provide in the living room for drinks or tea. The formal Japanese diner has a beautiful little lacquered table all to himself; he might even have two or three of them. Greeks in the Classical period each had a small oblong three-legged table. In these cases, the sharing which is universally important at mealtimes is expressed by passing the wine from one to another in a single cup, or by everyone bursting into song, or through complex interrelationships being continually stressed, as in the pouring of saké at a Japanese business lunch. In our own culture, we have worked extremely hard to achieve separation among the diners; but for the expression of unity we have the single, solid table.

Where tables are provided for every guest, they are rarely covered with cloths. The ancient Greeks, for instance, used their individual tables like large dishes, with some of the food placed directly on the wooden table-top; vase paintings show us loaves of bread in heaps, tidbits on the table or on plates, large cups, and long slices of meat, unwrapped from the spits on which they were cooked, and draped decoratively so that they hang down over the tables' edges. A new course was called second or third "tables," or "things brought next": either other tables were brought in, sometimes with food already on them, or the tables were all wiped down with sponges in preparation for the next round of food. Tables were light and portable: they were brought in and removed at the beginning and the end of every meal.

A distinction is always made between structured and unstructured meals: "structured" usually means "of higher status." We reserve a whole type of eating experience for "out of doors," where for once we eat seated on the ground. We are very self-conscious about picnics, and the freedom we grant ourselves to lounge about on a blanket eating cold food with our hands. We travel long distances and put up with a thousand risks and inconveniences to reach this state. The French might have invented the word "picnic," *pique nique* being found earlier than "pic nic." (The meaning, aside from the probable connotation of "picking," is unknown.) It originally referred to a dinner, usually eaten indoors, to which everyone present had contributed some food, and possibly also a fee to attend. The ancient Greek *eranos*, the French *moungetade* described earlier, or modern "pot luck" suppers are versions of this type of mealtime organization. The change in the meaning of the term, from "everyone bringing some food" to "everyone eating out of doors" seems to have been completed by the 1860s.

The impromptu aspect, together with the informality, are what the new meaning has in common with the old; there is a connotation too of simple food, which may be quite various, but which is not controlled, decorated, or strictly ordered into courses. Picnics derive, also, from the decorous yet comparatively informal sixteenth-century "banquets" mentioned earlier, which frequently took place out of doors. People often think that "there is nothing like the out of doors" for lending one an appetite. Fresh air and natural beauty, adventure, no cooking, and no tables and chairs—a good picnic is a thrilling reversal of normal rules. Not very long ago, picnics were rather formal affairs to our way of thinking, with tables, chairs, and even servants. But everything is relative: what was formal then made a trestle-table in the open countryside seem exhilaratingly abandoned. The general feeling of relief from normal constraints might even lead to the kind of liberty depicted in Manet's painting *Le Déjeuner sur l'herbe*, a faint and distant echo of the shocking behaviour of ancient Greek Bacchanals, who escaped the constraints of city living by going wild in the woods.

In societies where sitting on the ground is unexceptional, chairs and tables are regarded as stiff, formal, and status-ridden. Chairs and tables might be kept for extremely formal visits in the "public" part of the house, as they often were in China. An African chief might sit on a quite simple stool, but its being raised and decorated, perhaps covered with an animal's skin, made it a throne, an object of reverence. The fact is that chairs are extraordinarily constraining devices, and for that reason, in many societies other than our own, they are kept for exceptionally solemn occasions. They force us to sit where they are placed and, if we habitually use them, quite early in our lives they reduce the ability of our muscles to encompass the postures required for floor-sitting; a healthy middle-aged Westerner may expect to suffer agonies if forced to live even a few weeks without the use of any chairs.

Anthropologists tell us of at least 132 main ways of sitting; only about 30 of these involve anything resembling a chair. Among this restricted number of postures, many are thought impolite in our society, even for men. Women should strictly speaking sit in only very few of them, with legs either together or crossed; crossing their legs at the knee represented a revolutionary relaxation in quite recent times. Our clothing is designed with chairs very much in mind. Broad, flowing robes are required for floor-sitting, if much clothing be worn at all. The most "liberated" mini-skirted modern woman in nylon stockings is peremptorily forbidden the floor, even if she should be capable of sitting for hours with her ankles on the same level as her sitting bones and without leaning on anything. Shoes are a nuisance, and men's pants are quickly creased and stretched and usually become uncomfortable if worn on the floor.

Rigidity—sitting bolt upright *on a chair* and very still—is traditionally, with us, a sign of decorum. Never is this more so than at the table, where the need to show signs which conventionally demonstrate good will and self-control is, as we have seen, absolutely vital. Children are exhorted not to swing on chairs, not to lean over food. We must not put our elbows on the table—unless we can do so with an elegant lightness which makes it clear that we are not really supporting ourselves on the table and do not need to do so, and unless we demonstrate in everything else we do that we have *earned* this nonchalance.

Sitting, provided that it is on a chair, enhances social stature: people who can arrange to sit while everyone else is obliged to stand are usually eliciting respect. There is only one posture which can beat sitting erect for status, and that is lying down. The furniture must again, of course, be raised, and sufficiently luxurious; we recall that beds, like the most important person's chair at a banquet, used to be canopied. People lying down take up a lot of space; if nobody else is spread out full length, the distinction, and the focussing of everybody's attention, can be impressive. Anyone who has received visitors in hospital will know what I mean—although you have to be feeling reasonably well, of course, to notice your advantage. It is still one of the satisfying luxuries of life, and a clear enhancement of one's status, to be brought breakfast in bed.

In the eighth and seventh centuries B.C. the ancient Greeks came into fairly close contact with the eastern Mediterranean. There they saw people who ate, in formal gatherings, while reclining on couches. An Assyrian bas-relief shows us King Assurbanipal lying down to eat in the presence of his respectful, seated wife; and Phoenician ivory couches of the ninth century B.C. have been found together with luxury dinnerware. The Hebrew prophet Amos (ca. 640 B.C.) railed against the inhabitants of Samaria who imitated their neighbours the Phoenicians and Aramaeans of northern Syria: "Woe to them . . . that lie upon beds of ivory, and stretch themselves upon their couches . . . that chant to the sound of the viol . . . that drink wine in bowls, and anoint themselves with the chief ointments: but they are not grieved for the affliction of Joseph." He goes on to warn that "the banquet of them that stretched themselves shall be removed."

The custom, perceived at the time as the acme of prestige and luxury, was adopted by upper-class Greek men, except in such isolationist and conservative societies as Sparta and Crete, where everyone continued to sit as the Greeks had in Homer's day. The Romans learned the use of the dining couch from the Greeks and Etruscans in the second century B.C. Lying down remained *de rigueur* at formal banquets in the Roman Empire; it died out as late as the fifth century A.D. In Greek monasteries on Mount Athos there still exist halls containing couches on which monks may lie down and eat.

Reclining on a couch (a *kline* in Greek), always a status symbol, was confined in Greece to upper-class males. The Homeric days of the lord eating in his hall with his crowd of retainers had given way to a social system where aristocratic groups of friends, equal among themselves but considering themselves superior to *hoi polloi*, met to eat and then to participate in the drinking party, the symposium. Such groups had to be quite small and exclusive: it did not take many banqueting couches to fill up a room. A small dining room in the archaic period accommodated seven couches; a large room about fifteen, each wide enough to hold two diners.

Women lay down to eat where men were present only in exceptional societies such as that of the Etruscans, or if they were prostitutes. Upper-class women in Imperial Rome appear to have been allowed occasionally to lie down with the men, but for most of the history of the custom, "proper" women, if they ate with the men at all, sat on chairs with their small tables in front of them. It was definitely demeaning to sit while others lay: as late as the Hellenistic period in Macedonia, no male could recline at dinner until he had speared a wild boar without a net, and so initiated himself into manhood. "Cassander," Athenaeus tells us, "at the age of thirty-five continued to sit at meals with his father, being unable to accomplish the feat, though he was brave and a good hunter." When ancient Greeks portrayed the gods feasting together, they imagined them sitting, not lying down. This may have been because archaic, "Homeric" scenes seemed to them appropriate to the gods; Greek writings sometimes express a suspicion that reclining at dinner was a late, "soft" custom. But a British archaeologist has recently suggested that the goddesses would have had to be shown sitting rather than lying down in any convincing depiction of such a banquet, and that to apply human social distinctions among the gods, ranking females lower than males, would have been rude to the goddesses: the misogynist Athenians themselves had a female divinity for a patron.

An ancient Greek banqueter reclined on a couch so high that in some cases he needed a footstool to help him up onto it. He took off his shoes, climbed up, and then lay propped on his left elbow, facing his own small table which stood alongside his couch, and from which he took his food with his right hand. This posture required years of habit to maintain not only correctly but gracefully and without exhaustion. (One cannot, of course, rest one's chin on one's hand and still eat.) Greeks, unless they were feeling very amorous, usually had a whole bed to themselves, but Romans shared couches. One form of Roman dining room was called a *triclinium*, which as its name tells us held three couches, each sloping slightly downwards to the diners' feet. Up to three men reclined on a couch, nine often being said to be the ideal number for a dinner party. There might be only one table in a *triclinium*. The diners lay with their heads towards it, so that they could all reach it with their right arms. Servants were essential if several courses were brought in to the recumbent diners; the fourth side of the table was left free of couches and facing the room's entrance, to facilitate the presentation of successive dishes. Later the couches were placed in a semi-circle, or were melded into one semi-circular couch, with the table within the curve.

The close physical contact which fellow diners knew at a Roman banquet would seem exceedingly strange and uncomfortable to us today, after our habituation for several centuries to sitting on separate chairs to eat. Modern lovers who merely lean across a restaurant table to hold hands are making a heavily significant gesture just because our table manners work so insistently on keeping diners from touching while a meal is in progress. (Keeping "elbows in" is not only practical but also part of this taboo.) In one of Plutarch's symposiac conversations, the question discussed is "Why is there lack of space for the diners at the beginning of a meal and ample space later?" In general, one of the participants informs us, "each guest, while eating, assumes a posture almost flat, since he must stretch his right hand forward to the table; but after eating he turns back more upon his side, forming a sharper angle with the couch and occupying no longer a flat surface, but merely, one might say, a line." Then the down-filled cushions, used to prop people up and increase their comfort, slowly flattened out during the meal and left more space. And in any case, he continues, as the wine smoothed everyone's irritability out, people relaxed and did not perceive themselves as being squashed together.

In Palestine at the time of Christ, Jews normally sat in the ancient fashion on the floor round the trays of food; at banquets, however, they lay in the Roman manner, on couches. The Last Supper was a reclining meal, in a room larger than a *triclinium*. The apostle John lay alongside Jesus, each of them raised on his left elbow. John would have had to lean back, as the Greek says, "on [his master's] breast," that is, leaning against the chest of Jesus, in order to talk to him. The movement was quite unexceptional, and in fact necessary, given the table manners of the time; but several hundred years later, when depictions of the Last Supper became a favourite subject for artists, the Greek words had become completely baffling. Everyone was thought of as sitting on chairs, stools, or benches at the Last Supper, as people contemporary with the artists did. In order to accommodate the Greek text, John is made in these pictures to lean sideways, droop over, lean on Christ's shoulder, and even fall asleep in his master's lap or with his head on the table. Any of these actions would have displayed shocking table manners, of which the apostle was almost certainly quite innocent.

• The Prospect Before Us •

Tablecloths are first heard of in Rome at the time of the emperors. Gradually they became essential to the beauty of a banquet, and by the high Middle Ages they were even more expressive of the community of the diners than was the table itself. "To share the cloth" of a nobleman was to be seen to be treated as his equal. When a master dined with servants at the same table, either he was the only person with a cloth before him, or the whole table was covered with a cloth but at his place another small napkin was laid. One of the most horrible insults a medieval nobleman could endure was to be publicly humiliated and separated from his brethren by having the herald of an angry knight stride up to him at table and slit the tablecloth to the left and the right of his place, or across the top of it. Nothing but a sworn vendetta could redress honour smirched in this fashion. The host of the party must have been considerably irritated as well.

Damascus in Syria was where all the best tablecloths came from. "Damask" was patterned with lozenges and other figures; quite early on, purity and cleanliness won out as a most important message of the tablecloth, and it became almost invariably white. Today, damask is pure white twilled linen with only a discreet woven white pattern in it. Absolutely nothing else will do for a formal table setting. A good deal of its prestige rests upon the trouble such a tablecloth entails: it must be washed and pressed every time it is used, and a single stain ruins it. Chinese diners are said to rejoice in a messy table: the more bones, shells, pods, and crab-claws litter the table, the more fun the meal has obviously been. Nothing could be further from our own ideal. By the late seventeenth century, the tablecloth was no longer, as it had been earlier, "a space of common disorder," as the French historian Jean-Claude Bonnet puts it; it had become a pristine white space, separating out the place settings, and meant to be kept as clean and clear as possible.

Table linen was always a mark of wealth. Until quite recently in France, tablecloths and sheets were often handwoven, and made up a substantial part of the trousseau of a well-endowed bride. They could last for generations, and were handed down as heirlooms; the idea was to amass, if you could, a great deal of such linen. At late medieval banquets, splendid cloths were laid over the simple wooden boards used for tables: they were what made the setting luxurious. There were several of them, typically an undercarpet first, then a large cloth covering the whole table, then two upper ones each covering the table-top and falling to the ground of one long side. A "sanap" (French *sauve-nappe* or "tablecloth-saver") was a narrow strip of cloth lying along the table edge nearest the diners; it took most of the dirt from grubby or greasy wrists, and was presumably easier than damask to wash. The sanap could be made of several layers of cloth, and might be used only until the washing ceremony was over. From the sixteenth to the nineteenth centuries, when meals were divided into two set courses and then dessert, two tablecloths, or three, were laid one above the other; one was removed after each course, so that the succeeding course began with a clean cloth. Some modern restaurants have revived the practice by laying two cloths, the top one of which is removed before dessert.

When a substantial lunch became a regular feature of everyday life, which it did only in the nineteenth century, it was a meal to which guests could be invited far less formally than they were to dinner at night. A luncheon tablecloth was allowed to be only a runner, or lacy or pierced, so that the table showed through. By this time, of course, the dining-room table had become a valuable part of middle-class household furnishings, made of precious wood, polished till it gleamed, and proudly treasured. It became perfectly correct in the late eighteenth century to show off the table by removing all coverings for the last course, the dessert, of a formal meal, leaving only "doilies," rather substantial flannel squares, in place to protect the wood from being scratched by the plates. These doilies, named after a seventeenth-century London draper called Mr. D'Oyley, were the forerunners of our place mats.

The message of these mats, apart from their function and convenience, is clear: each person is as separate and self-sufficient as possible, given the unification represented by the table. For the past ten years we have found them perfectly acceptable even for formal dinner parties; but tablecloths have recently returned to favour. For some time these have not been always white except on the most formal occasions. Modern washing machines and detergents have made cleanliness easier to achieve, so that we no longer require whiteness, in sheets or tablecloths, to make the point as strongly as possible that the linen is clean.

The first objects set on the medieval tablecloth, after grace and the hand-washing, were the "salts," or containers for salt; the custom is recorded as being recommended by Pythagoras (sixth century B.C.). There are dozens of superstitions and ancient customs surrounding salt—a mysterious, powerful, pure, but dangerous substance which people have always treated with respect. At medieval banquets, salt had to be separately poison-tested. Families would prize their inherited cellar (a word, from French *sel*, which means "salt dispenser": saying "salt cellar" is strictly tautological). "Standing salts," stout cylinders of silver with a shallow depression at the top to hold the precious salt, were the custom at formal British banquets. Noble households on the Continent of Europe might possess a *nef*: a silver table-top ship which contained, often in a quite small compartment of the whole, some salt. It was occasionally fitted with wheels, and could be rolled along the high table to be admired for its value and splendid craftsmanship—and so that the diners could help themselves to salt. The lord and his special guests sat in the middle of the long side of the high table, as diners sit at high tables today; a standing salt or *nef* (sometimes several of them) would be set before the lord, and perhaps each of the highest ranking diners, as an "object of prestige" and indication of status. When the lord sat at what we call the "head" or the host's short end of the table, it became customary to place a standing salt as a marker, dividing the lord's intimates grouped at his end of the table from those who were not quite accepted into his inner circle and who sat "below the salt." As late as the Victorian period, the salt container might be combined with an elaborate centre-piece decoration, as when the pretentious Veneerings in Dickens's *Our Mutual Friend* (1865) had "a caravan of camels" to "take charge of the fruits and flowers and candles, and kneel down to be loaded with the salt."

At the beginning of the sixteenth century in England, dinner, the main meal of the day, used to begin at 11:00 a.m. Meals tended over time to be eaten later and later in the day: by the eighteenth century, dinner was eaten at about 3:00 p.m. French *déjeuner*, like "break-fast," once meant the first food eaten after waking from a long night spent foodless (*jeûner* means "to fast"). *Déjeuner* is now used for "lunch," and French breakfast, its name having been pre-empted, has now to be called *petit déjeuner*, while *dîner* is eaten at night. In English, lunch or luncheon (originally also called "nunch" or "nun-cheon") was in the first place a snack between meals. Dr. Johnson's *Dictionary* (1755) said Lunch or Luncheon was "As much food as one's hand can hold"; he suggests that it derives from "clutch" or "clunch." (The modern American term "munchies" for snacks points similarly to small amounts, although it refers, more openly than our ancestors might have liked, to mouths and chewing.)

By the early nineteenth century, lunch, what Palmer in *Moveable Feasts* calls "the furtive snack," had become a sit-down meal at the dining table in the middle of the day. Upper-class people were eat-ing breakfast earlier, and dinner later, than they had formerly done. Lunch having displaced the afternoon dinner (Jane Austen, in a let-ter written in 1808, could spell the older term "nuncheon" as "noon-shine"), and having become a substantial regular meal with a name of its own, "dinner" was now a late meal, and "supper" a snack taken at the very end of the day, before people retired to bed. For a long time luncheon was a very upper-class habit: ordinary working people dined in the early evening, and contented themselves as they had done for centuries with a mid-day snack.

By the late nineteenth century, luncheon had become a social occasion mainly for elite women; at this time of day their menfolk were busy seeing to their financial affairs; they might be doing so over meals at restaurants in "the city." The corresponding French institution was *déjeuner à la fourchette*, the lady-like "fork luncheon." Nowadays, lunch ("luncheon" sounds pretentious because of the eli-tist connotations of the term) has returned to its ancient function as a workday snack—unless it is a long heavy meal, taken if possible at the company's expense: it is then called a "business" lunch. Sunday lunch still survives, in England for example, as a weekly family cele-bration, a "dinner" in the middle of the work-free day. Since it is not the clock that gives shape to our day but our own repeated actions, the most essential and repetitive of which is undoubtedly eating, the gradual invention of regular lunch came to divide our day in two. Palmer calls the afternoon "the Nineteenth Century's great gift to mankind."

"Supper" now means a light evening meal that *replaces* dinner; such a meal is especially popular if people have eaten a heavy lunch. "Dinner," in North America, increasingly means any evening meal, light or heavy; the word "supper" is used less and less, and "dinner" can now be quite swift and small. Dinner parties must usually take place at night, when friends are free from work and can spend time visiting. Inviting friends to dinner is much more flattering than asking them to lunch, because night time is, except on yearly celebrations such as Christmas or Easter, the only free time. Meeting people for lunch on weekdays almost invariably means eating "out," while a dinner, carefully home-cooked with all the expenditure of time and trouble that such a project implies, is one of the highest compliments a busy modern person can offer to friends.

A dinner, then, when guests are invited into one's home, is now nearly always a night-time occasion. The table laid for it is lit, if at all possible, by candles in candelabra, even though we no longer use candles as our normal light source. Lit candles cast a flattering light on food, faces, china, and glass, and their use for evening meals and little else has become a marking ritual: "We now have gathered," they say, "for dinner." For millennia we sat round a fire to eat, and fires remain for us symbolic of the group which gathers round for light and warmth. Candles last their predestined, visible length. They represent spans of time for us: a lifetime, with the flame as life itself, fragile but still alight (they become, with this meaning, potent symbols during political demonstrations); or a significant period of time, as when candles on a birthday cake mean "years lived." A candle burning before a statue in a church represents for its duration the person who placed it there. A superstition common since Roman times is that snuffing out a candle (or the wick of an oil lamp) while a meal is being eaten means death to somebody present; again it is clear that a candle flame easily means "a life." Candles have a luxurious connotation, which is enhanced for us by the fact that they are now quite unnecessary. In the nineteenth century, an eminent host or "amphitryon" would go to enormous expense to provide as many candles as possible. The extravagant French literary gourmet Grimod de la Reynière liked significant numbers of them: 365, for example, for the days of the year. No description of a feast was complete without an enumeration of the candles.

Medieval banqueting trestle-tables had been narrow, seating diners along only one side so that they could be watched by a crowd of non-dining onlookers, and themselves enjoy the spectacles staged between the meal's courses. There were no plates, no glasses on the table, and not much cutlery either. Festive display was concentrated on the size and grandeur of the assembly, on clothing, table linen, the choreography of splendidly costumed servers, on extraordinary dishes and theatrical events, and on the pyramid of buffet shelves displaying the lord's family plate. When dining customs changed and the onlookers gradually retired from the scene of feasts, banqueters faced each other across the banqueting table as families always have done. The custom of mounting a buffet eventually died out, or rather the spectacle afforded by the buffet migrated onto the surface of the table itself. Decorations on the banqueting table were more and more lavish, while table surfaces became wider to hold them: the diners were now both partakers and audience at the feast.

At seventeenth-century banquets where tables were seated along one side only, and the diners themselves, together with the festive plenty, constituted the spectacle, the board groaned so that its surface was scarcely visible, but monumental centre-pieces were avoided because they would have obstructed the view. Tall pyramids of fruits and sweetmeats appeared at other kinds of dining events during the seventeenth century; Madame de Sévigné described a dinner-party accident, when a towering pyramid of fruit collided with the door-lintel as it was being brought in, and crashed to the floor: "the noise of [it] silenced the violins, oboes, and trumpets."

In the eighteenth century, a "centre-piece," or focal point, was felt to be necessary, to gather the diners round it; dinner guests, even at great banquets, were sitting all round the table. There were "middleboards," wooden shelved pyramids placed in the middle of the table and loaded with fruits; and *surtouts*, towering "over all" the table, as their name says, and demanding a great deal of room. Sometimes these were *dormants*, "sleepers," that stayed on the table throughout the meal. The grandest were sculptures—animals, temples, rocks and mountains, scenes from classical myths referring to nature, such as depictions of Flora, Diana, or the Seasons—of silver or silver-gilt; a great many of them are to be seen in the glass cases of our museums. Less spectacular *surtouts* were what the English call "epergnes," a word that looks French, but whose origin is mysterious. These were fanciful glass, silvered basketwork, or silver and gold salvers, lifted on branches, and containing sweetmeats and fruits or candleholders, and sometimes sugar, mustard, and other condiments; they were ancestors of the very homely cruet-stands mostly to be found in restaurants today, portable metal frames to hold salt, pepper, vinegar, and oil.

A fashion for low centre-pieces produced the *plateau*, a large flat tray which took up the centre of the broad table's surface. *Plateaux* were common, but almost none have come down to us. One surviving example is a flat mirror six feet four inches long, and bounded by a small gilt balustrade; it came supplied with twenty-nine porcelain figurines to be set out when the surface had been covered with a miniature "garden," complete with foliage, tiny hedges and walks, mirror ponds, and even streams and moving clockwork pieces. The early eighteenth-century French nobility delighted in "sand"-gardens as table centre-pieces, with elaborate patterns in various colours all dribbled onto the *plateau* by a professional *sableur* or "sand-man," a designer in sugar powders and tinted marble dust. The *sableur*, who sometimes performed his difficult craft before the assembled guests, would cover his creation with sheets of glass to keep it in place; on and around this he placed the sugar or biscuit-dough statuettes, the miniature urns and the fountains, in imitation of a formal French garden. These ephemeral fantasies later gave way to more durable and precious pieces of porcelain and sometimes silver.

Fresh flowers were used extensively as table decorations during the *ancien régime* in France, and in Germany and Italy. But they were not always the first choice: flowers could be thought rustic, not "cultured" enough. People loved silk, feather, cut-vegetable and other hand-made flowers, and revelled in their artificiality. It was only in the early nineteenth century that fresh flower decorations began to be *de rigueur* at dinner parties; by the end of the century they had taken over the table. While broad tables were still in use, flower decorations covered the surface previously used for epergnes, silver sculptures, and *plateaux*; places were laid for the guests round the perimeter of the garden display. It was difficult to talk to anyone other than those people sitting to one's immediate right and left. Modern manners emphasize conversation not only with neighbours but with guests across the table; we accordingly place flowers in vases, keeping them either low so that we can see over them, or standing tall in slender vases so that we can see past them. Flowers and candelabra constitute for us the vertical components of table decoration.

In ancient Rome, guests often used two table napkins each, one tied round the neck and the other for wiping fingers. Each guest brought at least one of these with him; his slave would use it to wrap round the food that was given to the guests to take home after the party. During the Middle Ages and later, napkins were not always provided for the diners, and tablecloths seem often to have been used for wiping hands and mouths. "It is equally impolite to lick greasy fingers or to wipe them on one's tunic," wrote Erasmus in 1530. "You should wipe them with the napkin or on the tablecloth." Late medieval table napkins were very large, luxurious, and fringed, more like a bath towel in size, and draped over the diner's left arm or over his left shoulder. By the mid-seventeenth century, napkins had moved to cover the eater's front, being worn quite commonly round the neck to protect elaborate lace falling collars when they were fashionable for men. By the early nineteenth century they were still very large, about a yard square, and being laid on laps; it was considered polite not to unfold them completely first. Fastening one to a button or tying it round the neck had become a sign of a lower-class upbringing—though at the time of the change, the gastronome Brillat-Savarin regretted the passing of yet another custom which contributed to prandial comfort.

Nowadays, in Anglo-Saxon countries at least, an expanse of napkin covering one's chest reminds us of a baby's bib. In Graham Greene's novel *Doctor Fischer of Geneva*, the malicious host, bent on demeaning his dinner guests, has his servants tie giant napkins round their necks. They think they are going to be served crayfish (a lobster, mussel, or crayfish dinner is one of the rare occasions when biblike napkins are still permissible)—but instead he gives them porridge. A napkin knotted round the neck also looks far too much as though the diner means business; and the expression of gross appetite is frowned upon in modern manners.

Napkins, in our culture, are to be kept *clean*—a wholly unreasonable requirement in view of the purpose for which napkins were designed in the first place, which is to wipe away spills and grease. The idea is that we do not wish to be made aware of grease, and spills ought not to occur; napkins should be used, if at all, merely to give the most unobtrusive dab to the lips. The movement towards the unneeded napkin began with the introduction of forks. Ben Jonson wrote in *The Devil is an Ass* (1616) that forks had arrived in England from Italy "to the saving of napkins." Montaigne had confessed to preferring the old-fashioned method of eating with his hands; he said he used his napkin a lot: "I would dine without a tablecloth, but very uncomfortably without a clean napkin German fashion; I soil napkins more than they or the Italians do, and make little use of spoon or fork."

Washing hands and wiping them is of course always important where people eat with their fingers. There is some evidence from several societies that people used quite commonly to wipe their hands on their hair—or on that of a slave if they were very grand. There could be prim rules, of course, limiting even this practice: the Flathead Indians of Montana thought it was very rude to wipe your hands on your hair if you had been eating fish. When people shared cups and spoons, it was polite to wipe them before passing them on; and before serving spoons were provided, diners were expected to take what they wanted from a dish with their own spoons, but to wipe them on their napkins before plunging in. Even when napkins were so heavily used, politeness manuals pleaded that diners should not dirty the *whole* cloth. Until the early nineteenth century, napkins were dipped into finger-bowls and then used to wipe mouths and chins at the end of dinner; the subsequent repression of this habit is a reminder to us of how very neatly and carefully we now cut up our food and place it in our mouths. The comfort value of a final wiping of the face, however, is not underrated by airline companies, which arrange for damp wiping cloths, heated and ceremonially handed to us with tongs, to be provided either before or after meals. Childhood memories probably survive in us of mothers cleaning us up after eating. Providing hot rough cloths for wiping hands and faces is a traditional Chinese custom.

For a very long time one of the virtuosities of the dinner table was the folding of the linen. Tablecloths when spread out were criss-crossed with creases; these had to be straight and clear (there was a superstition that a wrinkled fold, forming what was called a "coffin," meant death to one of the diners). The delight taken in effects derived from fastidious folding can still be seen in Tudor "linenfold" wood panelling. Until the eighteenth century, tablecloths were screwed into linen presses to keep them sharply folded when not in use. The cloth had to be laid with perfect symmetry on the table; we still like the central crease to lie down the exact middle of the table-top. But during the nineteenth century folds went so severely out of fashion that careful housewives kept their tablecloths rolled on tubes so that they would lie as smoothly as possible on the table.

However, the glory of linen-folding, beginning apparently in the late sixteenth century, was the napkins. In rich households and on special occasions, these were starched, then folded, bent, and twisted into enormously intricate shapes—"of Fish, Beasts, and Birds, as well as Fruit," wrote Giles Rose, translating from the French, in 1682, "which is the greatest curiosity in the covering of a Table well." Napkin-folding was an art and a profession in itself. One day before he was to give a dinner party, Pepys went home "and there found one laying of my napkins against tomorrow, in figures of all sorts, which is mighty pretty, and, it seems, is his trade, and he gets much money by it." At Versailles in the seventeenth century, nap-kin-folding probably reached its zenith. *Serviettes* were folded into frogs, fish, boats, herringboned pyramids, chickens with eggs, pea-cocks, swans, into the Cross of Lorraine if the duke of Lorraine was the guest of honour, and into a score of other shapes. It was a breach of etiquette to demolish these, however; other napkins were provid-ed for mere use.

During the nineteenth century, napkin-folding came to be consid-ered over-ornamental and pretentious, like crooking the little finger when holding a cup. Emily Post, in tune with the bare and functional ideals of the 1920s, pronounces that "very fancy foldings are not in good taste," and she also disapproves of what had recently been the custom, of folding the napkin simply and hiding the bread roll in it: she says the bread "usually fell on the floor" when the napkin was lifted. Napkins should be folded square and flat, she states, and laid *on top* of the place plate. *Never* put the napkin at the side, because it looks as though you are showing off the beauty of your place plate: "it is very much like wearing a ring over a glove." (We are talking of formal dinners, so there is no question of side plates on the table.)

At the end of dinner, it was an ancient practice—recorded for instance by Athenaeus in the second–third century A.D.—to wipe one's hands, and later one's knife and other implements, on bread which one then threw to the dogs. From time immemorial dogs, and often cats, have accompanied humankind at dinner; they are faithfully depicted on ancient Greek vase paintings of dinner parties, in pictures of the Marriage at Cana or of the Last Supper, in paintings of people at banquets in every age. The Greeks kept especially fine "table dogs," which the host would show off to the guests—and perhaps guests brought their own animals to the party. When there were several dogs present, they were often tied to different couches to prevent them from fighting. The famous sixteenth-century painting in Chantilly of the duc de Berry at dinner shows little dogs actually permitted to amble and root about among the splendid dishes on the table. Medieval etiquette manuals ask children to ignore animals at table, not to "stroke or cat or dog." The animals got not only "the children's crumbs," as the Gentile woman in the New Testament put it, but also all the bones, gristle, and fish heads anyone threw down for them. Ancient Roman dining-room floors often turned this litter into an artistic conceit: they were designed in mosaic to look scattered with refuse, which was skilfully made to appear as three-dimensional and as indistinguishable from the real mess as possible. A floor like this was known as *asaroton*, "unswept," in Greek.

But by the early nineteenth century throwing food onto the floor was considered quite barbaric, and dogs, which continued to be allowed in the dining room at some family meals and at country mansions, were less and less acceptable at city banquets. Knives, we are told by Branchereau in 1885, should be wiped on the napkin, not on bread: it was important to be very clear that you were neither wasting bread nor accustomed to throwing it to the dogs. Nowadays we still hate seeing an unwiped knife left on the plate after a meal and skilfully manage to get it at least fairly clean, if necessary by surreptitiously scraping it with the edge of our fork, but we would never wipe implements on the napkin.

When we rise at the end of the meal, we leave our napkins loosely rumpled on the table—never on the chair, presumably because it might look as though somebody has gone off with the hidden napkin. But chairs at dinner are, we recall, vibrant with taboo, and a European superstition has it that a guest who leaves his or her napkin on the chair will never come again to dinner at that table. In modern Portugal, it is correct to fold the napkin before leaving the table, but in most countries the unfolded napkin shows that you know your host will wash it, not give it again to someone else, and that you do not think you are to stay on for a second meal. Napkin rings may be provided for family members; it used to be a great honour, as a guest, to be asked to fold your napkin or to be given a napkin ring. Into this you slid your rolled and almost immaculate napkin (your modern manners having all but forbidden you to get it dirty), and it was saved for you, as family napkins are saved, for another meal in that hospitable house.

• *Fingers* •

One of the more spectacular triumphs of human "culture" over "nature" is our own determination when eating to avoid touching food with anything but metal implements. Our self-satisfaction with this marvellous instance of artificiality, however, should not lead us to assume that people who habitually eat with their hands are any less determined than we are to behave "properly"; for they too overlay "animal" instincts with manners, and indulge in both the constraints and the ornamentations which characterize polite behaviour. Forks, like handkerchiefs, look dangerously grubby objects to many people encountering them for the first time. To people who eat with their fingers, hands seem cleaner, warmer, more agile than cutlery. Hands are silent, sensitive to texture and temperature, and graceful—provided, of course, that they have been properly trained.

Washing, as we have already remarked, tends to be ostentatious and frequent among polite eaters with their hands. Ancient Romans, like the modern Japanese, preferred to bath all over before dinner. The etiquette of hand-washing in the Middle Ages was very strict. During the washing ritual, precedence was observed as it was in the seating of diners at the table; the bows, genuflections, and ceremonial flourishes of the ewerers or hand-washers were carefully prescribed. It was often thought disgusting, as it is in India today, to dip one's hands into the basin of water: a servant had to pour scented water *over* the hands so that it was used only once. (The modern North American preference for showers over baths is similar.) In modern Egypt, the basin is sometimes provided with a perforated cover so that the dirty water disappears at once from view. Hand-washing rules always insist that one must not splash or swish the water; be careful to leave some dry towel for the person washing next; and above all touch as little as possible between washing and beginning to eat. If an Abbasid (ninth-century Arab) guest scratched his head or stroked his beard after washing, everyone present would wait before beginning to eat, so that he could wash again. An Abbasid, like a modern Egyptian, host would wash first, so that guests need not look as though they were anxious to start the meal; alternatively, washing was done outside, and the meal began directly after the seating, usually when the guest of honour stretched his hand out to take the first morsel.

Desert Arabs go outside the tent, both before and after the meal, to perform ablutions by rubbing their hands with sand; they often prefer to perform this ritual before washing, even when there is plenty of water available. It is thought very rude to perform one's final washing before everyone else has finished eating; it would be the equivalent of our leaving the table while the meal is in progress. The corollary of this is that people who eat with their hands usually try to finish the meal together, since it is uncomfortable, for one thing, to sit for long when one has finished eating, holding out one greasy hand. Where family eating is done from a shared pot, there are rules about leaving some food over for the children, who eat more slowly than adults do. A great deal of attention, forethought, and control is required in order to finish a meal together, or at a moment agreed on in advance; it is a manoeuvre few of us have been trained to perform.

A monstrously greedy Greco-Roman banqueter is said to have accustomed his hands to grasping hot things by plunging them into hot water at the baths; he also habitually gargled with hot water, to accustom his mouth to high temperatures. He would then bribe the cook to serve the meal straight from the stove, so that he could grab as much food as possible and eat it while it was still hot—before anyone else could touch it. The story reminds us that eating food while it is hot is a habit both culture-specific and modern; a taste for it has developed in us, a taste which is dependent both on technology and on the little brothers of technology, the knife, fork, and spoon. People who eat their food with their hands usually eat it warm rather than steaming, and they grow up preferring it that way. (It is often said that one of the cultural barriers that divide "developed" from "developing" peoples is this matter of preference in the temperature at which food is eaten.) Where hot drinks are served, on the other hand (an example is the Arab coffee-drinking habit at mealtimes), people tend to like them very hot, as a contrast, and because the cups or glasses, together with the saucers under them, protect their hands.

Delicacy and adroitness of gesture are drummed into people who eat with their hands, from childhood. It might be considered polite, for example, to scoop food up, or it could be imperative to grasp each morsel from above. Politeness works by abjuring whole ranges of behaviour which the body could easily encompass—indeed, very often the easier movement is precisely what is out of bounds. It was once the mark of the utmost refinement in our own culture to deny oneself the use of the fourth and fifth fingers when eating: the thumb and first two fingers alone were allowed. Bones—provided they were small ones—could be taken up, but held between thumb and forefinger only. We hear of especially sophisticated people who used certain fingers only for one dish, so that they had other fingers, still unsticky and ungreasy, held in reserve for taking food or sauce from a different platter. This form of constraint was possible only if the food was carefully prepared so that no tugging was necessary: the meat must be extremely tender, cut up, or hashed and pressed into small cakes. None but the rich and those with plenty of servants were likely to manage such delicacy; it followed that only they could be truly "refined."

Distancing the fourth and fifth fingers from the operation of taking food can be performed by lifting them up, elegantly curled; the constraint has forced them to serve merely as ornament. A hand used in this manner becomes a dramatic expression of the economy of politeness. When a modern tea-drinker is laughed at for holding her cup-handle in three fingers, lifting the two unused digits in the air, we think it is because we find her ridiculously pretentious. What we really mean is that she is conservative to the point that her model of social success is completely out of date, and the constraints and ornaments with which she clothes her behaviour are now inappropriate—which is another way of saying that, although she is trying very hard to be correct, she succeeds merely in being improper. Modern constraints and ornaments are, quite simply, different. We should remember that snobbery has usually delighted in scorning what is passé.

Left hands are very commonly disqualified from touching food at dinner. The *Li Chi* tells us that ancient Chinese children were trained from infancy never to use their left hands when eating. Ancient Greeks and Romans leaned on their left elbows when reclining at meals, effectively withdrawing their left hands from use. You *had* to lean on the left elbow even if you were left-handed: if you did not, you ruined the configuration of the party by facing the wrong way. The same problem confronted, even more vitally, an ancient Greek hoplite soldier. He formed part of a phalanx of shields, all of which had to be held on left arms so that they could overlap; fighting was done with swords grasped in the right. A shield on the right arm would have created a gap in the closed phalanx. It must have been very difficult to be left-handed in the ancient world.

Abbasid Arabs used to hold bread in their left hands because this was the part of the meal not shared from a common dish, and even strict modern Middle Eastern manners permit the use of the left for operations such as peeling fruit; the main thing is not to take from a communal dish with the left, and to avoid bringing the left hand to the mouth. The left hand is traditionally discouraged at table because it is the non-sacred hand, reserved for profane and polluting actions from which the right hand abstains. One example of these tasks is washing after excretion. Now it is invariably important for human beings both culturally and for health reasons to understand that food is one thing and excrement another: the fact that they are "the same thing," that is, different phases of the same process, merely makes it imperative that we should keep the distinction clear, and continually demonstrate to others that we are mindful of it.

Eating together is a potent expression of community. Food is sacred, and must also be pure, clean, and undefiled. It crosses the threshold of the mouth, enters, and either feeds or infects the individual who consumes it: anything presented to us as edible which is perceived as impure in any sense immediately revolts us. Homage is paid to the purity of what we eat, and precaution taken to preserve it, in many different ways: we have already considered washing, white cloths and napkins, dish covers, poison-tastings, prayers, and paper wrappings, and we shall see many more of these. In our culture, lavatories (literally, "wash places"—only euphemisms are permissible for this particular piece of furniture) are kept discreetly closeted, either alone or in a bathroom; a "washroom" or a "toilet" (literally, a "place where there is a towel") is nearly unthinkable without a door for shutting other people out. The lavatory bowl is covered (sometimes the cover is covered as well), usually white, wastefully water-flushed (people even like to tint this water an emphatically artificial blue), and hedged about with special paper rolls and hand-washings.

Our fascination when we learn that people exist who will not touch food with their left hands is rather interesting. It begins with our conviction that "civilized" people (ourselves, of course) should eat with knives and forks in the first place—that is, try not to handle food at all. We do not like the reason left hands are most often said to be banned among certain "foreigners," fastening as we do upon one reason when it is only one from a whole category of "profane" actions, because our taboo about washrooms is so strong that we

cannot bear to be reminded of excretion—which we are, by the pro-
hibition. In other words, our taboo is even stronger than theirs.
Moreover, left hands have in fact an "unclean" connotation in our
own culture.

"Right," after all, means "correct" or "okay" in English.
"Sinister" originally meant "left." In French, a just man is *droit*,
meaning both "right" and "straight," while *gauche* ("left") describes
one who lacks social assurance, as well as dexterity and adroitness
(both of which literally mean "right-handedness"). We raise right
hands to take oaths and extend them to shake hands: left-handed
people just have to fall in with this. In fact, left-handed people, like
left-handed ancient Greeks, have always been regarded as an awkward, wayward minority, to the point where left-handed children
have been forced, against their best interests, to use their right
hands rather than their left. When sets of opposites (curved and
straight, down and up, dark and light, cold and hot, and so forth) are
set out, our own cultural system invariably makes "left" go with
down, dark, round, cold—and female. Males are straight, up, light,
hot—and right. Our metal eating implements free us from denying
the left hand—but most of us are right-handed anyway, and knives
(quintessentially "male" weapons, by the way) are held in right
hands. And as we shall see, North Americans still prefer not only to
cut with the right, but to bring food to their mouths with the right
hand as well.

Eating with the help of both hands at once is very often frowned
upon. The Bedouin diner is not permitted to gnaw meat from the
bone: he must tear it away and into morsels using only the right
hand, and not raise the hand from the dish in order to do so.
Sometimes right-handed eaters confronted with a large piece of
meat, a chicken, for instance, will share the task of pulling it apart,
each of two guests using his right hand and exercising deft coordina-
tion; no attention should be drawn to this operation by any movement resembling a wrench or a jerk. Even on formal occasions our
own manners permit us, occasionally, to use our fingers—when eating asparagus, for example (this is an early twentieth-century dispensation), or radishes, or apricots. But all of these are taken to the
mouth with one hand only. We are still advised that corn kernels

should be cut off the cobs in the kitchen, or that corn should, better still, be avoided altogether unless the meal is a very intimate affair. One reason why this vegetable has never become quite respectable is that corn cobs demand to be held in two hands. (More important reasons are of course that teeth come too obviously into play when eating them, and cheeks and chins are apt to get greasy.) When we chew, we should also be careful to fill only one cheek—not too full, to be sure. Two hands and two cheeks both signify indecent enthusiasm; cramming either hands or mouth is invariably rude.

People whose custom it is to eat with their hands make a further rule: Never take up and prepare a new morsel while you are still chewing. When left hands are allowed as well as right, it is quite dreadful to be feeding one's mouth with one hand while the other is groping in the dish for more. (We are far more lax than they on this point: we are permitted to use the knives and forks in our hands, and chew at the same time.) Ned Ward, in *O Raree Show, O Pretty Show, or the City Feast*, describes the dreadful manners of guests at the Lord Mayor's Banquet in London, 1704:

> Then each tuck'd his Napkin up under his Chin,
> That his Holiday-Band might be kept very clean;
> And Pin'd up his Sleeves to his Elbows, because
> They should not hang down and be Greas'd in the Sauce.
> Then all went to work, with such rending and tearing,
> Like a Kennel of Hounds on a Quarter of Carri'n.
> When done with the Flesh, they claw'd off the Fish,
> With one Hand at Mouth, and th' other in th' Dish.

Eating with one's hands is very often done from a common dish. "Rending and tearing," and hurrying of any kind, become absolutely shocking behaviour, because you look as though you want to take your companions' share of the food. You might also pay for such precipitousness by hurting yourself: Montaigne ate very quickly, and confessed in his essay "On Experience" that he sometimes bit his tongue and his fingers in his haste.

Teeth, among eaters with their hands, are even less on view than in our meals, partly because the kind of food politely eaten with the hands needs less immediate cutting and chewing than the slabs of steak or roast which we are often served. Hunks of meat are rarely taken up and bitten again and again by polite diners; this is the sort of behaviour which tends to be attributed to those whom people like thinking of as barbarians—Poseidonius reported with a thrill that the frightful Celts "clutch whole joints and bite." Those eaters with their hands who do consume a lot of roasted or dried meat may lift a manageable piece of it in the left hand, grasp a small bit between their teeth with the mouth closed decorously round it, and cut it off at their lips with a sharp knife, as Owen Lattimore saw it done in High Tartary, and as other travellers among nomad meat-eaters have attested. These travellers—French, German, English, Canadian, or American—love describing this action, precisely because it violates our own taboo against approaching the face with a knife.

In our own culture, knives are never used if we can possibly manage without them: they are sharp and dangerous, too suggestive of violence. A similar attitude obtains among eaters with their hands with regard to biting, and even chewing. Amazon Indians are reported, by T. Whiffen for instance, as finding the sight of biting so offputting that they manually tear their food into tiny pieces before putting it into their mouths. Many African tribes approve of swallowing porridge morsels without any chewing first. Something of the same aversion may be seen in our own dislike for the sight of teeth-marks left in food as yet uneaten: we prefer to break or cut bread into single morsels. People who take their food from a common dish must eat the whole of the piece taken; it is usually considered revolting to return a bitten morsel to the central bowl. (Natural circumstance may always mitigate these points: Farley Mowat describes an Inuit feast at which unfinished pieces of meat were allowed back in the boiling pot to keep them "warm between bites.")

It is a universal temptation to play with food before eating it. People pick their sandwich cookies open and scrape the filling off with their teeth; they make themselves rules about when and how to prick the yoke of a fried egg; they twirl and squish ice cream on their cones, pushing it down inside with their tongues and then eating the cone from the point up. Elizabeth Adler, analysing this phenomenon, concludes that we long to separate foods that have been combined in the cooking, and to mix those kept separate. We enjoy triumphantly destroying elaborate but fragile structures and creating new ones of our own; there is also a pleasant need both to challenge and to reward our sense of self-control by saving the best thing on the plate till last. We go so far as to ritualize this sort of behaviour, always playing in the same sequence and with the same rules. We might invariably eat, for example, first all the green vegetables, then all the starches, and finally all the meat. People may seize their food as ammunition for fights, as the seventeenth-century spectators would after a royal banquet, or as children might if they hate what they have been given to eat. Professor G. Nenci has pointed out that *tryphe*, meaning "luxurious living" in ancient Greek, derives from a verb meaning "to crumble or reduce to fragments": it almost certainly reflects the manners of the rich, who could bear to take their time when eating, and luxuriate in rolling food into balls or delicately breaking it into morsels of a "refined" size.

People who eat with their hands have far more opportunity for what Adler calls "creative eating" than we have. An Arab hostess of the feasts described by Aida Kanafani customarily stirs in with her hands the last-minute additions to a dish, such as sauces and juices, in front of the guests; this becomes a satisfying and appetizing part of the ritual "delay before eating." Diners themselves must manipulate their food, often being allowed—indeed, expected—to make artistic selections from what is available. For example, Arabs will create morsels of rice enclosing different fillings, chosen and juxtaposed at the will of the eater: a bit of meat, for instance, a date, a nut, and some rice. The whole is dexterously moulded into a self-sufficient "bite-sized" riceball, which may be different from all the other "creations" put together by the diner in the course of the meal. All this is done with one hand—it is nevertheless very rude among rice-eaters to drop any rice at all while doing it—and diners are conscious of enjoying the feel and temperature of the food before it goes into their mouths. In the creation of such a morsel (the Arabic word for it is a *logmah*), one must select, pinch, fold, and compress in the hand—but never fiddle, or smear; there should be as little disturbance as possible of the carefully decorative design of the various heaps of food set out in the centre of the group of diners. It is often the done thing to flick the finished ball into the mouth with the thumb. This prevents mouth and hand contact, and is performed with expertise and nonchalance enough to make it a politely ornamental gesture in itself.

Handling food is always tightly controlled by rules of etiquette. One is forbidden to play with food distractedly, or for its own sake. Europeans so often committed this fault before knives and forks became common that seventeenth-century French had a disapproving word for it—*gadrouiller* or *gradouiller*. *Civilité* books of the time say one should not dip one's bread into the sauce "too deeply," or the fingers will go in as well; neither should one turn and turn the bread so that it soaks up gravy on all sides. One should dip neatly and chastely, once. Licking fingers is either sternly forbidden or allowed only if certain constraints are applied. B. Meakin tells us for example that in Morocco in 1905, diners were allowed to lick their fingers, but only in this order: fourth (little) finger, second, thumb, third, first. Such a licker proved conclusively that he or she was not neglectfully lapsing from good form.

In our own culture, of course, we use our fingers only in special circumstances, or when the rules are being consciously ignored. Licking fingers is more deliberately relaxed behaviour still—even though we do not use our hands to take from a common dish, and other people do not therefore risk our touching their food with fingers we have licked. The marketers of a well-known brand of fast food, in claiming that the product is "finger-lickin' good," stress the informality with which they expect it to be eaten. (Even the "g" has gone from "licking." Rusticity is especially useful for advertising the most industrialized of foods: "country" people, we feel, are not only more relaxed and more cheerful than us, but must surely eat better than we do.) The advertisers also suggest that their customers will not be able to resist polishing the product off to the last smear.

The Table Boor, Gnathon ("Jaws"), among La Bruyère's *Characters* is revolting because he fingers all of the dishes, and not only those directly in front of him. "He paws them over and over again, tearing and dismembering them, so that if the other guests wish to dine they must do so on his leavings"; he spills the gravy over his chin and beard, and dribbles it over the other dishes and the tablecloth as he transports his handful to his mouth: "you can find him by following his track." Hands and fingers, so much swifter and more adept than knives and forks, must not only be kept under a tight rein, but everyone at table must constantly be reassured that one is exercising this control. And just because handfuls of food have constantly to be carried across the table, codes of manners warn that nothing should be spilled. Three centuries before La Bruyère described his Boor, Chaucer's Prioress, Madame Eglentyne, was being praised for having manners precisely opposed to his:

> At meat her manners were well taught withal;
> No morsel from her lips did she let fall
> Nor dipped her fingers in the sauce too deep;
> But she could carry a morsel up and keep
> The smallest drop from falling on her breast.
> For courtliness she had a special zest.
> And she would wipe her upper lip so clean
> That not a trace of grease was to be seen
> Upon the cup when she had drunk; to eat
> She reached a hand sedately for the meat.

It was our own choice to retreat, eventually, from the touching of food, but the process of giving up hands and taking up forks took many centuries to complete. At familial meals, it was common in Europe until recent times for a central dish of food to be placed in the middle of the table; from it everyone helped themselves. In medieval Hungary, for example, dining tables had holes cut in the middle of them to hold the communal cauldron of meat. Professor Robert Muchembled of Paris says that his own great-grandfather, in the second half of the nineteenth century, was the very first person in his village in Artois to renounce the traditional table with its thick top hollowed out in the middle to hold the food. He decided he would henceforth dine *à l'assiette*, "at his own place, and from his own plate." For a long time it was the height of sophistication to cut up our food with a knife and fork; but we would then put these instruments aside and lift the pieces with our fingers.

Sometimes individual foods would demand a retention of the old ways long after knives and forks were used for everything else: this was usually, but not always, for the sake of convenience. Lobsters and crayfish require both hands, as well as a napkin worn bib-style. Erasmus says that salt should be taken with the point of a knife, but "three fingers thrust into the salt-cellar is, by common jest, said to be the sign of the boor." Yet salt has often been taken from its dish with the fingers in very polite society, largely because at luxurious tables every person, or every couple, is provided with a salt dish; these were not always provided with little spoons. The salt shaker has still a rather new-fangled, vulgarly practical air; it has not yet been quite accepted into the conservative usages ordained for salt on formal occasions. Salt, Anglo-Saxons still feel, should be placed in a little heap on the edge of the plate, to be dipped into with each mouthful. Sprinkling it over the food may be less likely to ruin the taste of the food, but it is not strictly proper. It is even quite correct to revert to the ancient custom of piling salt on the tablecloth by one's plate at formal dinners—but, Emily Post warned in 1937, dipping celery or radishes into this pile "is never permitted."

Potatoes in their jackets, boiled or baked, were properly eaten at the turn of this century by being broken open in the hands, peeled, and cut (never mashed!), then lifted to the mouth with the fingers. We immediately note that they cannot have been preferred very hot, and that they were being treated as though they were bread. A more modern fashion, since our taste demands that a baked potato should be served hot, is to eat it out of its skin with a fork. It is still thought proper in some circles to break it open with the fingers in spite of the heat. It must not be attacked with a knife; any butter which is applied must be put on with the fork. Mashing, a whole new possibility which came in with the fork, has never been formally accepted at the dining table. It is both too destructive and too creative—too much like chewing done on the open plate; we shall look at the problematics of chewing later. Mashing leads to what Branchereau calls "mixtures unsuitable and contrary to good form." It should take place in the kitchen, firmly out of sight.

• *Chopsticks* •

The ultimately restricted—and therefore it may be thought the ultimately delicate—manner of eating with one's hands is to use the thumb and two fingers of the right hand, only the tips of these ideally being allowed to touch the food. This gesture, refined even more by artificially elongating the fingers and further reducing their number, is of course the origin of chopsticks. Once people become accustomed to fingers remaining clean throughout the meal, napkins used for serious cleansing seem not only redundant but downright nasty. Father João Rodrigues observed in the seventeenth century that the Japanese were "much amazed at our eating with the hands and wiping them on napkins, which then remain covered with food stains, and this causes them both nausea and disgust." Napkins laid on knees are still an "ethnic," Western affectation in China and Japan. There is, however, a tradition of supplying diners several times during the meal with small rough towels wrung out in boiling water, for hand- and face-wiping.

Chopsticks seem to have evolved in the East specifically for use with rice: the staple grain in China was originally millet, which the *Li Chi* insists must be eaten with a spoon, not with chopsticks like rice. Chinese rice is not loose and dry like that chosen by Indians, Arabs, and Africans, who prefer eating it with their hands, but sticky and slightly moist even without sauce; it is easily handled with chopsticks. The earliest word for chopsticks seems to have been $z\breve{i}$, related to the root meaning, "help." This is pronounced, however, like the word for "stop," or "becalm" used of boats. Chinese boatmen are said to have renamed them $kua\grave{i}$-$z\breve{i}$," which sounds like "fast fellows," because Chinese think of chopsticks as swift and agile, the very opposite of halting and being becalmed. This is now their Chinese name; "chopsticks" is of course a Western barbarism. In Japanese, chopsticks are called *hashi*, "bridge," because they effect the transition from bowl to mouth.

Chopsticks are thought of as fast, then, and helpful. Meals in China often surprise visitors by the speed with which they are eaten; chopsticks enable the Chinese and Japanese to eat food which is sizzling hot, but because it is often served in small pieces it gets cold if people dawdle. Chopstick-users remain more likely than we are to use their hands as aids in eating—but it is not at all advisable to get them greasy: chopsticks, and especially the lacquered chopsticks common in Japan and Korea, are extremely difficult to manage with slippery fingers. Porcelain spoons are used for soups and the more liquid dishes; children are allowed to use spoons for everything until they are about three or four years old, when chopstick training begins.

Chinese tables are round or square rather than oval or oblong: diners sit equidistant from the dishes of *cài* (meat, fish, and vegetables), all set out in one "course," in the middle. Each diner gets a small bowl for *fàn*, literally, "food," meaning rice. The rice is the substance of the meal; the *cài* is merely relish, unless the occasion is a banquet. The host, or the mother, doles out the rice into the bowls. Each guest must take the filled bowl in two hands: receiving in one hand shows disrespectful indifference. You never eat *cài* before being served rice, because that looks as though you are so greedy and selfish that you would be prepared to eat nothing but meat and vegetables, which are the expensive part of the meal, centrally placed in order to be shared with others.

When the host gives the sign, you may begin to take *cài* with your chopsticks. The gestures used by Chinese, Japanese, and others to do this are fascinating for Westerners. They look accomplished, delicate, precise, and gentle—much more polished than our own behaviour at meals. Roland Barthes in *The Empire of Signs* speaks eulogies on the Japanese manipulation of chopsticks: "there is something maternal, the same precisely measured care taken in moving a child . . . the instrument never pierces, cuts, or slits, never wounds but only selects, turns, shifts. For the chopsticks . . . in order to divide, must separate, part, peck, instead of cutting and piercing, in the manner of our implements; they never violate the foodstuff; either they gradually unravel it (in the case of vegetables) or else prod it into separate pieces (in the case of fish, eels) thereby rediscovering the natural fissures of the substance."

A Westerner feels like a brute butcher before this Oriental delicacy. Barthes says that we are "armed with pikes and knives" like predators rather than gentle mothers, our food "a prey to which one does violence." B. Y. Chao tells us that the Chinese are aware in themselves of a sequence of commands: "Await, avoid, attack!" You must pause, think of others, consider which piece you want, then zero in on it. You may have to stretch across the path of another's chopsticks—though Chinese, too, try to restrict themselves to taking from the side of the dish more or less facing them; fellow diners cooperate with each other and are not greatly offended by another's "attack." You should never look too intent on obtaining a particular morsel, however. Chinese children are taught that "the best mannered person does not allow co-diners to be aware of what his or her favorite dishes are by his or her eating pattern."

It is politer to transfer food first to your rice bowl, and eat it from there, than to take it directly from the *cài* dish to your mouth. Chopsticks must never be licked or bitten. Japanese bad manners include *neburi-bashi*: licking chopsticks with the tongue; *mogi-kui*: using your mouth to remove rice sticking to your chopsticks; *komi-bashi*: forcing several things into your mouth with your chopsticks; *utsuri-bashi*: one must not break the rule that a mouthful of rice is to be taken between every two bites of meat, fish, or vegetables; *saguri-bashi*: searching with chopsticks to see if anything you want remains in the dish; *hashi-namari*: hesitation whether to take one thing rather than another; and *sora-bashi*: putting back with the chopsticks food you intended to eat.

Mannerly diners with chopsticks never "fish about" for morsels; they must take the bit they touch first. This means that one begins by eyeing one's target carefully: if you prod it, you must take and eat it. Using chopsticks need in no way mean that people eat food touched by implements which have been in other people's mouths. Yet a very Western distaste for even the thought of touching the food of all with the utensils of each has spread. In 1984, Hu Yaobang, the former Communist Party Secretary, criticized the traditional Chinese way of eating and urged change on sanitary grounds. A good deal of such concern must in fact be a desire to participate in Western prestige as being somehow more ineffably "modern." The admiration of people like Roland Barthes for superior Oriental wisdom seems to be less satisfying than the allure of technological hygiene and "modern" metal instruments. A compromise with "modernity" is the Japanese pre-wrapped, disposable set of wooden chopsticks. But unfortunately there is an ecological price to pay for this, as hundreds of millions of trees are chopped down every year to supply throwaway chopstick wood—in 1987, 20 billion chopsticks were used and discarded in Japan alone.

It has never been acceptable to return bitten morsels of meat, vegetables, or fish to the common dish; but because the bowl of rice is "private territory," a piece of meat or vegetable may be held in chopsticks and bitten, and the rest put down on the rice in the bowl, to be finished later. One must never, in Japan, stick the chopsticks upright in the rice. This is done only when offerings are made by Buddhist mourners for their dead: standing chopsticks are rather like our own taboos about an empty chair at table.

With perfect propriety one lifts the small china bowl in the left hand and sweeps the contents into the mouth with precise, busy movements of the two sticks together, held in the right. Barthes's delicate gestures suddenly become swift and purely efficient; the bowl held under the chopsticks is moved dexterously about so as to prevent food spills. We ourselves are surprised to see this done because we are never allowed to lift dishes containing solid food— and we count soup, unless it is in a cup, as "solid food"—to our lips; we gave up doing this when we agreed that formal politeness involves using our cutlery. The Chinese may be thought of as treating the little bowl like a cross between a teacup and a large spoon, with the chopsticks as "helpers." Table manners always impose difficult restraints: "If you rattle your chopsticks against the bowl," says a Chinese proverb, "you and your descendants will always be poor." Whatever happens, however, at an ordinary meal every single grain of rice in one's bowl must be eaten before dinner is over. Leaving rice is disgusting behaviour, because it shows a lack of knowledge of one's own appetite in the first place, together with greed for meat and vegetables, and no respect for rice—its culture, its history, and the hard work that has been involved in getting it to the table.

Rice is never to be gripped, lifted, and eaten grain by grain, as Western novices in the art of chopstick-handling find themselves doing with so much frustration and so many complaints. "Picking" at one's food is very rude, in fact, for Oriental manners, more than our own, demand demonstrations of delight and pleasure in eating, and inept fiddling with one's chopsticks is apt to be interpreted not merely as a want of competence but as a depressing unwillingness as well. The problem that Westerners experience is often the result of attempts to eat rice with chopsticks from flat plates: the small bowl raised towards the face is far easier to manage with the proper zest. Chinese themselves, given food on a flat plate, prefer to use a porcelain spoon (to stand in for its sister, the bowl). This spoon, like a bowl, has a flat bottom, so that it can be laid down without spilling the contents.

The kind of food we ourselves eat, together with the way we cook and serve it, predisposes us to use knives, forks, and spoons, and our idea of what constitutes a "place setting" also influences our food choices. Oriental food is cut up in the kitchen so that it can be eaten with chopsticks—but also, as Barthes points out, chopsticks came into being because each mouthful is regarded as comestible partly because it is small; being confronted with a large slab of meat on a dish can be a disgusting experience for people from rice-and-chopstick cultures. In addition, rice-growing is a land use which reduces the amount of fuel available, so that meat and vegetables must usually be cooked quickly to save wood. Cutting them up small facilitates stir-frying and other quick-cooking methods.

· Knives, Forks, Spoons ·

The Chinese knife is a cleaver, useful, so the Andersons tell us, for "splitting firewood, gutting and scaling fish, slicing vegetables, mincing meat, crushing garlic (with the dull side of the blade), cutting one's nails, sharpening pencils, whittling new chopsticks, killing pigs, shaving (it is kept sharp enough, or supposedly is), and settling old and new scores with one's enemies." Keeping this all-purpose tool apart from the dining table shows a resolute preference, in the table manners of the societies which use chopsticks, for polite restraint.

Men in the West used always to carry knives about with them, finding them indispensable for hundreds of purposes—including that of slicing food at the table. St. Benedict's *Rule* (sixth century) requires monks to go to bed dressed and ready to rise the next morning, but advises them to detach their knives from their belts in case they cut themselves during the night. In the Middle Ages only the nobility had special food knives, which they took with them when travelling: hosts were not usually expected to provide cutlery for dinner guests. To this day in parts of France, men carry with them their own personal folding knives, which they take out of their pockets and use for preference at intimate gatherings for dinner. Small boys love being given folding pen-knives with many attachments; these are the descendants of this ancient male perquisite.

Women must also have owned knives, but they have almost invariably been discouraged from being seen using them. Swords and knives are phallic and masculine. In ancient Greece, when women committed suicide, people hoped they would politely refrain from using knives and opt for poison or the noose instead. At many medieval dinner tables men and women ate in couples from a bowl shared between them, and when they did, men were expected courteously to serve their female partners, cutting portions of meat for them with their knives.

Prevention of the violence which could so easily break out at table is, as we have seen, one of the principal aims of table manners. In the West, where knives have not been banished, we are especially sensitive and vigilant about the use of these potential weapons. "When in doubt, do not use your knife" is a good all-purpose rule. We must cut steaks and slices of roast with knives, but the edge of a fork will do for an omelette, or for boiled potatoes, carrots, and other vegetables, especially if no meat is being served with them. If a knife is needed, in a right-handed person it will be occupying the right hand. The American way is to put the knife down when it has done its work, and take up the fork in the right hand; the fork is now available for breaking vegetables as well as lifting what has been cut. Europeans hold on to the knife and have to cut vegetables with it, since the fork is kept in the less capable hand.

Fish may be gently slit down the side facing upwards and separated into portions with the help of a knife, and a knife-blade held flat is useful for lifting fish bones; but everything has been done to bypass knives, because they are not necessary for cutting, at the fish course. Cooked fish must not be cut into fillets, for instance, but lifted from the bones bit by bit. Being gentle with fish had its aesthetic aspect. "In helping fish," pleads a cookbook in 1807, "take care not to break the flakes, which in cod and salmon are large and contribute much to the beauty of its appearance."

Before the invention of stainless steel in the 1920s, the taste of blade metal was often said to ruin the flavour of fish, especially if it was seasoned with lemon. (Fruit-knives were made of silver because of the acid in fruit.) Special fish-knives were invented in the nineteenth century: they were silver or silver plate, ostentatiously unsharpened, and given a whimsical shape to show that they were knives whose only business was gently deboning and dividing cooked fish. Before fish-knives, fish was eaten with a fork in the right hand and a piece of bread, as a pusher, held in the left. Two forks were used to serve it, and sometimes to eat it as well. Eating fish with forks long remained the choice of the aristocracy: silver fish-knives and their matching forks were middle-class, a *parvenue* invention. Laying one's table with them was a sign that one had *bought* the family silver, instead of inheriting it and the ancient ways that it was made to serve. Fish-knives have often been frowned on during this century, being thought quaintly decorative, too specialized, or over-refined; they are said to be reasserting themselves on middle-class tables.

The French insist that salad should never be cut with a knife: it must be torn in pieces by hand before it goes into the salad bowl, and then, after dressing, eaten with a fork. The rule probably arose from the taste and stain of metal from a steel knife, an especial danger for French lettuce because it was always dressed with oil and vinegar or lemon. The British and Americans, who used far less "French dressing," have always found this French fashion effete. We ought to be given a silver knife to eat lettuce (since we cannot count on salad being torn into little pieces in advance), says Emily Post, but if not we should simply go ahead and cut each leaf into "postage-stamp samples." We should not be misled, she adds, by falsely French manners into eating large lettuce leaves with a fork, "wrapping springy leaves around the tines in a spiral. Remember what a spring that lets go can do!"

Lettuce is not cut in France partly because lettuce leaves are supposed to be too tender to need cutting; in the same way, the French—overturning Erasmus's advice in his famous book on the manners of boys—are shocked by knives being used on bread at table. The change to breaking rather than cutting bread, among the eighteenth-century French aristocracy, seems to have been part of the move towards an elegant simplicity in manners as the new hallmark of good taste. French bread is not usually sliced for buttering or for toasting; Anglo-Saxon methods of eating bread often require knives for spreading as well as cutting, and also the provision of butter plates. *Pain de campagne*, the large, solid, round country loaf of France, is correctly cut in pieces: a man may whip out his pocket knife, grip the loaf under his arm, and carve out a slice. He must cut from the outer edge and towards his own body, so that no one else is endangered by his exploit. "Viennese" *baguettes*, on the other hand, are soft white table bread; they are sliced, but away from the table, and served in a bread-basket. The refusal to cut them at table is a statement about the kind of bread it is, and a distinction that is being made between it and *pain de campagne*. In Germany, it is rude to cut potatoes with a knife, or pancakes, or dumplings; it looks as though you think they might be tough, and also these starchy foods are thought of as almost like bread. In Italy, it is never "done" to cut spaghetti.

Ever since the sixteenth century there has been a taboo against pointing a knife at our faces. It is rude, of course, to point at anybody with a knife or a fork, or even a spoon; it is also very bad form to hold knife and fork in the fists so that they stand upright. But pointing a knife at *ourselves* is viewed with special horror, as Norbert Elias has observed. I think that one reason for this is that we have learned only very recently not to use our knives for placing food in our mouths: we are still learning, and we therefore reinforce our decision by means of a taboo. We *think* we hate seeing people placing themselves in even the slightest jeopardy, but actually we fervently hope they will not spoil the new rule and let us all down by taking to eating with their knives again.

For the fact is that people have commonly eaten food impaled on the points of their knives, or carried it to their mouths balanced on blades; the fork is in this respect merely a variant of the knife. With the coming of forks, knife-points became far less useful than they had been; their potential danger soon began in consequence to seem positively barbaric. The first steps in the subduing of the dinner knife were taken when the two cutting edges of the dagger-like knife were reduced to one. The blunt side became an upper edge, which is not threatening to fingers when they are holding knives in the polite manner. According to Tallement des Réaux, Richelieu was so appalled by the sight of Chancellor Séguier picking his teeth with a knife, that he ordered all the knife-blades in his establishment to have their points ground down into innocuously rounded ends. It later became illegal in France for cutlers to make pointed dinner knives or for innkeepers to lay them on their tables. Other countries soon followed suit. Pointed knives for all diners were later to return to the dining-room table, but as "steak" knives, which have a special image, linked deliberately with red meat and "getting down to business" when hungry. They are still quite rustic in connotation.

Cheese, which can be a very hard substance indeed, has usually required a knife to cut it, and as long as knives were pointed, hard cheese was spiked and moved to one's plate or bread slice, or passed on the knife-point to a neighbour. So obvious and natural was this action that the Victorians found it necessary, despite the acceptance of the rounded knife-blade, to invent a special cheese-knife. It has a blade, but more than one point, like a fork; the points for impaling the cheese, however, are turned to one side, thus ingeniously preserving the blunted tip of the knife. People had repeatedly to be reminded by etiquette manuals in the late nineteenth century only to *transport* the cheese with this knife or any other, and not to eat it from the point: "When eating cheese, small morsels should be placed with the knife on small morsels of bread, and the two conveyed to the mouth with the thumb and finger, the piece of bread being the morsel to hold. Cheese should not be eaten off the point of the knife." The morsels of bread were to protect the fingers from touching smelly cheese. In France, cheese must always be handed with a knife, exceptions being made only for Gruyère and Cheddar, which may be lifted, after cutting with a knife, by piercing on forks.

French children are carefully taught never to serve themselves by cutting off the point of a triangle of cheese: in something like a Camembert or Roquefort this would be to take the delicious centre for yourself, under the noses of the furious other guests. Triangles of cheese must be cut like cake, in slices which include a substantial amount of edge, and taper to the middle.

An interim period followed the introduction of rounded knives, as forks began to make their way in the world. For a while, people were occasionally exhorted to eat only with the back of the knife-blade, blunted as it now often was. (As late as 1845, American eaters with their knives were advised, when putting a blade into their mouths, to "let the edge be turned downward." For some reason, during this operation upper lips stood in greater need of protection than lower lips did.) Special knives appeared with widened, not merely rounded, blade ends. The English in the eighteenth century, so Le Grand d'Aussy tells us, were given to using this knife like a sort of flat spoon, even for eating peas. It was an anonymous Englishman who expressed the frustration of many by imagining a heroic solution:

> I eat my peas with honey—
> I've done it all my life.
> It makes the peas taste funny
> But it keeps them on the knife.

Yet it is the English who have insisted for at least a hundred and fifty years on trying to pierce peas with their fork tines, and balance them or crush them on the humped side of a fork, instead of sweeping them onto a fork held in the manner of a spoon.

When Sigmund Freud explained his theory of "symptomatic acts," he gave an example supplied to him by Dr. Dattner of Vienna of a colleague, a doctor of philosophy, who was holding forth while eating cake. This gentleman was talking of a missed opportunity, and as he did so he let fall a piece of cake, an unintentional but perfect "pun" expressing his idea. "While he was uttering the last sentence," the doctor wrote, "he raised a piece of cake to his mouth, but let it drop *from the knife* [my italics] in apparent clumsiness." The slip reveals to us that in Vienna in 1901, eminently bourgeois people were carrying cake to their mouths with their knives. Cake-forks were to become the solution—or simply fingers, as the British insist—and not providing knives with cake at all.

Spikes, not only for spearing meat that is roasting but also for lifting food from the fire or from a food heap and carrying it to the diner, are at least as old as the first knives and spoons; a sharp stick must have been one of mankind's earliest tools, in cooking and eating as for other purposes. Ancient Romans had spoons with one prong or two at the end of the handle for winkling out shellfish, and one-pronged dinner spikes survive from the Middle Ages: a *perero*, for example, was a spear on which one impaled fruit in order to peel it. A fork most simply splits into two tines; early dinner-table forks were generally two-pronged, large, and used mostly to help in cutting, and for serving, not eating, food—our carving forks still keep the size, shape, and original function. Or they were small "suckett" forks, used to lift preserves like ginger out of jars, or to eat fruits, like mulberries, which might stain the fingers.

The fork revolution did not, then, present the world with an utterly strange new implement; what did constitute an important change in the West was the spread of the use of forks, their eventual adoption by all the diners, and their use not only to hold food still while it was cut, but to carry it into people's mouths. The first modern fork, as far as we can at present ascertain, is mentioned as having been used in the eleventh century by the wife of the Venetian Doge, Domenico Selvo. St. Peter Damian, the hermit and cardinal bishop of Ostia, was appalled by this open rejection of nature; he excoriated the whole procedure in a passage entitled "Of the Venetian Doge's wife, whose body, after her excessive delicacy, entirely rotted away." Forks are mentioned again three centuries later, in 1361, in a list of the plate owned by the Florentine Commune. From this time onwards, forks are spoken of frequently; more than two hundred years were to pass, however, before they were commonly used for eating. In Bartolomeo Scappi's book, 1570, there is an engraving depicting a knife, a fork, and a spoon. King Henri III of France and his companions were satirized by Thomas Artus in 1605 for their fork-wielding effeminacy. "They carried [their meat] right into their mouths" with their forks, exclaims the author of *L'Isle des Hermaphrodites*, "stretching their necks out over their plates. . . . They would rather touch their mouths with their little forked instruments than with their fingers." They looked especially silly, the satirist goes on, chasing artichokes, asparagus, peas, and broad beans round their plates and trying without success to get those vegetables into their mouths without scattering them everywhere—as well they might, given that early forks had long, widely separate prongs made for spearing with their very sharp points; scooping with them was impossible. An early nineteenth-century American complained that "eating peas with a fork is as bad as trying to eat soup with a knitting needle."

Italy and Spain led the world into the adoption of forks. In 1611, the Englishman Thomas Coryat announced that he had seen forks in Italy and had decided to adopt them and continue to use them on his return home. The reason for the Italian custom was, he explains, that these extremely fastidious, ultra-modern people considered that any fingering of the meat being carved at table was a transgression against the laws of good manners, "seeing all men's fingers are not alike cleane." Even Coryat, however, does not seem to think of forks as for eating with, but for holding the meat still while carving oneself a slice from the joint intended to be shared by everyone.

The use of individual forks began to spread as the seventeenth century progressed. People would often share forks with others as they would spoons, wiping them carefully on their napkins before passing them on. Antoine de Courtin, in the late 1600s, advised using the fork mainly for fatty, sauce-laden, or syrupy foods; otherwise, hands would do. It was in the course of the seventeenth century, again, that hard plates—prerequisites for the constant use of individual knives and forks—began to be provided for every diner at table. At medieval banquets, plates had been trenchers (from the French *trancher*, "to slice"), made of sliced bread: they were for receiving morsels of food taken from a central dish with the hand, and for soaking up any dripping sauces, not for holding portions which needed subsequently to be pierced and cut up. Trenchers started to receive pewter or wooden underplaques, also called trenchers, in the fourteenth century; cut-marks found on some of them show us that people were beginning occasionally to use them to slice food. The solid non-serving dishes at this time and later were bowls shared between couples, as was the platter of Jack Spratt and his wife in the nursery rhyme.

It is said that the earliest flat modern plates so far known (the word "plate" means "flat") are depicted standing on a buffet in a fresco of the Palazzo del Te at Mantua which dates from about 1525; they are made of metal. (These could be serving dishes, however, and not meant for individual portions.) King François I of France ordered a set of six plates for separate servings (*assiettes*—from *asseoir*, "to sit": the word originally meant both a course or "sitting" and an individual place at a meal). The date was 1536—about a generation before that of Henri III, the king who was laughed at for introducing individual forks at his table. The French, who made superb silver dinnerware in the seventeenth and eighteenth centuries, ended up melting down most of it to defray the cost of wars. But during that period the rising bourgeoisie could afford to buy more and more silver dishes; they were steadily closing the gap that separated their acquired wealth from inherited riches. The aristocracy retaliated by opting for simplicity, and ceramic plates. ("Good taste," as we saw earlier, can be the last bastion of privilege.) But whatever the material used, individual knives and forks required a hard surface to cut on, for every diner served.

Flat ceramic plates were fairly common in France by the end of the seventeenth century, but they completed their general acceptance, replacing bowls for all but soup and certain desserts, only in the nineteenth century. The French still like drinking their breakfast coffee out of bowls. It is a custom under heavy attack at present, because it encourages the downing of copious draughts of very milky coffee in the morning, and the taking of time. In any case, bowls are far too broad and comfortable-looking, and have no handles; two hands are required to lift them. They do not suit the brash new rushed and masculine image, the longing to be "on the cutting edge."

By the beginning of the nineteenth century, North Americans generally were beginning to replace wooden trenchers with pewter and china dishes, and the use of forks was spreading. As late as 1837, however, Eliza Ware Farrar still recommended "the convenience of feeding yourself with your right hand, armed with a steel blade; and provided you do it neatly, and do not put in large mouthfuls, or close your lips tightly over the blade, you ought not to be considered as eating ungenteelly." But the book was edited, by 1880, to exclude her suggestion that one might with propriety eat with the knife-blade: forks have conquered the field they are henceforth to occupy. For a long time forks usually had two prongs, very separate, long, and sharp-pointed. They were often used in conjunction with the English "eating" knives. In this operation the fork, held in the left hand, served to keep the meat still while it was being cut, and then to raise the morsel from the plate. The food was then transferred to the knife's rounded blade and placed in the mouth: the knife was being used like a spoon.

The fork soon fought back. It had often been made with three prongs; now these were shortened and moved closer together, and a fourth prong more commonly added. (Five prongs were also tried, on an analogy with hands, but custom soon decreed that four would suffice. The fashion at the time was for small mouths, and hands were no longer supposed to be feeding them.) Now the fork resembled a spoon, if it was held with the tines facing upward; the knife-blade's spatula end gave way and narrowed to its present shape, and forks more authoritatively took over the function of introducing food into the mouth.

There was a fashion in Europe during the nineteenth century for downplaying the knife to such an extent that one was not only to use it as little as possible but also to put it aside when it was not in use. You cut up your food with the knife in the more capable hand and the fork in the other; you then put down the knife, being careful to place it with the blade's edge towards the centre of the plate, not facing neighbours. Then the fork changed hands, and was used to take the cut food to the mouth. More elaborate manners demanded that one should perform this manoeuvre for every mouthful consumed. Using only one hand is commonly thought polite, as we have seen, and the right hand only is often *de rigueur*. Eaters adhering to this fashion thought that people who ate with both hands holding on to the cutlery were gross and coarse. What Emily Post calls "zig-zag" eating was still customary among the French bourgeoisie in the 1880s, when Branchereau describes it. He says, however, that the English are successfully introducing a new fashion: they hang on to their knives, and take the food to their mouths with the left hand which is still holding the fork.

Eating in the "English" manner means that the fork, having just left off being an impaling instrument, must enter the mouth with the tines down if it is not to be awkwardly swivelled round in the left, or less capable, hand. Food must therefore be balanced on the *back* of the rounded tines. This has two advantages for polite behaviour. First, a fork thus held encourages the mouth to take the food off it quickly and close to the lips—it is quite difficult to push the fork, with its humped tines, far into the mouth. "Weapons" should not be plunged into mouths; we now keep this rule faithfully, hardly needing it to be enunciated. The second advantage is that denying a modern fork its possible spoonlike use is wantonly perverse: it forces us to take small mouthfuls and to leave some of the food, unliftable, on the plate. It is difficult to get the food onto the fork, and harder still to balance and raise it faultlessly. Managing to eat like this with grace is a triumph of practice and determination, and therefore an ideal mannerly accomplishment.

The former way of eating was not dislodged in North America as it was in the rest of the world. It has been suggested by James Deetz that the old way was more deeply entrenched in America because forks arrived there relatively late. According to this theory, Americans remained attached to eating with their spoons; they would cut food (probably holding it still, when necessary, with their fingers or their spoons), then lift it in the spoon, first shifting it if necessary to the right hand, to their mouths. Forks, imported from Europe, were certainly used sometimes not only for impaling food but for transporting it into the mouth. Charles Dickens visited America in the early 1840s and witnessed eating with both knife and straight, long-pronged fork: he says in *American Notes* that people "thrust the broad-bladed knives and the two-pronged forks further down their throats than I ever saw the same weapons go before, except in the hands of a skilled juggler." But soon forks took their modern spoonlike form, so that they could be treated, after the spearing and cutting was done, as though they were spoons. Europeans, meanwhile, kept eating food impaled on the tines.

Americans have been badgered and ridiculed about their eating habits for over a hundred years. They have refused so far to change, not seeing any need to do so, and out of patriotic pride in non-conformity. In any case, as Miss Manners (1982) says, "American table manners are, if anything, a more advanced form of civilized behavior than the European, because they are more complicated and further removed from the practical result, always a sign of refinement."

The spoon is the safest, most comfortable member of the cutlery set. It is the easiest implement to use—babies start with spoons—and the one with the most versatility, which is the reason why its employment is constantly being restricted. Spoons are for liquids, porridge, and puddings—even the last being often given over to forks. Insofar as spoons have an infantile image, they lack prestige. (A Freudian analysis of the knife, fork, and spoon gives the spoon the female role in the trio; the fork, if I understand the writer correctly, is a male child of the knife and the spoon, and, like a little Oedipus, resentful of the knife and jealous of the spoon.) Social historians are puzzled by medieval paintings of banquets, which show knives but seldom spoons, although we know that spoons were often used. It has been suggested (unconvincingly, I think) that knives might simply have impressed the painters more. Spoons seem, at any rate, not to have been laid down on the table's surface as knives were.

But spoons can inspire affection as knives and forks cannot; they are unthreatening, nurturing objects. Superstitions about them show that they are subconsciously regarded as little persons: two on one saucer means an imminent wedding; dropping one on the table means a visitor is coming; and so on. Spoon-handles, more than knife- or fork-handles, are made in the shape of human figures, as in the sets of twelve apostle spoons. The Welsh traditionally made love-spoons carved with the lovers' hands, which they gave to each other as tokens, and an old English custom at Christmas was for all the diners to hold up their spoons and wish health to absent friends (spoons were customarily classed with cups and bowls). Spoons have always been popular as presents and commemorations, whereas knives are often superstitiously avoided as gifts, and forks somehow fail, still, to stand on their own as spoons and knives can.

A spoon is a bowl with an arm attached, the earliest spoon being a cupped human hand. Every race on earth has made itself spoons, out of seashells, coconut shells, bones, gourds, amber, ivory, stones ranging from agate to jasper, many kinds of wood and metal, porcelain, tortoiseshell, either cut or boiled and pressed horn, and even basketry. The word "spoon," however, means in Old English a chip of wood, and many spoons have been flat spatulas, like those provided with ice-cream tubs, or like the blades of "eating" knives. The flat spoons of some North American Indian bands could be so large that they were used partly as plates. Spoon bowls have been made in many forms, from round to banana-shaped.

The fig-shaped spoon bowl was roughly triangular, with the handle attached to the pointed end and the front end almost straight. It was introduced into Europe during the Middle Ages from the eastern Mediterranean; only wooden cooking spoons are still commonly made in this ancient shape. It probably reflected the practice of drinking from the front end of the spoon, a usage which is still correct in many European countries. The British and North Americans treat the bowl of a soup spoon like a cup, and drink from the side of it; French visitors to Britain often express their fascination with this mannerism. The word "ladle" means the bearer of a larger-than-usual "load" of food or drink; ladles, like most spoons made for dipping into deep bowls, are usually provided with upward-turning stems. (Modern oval-shaped spoons with horizontal handles became conventional in the eighteenth century. They mark the transition to the custom of eating most commonly from flat or shallow plates.) Persians and Arabs have traditionally drunk water from a large wooden ladle (Mohammad forbade Moslems either to drink wine or to use gold and silver spoons), which they passed round the company as cups were passed in Europe. Care was taken in polite society to pour water into the mouth so that the ladle never actually touched the lips of anyone.

A serving of tea or coffee, like soup, is provided with a spoon— but not to drink from. A good deal of sipping from teaspoons used to go on, perhaps because people were less accustomed than we are to consuming hot liquid. Manners books warn their readers not to "pour hot tea or coffee violently from spoon to cup" (in order to cool it). For about a hundred years it has been forbidden to leave teaspoons in cups, partly to make it clear that we understand they are for stirring only. The saucer (which was once, as its name shows, a small dish for holding sauce) has migrated to its present position under the cup, which is now regarded as incomplete without it; upon this saucer we must also place our teaspoon, out of temptation's way. "Never," says Andréani's French guide to etiquette (1988), "leave your coffee spoon in your cup when you lift it to your lips." It was once perfectly correct to stand your teaspoon upright in your cup to show you did not want any more tea, just as it was once correct to pour a hot beverage into your saucer—which was deep then, more like a bowl—to help it lose heat. A side plate or table mat was thoughtfully provided, to take the cup until the drink, once it was thought cool enough, had been ingested from the saucer.

• Sequence •

"A Western banquet," says the narrator of Anthony Burgess's novel *Earthly Powers* (1980), "recapitulates the history of the earth from primal broth through sea beasts to land predators and flying creatures and ends with evidence of human culture in cheese and artful puddings." The German Romantic poet Novalis felt that the course of dinner was like a human lifetime—"The dinner itself is, like life, a curve: it starts off with the lightest courses, then rises to the heavier, and concludes with light courses again." "The full Tuscan dinner," according to N. Newnham-Davis, "does not follow in the order of fish, entrée, roast, pièce de résistance and game, but of boiled (*lesso*), fried (*fritto*), stewed (*umido*), and roast (*arrosto*). Fish, for example, might be found under all four headings." Such perceptions of the nature of dinner—it is always a "full" or formal or "proper" dinner which is meant—show us how fundamental to a meal is a sense that it evolves and progresses in an orderly fashion, tells a tale, symbolizes life, society, the cosmos, Paradise. A well-planned meal must contrive to provide variety, contrast, and completeness, to range from liquid to solid, cold to hot, and through all the flavours from savoury to sweet.

The "plot" of the meal can vary enormously from culture to culture. We have only to recall that a Chinese banquet often begins with fruit and ends with soup; there may or may not be dessert in the middle—but not at the end—of the meal; and conversation tends to take place before eating begins, rather than during the chewing or after the meal is over, when the Chinese feel that everyone is too replete to start discussing business or the meaning of life. We shall look first at fully fledged feasts as they have evolved in our own immediate past. One of the purposes of feasts is to dwell on ritual, including the order of the proceedings. Deliberately "non-ritual" meals are discussed later.

The programme for a feast goes by the French name, *menu*, which derives from the Latin *minor* or *minutus*: it gives the details of the performance, as do the "minutes" of a meeting, but gives them prophetically, before eating starts. Menus are polite provisions at large feasts, because they enable guests to judge how much of everything they can eat and still find room to do the meal justice. They were used by restaurants from the beginning, as a list of the possibilities available, and as a form of advertising. Nineteenth-century restaurant menus were huge and often entirely wishful fictions, offering, according to Emile Goudeau in 1893, "a hundred soups, a hundred removes, three hundred entrées, two hundred roasts, four hundred side-dishes, and two to three hundred wines." The idea that *all* restaurants should have a menu, and that customers should expect everything on the menu to be available (though some dishes might still be subject to seasonal availability), became conventionalized only in the 1890s in France. "Today," Goudeau continues, "the short menu of a single sheet . . . offers only what it can produce: fifty to sixty dishes."

Menus written on tablets were known in ancient Greece and Rome, but far more common at feasts was the custom of someone—either the host or a specially instructed slave—pointing out the different dishes, explaining on occasion what each contained and how it had been made, and informing guests of the provenance, the freshness, the age of the foods and wines. The need for written menus at modern feasts is the result of an important change in the way formal meals were constructed, which spread in Europe and

America from about the mid-nineteenth century. The earlier presentation, known as dinner *à la française*, was divided, much as the Roman banquet had been, into two courses—three, if the introductory soup and fish is counted as a separate course—and dessert. But on the large table at which everyone sat stood a throng of dishes of many culinary varieties. The food itself lay there, to be described. Menus had to be written down for the guests when the new serving system was introduced: dishes then appeared in succession, from backstage as it were, and diners needed to be informed about what they could not yet see.

Formal dinners in the old style, *à la française*, had evolved from earlier medieval and Renaissance models, and "set" as a system in the course of the eighteenth century. Diners, let us say about twenty-five of them, would arrive at table to find it laden with food. Dishes, candles, salts, and ornaments had been placed with careful attention to the hierarchy of dishes and the position they could therefore command upon the table, to symmetry (dishes for dinner *à la française* often came in pairs), and to the relative heights of fruit pyramids and decorative objects. Order was especially important because of the crowding of the table: table-setters are warned to take care lest dishes "look as if they had fallen down like hailstones." The whole was designed to give an impression of opulence and abundance. And this, everyone knew, was but the first, the introductory course of dinner.

Among the dishes on the table were tureens containing two or more varieties of soup. These would be served first, then the tureens and the soup plates were removed and the former replaced by dishes called *relevés*, "removes" in English—perhaps roast mutton and turkey *en daube*, or two large fishes. The guests could also begin eating the *entrées*, the "entries" to the meal proper, which might include cheek of veal, cutlets, tongue, vol-au-vent, sole, chicken, sweetbreads, and eels. Two large *entremets* completed the picture: say, a cake and a fish. Around the large creations clustered little dishes, the *hors d'oeuvres*, placed literally "outside" the main "works": *hors d'oeuvres* stood spatially apart, not temporally first as they do today. They were what we might call "side dishes," and consisted of such things as small pies, anchovies, tuna in marinade, oysters, eggs, artichokes, and radishes. They sometimes remained in place during the first and second courses, while the larger dishes were changed.

The second course began after all or most of the dishes of the first course had been removed from the table. At this point the top tablecloth was rolled away, revealing a clean cloth underneath, to provide a pristine start to the second course. This consisted of the really big pieces: Jean-Paul Aron says that if a meal were a musical offering, this part of it would have had to be an organ chorale. In came various roasts, and the spectacular items which the French call *pièces de résistance*. (Nineteenth-century French *gourmands* loved to see themselves as "attacking" a particularly splendid dish, as if it were a fortress; a *pièce de résistance* was worthy of the siege machines and armed might of even the doughtiest *gourmand*. Another theory to account for the phrase is that diners had to "resist" eating too much from the lesser dishes and wait for these climactic creations to arrive.) Accompaniments to these large dishes were salads, vegetables, and sweet *entremets*: creams, jellies, ices; to our way of thinking, the second course was like a second complete meal. The last course, dessert, was cheeses, sweets, pastries, and fruit—but might include meat pâtés as well. It was set out on another fresh tablecloth, or on the gleaming bare wood of the mahogany table, each dish resting on a protecting mat. Dessert plates, knives, forks, and spoons were brought in especially for this course.

Dinner *à la française* could be adapted to special circumstances, such as the availability of a huge West Indian green turtle. In the mid-eighteenth century it was discovered that these turtles could be transported live to England, if kept in fresh-water tanks during the journey. A sixty- to one hundred-pound turtle could make a whole first course at a particularly splendid feast. Here the soup was the climax, and set in the centre of the arrangement. It was made from the head and lights of the animal. The belly was boiled, and the back roasted; these were two separate dishes, laid at the top and bottom of the table. Corner dishes or *hors d'oeuvres* were concocted of the fins and guts, done in clever rich sauces. Turtle dinners, and especially turtle soup, became signs of enormous prestige. Since not many people could find or afford the real thing, mock-turtle soup was devised, using a calf's head and plenty of Madeira. In the early days one did one's utmost to procure a turtle shell in which to serve it; people who had access to the genuine article could be relaxed on this point, and often served their soup in a tureen.

The two first courses each comprised a *mets* in French (something "placed" before the diner); the sweet, light, or amusing dishes which they included were intended to provide a break, or *entremets*, "between the *mets*." In the Middle Ages *entremets* were entertainments, put on for the guests while they were digesting one *mets* and getting ready to attack another. These theatrical presentations, called "sotelties" in English because of their subtle or ingenious inventiveness, could include singing, juggling, sword-dancing, mock battles, and masques symbolically representing the politics underlying the feast. Olivier de La Marche, maître d'hôtel to Charles the Bold, described an *entremets* during which he himself entered the dining hall sitting "on an elephant" led in by a giant in Saracen dress. Olivier represented the Eastern Church held captive by the Mohammedans, and, wearing a long white dress, he pleaded in a falsetto singing voice with the duke of Burgundy, lord of the feast, to undertake a crusade. When Charles the Bold married Margaret of York at Bruges in 1468, the *entremets* included a dwarf riding into the banqueting hall on a gilded lion, a pedlar pretending to sleep while monkeys stole his wares and gave out purses, brooches, lace, and beads to the company, and a dromedary ridden in by a wild man who threw coloured balls among the guests.

A "soteltie" could also be an entertainment in the form of a dish decorated to resemble a castle, or the Four Seasons personified in sculptures, or a series of warlike tents. Sotelties could equally be made of carefully carved wood and embroidered banners; very magnificent table decorations of this kind would often be given away after the dinner to favoured guests. But edible triumphs of the imagination were more appropriate, and more obviously created for this special occasion alone; they could be combined with the theatrical element, as when a jester leapt into a giant tureen full of custard, or when four and twenty blackbirds flew out of a pie. Bartolomeo Scappi describes a feast he organized in a garden in Trastevere, on May 31, 1536, at which there figured nine elaborate scenes which he had designed and created for the table. They included a sugar Diana with moon, bow, and dogs on a leash, accompanied by five Nymphs, each with appropriate attributes. There were butter sculptures of an elephant with a palanquin, Hercules with a lion, and a Moor seated on a camel, together with a pastry Paris holding his apple, confronting Helen and the three goddesses who sought to please him. The purpose of these creations was simply to impress and delight the guests, to give them something to talk about and to remember. (It will be noted that we are still describing them.) The *entremets* at eighteenth- and nineteenth-century meals had dwindled to dishes definitely meant to be eaten, but as a break in the proceedings, not to be taken seriously or "attacked" like the *pièces de résistance*.

The cleared or "de-served" table (*desservie* in French) is the origin of the term "dessert" which was given to the course brought on last. Dessert was intended in some measure to clear the palate. Scappi says that after the table has been cleared, hands are washed, clean napkins provided, and guests are presented with toothpicks in dishes of rosewater, stalks of fennel to chew, bunches of scented flowers to refresh the nose, and small comfits and confections. Anise and peppermint candies with the same purpose as these are still offered at the end of Indian dinners, and often after our own restaurant meals. Dessert, which descended from the post-prandial, mainly sweet "banquet" and "voydee," described earlier, became much more substantial than this, but it is still intended to be a light-hearted flourish to finish off the meal.

The guests at Baroque and Rococo dinners *à la française* sat much closer to each other than we do, round the edges of the huge table which was required for the laying out of all the dishes, candles, and elaborate centre-piece decorations. They were expected to eat from the dishes placed in the immediate vicinity of their places. It was permissible to ask a servant to pass a helping of something placed some distance away, especially if the host had recommended it as he spoke his "menu" at the beginning of the feast, but it was not done to ask too often. People were more obliged than we are to notice what neighbours were missing and could not reach, or carve, or cut without their help. The arrangement makes it easier for us to understand how the custom had arisen of sending morsels of certain delicacies as signs of favour towards friends seated at a distance; part of one's education in manners was learning which were the "noblest" morsels of meat, so that one could offer them to one's neighbours.

The enormous banquet-menus which have come down to us, listing a plethora of dishes, roasts, soups, game, fish, cakes, blancmanges, pâtés, and fruits in a seemingly horrific abundance and confusion, make more sense if we consider the way in which these were served, as parts of courses, each of which constituted what would today be a complete meal in itself, in its variety and range. But nobody was expected even to try all of the dishes; in spite of the spectacle which was considered *de rigueur* for a feast, one could, if one wished, eat very abstemiously indeed at a dinner *à la française*.

The Russian Prince Kourakin was credited, in the 1830s in Paris, with first introducing an entirely new way of serving feasts, the ancestor of our own. (Antonin Carême had observed the method when he was at the court of Alexander I in 1818, but had thought it unsuitable for French cuisine.) Félix Urbain Dubois, who served as chef to Prince Orloff in Russia, did a great deal to popularize the "Russian" method of service when he returned to Paris in the 1870s. Germans also frequently served their meals in this manner, and sometimes the new dinner sequence was called *à l'allemande*. Dishes began increasingly to be served in succession. After the soup followed by the *entrées*, a joint or large fish was typically brought in whole and first presented to the host and guests so that everyone could see it in its magnificent entirety. It was then either carved by servants at a side table or taken back to the kitchen to be divided into portions. These were carried round on platters to the diners, who took what they wanted and placed it on their own plates.

Ordinary, non-festal behaviour at meals had doubtless always relied on courses following one another, one course comprising one shared dish at a time. Feasts, however, demanded plenty, and dinner *à la française* offered that plenty as a feast for the eyes as well as the appetite; it also offered broad and immediate choice. The arrival of feasting *à la russe* made extravagance a matter of the number and quality of dishes appearing in succession; it also enormously increased the number of the personnel needed for the last-minute preparation and serving of all the dishes individually to the diners.

The more servants you could provide, the more impressive your dinner *à la russe*—and the more different from normal everyday eating. Among the rich it soon became polite to impose utter helplessness upon formal diners at table. No one was allowed to help themselves, or to pass or ask for anything: the numerous servants were there to be depended upon. An early complaint about the new system was that owners of enormous numbers of serving dishes were no longer able to display all their silver and valuable porcelain. Individual choice was abruptly curtailed, and hierarchy—apart from precedence in being served—was forced to become far more subtle than it had been: everybody was offered the same food.

The first course was soup and *entrées* (*hors d'oeuvres* soon became permissible, as first courses, only at lunches or informal suppers; and at modern dinners, egg or fish "entrées" follow the soup as a separate course). The plates were removed, and the next course appeared, then the next. Dessert, being the most decorative part of the meal, was sometimes on the table from the beginning, as in the version of dinner *à la française* which was called an *ambigu*. But dessert was never eaten until the table had been cleared and swept free of crumbs. On entering the dining room, guests at a banquet found at their places written menus, rather like theatre programmes; by the end of the nineteenth century, a special dessert menu was provided for an especially grand dinner.

Under the new system every course had to be a culinary triumph, because all of it was offered to everyone. Variety now lay in *temporal* juxtaposition and range, the decoration and presentation of each dish, and careful attention to overall structure as sequence. There was far more space left on the table now that it was not encumbered with many dishes; this was taken up in the 1890s by a new richness in floral decorations. Soon thereafter taste veered towards preferring plenty of free white space: guests were sitting further apart and concentrating more on keeping out of other people's way than on looking for opportunities to help them. And in any case tables, even for banquets, were becoming narrower, and adorned with fewer large silver and gilt objects.

Carving the meat at the table could be by-passed. Dishes did not have to stand on the table, waiting for people to help themselves;

they could be served at once, and hotter than ever before. No second helpings were offered round the table at formal meals. Very soon the long-drawn-out banquet was a thing of the past, and speed was prized as a sign of control and efficiency of service. (It should be mentioned however that as early as 1680, swift, choreographed battalions of footmen were greatly admired: one huge Parisian banquet was proudly reported to have taken only two hours to eat, even though it featured more than six hundred dishes.) By the 1920s in America, Emily Post was recommending that a formal evening, beginning with the arrival of guests at eight, should be over at no later than ten-thirty: introductions and pre-dinner talk, dinner with several courses served in succession, coffee and liqueurs (the women and the men taking these in two separate rooms), and general conversation afterwards had all to have been completed within two and a half hours. Luncheon parties began at 1:30 p.m. and "by 2:45 the last guest is invariably gone"; lunch itself consumed no more than thirty to forty-five minutes of anyone's time.

The formal dinner parties we have been considering cost a great deal of money, and were not expected to be everyday occasions, even for the rich. The formal dinners held today continue to be ceremonious expressions of various kinds of consensus and relationship. The food at a large banquet may struggle against being a mere pretext through its copiousness, complexity, and magnificence. A "buffet" meal foregoes table, immobility, and precedence, but partly compensates for loss of formal éclat by means of the display of food; it is a return to some of the principles of dinner *à la française*. But ceremonial intensity need not be commensurate with the quantity of food consumed: it is possible for a meal to consist of very little, as for example in the Eucharist or in the Japanese Tea Ceremony or Cha No Yu, where the simplest elements bear all the ceremony of a huge banquet.

The recent fashion for *nouvelle cuisine* is a social expression of the modern ideal that successful people ought to contrive to be not only very rich but also very thin. Food is not mounted in an extravagant and copious display, to be divided among the guests; modern individualists receive individual plates, each already bearing its exquisite and exotic, though meagre, portion. This might consist, for example, of a scattering of colourful shreds of vegetables and flowers. Or there may be three slices of duck breast lying on a sheet of concentrated but unthickened sauce; this sauce may be streaked or dotted with sauce of a different shade, *ton sur ton*. Sauces go under, not over, the food, lending it background and visual enhancement rather than comfortably cloaking it; the sophisticated skimpiness, expensive simplicity, and image-consciousness of *nouvelle cuisine* remind us of the fashionable clothes designed for its consumers. Japanese restraint and refinement of taste are suggested by layout, conscious juxtapositions, and the attention to colour, shape, and texture. Restaurants love *nouvelle cuisine* because anyone tempted to pander to an appetite must order several artistic creations in order to make up a meal.

The ancient three-fold pattern of the formal European dinner, even the dinner *à la française*—overture, climax, sweet final flourish—provides the structure for much simpler, and more simply filling, family meals: soup, meat and two veg (notice the three-fold principle in microcosm for this central course), and dessert. Tea and a biscuit do not constitute a proper meal; nor would a series of sweet dishes, or nothing but greens. Soup is a meal, but only if it is thick enough, and accompanied, say, by bread and cheese. Breakfast often fails to be considered a meal. The French are amazed by the British breakfast because—unlike the "Continental" repast consisting of coffee and a roll—a traditional British breakfast is a real meal, with cereal and milk or grapefruit in the place of soup or *hors d'oeuvres*, then eggs and bacon, and finally toast and jam (for dessert). For many people a meal is not really a meal unless it features something hot. And leaving out meat changes the entire structure of the proceedings. Vegetarian dishes cost less, are shared more easily, and can be cooked more quickly, in spite of the peeling and chopping, than meat. But they generally force us (to whom vegetarianism is not traditional) to use considerable imagination and effort to keep everyone happy, and convinced that they are eating a *meal*.

An airline dinner is a useful device to keep passengers pinned to their places and occupied for an appreciable length of time. People hurtling through the air in a metal tube, both uneasily aware of what could go wrong and stupefied with boredom, are deemed to require solace. Eating is comfort—provided that nothing untoward or unexpected occurs during dinner. In the early days of air travel, until the early thirties, travellers ate at tables set out in the plane, as in a restaurant. There were wine bottles, flowers, cloths on the tables, and male stewards (then called couriers) in white jackets, serving the meals. The shuddering and dipping of the aircraft caused spills, and the noise was so infernal that conversation had often to be carried on by means of written notes—but still things were done "properly," which is to say as far as possible as they were done on earth.

The first passenger aircraft in service after World War II fitted people into planes as though they were in a bus: airline management had realized that the future lay in cutting corners, increasing the numbers on board, and relying on the prestige of technology to make up for any loss in luxury. The gamble paid off. The new air travellers packed themselves into small spaces with a sense of fun, awe, and excitement. At first, seats were reversible so that passengers could turn them round and sit facing each other for meals; soon even that kind of encouragement to companionship was denied. But a three-course dinner with a hot meat component is still provided for everybody (except those who exempt themselves on health or vegetarian grounds), whether they are ready to eat or not, on the fold-out flap which anchors us to our places while dinner is served.

No effort is spared to impress upon us that we might be cramped and uncomfortable, but we are certainly experiencing a technological miracle. A tray is usually the receptacle for dinner, with pre-moulded compartments or fitted containers keeping every course separate. The separateness is spatial, not sequential: an airline meal is one course of a tiny dinner *à la française*. There will be cellophane coverings and plastic lids (we are hygienic, we are safe) and cutlery, pepper, salt, and paper napkin in a neat bundle. Until air travel became entirely banal, people used to save their little plastic knives, their mustard packets, and swizzle-sticks stamped with airplane motifs, as souvenirs; they were familiar objects, but small and sufficiently odd-looking to remind us of those strange meals aloft, and to prove to others that we had been there. The knife, for instance, often has an almost triangular blade: its bizarre shape looks convincingly modern, but it is actually designed so that we can eat with elbows so tightly compressed to our sides that the blade must descend almost vertically upon the meat. Nobody with any sense would eat the *hors d'oeuvres* of an airplane meal first. They are almost always cold, and the heated meat and two vegetables will cool off in a matter of minutes. We therefore attack the main course first, then rip open the *hors d'oeuvres*, toy with the stiff lettuce (most of us leave this "*entremets*" uneaten), then attempt the block of cake.

For the higher price of their tickets, first class and "business" class passengers get better food as well as wider seats. In their anxiety to please their richer customers, and to mark as clearly as possible the difference between them and the mere "economy" or "coach" class, airlines spend as much as four times the amount on meals for the well-heeled in their curtained-off enclosure up front as for those in more straitened circumstances behind. In North America food service is becoming an important selling point on aircraft, now that the few airline companies which are left have agreed among themselves to refrain from the turbulence that used to be caused by competitive fare cuts. So more imagination is being tried when compiling menus, china and metal cutlery are increasingly supplied, and meals, especially in the upper class, may even be served in courses (*à la russe*).

The "companions" close to our sides (we face other people's backs) are likely to be strangers. Meals are provided in strict accustomed sequence: breakfast, lunch, dinner, with "proper" tea-breaks and drinks, in spite of time changes, and regardless of the fact that eating events may take place with very short periods of sedentary time between them. An airline meal is not large: who would expect a large meal in our cabined and confined state? But it is invariably complete, and as complex as possible. It tries to carry all the connotations of a shared, comforting, "proper" dinner. It is supposed to supply a nostalgic link with the cultural presuppositions with which flying conflicts, such as warm kitchens, stable conditions, and the products of the earth. Manners, here, impose passivity and constraint; ornamentation is taken care of by the oddity of our being served dinner at all in such circumstances. There is no question of argument, and only very limited choice. Airline passengers are extraordinarily docile and uncomplaining. They give up space and ceremony, believing that this is only fair since they are gaining time and ought to be grateful for safety.

The three-part meal turns up again in another "food event," the time-saving hamburger. Here we have a meal wherein all references to companionship have been firmly deleted. Circles are symbols of completeness and self-sufficiency. The traditional European plate is round: diners at table are separated from one another, marked off by the cutlery, and expected not to trespass upon others' places. Circular hand-held hamburgers make the most individual and unshared of meals; table, tablecloth, conversation, and cutlery are all unnecessary. Utterly round buns (giant hamburger industries destroy every imperfectly circular bun) enclose disks of ground meat, every one of them exactly alike in weight, consistency, and colour. Subordinate to bread and meat, but colourful, glistening, and frilly, are the tomato slices and lettuce leaves. Trimmings may be chopped onions, ketchup, pickles, or mustard; a slice of processed cheese can supply an extra course.

Every burger is as self-contained, as streamlined and as replete as a flying saucer, and just as unmistakably a child of the modern imagination. Yet its substance is no more novel than hot meat and two veg, with sauce, condiments, and bread; and the roundness is not only self-sufficient but also old-fashioned, plump, and comforting. The middle section of the traditional three-course meal is piled up, each part clearly identifiable and contrasted with each, the whole symmetrically bracketed with bread. Our teeth bite down through the lot, as we skilfully hold it all together with fingers which must simultaneously contrive not to get bitten or to let parts slide out from the whole. The formality of hamburgers lies in their relentlessly predictable shape, and in the superimposed and separate layers of food which make sophisticated references to parts of the sequential model for a formal meal. Hamburgers are ready very fast (we do not see, and therefore discount, all the work which this speed and availability presuppose), and they take only a few minutes to eat: informality in this case cuts away time and clearly signals a disinclination to share.

The native Cantonese institution of *sihk puhn* uses informality to achieve something very different. A *sihk puhn* (literally, "eat pot") takes the sequence of nine courses which make up a formal Chinese banquet and collapses them all into one mass of food. (The English word "mess" originally designated a portion of food or a course; then it came to mean a portion shared among two, three, or four people; then a number of people eating together; and finally—perhaps because of a set of ideas similar to that expressed by *sihk puhn*—it signifies structure destroyed.)

Into a large wooden basin go bits of fat back pork, white turnips, chicken, dried beancurd skin, fish balls, dried pork skin, dried fish, fresh fish, and dried squid. Each ingredient is fried separately in peanut oil, and all are mixed together at the last moment—rather as a hamburger is assembled before the customer's eyes. A sauce is made of chopped green onions, sugar, black peppercorns, dried cassia bark, cloves, fennel, star anise, rice wine, fermented soy beans, fermented beancurd paste, garlic, and water; this is poured over all. *Sihk puhn* is consumed at a great concourse of people, and each bowl is shared among about eight of them. Every person takes a pair of chopsticks and an individual portion of rice. A party might sit at a table or squat on the ground; the first to come are the first served. People root about in the bowl with their chopsticks for bits of food; they eat at their own pace, and leave whenever they feel like it. There are no hosts for the groups (and we have seen how important the leadership of the host is to the conduct of a formal Chinese meal), there are no speeches, very little talking, no toasts, no precedence or places of honour, no dressing up, no head table, no waiters.

The point about a *sihk puhn* is that it is most emphatically not formal; and this expresses the intention of everybody at the feast to practise equality. As a local rice merchant told the anthropologist James Watson, "It shows that we all trust each other." Factory workers, bank managers, and farmers sit or squat side by side; the destruction of sequence is symbolic of the (temporary) collapse of distinction among the people present. *Sihk puhn* banquets are used to legitimize social transitions, such as marriages, the birth of male children, the "coming to personhood" of all babies thirty days after birth, and the adoption of male heirs.

While hamburgers demonstrate an agreement to be separate, *sihk puhn* signifies cohesion and trust. In both cases, equality is expressed not only through informality but also through careful attention to the principle of simultaneity, in one case through the careful stacking of the ingredients, and in the other through the wanton mixing of them. Hierarchy, both in America and in the Canton Delta, is expressed by formality, and therefore informality breaks down rank. And where formality takes time, its relaxation requires speed.

• *Helpings* •

We no longer eat from a common dish, but are each served, or each take, a portion on a plate. Seated upright on our separate chairs, we keep elbows in and hands off anybody else's dish. It was once a friendly gesture to give fellow diners choice morsels from our plates or from serving dishes set near us on the table, or for the host to express esteem for particular guests by passing them special delicacies. It is now permissible only where there is considerable intimacy for fellow diners to give each other "tastes" from their plates. Correct behaviour guarantees the absolute sovereignty of every diner over his or her domain: the individual plate in its designated "place," an area of the table safely bordered by its metal implements and impermeable to incursions from without, except for supplies and replenishments of food as permission for these is given.

The "place," at formal dinners still, is never permitted to stand empty. On entering the dining room, and nowadays on entering many an expensive restaurant, the prospective diner finds a "place plate," and upon it a napkin, filling the area of the "place." (If there is no place plate, a compromise may be made by having the napkin alone fill this space.) A place plate is often elaborate: it never has to submit to scraping and scrubbing, for it is never used for actual eating. It has no function but to ensure that the designated area does not lie empty; it will be removed when food is brought in. As each succeeding course is finished and the dishes are taken away, a clean place plate should always fill every place until the next course arrives—"A plate with food on it can never be exchanged for a plate that has had food on it; a clean one must come between." It is as though these patches of bare tablecloth cry out to be filled, like guests who must not be left unsatisfied lest they become "demanding" and a source of future trouble.

A place is not a place at a formal dinner without its plate. Formal etiquette is said to require that, when a very correct diner eats alone, four places should be laid, one at each of the table's four sides, and four even at a round table. Emily Post's 1928 edition shows a picture of such a table laid for the lady of the house lunching alone. The objects customarily found on the dining-room table at meals, such as places laid for other people, or side plates even when no bread and butter is being served, are often necessary to a diner's sense of well-being. An extreme example of this principle was the decision of the Igbo of Nigeria in the nineteenth century, made in a time of famine so serious that no coco-yam fufuu was available, and the people had to content themselves with soup. At the left-hand side of each diner, where comforting balls of fufuu would have been heaped up when people could eat their fill, a pile of stones was placed instead, and the soup was eaten with spoons since there was no food to dip into the bowl. In 1922, Emily Post suggested to Americans that hosts who could not provide wine set out at least two wineglasses and "pour something pinkish or yellowish into them" so that appearances at least would live up to expectations.

In fourteenth-century Europe, there were no "covers" or place settings as we now know them, set out at banquets for every diner. The "cover," as we have seen, referred only to the king's or the lord's food and utensils, which were covered with cloth to prevent tampering en route from the kitchen. Goblets for drinking did not stand on the table: wine was something you specifically asked to be served. Utensils were extremely simple—knives usually brought with them by the guests, and spoons, also occasionally the personal property of the diners, or shared with one or more companions. Soups and stews with their liquid sauces were served in bowls, one for every two diners; male and female couples shared, the men bringing out their knives to cut their partners' meat for them. The size of a banquet was estimated by counting these bowls, or *écuelles*: a thirty-*écuelle* meal, for instance, was a banquet for sixty. In England, two or four people would commonly share a "mess" or portion.

There were platters or "chargers" of food from which to choose what to eat, and before each diner his or her own trencher, of whole wheat bread about four days old; it was cut from a *boule* (a "ball" of bread; hence the French word *boulanger* for a baker) with a wide-bladed knife called a *tranchoir* or "slicer." Fresher, softer bread was also provided to accompany the meal. The trencher slices—often coloured a festive yellow with saffron, green with parsley or spinach, or pink with sandalwood—were trimmed into squares or rectangles roughly six inches across, and used by the diners as bases on which to place fairly solid pieces of food such as slices of meat cut from the roast. (A relic of this custom remains in the rounds of toasted bread upon which we serve certain kinds of meat, such as tournedos steak or game.) Thick sauces, into which pieces of meat could be dipped, were also placed on the trenchers, which might be changed several times during a meal. Lordly diners' left-overs, together with their trenchers soaked in meat juices, were commonly given to the poor after a banquet. Alternatively one could, as we have seen, wipe one's hands on the bread and throw it to the dogs. Bread could be used not only as a spoon and a plate, but as a napkin as well: waiters at table often used bread to protect their hands from hot dishes, though they were advised not to make the device too obvious. Firm trencher-bread was also hollowed out to make simple salt cellars or candleholders.

In Vergil's *Aeneid*, the hero receives a terrifying prophecy both from his father and from a harpy: that his company of refugees would not find a home until they had reached the point where they would "gnaw and devour their own tables" out of sheer hunger. One day years later Aeneas and his men realize with enormous relief that they have just fulfilled the prophecy: after eating what modern people would call a picnic on the banks of the Tiber, the company proceeded to finish off the bread upon which they had set out the meal. Having "eaten their tables," the founders of the future Roman Empire knew they had reached their fated goal.

Many modern societies still eat their meals off bread, baked broad and flat like large pancakes. Just as the Chinese believe that a meal should consist mostly of their starchy staple, rice, and expect it to be eaten to the last grain, so people who eat off bread "tables" often make it a point of etiquette to eat plenty of the bread. Traditional Rwala Bedouin make each diner eat a pathway through the bread, starting from a point near him on the edge of the food tray, and heading towards the central mound of meat and vegetables. The bread is torn swiftly and silently into bits, squeezed into pellets, and swallowed without chewing. When the eater finally reaches the meat he may not grab or even choose a piece, but must work his way under the heap and take whatever falls into the gap he has torn in the bread.

Medieval bread trenchers were sometimes placed on top of wood and pewter bases; these gradually in the course of the sixteenth century came to replace the bread. The extravagant dukes of Burgundy boasted trenchers made of silver-gilt. With individual knives and forks came hard dishes for everybody at the table; for ordinary people in England this could mean a square wooden plaque (the same shape as most bread trenchers, but larger), which might be hollowed out to hold food both solid and liquid, and fitted with a small separate hollow for the salt. Sometimes a wooden trencher could serve for two courses: you cleaned one side of it thoroughly, and turned it over to be used again. During the seventeenth century—a century earlier in Italy—trenchers became circular, which is now the traditional European shape for plates.

Spoons for everyone meant no more lifting of soup bowls to drink their contents. You *ate* your soup, even though soups had become far more liquid than they had formerly been—and "eating" now meant using a spoon. Our words "soup" and "supper" both come from "sop," the soaked bread that so often used to fill out the broth in its bowl; "soppy" people are as squishy as this bread. The bread left the soup as courses at banquets multiplied. Soup at a formal meal had never been a dinner in itself, as it most often was at simple and informal tables; and now it became merely a liquid overture to a banquet. It remained a fortifying "food," however.

A French etiquette manual of 1782 enumerates *serviette*, plate, knife, spoon, fork, and goblet for every guest, and warns that "it would be utterly gross-mannered [against *honnêteté*] to do without any one of these." The "cover" had been standardized, and the move towards the diversification of implements was already under way. It coincided with the specialization of the rooms in the European house, and with the proliferation of furniture with specific uses: different tables for dining, writing, kitchen, drawing room, cards, by the bedside, for tea, and so on; chairs made especially for the living room, dining room, kitchen, parlour; rocking chairs, couches, love-seats, and chaises-longues. By the mid-nineteenth century, the dining-room table set for a formal banquet was laden with floral arrangements, centre-pieces, and ornaments (epergnes, *plateaux*, silver and silver-gilt trees and animals, "compotiers" or large glass footed bowls), candelabra, glasses, serving dishes, and plates. All were laid out in an orderly fashion which still left defining areas of clear white tablecloth. The table bristled with cutlery. There were knives and forks made especially for cheese, for fruit, for fish, for shellfish, salad, melons, ice cream, cakes. Apostle spoons, or little Dutch spoons crossed, were laid on the table as ornaments. Ranks of glasses were set out for every guest, with distinctive shapes and sizes depending on whether they were to hold brandy, wine, champagne, sherry, or water. In 1890, Madame la Baronne de Rothschild owned a vast silver service which included, as serving dishes alone, a roast beef platter, lots of other covered meat dishes, two salmon dishes, a turbot dish, ten different dish covers, several serving dishes provided with warming devices, eight champagne buckets, numerous sauce dishes and dispensers, vegetable dishes of various kinds, eight dessert presenters, and much else besides.

A full dinner service now included soup bowls, dinner plates, and dessert plates; it became essential that formal dishes be given a rim, to distinguish them from merely "luncheon" dishes. No bread and butter plates were supplied at formal meals. It is still "not done" at formal dinners to provide butter, or side plates for spreading it on bread: a banquet is supposed to be rich enough not to need more butter; bread is broken and laid on the tablecloth in the French manner. The custom has for Anglo-Saxons an obstinately archaic air—which is often just what formality demands; it is like the aristocrats clinging so long to trestle-tables for dining, or modern women wearing veils at their weddings.

Bernard Gille, a Frenchman writing on English manners in 1981, explains to his countrymen that the English think of food as a matter not usually important enough to treat as a ritual, or worth interrupting other activities for; the English might, for example, watch television while eating. His French readers are warned that

Anglo-Saxons lay their cutlery upside down, with spoon bowls and fork tines facing upward. (The French custom, bowls and tines down, used to hold in Britain, too. British and North American owners of very old silver may lay their cutlery in the French manner in order to make sure no one misses the monograms, which were placed on what are now, for us, the backs of the forks and spoons.) The English, Gille goes on, lay the table for an ordinary meal with no plate in the space surrounded by cutlery; the French are accustomed to entering the dining room to find plates in place. French visitors to England typically feel their worst suspicions confirmed when they see the side plate, take it for a dinner plate, and think they will not be getting very much to eat. Not being used either to side plates or to cutting their bread, they often fail to leave the tablecloth crumbless and fear that Anglo-Saxons judge them unkindly for it.

Our system of serving the meal in courses means that we must supply many eating plates; but they are all very similar, their shapes corresponding to the three main sections of a meal: soup, main course (*hors d'oeuvres* are served on plates similar to, though often smaller than, those of the main course), and dessert. The French custom of supplying knife- and fork-rests, so that diners might use the same utensils for more than one course, was common in Britain and America during the eighteenth and nineteenth centuries. For some time it has not seemed proper to Anglo-Saxons, for whom formal hospitality should be expressed through the marshalling of as many dishes and implements as one can muster. Among family and friends, people have doubtless always saved their cutlery for another course. The story continues to be told, because of the charming informality, the consideration, and the insouciance about formal manners which it displays, that a Canadian waitress once advised visiting British royalty: "Keep your fork, Duke, there's pie."

We now use fewer implements at banquets than we did in the nineteenth century, but there are still so many of them that correct table manners are often described as "knowing which fork to use." At a correctly laid table there is supposed to be no problem whatever. The diner starts with the outermost knives and forks and moves inward, the innermost pieces being the last used. In countries where it is the custom not to lay the dessert spoon across the top of the "place," this spoon lies at the right, closest to the plate. One formal rule is that there may never be more than three knives laid at any one place; if there are more courses than three, a servant must supply the other knives. This seems to be another example of the curb on knives, a small and rather feeble complication one would have thought, but a rule which has nonetheless stayed in the book.

At a Japanese meal, chopsticks never vary except in size (hosts may use extra-long ones for passing on delicacies to guests), and spoons are occasionally needed. It is the shapes, sizes, and colours of plates, trays, bowls, boxes, and stacked drawers for food which are extremely variegated. The Japanese feel that the shape of a container and the material from which it is made should determine what food it shall carry; that taste, as well as factors such as seasonal changes and the character of festivals and occasions for celebration, should be reflected in the dinnerware chosen for a particular meal. Bernard Rudofsky (1965) quotes a *haiku* by Jûgaya, expressing Japanese astonishment at our lack of imagination in this regard:

A European meal:
Every blessed plate and dish
Is round.

Japanese pride in their porcelain, glazed pottery, and lacquer dishes leads them to make a special point of contemplating and praising the dinnerware, quite apart from the food or drink served in it. The Japanese Tea Ceremony, Cha No Yu, raises these civilities to a sort of sacramental ritual. (Praising the utensils is of course only one among the many strands of ceremony which make up Cha No Yu.) The host of a Tea Ceremony takes enormous trouble first to lay out cups and other objects which are "of a nature to harmonize with the probable thoughts and moods of the guests." They, in turn, must react and respond to his or her thoughtfulness. Once all have taken their carefully pre-ordained places—there is a special spot created by the seating rules for anyone present who might be the owner of a celebrated tea utensil—the person being honoured as "superior guest" must praise the arrangements. An extremely polite host will absent himself or herself while this is going on, so that the guests may be left at liberty to look around and comment on the dishes, the room, and its furnishings without embarrassing the host.

Later, as the host is making the fire so that incense may be lit and the kettle set to boil, the superior guest must ask to see the host's incense-burning equipment; the other guests should then manifest curiosity and admire it. If Cha No Yu takes place at noon, a few morsels of food may be eaten, and the guests go for a walk in the exquisitely laid-out garden while the host completes preparations for tea-drinking. He or she adorns the room with flowers and changes into different clothes, strikes a gong, and the guests return. The contemplation, admiring, and commenting begin again—the vases, the tea canister, the water-jug, everything is noticed, experienced, appreciated. The host traditionally provides only one special, simple, but intensely valued cup. It is filled with tea and each guest, beginning with the first, sips two or three times from it, wipes its edge carefully on a napkin, and passes it on. The first guest asks questions about the tea: where it came from, its name, its properties; the other guests silently savour it. The host drinks last, and—invariably—apologizes for the poorness of the infusion. The cup is then handed round the company, turned over, examined, and exclaimed over. Smoking may follow, then sweetmeats are served, with more, weaker tea in small cups, one for each person.

A traditional Chinese banquet takes a form that deliberately contrasts with an ordinary meal. Rice no longer *is* the meal, with all other food being thought of as luxurious relishes; at a banquet, eating too much meat and too little rice does not constitute extremely bad form. Instead, rice may not be eaten at all until the banquet is over, and asking for rice means you intend to stop eating—or drinking, if a drinking party follows the meal. Even at the end, you should not eat more than a mouthful or two of rice for fear of accusing your host, by implication, of not supplying you with enough special meats, vegetables, and fish. At a banquet, guests praise the food unstintingly; they apologize for putting the host to so much trouble, and wonder what they can have done to deserve such generosity, to become the recipients of so much skill. The host responds that they shouldn't be polite—it is they who honour this small and simple house. They then protest that they would never be merely polite—they really mean every word: the food is utterly extraordinary. One Chinese writer explains to Westerners that there are "no rules" to follow at a Chinese meal. You just do whatever you like (we have seen that this is far from being the case) and *show appreciation*. It is not enough, in Oriental manners, to "do the right thing": you must convince everyone present that you are impressed and delighted. Hosts work hard to earn this praise—and then respond to it by deprecating themselves and apologizing for their insufficiency.

In the West, wealthy hosts once grandly displayed their silverware on buffet shelves erected in full view of the banqueters, who were expected to be impressed. Yet today we do not lavishly praise the food—let alone the dishes it is served in. In France, for instance, a reverent silence might fall over the company as a magnificent instance of culinary art arrives on the table, and the *convives* might permit themselves murmurs of approval. But actually to praise the food, says a modern French work on manners, "makes you look as though you want some more." There is also, surely, a kind of inverted politeness involved: receiving food with exclamations of joy could be taken as surprise, or relief. *Not* praising it (while showing unmistakable if carefully subdued appreciation) shows that you would expect nothing less than excellence from your host. "Did you expect," one Victorian hostess is said to have asked with acerbity, "not to eat well in my house?" The host, similarly, must under no circumstances praise his or her own food, or comment upon it. "One rejoices silently in one's success," lays down the Baronne Staffe.

Given their officially cool and distant attitude to food, carefully instilled as it has been by education and relentless social pressure, Europeans and Americans are shocked and self-righteous when they encounter the other point of view. In many societies, guests are expected to express their appreciation not only verbally but also through inarticulate sound and action. Persians and Arabs are asked to slurp their tea or coffee with sighs of satisfaction, and always to drink more than one cup or risk offending. (Slurping tea and other drinks is very common; practitioners claim that it improves the actual flavour of the beverage enormously.) It is often customary to suck every scrap of meat from the bone, or to belch at the end of dinner, in order to gratify the hosts.

English and North American manners, on the other hand, insist that one be prepared to forego even the most delicious final morsel if it should prove difficult to raise it from the plate with a correctly constrained fork. (This is in complete contrast to the Chinese attitude that not a grain of rice should be left in the bowl.) The French share the general European reticence about showing enjoyment for food, yet feel at the same time that their sauces, and everything else they serve, deserve more respect: is it not polite to show an inability to resist eating everything because it is so good? On informal occasions they may take bread in one hand and wipe up the remains; it is more polite (because it denies the fingers and their facility) to break small bits of bread, impale them on a fork, and use these to mop up the sauce. One Parisian restaurant tried a few years ago to introduce a special spoon, to be used for collecting every last drop of their renowned sauces. It is a brilliant idea, but does not appear to have "taken."

Guests should never criticize the food. This is based on the same principle as not praising it, distance being the goal in both cases. Equally, distaste must be disguised out of consideration for the host. "If dishes are failures, you do not notice," states the Baronne Staffe with her customary firmness. "You eat bravely what is offered, as if it were good." She tells the story of a heroic Frenchman visiting England, who drank and (with perhaps excessive politeness) pronounced excellent a "frightful beverage" offered to him as a rare wine—he had been served medicine by mistake.

One should, in many societies, try at least a taste of all the dishes presented, on pain of offending the hosts. Even to hesitate is sufficiently reprehensible to be given a name in the Japanese list of faults. In our own culture, a guest may "beg off" a particular dish, especially if he or she can think of a reason with even vaguely medical associations. The excuse must be very sound if one is to escape eating the soup, however: soup is a basic foodstuff to our way of thinking, a symbol of love, and often thought of as a *remedy* for ill health. Served at the beginning of a meal, it is supposed to take the edge off everyone's hunger, so that refusing the soup is a little like avoiding rice at an Oriental meal. The corollary of this is that hosts must not serve too much of it—"to fill, or even to half fill, a soup-plate with soup would be in very bad style," says a nineteenth-century English book of etiquette. Full bowls of soup could conceivably represent a host's hope that the guests will not eat too much thereafter.

It is possible to criticize by eating "with the ends of the teeth," as the French put it, and this is strongly discouraged by the etiquette manuals. Even if an insect is discovered, says Branchereau, behave as though nothing has happened; hide it under a leaf at the side of the plate and carry on. A children's manners book (1701) recommends that one should eat without investigating too closely: "Smell not to thy Meat, nor move it to thy Nose; turn it not the other side upward to view it upon the Plate." It is rude in China to make obviously for the fresh and sizzling dishes; if there are warmed-up offerings from a previous meal, a polite guest will show equal interest in those—and others at table will notice whether or not he or she does so. Another thoughtless action is to reach for the salt or to sprinkle it over the food before you have tasted it. Different societies exhibit varying degrees of sensitivity to this. Visitors to Hungary, for instance, are advised to taste food before adding salt or paprika, otherwise the hosts might be insulted. According to the *Li Chi*, a guest who adds salt should elicit heart-rending apologies from a polite host.

Power struggles between men and women are frequently expressed through the medium of food. Wives may, subtly or not, raise or lower their cooking standards to express their pleasure; husbands may make it obvious that they appreciate or hate the food offered them. Children too can cause a flurry of parental concern by refusing to "eat properly." The eating disorder called anorexia ("not stretching forth the hand and taking" in Greek) usually includes love-refusal as part of its original strategy. Fasting is an ancient form of political protest, a way of withdrawing from society in order to think over one's life, or to demonstrate that one disapproves of what is going on; we have seen how eerie an empty chair can be at a feast.

Because food is such a powerful metaphor for love, and sharing it such a binding force, refusing to eat is often one of the most wounding insults one can wield. In Nigeria, for example, where anyone visiting must be offered food, a guest's saying that he has already eaten and wants no more food is interpreted as an expression of great anger on his part. A traveller in Iraq during the thirties described a Bedouin "enemy feast," where the rage of the guests was displayed by their taking up handfuls of the food, rubbing it over their shut mouths, and dropping it in the dust at their feet. (These men, everybody knew, were famished, which was why they had been invited. Desert hospitality enjoined that hungry people must be fed, even if they were known enemies.) Then, claiming, "We have eaten," they strode out of the tent, wiping their hands on their clothes or in their hair; contempt could not be more graphically expressed. Where a male holds great power over his womenfolk, he may make his displeasure with the cooking brutally clear: a Pedi husband, for instance, could cause consternation by ploughing his finger through the porridge in his bowl. "With the first offence he will eat some of it," but there will be serious trouble if it happens again. "Good cooking on the other hand is an accepted fact and will cause no comment."

The modern convention is to serve a meal in courses, the dishes being taken round the table by servants on formal occasions so that diners may take what they want; only the obligatory soup is presented already in its plate to a guest. At the usual servantless meal, platters are passed round the table for people to "help themselves." In this way, the hosts make it clear that they relinquish control over the quantities which guests may eat. Having sized up their own appetites and fitted their portions to them, guests ought to eat everything they themselves have put on their plates. Less formally, the host may rise to his or her feet and place food on the plates for the others, sometimes asking them how much they would like. Portions may be served directly onto the plates and then brought into the dining room, so that there is no choice involved. The obligation to eat what is placed before one then becomes ambiguous: eating everything shows appreciation—but then, the quantity served was not in the guest's control. Where people eat in the kitchen, as they do more and more commonly nowadays, either they are served from the stove and can state their preference, or they take food from dishes set in the centre. Choice, regarding quantity at least, returns to the serving ritual.

The word "helping" points to one of the most important kinds of table manners: companions must learn, or be pressured, to notice their neighbours' needs and supply them where they can. The Abbasids in the ninth century were enjoined to see to it that the people sitting near them lacked for nothing; they were to be encouraged to eat more, and to try dishes they had not yet tasted. All over the world, good manners tend to require that diners should offer food to their neighbours before taking it themselves. The Chinese must offer to pour tea for others every time they top up their own tiny cups; Nigerians should never dip porridge morsels into the relish before they have asked their neighbours to do so first.

Inferiors may be forbidden to ask for anything at table. It will then be incumbent upon others to demonstrate their superiority by watching out for them, an excellent device (provided that everybody works at it) for bringing lower ranks to the attention of higher at table. We have seen that a man sharing an *écuelle* with a woman was expected to cut her slices from their common portion, since he was the official wielder of a knife. Helping another with one's knife without asking their leave was a sign of great condescension. *The Court of civill Courtesie* (1591) explains: "Item to have an eie to such as sit nere beneath him and cannot reach, and peradventure for good maner (if they be any thing his inferiors) wil not speake; and if they eat not, to aske whether he shall be their Carver. But I would not have him be any mans Carver, without asking him first, except it be to one so much his inferiour, as he knoweth wil be glad of the curtesie he sheweth him, though hee like not the meate. For as to carve to a mans better is presumption, so to ones equal, except by asking first the question. . . ."

Children, like women, had to be helped, and could not serve themselves; they were also forbidden (at least according to the rules) to ask for anything. The monastic orders which impose silence at meals do so not only to enable the monks to listen to the texts customarily read aloud in the refectory; they are also enforcing the ideals of humility and consideration for others. A monk depends entirely on his neighbours to notice what he needs, to serve him with food and drink, and to pass the salt. A willingness to notice other people is essential to polite behaviour of every kind. A game is sometimes played during meals at summer camps in Canada: someone starts by doing something peculiar, say putting her finger on her nose. As soon as the others notice, they do the same, until only one camper remains oblivious to what is happening and over-absorbed in eating. The others point to him and shout, "Pig!"

Until the late eighteenth century in Europe, when "covers" were conventionally provided for everyone present, guests often brought their own spoons as well as their knives to dinner. They served themselves from the more liquid dishes with their spoons; the manners books exhort their readers either to wipe them carefully before plunging them into the central bowl, or when the food has been eaten to send them to the buffet to be washed before taking a second helping. Serving spoons began to be supplied first in Italy; they had become common in France by the late seventeenth century, but even then guests were at liberty to bring their own spoons and use them in the common dish. One must not slide food from serving dish to plate, says Branchereau at the end of the nineteenth century; serving implements once provided must be put to use, for dexterous *lifting*.

At formal dinners today, no one may take a second helping: dishes are passed but once. The emphasis is on speed and variety. Eating a lot—of one dish, anyway—is not elegant. (This was not the case at dinners *à la française*, where, just because everything was laid out on view, diners were thought to be especially polite if they ate—repeatedly if they liked—from only one or two of the dishes standing near their seats.) At family meals or dinner with friends, on the other hand, it may be important to the self-esteem of the hosts that guests should eat more than one plate of food. In Denmark, at least some seconds must be accepted, and visitors to Bulgaria are warned to take small portions, because they must eat several of them, and even then, "don't just nibble." At an ordinary meal in China, taking more *cài* or relish is conditional upon there being rice still in one's bowl—it is rude to "fill up" on *cài*. It is an ancient rule in Japan never actually to ask for a second helping of anything but rice or soup. In France, a female guest of honour must accept an offer of a second helping, because only if she does so can anyone else have one.

A host, to show his or her generosity, may urge guests repeatedly to eat. The host wants to give, and acceptance of the food often means a strong though vague obligation incurred by the guest. We have seen that in many cases the host will go so far as not to eat anything himself; but guests in another's house may not, except for reasons of health, great grief, or an officially declared state of fasting, claim the same prerogative. A game with tremendously complex rules and innuendos may have to be played: Guests will refuse more food; hosts will press them to eat. Ritual might decree that three refusals are required. A host who fails to reiterate his plea can therefore show real malice.

The Sherpas, Sherry Ortner tells us, are culturally imbued with resistance to receiving anything from others in everyday life; the host's pressure is necessary, or the reluctance of even the most well-intentioned guests would prevent them from enjoying his party. On the other hand, the host never *really* knows why his guests are so hard to persuade—are they being hostile, or merely polite?—and he may become genuinely anxious. He must ensure that he wins in the contest of wills, however, or a guest might go away with "an empty mouth"—a condition that ineluctably spells trouble.

Ritual refusals work only when pressure is also exerted to override them. The British custom is that one should not force food upon people; it is part of the whole elaborate scheme in which one should appear to consider food to be relatively unimportant, and assume that nobody is obsessed with eating. Henry Fielding wrote in the eighteenth century that no host should urge his guests to eat more than once, and that he should never complain that they have no appetite: such importuning, in his opinion, is "sometimes little less than burlesque, and always impertinent and troublesome." The English still baffle foreigners by the *unspokenness* of their preferences and resentments, and the extraordinary sensitivity to non-verbal signs which this necessitates in everybody. French visitors intending to stay with families in England are warned by Bernard Gille in 1981 that the first meal eaten with hosts is vital. You absolutely must eat as much that first time as you usually do, even if you are exhausted from the trip—under pain of being underfed for the rest of your stay. For your hostess will watch closely what you eat the first time, and base her estimate of your appetite, when planning subsequent meals, upon that information. He suggests that you might say, "No thank you! Excuse me, I am not very hungry tonight. But I like it very much and I will eat far more tomorrow." And never, he warns, refuse a second helping if you really want it; your hosts will maddeningly take you at your word.

In most cultures, however, hosts are expected to go overboard to make their magnanimity felt. Arabs heap guests' plates with food and beg them to eat (a manners book for foreigners assures us, however, that it is not necessary to consume everything). It is polite also to pour tea into glasses until it slops into the saucer—precisely as Europeans and Americans are taught *not* to do. The Arab custom continues to express the idea of generosity experienced by the Old Testament Psalmist who rejoices because his "cup runneth over."

One of the many legends about Napoleon's friend the archchancellor and gourmand Cambacérès is that he once provided a magnificent sturgeon for a dinner in honour of the tsar. (An alternative version of this story makes the host Talleyrand and the fish a giant salmon.) The great fish, weighing 162 pounds, was carried round to be viewed before serving, with the accompaniment of a flute and violins (Athenaeus says that sturgeon was always served to music at Roman banquets). Besides the musicians dressed as chefs, there were four footmen bearing torches and two kitchen assistants wearing knives and carrying the sturgeon laid out on leaves and flowers, resting on an eight- to ten-foot ladder; the head porter, ornamental axe in hand, marched at the head of the procession. Guests stood on their chairs to see the fish, correctly overlaying restraint with admiration for this special occasion. When the mighty dish had been borne round the table and was being carried out of the dining room for carving, one of the bearers made a false step, and fell on one knee. The fish slid from its garnished ladder to the floor. The horrified guests struggled to hide their disappointment and embarrassment, cried out in despair, shouted advice about how to save the situation. But Cambacérès, with ancient Roman simplicity and dignity, quietly said, "Serve the other one." It was even larger (187 pounds) and more splendidly adorned than the first. The intentional accident had served merely to thrill the guests and magnify their host; the first fish had been "sacrificed to honour the second."

Guests in many cultures are given food to take home with them. Accepting the rest of one's portion as a takeaway parcel is apparently the only way to appease an anxious Sherpa host when a guest really cannot eat another thing. We have seen that in ancient Rome guests brought napkins with them, which they filled with food and took home to their uninvited wives and families. Hosts may, as we have mentioned, show their esteem during the meal by passing delicacies to certain guests; the recipient, of course, is absolutely bound to accept and eat. The *Li Chi* says that if you are fortunate enough, as a guest, to be given a piece of fruit by the ruler, you should suck the kernel clean and put it down the front of your robe, to show that you are not throwing any of his gift away.

When giving is seen as the first move in a chain of reciprocal obligations, it is a sign of strength. The host, giver of the dinner party, often makes his position clearer still by bestowing food directly upon certain guests. King Menelaos, in Homer's *Odyssey*, honours two special guests by giving them the largest and choicest portion, the "fat roasted chine of an ox," which was his because he was the king. Among Jews and Greeks the host's gift, selected and presented (however this was done) to a guest singled out by his attention, was thought of as itself a token meal; in Greek it was known as *psomis*, "the morsel." Jesus gave Judas "the morsel" at the Last Supper, when the time for the betrayal came. In the Book of Genesis, Joseph, a prince in Egypt, sent food from his solitary high table to where the visiting Hebrews were sitting at dinner; he ordered five times as much to be given to his brother Benjamin as to anyone else. Xenophon describes how the magnanimous Thracian Prince Seuthes "would take the loaves lying in front of him, break them into small pieces, and toss them to whom he liked; the meat likewise, leaving only enough to taste for himself." Then the other diners were expected to follow suit.

Modern Western custom is, of course, for each person to control his or her own "place" and portion, and to show politeness by not impinging on others. Sequence may be hierarchical, but substance never—except insofar as the best pieces may be taken by those first in line. We must watch for anything we can offer our companions, pass what they need, ask if we may fill their glasses—but giving them a piece of our portion and expecting them to eat it seems to us either importunate or a sign of favouritism. We are expected, while at table, to treat everyone with equal benevolence, and not to single anyone out even in conversation, let alone in the matter of servings and slices. The rule is that food may go from serving dish to plate and thence back to the kitchen—but not from plate to plate: there must be no crossing over the boundaries laid out on the table by means of the cutlery. A feeling of dismay or even disgust (hastily thrust out of sight, of course) may arise at being presented with something from another's plate, and probably transported by means of another's cutlery. It follows that *breaking* the rule, by giving someone a piece of food from our plate or receiving one with pleasure, is a sign of intimacy. In India, where the "apartness" of diners is upheld by pollution avoidances, such an act would be unthinkable except between mother and child.

• *Carving* •

Before 1500, the Indians of South Dakota depended for their meat meals mostly on bison and antelope, which the men would hunt and kill, or drag from the rivers in winter when animals fell through the ice and drowned. Hunting usually took place a long way from the home base, mostly in order to avoid packs of dogs and wolves which lived at the edges of human territory, scavenging and hoping to share the results of the hunt. Having obtained the prize of a large animal, the Indian band would have to transport it very quickly home over a considerable distance; as meat became high, dogs, wolves, and bears would be drawn to it by the smell.

In order for the men to move quickly, the burden had first to be lightened. Archaeologists have found heaps of bones at the sites of Indian villages, and worked out which parts of the beasts were customarily left behind at the hunt-site. These included: the heavy heads (though muzzles were cut off and taken home to become ingredients in stews and soups, and one jaw, the lower, probably with the tongue attached, was often brought back); the vertebrae; the pelvis; and the rather meatless lower limbs. It is known from early ethnographic descriptions that the butchered meat would probably have been cut in great hunks and piled into one half of the split hide and covered by the other half. Some of the bones were transported back for extracting the marrow, for use as hoe-blades and hide-scrapers, and for pounding into small pieces and boiling down to produce bone-butter. A few bones and meat scraps were carried back to be fed to domesticated dogs. The more careful carving, and the dividing of the meat among the village inhabitants, would be the women's job after the meat had arrived safely home.

But before the animal was hauled back, the men must have feasted on its inner parts, the brains, heart, liver, kidneys, and sometimes the tongue; these portions would go "off" quickly and tasted best when absolutely fresh. This was the hunters' prerogative. Hunters were mostly male, though some women might also have taken part in catching and carrying prey. Eating the innards together was an immediate and handsome reward for the group's success.

In Europe during these same centuries, hunting was still fairly common, and a sport for the nobility. The equipment for an aristocratic medieval huntsman always included a *trousse*, a leather scabbard containing a chopper, a saw, several different knives for hide-stripping and specialized cutting tasks, and spits for grilling offal over a fire before the triumphant return home with the rest of the animal carcass. Possession of a *trousse* expressed the hunter's optimism as he set out; it was part of a nobleman's personal equipment, and could be indispensable to his honour. The inner parts of the animal which the noble hunter cut out and ate at the site of the kill were called in French the *parties nobles*; they included the brain, the dark, bloody, shiny bits which were clearly essential to the animal's life, and sometimes the genitals. The "vitals," apart from the brain, are equated in many languages with personal courage: in English, a brave man has "pluck" and "guts," whereas a coward could be mocked as "lily-livered." Hunters, eating the viscera of their victims, were consuming the essence of strength and bravery.

These once-precious animal parts seem to have become devalued in England towards the end of the eighteenth century; in about 1800, city slaughterhouses were giving them away to the poor. Hunting was no longer economically important as an ordinary source of protein. "Organ meats" were difficult to transport to points of sale while still fresh (they had very poor "shelf life"). Their fall from favour was so precipitous that, for instance, an old collective term for the viscera, "numbles" ("umbles" in some dialects), came to be thought of as a version of "humble." A person, therefore, who "ate humble pie" (with a filling of kidneys, liver, and so on) was joining the ranks of those whose status was low. Butchers called viscera "offal" (they fall off in the butchering); and "garbage," meaning viscera and entrails, began to signify refuse of every kind. In any case, there was in Anglo-Saxon countries an increasing distaste for thinking about what meat had been before it was slaughtered; and the trouble with the inner organs is that each of them has its own peculiar texture and shape, and every one has a function that is all too familiar. The ancient distinction between "meat" and "innards" was maintained, although the value system was reversed. Offal tends still to be called by a term which covers all of the inner organs; such terms preserve the distinction between "innards" and "meat," but euphemistically help the mind to slide past the particularities by refusing to name them.

In the modern ceremony of the barbecue, there remains an echo of the ancient ritual of the impromptu meal at the scene of the hunt. Barbecues are special; they are weekend treats, celebrations of good weather. The fare is "party" and "picnic" as opposed to "everyday." These are therefore occasions when men may jocularly don aprons and set about enjoying the process of cooking. Barbecues begin with male-dominated firemaking. They take place outside the house— though not necessarily very far from it—and the "masculine" live fire is accompanied by the special grids, knives, and skewers. The women tend to take care of the salads, the plates, the dessert, and washing the dishes afterwards.

In many societies that depend upon success in the hunt for survival, the sharing out of meat becomes an exciting event, with enormously complex rules and meanings applied to it. Among the Copper Eskimo of the Canadian North, for example, the division and distribution of the flesh of a ringed seal is turned into a sophisticated expression, offered by the lucky and the skilful, of friendship, generosity, and orderly care for the good of the entire group. Any ringed seal caught must be shared. Men in the village belong to a *piqatigiit*, or system of associates, membership in which is linked directly to the body parts of the seal. When a dead seal is towed into the village by one of the hunter's dogs, the men who are related in this manner (it is a matter of friendship, not kinship) send their sons, daughters, or wives to the returning victor's house with skin buckets for the parts of the seal that are due to them. There are flipper associates (entitled to hind flippers from the animal), liver companions, hind-quarter companions, associates of the sides of the breast, and so on. As many as fourteen bonds of friendship may be expressed by the body of each ringed seal. The hunter keeps a portion of meat for himself and his family, and gives everything else away; if associates are absent from the village, their pieces go to villagers not entitled to them by special companionship. Sharing, the ethnographers report, is *strictest* when returns from the hunt are just equal to food needs, or fall behind them.

Other hunting groups have similar systems of food distribution. Australian Aborigines, for instance, are very particular about how they cut and share the kangaroo. All their meat-division and cooking techniques are laid down in traditional law, established by the creation ancestors. A kangaroo is split in two parts—body and tail—and fitted into a pit with live coals surrounding its flesh. Earth is piled on top, leaving only the kangaroo's feet protruding. Once the cooking is finished, the pit is uncovered and the meat is cut along the ritually correct dividing lines by the hunter, who hands out the meat which is traditionally their portion to his male relatives. The hunter himself might get very little: he relies on those he is feeding to give to him when they are successful in a later expedition. Women wait in the background to be given pieces of meat by their menfolk; this ceremony has been described as "men's time."

In south-eastern Algeria, non-nomad Touaregs club together to buy and share out a camel. The heart of the animal goes to the village chief, and a kidney to the scribe, or to the chief if he is lettered. The rest is divided into eight parts, and then the systematic ensurance of equality in the shares begins. Each part is divided also into eight, and eight piles of meat are formed, with pieces from all the original eight sections in each. Several people will contribute the money to buy each pile of meat. These groups now choose tokens to represent them (a stone, a knife, a straw); then someone—preferably a child—is blindfolded and led to the mounds of meat in turn, to drop one token at each heap. The group must accept its meat as a fair share; they then set about dividing it among themselves. The butchers who are essential to this elaborate performance are not paid, but allowed to buy fat from the hump, liver, and tail; the burier of unwanted remains receives the right back foot; indivisible parts like the head and the skin must be sold separately.

Civilized people are easily reminded, when they share out the flesh of animals, that they have killed, or sacrificed, in order to feed themselves. An animal, moreover, has an awkward shape: it has only two buttocks, two hind legs, a limited number of ribs. The quality of the meat varies greatly from cut to cut; forethought must be given to how people are to be served and satisfied. Hierarchy can be expressed by the allocation of pieces in descending order of desirability, and even of size. Meat is good to use for this solemn ceremony because it is rich and expensive; it used to be eaten comparatively rarely, and then on special occasions. Until recent times, meat has had exceptionally poor keeping qualities, which meant that it had to be disposed of quickly—all of it tended to be divided out in one operation. For thousands of years it was placed before the family as a result of male enterprise and triumph; and men, with their knives, have insisted on carving it up, and even cooking it before the expectant and admiring crowd. Vegetables, on the other hand, were most often the result of the steady, unexalted, cooperative, and often mainly female work required for collecting them, or for tending them in the fields. Vegetables cost plenty of effort and care, but far less guilt, drama, and intensity than that which attends the catching and slaughtering of animals. A joint of meat served for dinner restricts the number of guests invited; vegetarian meals permit far more elastic arrangements because they are easily shared and extended.

Sharing meat *can* be made into an expression of egalitarian ideals—but only if the flesh is reduced to small fragments, as relish, soup, or stew to be eaten with vegetables, as pie filling and stuffing, or as minced and re-formed meat cakes. A whole beast cut up in public, on the other hand, expresses the unity of the group that consumes it; but if the pieces offered retain their character and everyone gets something different, then meat division can dramatize at the same time the individuality and the ranking of everybody at dinner. The hunters who gathered round to roast the fresh innards of their prey felt themselves to be a close inner group, both set apart and deserving of their privilege. (They also, as Walter Burkert points out, shared the guilt of the killing.)

Ancient Greeks normally dined on red meat only when the animal had first been ritually sacrificed. A sacrificial beast was usually a domestic animal, chosen as a perfect male specimen among the herds and flocks; meat-eating after sacrifice was, in Greece as in ancient Israel, an integral part of a farming, rather than a hunting, economy. After the killing (about which the Greek texts are always extremely euphemistic—vase paintings may depict mythic scenes of human sacrifice, and also killing as a climax to the hunt, but they never show an ox being ceremonially put to death, even in otherwise detailed sacrificial scenes), the animal was laid on its back and the *mageiros*, the "knife-wielder" or butcher, slit its torso up the middle. Heart, lungs, and liver were removed in one piece, then the spleen; the digestive organs, stomach, and intestines were set aside to be turned later into sausages; and finally the kidneys were revealed and extracted.

The liver was immediately examined for its prophetic properties. The lobes, the portal vein, the gall sac, the shine of the liver's surface were all portentous. The backbone and thigh bones were cut out and covered with fat, to be burned in the fire for the gods, who doted on the aroma of their smoke. The priests and other important people present at the sacrifice made shish-kebabs of the prized viscera, grilled them at the fire, and ate them. Occasionally the priests would later cook and eat the unburned offerings set aside for the gods; they received the animal skins in payment for their office. The bulk of the other, ordinary meat was set aside to be eaten later by *hoi polloi*. Hierarchy having been given its due in the eating of the sacred innards (some etymologists believe that the very word "hierarchy," in Greek "charge over sacred things," came from priestly superintendence over animal sacrifices), the rest of the meat was cut up into fairly equal pieces and threaded onto skewers to be carried off and sold or eaten elsewhere.

The Greeks also knew the carving of a whole sacrificed animal, skinned and roasted, before the assembled company of diners. Here the group was clearly ranked according to the pieces allotted; these kept their whole original shape rather than being cut into collops. An especially good piece, such as a large chine of pork, was a *geras*, or gift denoting honour. The privilege represented by a piece of meat was expressed by the superiority in tenderness and savour of the portion, its size, or its singularity. (The viscera were prized for existing in smaller quantity than the rest of the meat, and also because there is only one heart and one liver; each of these could be presented to someone as a special privilege.)

The ancient Greek word for "fate," *moira*, means literally a portion, a piece of meat from the ritually sacrificed animal. This serving expressed the recipient's honour among the assembled guests, their estimation of him: it amounted symbolically to what we still call his "lot" or his "portion" in life, his "slice of the pie." A *moira*, as portion of a whole, could also be a piece of land, or a section of the universe. When the three eldest brothers, the greatest of the Olympian gods, drew lots for the three main divisions of the world, Zeus received the heavens, Poseidon the sea, and Hades the Underworld (Earth was herself a goddess, or, belonging to Gaia, was a portion already "served"). A shared sacrificial meal was a *dais* or "division," from the verb "to cut up"; it is meat which informs the metaphor. The distribution of meat, at a civilized meal or *dais*, was supposed always to be "equal." This meant either that everyone received the same amount (an egalitarian arrangement), or that everyone's part was equal to what he *deserved* (which is hierarchical or meritocratic). Both points of view might be expressed in the same meal, as we have seen, by the exclusive allocation of the "innards" to a privileged group, as opposed to the equal sharing of the "meat." The slight to one's honour which could be suffered through getting a portion of meat beneath one's due can be represented by the rage of Heracles when, after the completion of his Labours, he was invited to dinner but served a "lower" helping of meat than those given to the three sons of his tormentor, Eurystheus. He slew them all.

Fate or *moira* is closely linked to the idea of drawing lots (as in the myth of the dividing up of the world), and to oaths and curses—words which create ineluctable events in the future. When Atreus chopped up his brother's children and served them up to their father as his portion at dinner, Thyestes cursed his murderous brother and all his house. This curse was to operate relentlessly for generations, as the fate of the House of Atreus. Thyestes accompanied his utterance with its perfect physical embodiment, the destruction of the dinner-time civilities: he kicked over the table and sent the dishes crashing to the floor.

In medieval France, there appears to have been a fashion for swearing at dinner over the meat before it was carved. A "great bird" was chosen for this solemn ceremony: a peacock, swan, heron, or crane—or a pheasant, as in the famous Vow of the Pheasant made by Philip the Good, duke of Burgundy, at Lille in 1454. The guests one by one made a vow over the fowl, in the presence of their fellow diners and co-conspirators. The bird was then cut up and everyone ate their portions. (At Philip's Pheasant Banquet, the bird sworn over was alive and wearing a jewelled collar. It does not appear to have been eaten—at least not immediately.) The vow was intended to be irrevocably binding and, as such, fateful.

A peacock, the "greatest" of birds, was prepared for an important banquet by being skinned carefully so that its feathered mantle remained intact. The flesh was then stuffed, roasted, "endored" or gilded with egg yolk, and sewn back into its feathers, with the tail splendidly raised, the feet gilded, and the head, complete with its aigrette, restored. On especially magnificent or dramatic occasions the peacock, holding in its beak a wad of flaming wool, was brought into the hall on a gold or silver dish by a beautiful young female member of the host's family, and presented to the most honoured male guest. He had to pronounce a vow, holding his hand stretched over the bird— that he would, for instance, be the first to strike an enemy with his spear, or the first to plant his standard for the honour of his lady upon a besieged town—and he then had to demonstrate, before the assembled company, his skill at carving the fowl over which he had sworn. The carver might be expected to wear an iron band on his arm thereafter, to symbolize his fateful vow and remind him constantly of it.

A carver, where meat is ceremonially divided before the company, is the focus of everyone's attention. In the Middle Ages he was one of the lord's friends, a nobleman, a relative, perhaps his son. The carver alone handled unsheathed knives before the eating began; and only he could keep his hat on where all the other servers at table had to remain bare-headed in deference to the diners. He walked into the hall at the head of a procession, lit with flaming torches in winter, which included the Taster (sometimes the Carver carried out the tasting as well as the cutting), the Cup-Bearer, the Butler (the "bottler," who saw to the drink), and the Panter. The last-named official was in charge of the pantry and the bread (*pain*). He too wielded knives: one for large loaves, a special parer, a trencher knife, and a "mensal" knife for cutting the value-laden upper crust off the bread and presenting it to his lord.

To cut and present meat, first to the lord and then to the company according to their rank, was to "do the honours." Honour, writes Giles Rose in 1682, "is more Spiritual than the material," and the carver was therefore higher in rank than "those that employ themselves in nothing but what is meerly corporal." Since his role was theatrical and ornamental as well as practical, he should be a "handsom comly person of a good behaviour and well clad"; one sufficiently educated in the niceties of portions; and sensitive enough to "study the appetite of his Master, to the end that he may always present him with that bit which is most agreeable to his Princes Stomach." By the sixteenth century, the "prince's" carver was a professional, well born but not necessarily of the nobility. He had, if he was to hold a position at an Italian court, to learn his craft and perform it with the panache and the skill of a juggler.

A manual for carvers, from the pen of Vincenzo Cervio (1581), is one of the earliest absolutely specific and detailed instruction books we possess in any field. Cervio takes nearly two thousand words to explain how to divide a pheasant in four, and four thousand for the carving of six platefuls of peacock. He "does not wish to discuss" the carving of an old, tough, and ill-adorned peacock, except to say that in such a case you should not bother to try cutting off slices of anything but breast, and you could leave it on its dish for carving, in the dreary manner of the French or the Germans.

No carver worthy of the name, in Cervio's book, cut up meat on a dish. He lifted the entire joint or fowl up into the air, speared on the carving fork held in his left hand, and sliced pieces off it by wielding an extremely sharp knife in his right; wafers of meat fell to the small plate underneath (a *tondo*: Italian plates were round), in perfectly organized patterns—not overlapping too much, warns Cervio, so that the plateful would look "more ample." A swift tidying of the slices with the knife-point was permissible, before salt, lifted from its receptacle with another knife, was sprinkled over them with a flourish and plenty of *grazia*, and the dish presented to the diner.

As a carver, one had first to decide exactly how to divide a bird among the number of people to be served; and then there were questions of who got what. It was best to give pieces from several parts of the body to each—say a bit of breast, some wing, some thigh. It is clear that noble diners ate very sparingly of each of the many animals which figured at any meal: merely slivers and tiny morsels of as many different "honourable" meats as possible. Birds were almost never completely consumed at table; often only the breast was eaten, and the rest was removed to the kitchen, perhaps to be made into soups, and perhaps to feed servants and retainers. Good carving, Grimod de la Reynière was to point out in 1808, permitted great economy; messy carving caused waste.

Spearing the animal was especially important, Cervio wrote: there was intense shame to be endured if the meat fell from the fork in front of the assembled company, most of whom were presumably watching the carver intently; such shame was proportionate to the glow of pride he enjoyed when he performed his feat perfectly. It was not uncommon that the high table would applaud an especially fine demonstration of carving technique. As carver, one had to know exactly where to drive in the tines; how to stand, for the whole of one's body was on view: one was not to twist the torso or agitate the head, no matter how contrary the joint proved to be. Then there was the manner of lifting the roast from its dish, touching it with the knife's point in a beautiful gesture; the skill involved in turning the heavy burden on the fork with precision and an appearance of effortlessness, so that the knife could pare the surfaces as thinly as possible and dispatch the slices to their best positions on the *tondo* lying on the table below. Everything had to be done as speedily as possible, for a roast in mid-air is a roast that cools fast. An especially impressive trick—performed, admits Cervio, out of pure *galanteria*—was to cut with two knives at once, both gripped in the right hand with one finger separating them. One could of course give in when confronted with something as large as a shoulder or leg of mutton, and facilitate matters by wrapping a napkin round one end and holding the joint up to depend from the left fist while it is cut with the knife in the right; but brandishing meat aloft on a fork must always remain *più bello*.

Meat could be carved away from the table, on a *credenza*, but Cervio is contemptuous of would-be carvers who are not prepared to perform in full view. One could also cut the meat on the dish and present slices to the lord on a wide-bladed "presenting" knife, or even on a fork. The almost invariable scattering of simple salt over meat, as Cervio repeatedly recommends, was new; medieval carvers had been expected to know just what sauces each morsel necessarily required, and to slice or mince and sauce portions before serving them. (Especially large establishments sometimes employed a Saucer, working in tandem with the Carver, to prepare and serve these relishes.)

Some echo of the mystique attached to the carver's art reaches us from sources such as John Lydgate's poem, *The Hors the Shepe and the Ghoos* (1478), and Wynkyn de Worde's *Boke of Kervynge* (1508, 1513). In such works, the carving of every bird and fish, and some meats and pies, is given a separate English verb, the effect being to make its performance a separate object of admiration. The carver is exhorted to "*alay* that pheasant" (remove its wing, *aile*), "*rear* that goose, *lift* that swan, *raise* that capon" (each of these terms perhaps refers to cutting upwards from underneath the joints, or to the methods Mrs. Beeton was later to advocate, such as lifting the body of a partridge from its rear end, up and away from the legs, which are held fast to the plate). "*Untach* [untie] that bittern," the list goes on, "*unbrace* that duck, *unlace* that coney; *leach* that brawn" (slice it, from the Catalan term *llescar*; "brawn" means lean meat, usually pork), "*frust* that chicken" (reduce it to *frusta*, or fragments), "*spoil* that hen, *disfigure* that peacock, *dismember* that heron, *brawn* that gull" (slice the breast only), "*thigh* and *shred* that pigeon, *wing* that partridge and that quail, *splay*, *splat* and *chine* that bream, *gobbet* that trout, *unmail* that crayfish, *tame* and *mine* that crab" (broach it—French *entamer*—then take the flesh from the shell). A crab, says John Russell crossly in 1460, is "a slutt to kerve and a wrawd wight" (a froward or perverse creature).

Heads were always difficult to serve, and sometimes not worth eating at all, but the larger animals' heads were well worth mastering, for everyone knows that the head is the most honourable part of the body. People ate many different parts of a head, and the conscientious carver had to know which bits were best and who deserved to have first refusal of them. John Trusler, who was writing in 1791 for people who carved in far more relaxed and intimate circumstances than were customary for the readers of Wynkyn de Worde or Cervio, explains in *The Honours of the Table* that "many like the eye" of a calf's head, "which is to be cut from it's [sic] socket by forcing the point of a carving knife down to the bottom on one edge of the socket, and cutting quite round, keeping the point of the knife slanting towards the middle, so as to seperate [sic] the meat from the bone." The palate, "a crinkled, white thick skin," required some adroitness to get at it, as did the sweet tooth: "There is a tooth in the upper jaw, the last tooth behind, which having several cells and being full of jelly" is a favourite of some, though Trusler himself thinks that "It's [sic] delicacy is more in the name than any thing else." When all the other edible pieces have been distributed, what is left of the head should be set before the most honoured guest, who will be invited to spoon out the brains. (It was often considered crude, on the principle that knives suggest nastiness and are to be avoided wherever possible, to insert a knife into a brain.) Kitchen staff had probably been instructed to saw off the top of the skull in advance, and replace it carefully so that it could be lifted off at the end; in other places and times, the opportunity to cleave the skull was itself a part of the honour of being invited to eat the brain.

It was always important to include morsels of fat on every polite plateful, and carvers are told to establish the diners' tastes, for, Trusler wrote in 1791, "there are some who prefer soft fat, and others the firm." A special flame was provided to keep some kinds of fat warm, for instance, that of venison, which was appreciated only in a fairly liquid state. "There is some nice, gristly fat to be pared off

about the ear" of a calf or a pig. Ears were great favourites, especially those of the hare: "Before you dissect the head, cut off the ears at
the roots, which if roasted crisp, many are fond of, and may be asked
if they please to have one." A medieval lord, or an honoured guest,
expected to be given a fish's head, with "a finger [width] of flesh"
attached to it, mostly because of the honour it signified. But a cod's
head and shoulders was a dish itself to be carved. There were liver,
palate, roe, and tongue to be offered to those favoured, the sound or
swim-bladder lining the fish beneath the backbone, and certain
"gelatinous parts" about the head and neck. "The jelly parts," writes
Trusler, "lies [sic] about the jaw-bones, the firm parts within the
head . . . the green jelly of the eye is never given to any one."

A nobleman's education was never complete until he had learned
to carve. Gradually noble women were given this training also, so
that they could "do the honours" at family dinner parties. Carving
masters, like fencing and dancing masters, gave classes to their
charges, often several times a week. As ancient Roman teachers had
done, they appear to have used wooden demonstration models of
various fowl and joints, carefully marked out so that students could
learn the placing and order of the cuts. As the rise of monetary
wealth spread "the civilities" of the nobility among the bourgeoisie,
it became necessary that every gentleman worthy of the name
should know how to carve. "How would he be put to the non-plus,"
wrote Giles Rose in 1682, "for shame, that he knows not how to
make the dissection of a Fowl." The eighteenth-century gentleman
might find carving a bore, and consider it beneath him, but Lord
Chesterfield thought such an attitude a mistake: "To do the honours
of the table gracefully, is one of the outlines of a well bred man, and
to carve well, little as it may seem, is useful twice a day, and the
doing of which ill, is not only troublesome to ourselves, but renders
us disagreeable and ridiculous to others."

Grimod de la Reynière reminded post-Revolutionary French
gourmands that although carving might be troublesome to learn (he
admitted that the days when one could recognize a man's breeding
by his carving skills were now gone), it was something which added
prestige to a man of accomplishments. A host or "amphitryon"
might, in 1808, be permitted to carve at a side table, and Grimod

advocated standing up while doing it. (It had become very chic to sit down to carve, because it was difficult and required practice, and perhaps also because it looked less histrionic and less formal.) The *Manuel des amphitryons* even suggests that a carver should spread a large napkin over his chest so that the fear of getting splashed might not prevent freedom of movement; polite guests ought to refrain from staring at him while carving proceeds. Everyone should learn to carve, Grimod adds, because this is a skill that often makes one a useful guest, and highly *recherché*.

Grimod's remarks make it clear that virtuoso carving had begun its long decline; it is less and less an entirely necessary part of a "polished" man's education. Mrs. Beeton, in the mid-nineteenth century, gives a good deal of information on carving (which she says should be performed sitting down). Britain clung to carving ritual long after Continental dining custom had delegated it almost invariably to kitchen staff. In her day, when roasts were served at middle-class dinner tables they were cut and distributed by the knife-wielding chief male of the family. "We can hardly imagine," she says, "an object of greater envy than is presented by a respected, portly paterfamilias carving . . . his own fat turkey, and carving it well." Yet she fears that the new fashion of serving dinners *à la russe* "may possibly, erewhile, save modern gentlemen the necessity of learning the art which was in auld lang syne one of the necessary accomplishments of the youthful squire, but until side-tables become universal or till we see the office of 'grand carver' once more instituted, it will be well for all to learn to assist at the carving of this dish"—a roast hare, which had always been for the carver "an opportunity of display."

Beeton proposes several other occasions for demonstrating a knowledge of etiquette in the distribution of meat: in the still-ritual carving of the forequarter of lamb, for example, where the shoulder has first to be removed, and the cut sprinkled with lemon juice and salt before proceeding; and in the knowledge of "best parts"—skin and thick parts of fins in a turbot, backbone of grouse, thigh of blackcock, and "the finely grained meat lying under the part . . . called the Pope's eye" in a leg of mutton. A rule of thumb for the best part of ducks was "the wing of a flier, and the leg of a swimmer," with ducks' feet a particular delicacy for some. One must *never* give a lady a bird's leg: legs were much too corporal, and suggestive of what lay under skirts. Women might be helped to breast (delicately referred to, in some circles, as "white meat"—though Mrs. Beeton is robustly forthright with this word), wings, and merrythought or wish-bone. Beeton says that Byron did not like dining with ladies because "they always had the wings of the fowls, which he himself preferred." And of course one's carving should always be cool and assured; she recommends a "fine keeping of the temper," even if a tough chicken or an old goose proves hard to disjoint.

In 1922, Emily Post complained that carving was "an art being lost." In 1928, she still preferred that carvers should perform while seated; but it was perfectly in order for Cook to carve the meat in the kitchen to keep it warm, reassemble it on a hot platter, then bring it into the dining room to be served. In 1945, Post dropped the section on carving technique from her handbook on etiquette; she did not reinstate it. The finer points of carving are now the province of cooking professionals. These may still on occasion show off their expertise before a fascinated audience, even holding a bird up in the air to slice it, as is traditional with Rouen or American canvas-back ducks. Proust provides us with a picture of Aimé, the maître d'hôtel at Balbec, taking on the role of "hierophant" and himself carving the turkey-poults in the restaurant: "He carved them with a sacerdotal majesty, surrounded, at a respectful distance from the service-table, by a ring of waiters who . . . stood gaping in open-mouthed admiration."

At family festal dinners, fathers may still be called upon to stand and divide the turkey or the joint. Very often family traditions are adhered to, such as the ceremonial sharpening of the carving knife; ritual questions about preferences, asked in a hierarchical order; joking phrases: "Little fat, Mummy?"; and "red gravy" from a spoon for the smallest child at the very end. But such occasions are rare. Indeed, they tend to be kept for festivals, precisely because festivals demand unusual, though traditional, behaviour. Families are mostly too small nowadays regularly to require large joints of meat; festivals bring together the numbers, making it worthwhile (it being a holiday) to take the time and trouble roasting, gravy-making, baking, and attending to ceremony.

The very idea of seeing our portions being cut and prised from something as vividly recognizable as a whole calf's head has become strange and unpleasant to most of us. Carvers no longer "perform," and "amphitryons" never permit themselves to rank their guests with the devastating clarity of Talleyrand, who taught a young protégé the famous "beef lesson" by his example at dinner one night.

"Monsieur le duc," said Talleyrand, with an air of deference, picking out the honourable piece (*le meilleur morceau*) for him, "may I have the honour of presenting you with a little beef?"

Then, with a graceful smile, "Monsieur le marquis, may I have the pleasure of offering you some beef?"

To his third guest, with a familiar, affable gesture: "My dear Count, shall I offer you some beef?"

To the fourth, with a benevolent air: "Baron, will you accept some beef?"

To an untitled though upper-class fifth: "Sir, would you like some beef?"

And finally, to a man at the end of the table (table ends are "low" in France), he raised his eyebrows slightly, smiled, and said: "Beef?"

• *The Red, the White, and the Gold* •

The liquid element in a meal is either placed first and "eaten" as soup, with a spoon, or it is poured over the solids as sauces, gravies, creams, or syrups. The accompanying drink is kept very separate, standing outside the meal: literally standing in a high glass, and literally outside, beyond the cutlery fence bounding the "place." One ancient way of drinking beer is for people to distance themselves from the brew by means of sucking straws, as the Sumerians did and as many modern Africans still do. The reason is partly that straws may be attached to sieves, and many beers require straining; but also the straws can permit everyone present to drink from one container, while separating drinkers from what they imbibe, much as chopsticks and forks mediate between eaters and food.

We, however, carry the liquid in our beer and wineglasses directly to our mouths. Modern commercial beer is clear of solid matter, and we drink it from tall mugs or vaselike glasses which are often designed to enhance the colour and brightness of the liquid, and the sight of its foaming. Early northern European beers were often mixed with egg, and not attractive to look at; they were drunk from leather jacks in the Middle Ages, and later from pewter pots—the liquid in them was not visually stressed. The glass pint beer mug became conventional during the mid-nineteenth century, just when dark, opaque beers began to fall in popularity and seriously to give way to lighter, clearer, golden beers which were actually enhanced in appearance by faceted glass.

Wine-drinkers supply themselves with special goblets for all but the least formal occasions. A wineglass is like a flower, springing from a stem which not only lifts the wine from the table but provides it with a long, slim, distancing device. A glass of cold white wine—always more "lady-like" and ethereal than red—must be held by the stem; its bowl should not come into contact with our fleshy, warm fingers. The bowl of a glass of red wine (which is heartier, and better if *chambré*) may be touched, even lovingly cradled; but the fingers nonetheless remain aware of that stem, which subliminally signifies to us both refinement and respect. In Europe and America, beer, even for those of us who prefer beer, never achieves the kind of ineffable prestige that is granted to wine. Even if we did not know this, we would be able to deduce it from the difference between the glasses in which beer and wine are served, from the firm capacious utility of the one and the purely ornamental pedestal supporting the thin, fine glass of the other.

Wine and beer are alcoholic. This makes them as "cultural," as dependent upon civilized control and organization as bread, in that human beings have to work hard and long to grow, pick, crush, and ferment the must and the malt, and then patiently let them lie till they are ready, just as bread must be grown, harvested, ground, "fermented" with yeast, kneaded, left to rise, and baked. Care, planning, technology, and organization are required for both. Alcohol is to be treated with respect, not because it is "the staff of life" like bread, but because it is exactly the opposite: it gives pleasure, but is usually unnecessary and potentially dangerous. In ancient Greek myth, wine was a "latecomer" in human history, which meant among other things that people could live without it. Drinking it induced religious awe and direct acquaintance with Dionysus, the god of the vine, of ecstasy, of the group acting as one, of the loss of individual identity.

At Greek and Roman banquets, the drinking proper (that is, apart from the occasional mouthful of wine or water taken merely to wash down food) was set entirely apart from eating. It took place at the *symposion* ("drinking together") after dinner, the guests having wreathed themselves, reapplied the perfumed oils to their persons, and lit the incense on its stand. The dishes were cleared away, and in came the cups, the crater (for mixing water and wine), the water-pots, pitchers, coolers full of snow to be floated in the mixed wine (or alternatively, pots of ready-mixed wine floating in iced water), and ladles for serving from crater to cups. A *symposiarch*, or leader of the drinking party, was chosen by lot from among those present; he judged amounts, allocated roles, and maintained what was considered to be a truly Hellenic triumph, the sympotic balance between the structured and the loose, the organized and the heady. First a libation was offered to the gods. This was an ancient Greek version of grace, a sort of "first fruits" taken from the wine to be drunk, and poured out over the altar if there was one in the dining room, or onto the floor. In this way the gods were given their share first, as though they were guests of honour. Then a hymn was sung, and drinking began.

Alcohol has been known and used by human beings for thousands of years, mostly as a lubricator for social events. It relaxes people and lowers their inhibitions; the desirable end is that of helping individuals to soften their edges and meld better into a group. Eating together intends to achieve this also; alcohol can speed and heighten the effect. Nevertheless, inhibitions are not lowered with impunity, and alcohol introduces an element of danger to a feast—a danger which, we have seen, lies always close, no matter how dormant, at mealtimes. Drinking on one's own is almost invariably castigated by society. Social rules insist that drinking must always be done for social reasons, and never for solitary escapism or need. Where drinking is often done in common, the company evolves methods of controlling drinking behaviour and sharply discouraging excess; it may indulge in a certain decorous jollity, but it despises loss of control.

The Iteso of Kenya and Uganda admire a person who is *epaparone*, one who is "happy with himself," and "likes talking to others in a gentle way, drinking with others, without causing trouble." An Iteso beer party lasts between five hours and three days. People sit down in two concentric circles round a large pot of beer, drinking from straws often shared among two or three people. There is music, drumming, singing, dancing, and the whole affair is governed by a strict code of etiquette. Never hold your straw with your left hand; always ask permission to speak; anyone who speaks without asking first must take the straw out of the pot and not drink for a while; if you go out and come back in again, thank everyone before sitting down; women must not crawl under straws; no one must step over the straws; pull your straw out of the pot if you sneeze; if a straw is removed, do not pass between it and the pot; never blow bubbles in the beer; always sit facing the pot; never wipe the drinking end of the straw before passing it to the person you share it with; do not stand and stare at the pot.

A "sergeant at arms" is delegated to draw attention to drunken behaviour and eject anyone who loses control. Sucking straws is a knack quite difficult to learn—just as is the correct use of forks. A host must place his guest's straw in the pot and get the beer moving through it; the guest must competently keep up the flow. The seating of the circles of participants expresses the kinship system of this society: it is all arranged so that each person sits in the half circle that does not contain his parents or his children. The seating separates people and underlines distinctions; yet all share the same pot of beer, and the straw system enables a good many of them to drink of it at the same time. Careful manners meanwhile maintain a lively consideration for others.

The Iteso practise drinking together in order to reach a state of what they call "much understanding." But they know that a drinking party is a dangerous business: it opens up possibilities of violence, and hatred issuing in sorcery is to be expected. (Many of the rules of etiquette are said to be ways of avoiding sorcery.) The host who gets the beer flowing through the straw for his guest is simultaneously "tasting" his brew to show it is not poisoned. But a guest can show distrust, and so insult the host, by bringing his own personal straw to the party. And as always with manners, the Iteso fear that only lip service may be being paid to fellow feeling—they fear that keeping the rules of courtesy might simply be a disguise for real underlying antagonism. A good drinking party, therefore, is never a foregone conclusion: meeting in this way is a testing as much as it is a gentle, courteous expression of oneness. Coming together is fraught with danger, but we cannot be one without taking the risk and working to achieve that blissful state.

Sharing, which makes eating such a powerful symbol of community, is in some respects more perfectly performed when people drink the same liquid, even if we leave out of account the extra "punch" administered by alcohol. Even if we pour out separate drinks rather than suck the liquid from a single source, what runs from a single bottle into the different glasses is "all one": it is *seen* to be one, and remains the same in every glass; no cutting or choosing is even possible. It has been rare among us until fairly recently for each person to have his or her own glass at table; often drink was imbibed from a single cup, passed round the company. As late as 1855, the American *Illustrated Manners Book* speaks of sharing a drinking vessel as a sign, quite commonly desired, of closeness: "Two persons may drink from the same glass, but this intimacy should never be forced on anyone." And Gabriel Oak in Thomas Hardy's *Far from the Madding Crowd* (1874) was thought "a nice, unparticular man" for refusing a clean cup for his ale. "No, not at all," he said in a reproving tone of considerateness, ". . . I never fuss about dirt in its pure state, and when I know what sort it is."

In spite of the modern terror of germs, the power of ceremonially sharing one cup to induce what anthropologists call *communitas*, or the sense of togetherness, at table, is probably even greater now that we are all used to having our own glasses; it can be used at celebrations of the Eucharist, and of passing the "loving" cup. (A similarly powerful symbol of unification is the circulation of the North American Indian tobacco pipe, where the smoke from the burning weed—also a mild drug—takes the place of alcohol.) Greeks at a symposium celebrated the bonds of friendship and likemindedness which held the group together by passing a capacious pottery cup of wine "in a circle," as they said, from left to right, from person to person. The wine was mixed with water first, the proportions of water to wine being decided by the symposiarch. A liquid once mixed becomes again "all one," and so perfectly expresses the agreement of everyone to abide by the rules.

Expecting to drink from a separate vessel, on the other hand, where sharing cups is the custom, signifies that one is hostile and distrustful: it is similar to demanding that one's food should be tested for possible poison, or bringing one's own straw to an Iteso beer party. A very grand person may be allowed to cut himself off from others by bringing his own cup—just as a great lord could once demand to have his food poison-tested. Among the Igbo of Nigeria, titled men are allowed their own gourd cup or horn *mpi*, but anyone else who brings his own shows distrust and a strained relationship with his host. In ancient Greece, a dinner party without singing or discussions, with no sharing wine mixed in the crater, or letting cups occasionally circulate among the group, produced a sense of stifling gloom. Orestes, who arrived in Athens pursued by the Furies for having murdered his mother, was received and given dinner; but the horror and fear which his polluted state inspired was expressed by every person present at the meal having to eat in silence and drink from a separate pitcher. Symposiasts seem to have been supplied with small individual cups in addition to the large shared ones; they may also have been allowed to bring their own cups to the party without causing offence. Athenian courtesans (they were called *hetairai*, "companions") could attend banquets as respectable women could not; but they apparently had to bring their own cups. Some of these have survived, inscribed with their owners' nicknames in the trade. Typical examples of such names meant "Lioness," "Mania," "Couchy," "Skinny," "Sweetie," "Mouthy," "Tipsy," and "Toad."

The patrons in certain popular restaurants in the South of France are all seated in close proximity to one another, and each is provided with a one-glass flask of the same cheap wine. A diner, Claude Lévi-Strauss tells us, may pour this wine not into his own glass but into that of his neighbour; the latter will courteously respond by returning the favour. It is the custom in Europe to ignore strangers; it is good manners to offer them "polite inattention," in Goffman's phrase. But in the action of pouring wine for each other these temporary neighbours alter their relationship, replacing fortuitous physical juxtaposition with social bonding; they dispel the awkwardness of feeling "at the same time alone and together." The first person to pour implicitly calls upon the other to respond with good manners and cordiality, and do the same for him; he risks being rebuffed, of course, by indifference or boorishness. But if he succeeds—and the call, in this open arena, is strong: both the giver's glass and his bottle stand glaringly empty—he may then start a conversation, having "broken the ice." After the action of filling that first glass, there must follow either increased fellow feeling or hostility; there can be no going back to the original indifference.

Wine and beer can support powerful social roles like the one just described because people have chosen them to do so. These drinks, in Europe, accompany food because they are fermented rather than distilled, and considered nutritious and healthful, like dinner itself. They then seem more innocuous than other liquors because they are consumed at table. Beer is cheerful and convivial, and thought of even as a sort of liquid bread; dinner wine in France can arouse what Lévi-Strauss calls "a sort of mystical respect," even if it is "more than often very bad." But wine drunk by a tramp in a parking lot, or beer swilled on a doss-house bed, are different substances entirely; they become social problems, the objects of moral crusades to ban them. In our own day, of course, even drinking at meals can become a menace when people drive their cars immediately afterwards.

The measures taken by groups of drinkers to repress drunkenness are enormously various, and always culture-specific. Modern Westerners increasingly drink water at table; guests often express a preference for water even at a formal dinner party. The water chosen is fizzy "mineral" water, or flat water from a named spring, bottled and perhaps imported—ordinary tap water will seldom do. As usual, we make health the reason: we protest that tap water is full of chemicals, and believe that "mineral" water is better for our livers and digestive systems. It certainly costs money, and the bottle and the fizz feel slightly festive. Marketers may also add faint fruit tastes to bottled water, to give it a suggestion of wine.

Enormous research funds have been poured into finding out what appeals to us in a mineral-water bottle. Some of us prefer green bottles (cool, old-fashioned, and rustic); others like white (clean, clear, and modern). Labels, especially those on white glass, are in pastel colours: as little like wine labels as possible, yet—presumably to balance the modernity—old-fashioned in style. Plenty of writing—lists, for example, of the minerals contained and the encouragements they offer to various parts of the body—gives labels an archaic, European air with suggestions of the tried-and-true and the safely gourmet. Wine and especially beer are feared because they are fattening; they also make us sleepy, which at lunchtime on a working day is ill-advised. Even the French, these days, increasingly forego wine with any but the most celebratory meals. No French dinner, however, is really complete without cheese, and the French drink wine with ritual fervour, even if it is only a few mouthfuls of wine, when they reach the cheese course.

At ancient Greek symposia, wine was always "cut" (as we say) by the addition of water. The most common proportion was in fact more water than wine: three parts to two. A mixture of half water, half wine was daring, while unmixed wine was regarded as perilous. Quite commonly the wine was diluted with salt sea water or treated in the making with brine. Nobody has ever been able to account for this taste, which was an enthusiastic and long-lasting one. The Greek doctor Dioscorides complains that "sea-watered" wine causes stomach aches and nervousness; it also makes people thirsty, which could produce the opposite effect from that intended, which was to avoid, or at least postpone, drunkenness. Ancient Greeks were very messy drinkers. We have seen them flinging wine across the room in the game of *kottabos*, and repeatedly pouring libations over the altar or onto the floor; passing big flat pedestalled dishes of wine from couch to couch, while lying down, using only one hand, and becoming increasingly merry, surely cannot have been achieved without frequent mishap. Aristotle (*Problems*) and Plutarch (*Symposiacs*, 9) assure us that Greek habits of both mixing wine and using salt water for washing made the stains harder, not easier, to remove.

Wine which was *akratistos*, "not mixed with water in a crater," was a special substance, sipped cautiously during only one drink offering at the symposium, that to the "good Daimon" of the house. It was also used for soaking one's breakfast bread, the Greek word for breakfast being *akratisma*, an "unmixed wine" snack. Barbarians were known to drink their wine neat; the gruesome Scythians and Thracians even invited their wives to join in doing so. Obviously only Greeks were capable of conducting a proper symposium, where men revelled in clever talk (impossible if you were drunk), while under the influence of both Dionysus (wine) and his sage nurses the Nymphs (water). Romans proudly adopted most of the Greek drinking customs, and spread their use throughout their empire. A little water is always mixed with the wine in the Catholic Mass, where the correct manner of drinking at the time of Christ is remembered— and given a new significance: the water is the humanity of Christ, the wine his divinity, and both are definitively intermingled.

The Chinese and Japanese normally drink tea with their meals; alcohol is reserved for festive occasions. And at banquets, saké and *jiŭ* consumption is limited, while the imagery of interaction is multiplied by the provision to everyone of tiny porcelain cups for alcohol. There can be no "drinking deep," as the Greeks did from their large cups, or in the manner of the Saxons, the Teutons, or the Scandinavians. Saké is taken in sips, with much decorous consideration of who should drink first, and who of the other *convives* should sip before or after whom. The ancient Chinese *Li Chi* prescribes constant bowing, whenever the cup is washed, taken, filled, and during the many exclamations of gratitude for having the drink poured by a neighbour; it is suggested that one might "drink all day without getting drunk" if enough bowing is done. Drinking "valour" is played down in favour of a set of polite reactions, in numerical order. On receiving the first cup, the *Li Chi* says, you should look grave; at the second, be pleased and respectful; and at the third, "look self-possessed and prepared to withdraw."

A Greek version of the limits to be observed, and the consequences of breaking them, is expressed in the words which the poet Eubulus puts into the mouth of Dionysus: "Three craters only do I mix for the temperate—one to health, which they empty first, the second to love and pleasure, the third to sleep. When this is drunk up the wise guests go home. The fourth bowl is ours no longer, but belongs to *hybris*; the fifth to yelling, the sixth to prancing about, the seventh to black eyes. The eighth brings the police, the ninth vomiting, the tenth insanity and hurling the furniture." Ancient wine mixed with water had roughly the alcoholic strength of modern beer; a guest's share of three mixed craters was about six pints of liquid.

Even where temperance is not the main goal, demonstrations of reluctance may be correct etiquette. Japanese at a business lunch are expected at least to feign increasing merriness and submission to the influence of alcohol. One may pour saké for oneself only on very intimate occasions; other guests should be depended upon to fill one's cup on formal occasions, as a sign of social awareness and good will. It is one's duty to struggle against their importunate offers of more saké, while seeing to it that other people's cups are repeatedly filled. Saké cups may be filled while they are standing on the table only when one is pouring for oneself; a person being served by someone else must lift the cup in his or her hand. One is obliged in consequence to notice the favour and take the opportunity to bow and express thanks. One may raise the cup against the pouring bottle to cut off the flow, all the while protesting fluently; but a dexterous saké-pourer will simultaneously raise the bottle and keep pouring. And in spite of the difficulty of these manoeuvres, and the increasing tipsiness of the diners, they must all do their utmost to avoid spilling anything: spilling is very bad form. The rules impose intense concentration and careful cooperation, and the result is a necessary awareness of other people, their considerateness and their needs. The Chinese host "leads" his guests much as the Greek symposiarch governed the party: no one must drink until invited to do so by the host, and the frequent celebratory drinking all together is usually initiated by the host as well. In many cultures it is very boorish to pour drink for oneself at a party. We ourselves might be permitted attention to our own glasses, but only when pouring for everyone seated nearby; and glasses must not be filled to the brim.

It is almost invariably rude to begin drinking before some food at least has been consumed—eating something before drinking is known to "line the stomach" and help prevent drunkenness. In both China and Japan, food is classed in a completely different category from drink and this affects table manners; the serving of rice at the end of a banquet, for example, stops the consumption of alcohol then and there. Our own insistence is that wine cannot be drunk with soup. (It is an old English custom to serve Sherry or Sauternes with soup, but this is being increasingly replaced by the French rule of abstention from wine until after the soup course.) Broth, in spite of counting as food, is liquid already and therefore drinking wine with it may be considered inappropriate, although a rustic French custom (*faire chabrot*) actually encourages the dilution of the soup remaining in one's bowl with wine; but the resulting mixture is then thought of as drink, not food, and the bowl is therefore lifted, like a cup, in the hands to the mouth. Soup should be served at a formal meal, and must at least be tasted: it is rude to leave it untouched. By this means we delicately ensure that everyone present is fortified before wine is served; we also enforce the highly civilized impression that nobody present is anxious to get started on the wine.

At some Chinese restaurants patrons leave the teapot with the lid raised to show that more tea is desired. German beer steins have covers to them, traditionally to signal whether or not the customer wants more beer. It used to be correct to place one hand over our glasses to show we wanted no more beer or wine, and Victorian women, who wore gloves to the table and took them off to eat, could cover the glass with a glove. It is now politer simply to refuse, or if this fails, to leave some liquid in the glass undrunk: we no longer expect guests to eat and drink up in order to show respect for the host's generosity. Even worse than covering the glass is turning it upside down to prevent anyone pouring wine or beer into it; the gesture may be efficient, but statements of refusal must not go too far. The ancient Illyrians wore loosely tied belts to drinking parties. As drinking became more intense, belts were tightened, an action which presumably both signalled a desire to stop and reduced the ability to continue.

Another ingenious method of repressing too much drink is to supply it sporadically, and prevent people from asking for it. Among the Newars of Katmandu, the women who make the beer usually pour it. A woman squats in front of a guest, places a bowl for him on the ground, and pours from the jar resting on her hip. (In the language of the Newars, there are different words for the verb "to pour," depending on whether the liquid is water or alcohol.) The drinker, squatting on his heels, must dip the middle finger of his right hand into the beer, offer a drop to the gods by letting it fall to the ground, then lift the bowl in his right hand and finish it all in one draught. The server offers him a second cup, then a third. He may accept or refuse—but it would be unseemly to drink more than three times. She then moves on and out of his reach, serving the other guests.

In our own culture, women are never encouraged to ask for a drink; men are supposed to see to their needs, and women themselves are made to feel that alcohol ruins their appearance, by making them fat or flushed or both. The number of times one was allowed to request wine or beer has often been limited: in Tudor England, for instance, it was rude to ask for it more than twice. Erasmus recommended that a boy should not taste any drink at all until sometime during the second course of the meal; he should drink only once more, at the dinner's close, and "he should take it in moderate sips, and not gurgle it down sounding like a horse." Undiluted wine, he warned, caused "decaying teeth, bloated cheeks, impaired eyesight, mental dulness—in short, premature old age."

From the fourteenth until well into the nineteenth century with the arrival of dinner *à la russe*, goblets and glasses seem often to have offended people's sensibilities if they stood on the table at a banquet. Even when many glasses were available, they were kept in a cooler at a separate side table, and had to be asked for. Servants would mix wine with water in the desired proportions for each guest: it was always considered very coarse, where French manners were followed, to drink wine undiluted. The waiter or cup-bearer would then give the filled vessel to the drinker, and wait until it was finished; then he took it away to be washed and replaced in the cooler. When a woman took a drink, the attendant might actually stand beside her holding a napkin under her chin until she had finished and handed back her glass. In this manner every drink was turned into a performance: unconscious or uncontrolled tippling was rendered impossible.

But banqueters have always been quite capable of deciding that drunkenness, not sobriety, was the order of the day; the Mongols, for instance, thought hospitality had been achieved if the guests got

well and expensively drunk. In these cases, people might be forbidden *not* to drink as much as they could. The cylindrical tumbler
which we now use for drinks on ordinary occasions, especially if the
liquid is not wine, was once a member of a special class of cups that
demanded to have their contents drained. Frankish glass tumblers in
the fourth to seventh centuries had rounded bottoms, and were
designed to tumble and spill what was in them if set down. Bell-
shaped drinking glasses made in Venice in the sixteenth century
belonged in this category; they had a footless stem, and could only
be set down reversed, like a bell. The Prince Regent was supposed
to have begun the custom in England of snapping the stems of wineglasses at especially raucous parties, to ensure that they were emptied. Drinking horns with pointy ends were both huge and meant to
be finished or handed on to others, but never put down till empty.
Philip of Macedon used a horn for toasting people to whom he
wished to pay a compliment, being very aware that this drinking
vessel, antiquated as it already was in classical Greece, had the connotations of heroic prowess. The Greeks, in spite of, or because of,
their tradition of watering wine, were capable of worshipping the
Hero Akratopotes, "Drinker of Wine Unmixed." They loved imposing—as a forfeit for those who failed at sympotic games and contests—the task of downing a large cup of wine to the dregs without
once drawing breath; this feat was accompanied by wild music.

No less than three shots of Schnapps are customary. But a modern
dispensation allows that drinkers must drain the first glass, but may
"bite" the second in two (that is, take it in two mouthfuls) and the
third in three. A man used to have to drink as many whole glasses of
Schnapps as he wore buttons on his waistcoat: a lot of buttons was a
boast of drinking prowess. Guessing games frequently break out at
Chinese and Vietnamese dinners; they consist of calling out the correct number of fingers an opponent holds out at the precise moment
he does so, and the loser (the one who calls the wrong number, or
the one whose fingers tally with the number called) has to drink a
whole fresh cup of wine. Some fingers may never be held out together, because of their obscene suggestions. Only careful training from
childhood can keep the taboos unbroken during the heat of combat:
foreigners are advised not to try Chinese finger-games. Several pairs

of diners might be going at such contests at any one time, with all the noise incident to the game. The guessing goes on until the capitulation of one or both sides.

Being able to "hold one's liquor" and "drink everyone else under the table" are still signs of a certain type of macho vigour: in a very primitive sense they show such a person to be more capacious and self-controlled, or at any rate more impervious, than other men. It used to be expected at heavy drinking and toasting bouts that one or more men would fall to the floor in a drunken stupor; a servant would automatically step forward and loosen the necktie of anyone prone and insensible. (The philosopher Socrates was famous for remaining unfuddled by liquor and continuing relentlessly to philosophize when almost everyone else at the symposium had either left or passed out.) Men in groups have often found it irresistible to boast of their drinking valour, and to challenge others to see who could "take" the most. It could be impossible to turn down such a challenge without losing face; Alexander the Great is said to have died by returning one pledge too many.

An ancient Greek libation was a sort of concrete prayer, a sharing of wine with the gods. The Homeric ritual for this act entailed rising to one's feet holding a cup full of wine in the right hand, looking up into the sky, deliberately spilling some of the liquid, praying with both arms and cup raised, then drinking. The Olympian gods were not necessarily thought to have imbibed the wine—but they accepted the gift, the sacrifice of that all-important first mouthful, and a connection with them was thereby established. "Drinking to" people was, and remains, in some respects similar to pouring libations. The toaster rises to his or her feet as a gesture of respect, and everybody else rises too, if the recipient of the honour is important enough; all must certainly raise their glasses. When men wore hats at meals, hats had to be removed. The toast is spoken, and it is very important to look the person being toasted in the eyes. A bow or nod of the head follows, and everyone sips wine. Taking only very little wine at this point is a modern constraint: toasting in the past has often meant draining the whole vessel. Because we all now have our own glasses, we substitute drinking simultaneously for sharing the cup.

The Saxon "wassail" bowl was named after the toasting formula,

"*Wass hael!*"—"Be hale!" or "Be healthy!" (The favourite toast has always been to wish for the good health of the person being toasted.) The Saxon host's wife or his daughter would enter the hall with a large bowl, sip from it as a taste test proving there was no poison in it, and offer the cup of welcome to the guests, toasting each one. Later, the cup-bearer would ladle out spiced wine or mulled ale into each person's own cup. But the custom of everyone partaking from the single bowl was remembered and survived, for example, as the British ceremony of passing the "loving cup" from person to person round the whole company. Three people stand up at a time, one to pass the cup, one to drink, and the third to "defend"; the defender once had to draw his sword and hold it at the ready as the huge two-handled cup took all the attention of the drinker and left him vulnerable to attack. As always, love and the possibility of violence walk hand in hand at table. Today, the defender merely turns to face the company, "guarding the back" of the drinker. When he receives the cup, its lip having been wiped on the napkin which is tied to one of the handles, the person next to him stands to act as "defender," and so on round the company.

Toasting can be done between two persons only. The ancient Greek version of this was called *proposis*, "the drink before." The toaster sipped first, then handed the vessel containing the rest of the wine to the person honoured; on especially dramatic occasions the cup itself was a permanent gift to the receiver. At a wedding, for example, a golden libation bowl full of wine might be given in this manner from father-in-law to son-in-law. The bowl became a symbol of the bride, "given away" (as we still say) by her father; the two men, the two families were now one in the shared wine. Many quite different wedding ceremonies still involve a sharing or exchanging of drinks, symbolizing unity.

A gift entails a response. The Greek pourer of a libation expected the gods to reciprocate, in much the same way that the Provençal restaurant patron feels he must pour wine for a neighbour who has made the first move and filled his glass. But a gift, where obligations are powerfully felt, can also be a challenge, and toasting, because it had to be returned, could quickly turn into a provocation. Toasts were not, as we have seen, always discharged with a mere sip: the ritual in seventeenth-century Ireland, for example, insisted that the toaster "sups up his breath, turns the bottom of his cup upward and in ostentation of his dexteritie gives the cup a phillip to make it *twange*, and thus the first scene is acted." The person toasted had to perform a second "scene," equalling the exploit, as often as he was so honoured. A "toasting glass" had a ball instead of a foot at the base of the stem; finger-bowls, or the individual glass wine-coolers that became popular in the early nineteenth century, could be provided for these glasses to be set upside down in; at least this preserved the table-top from some of the drips. Men were not so lucky in seventeenth-century Russia, where both toaster and toastee had to turn their beakers upside down on their heads to prove that they were empty.

Modern European toasting rituals are strongest and most formal in Germanic, Scandinavian, and eastern European countries. No one should taste wine or other alcohol in Scandinavia until the host has made a toast. All lift their glasses and look around at everyone present; they toast, taste, then look around at everyone again. Guests in Denmark may give subsequent toasts; the guest of honour is expected to express thanks to the hosts by tapping his or her glass to attract attention, and then proposing a toast. The drama of toasting has never been very strong in Mediterranean countries since the rise of Christianity, which gave to wine a gentler (though still sacred) mystique than the one it had enjoyed in the classical world. Toasting is given German names in French, Italian, and Spanish: the custom seems to have been reintroduced, in Germanic form, to those countries during the sixteenth century, probably by the Landsknechte, bands of German mercenaries who fought wherever they could find employment. So in Spanish and Italian "to toast" is *brindar* and *brindare*, from German *ich bring dir's*, a toast meaning "I bring it to you"; French *trinquer* is from German *trinken*, "to drink." In English, the word "toast" comes from the British practice of floating a piece of toasted bread on top of the wine, ale, or mead of the loving cup. Once the bowl had gone round, the host was expected to drain the last drops and consume the toast in honour of the guests.

Today, the custom of toasting includes the clinking of glasses. Drinking wine, people have often remarked, is an action pleasing to four of the senses: taste, smell, touch, and sight. Clinking provides

sound as well. Glasses gradually replaced pottery cups, metal goblets, and other kinds of containers on European tables, beginning
with the establishment of Venetian glass-blowing expertise in the
sixteenth century. They grew in popularity from the seventeenth
century as people were increasingly provided with individual drinking vessels. Glasses, from the beginning, were prized for their
"ring," the sound they made when tapped. "Ring" improved where
the raw material for making glass contained plenty of lead oxides;
British and Irish glass of the seventeenth, eighteenth, and early
nineteenth centuries is still famous for its "rich bell-notes of F or G
sharp . . . which throb themselves out with lingering resonance."

Clinking glasses—rapping them to call everyone present to attention, or tapping them together when toasting—has always given
people pleasure. Clinking one glass against another is *making contact*,
an action we perform precisely because we are not sharing one cup;
in doing it we remind ourselves that the wine, now separated into
glassfuls, is still one, and we reach out to each other even though we
do not hand our glasses on. Russians go one further and smash their
glasses after particularly fervent toasts, vows, or oaths. The half-
Russian poet Apollinaire loved using the image of a smashed glass to
express exultant joy. People have often felt that disposing of the
wine in a toast was really not sufficient: the cup should go too—
either broken or given away—otherwise the words symbolized in
drinking are not finalized, and the action is lacking in generosity.
Smashing the glass also ensures that no less worthy toast shall ever
be made in that glass.

Toasting was used during the eighteenth century to force guests to
learn each other's names—everyone knew that when toasting began
they would have to drink healths, calling out their companions'
names. An early form of invitation to make a toast was "Let us hob
and nob," roughly, "give and take" ("hab" and "nab" meant "have"
and "not have"). "Hobnobbing" with people was repeatedly being in
a position to toast them, and specifically to clink glasses with them.
Charles Dickens, in *Little Dorrit* (1857), tells us how the Victorians
toasted with "bumpers"—a term that appears to refer to the clinking
of glasses, though some claim that it means glasses so full of wine
that their surfaces bulge slightly, surface tension preventing them

from actually spilling over. "The bumpers filled, Mr. Blandois, with a roystering gaiety, clinked the top of his glass against the bottom of Mr. Flintwich's, and the bottom of his glass against the top of Mr. Flintwich's, and drank to the intimate acquaintance he foresaw."

Being allowed to propose a toast to somebody present, and therefore to call forth a response in kind from him, expressed a sense of being on an equal footing with that person. When society was fiercely hierarchical, who could toast whom, and so demonstrate equality, was a matter of punctilious etiquette. *The Court of civill Courtesie* (1591) says that toasting is to be done only to please inferiors "to whom we mean not to use speach of familiaritie," or to congratulate peers. "A man must never drinke to his better, except he be sure, that by way of friendship and familiaritie hee be content to become his equal"—and even then care must be taken that everyone present is aware of the new intimacy between them, that "it proceedeth . . . not of presumption." The seventeenth-century French rule was that one could toast a superior, provided that he was not addressed directly. A third party received one's words ("Sir, it is to Monsieur that I drink"), so that no boundaries separating ranks were impudently crossed. Hosts could toast guests, but never the reverse. (Hosts had of course to control the number of toasts they drank because if guests kept toasting, the host, being required to respond to every "health," would quickly find himself incapable of hosting at all.) It is apparently still impolite to take away the host's prerogative by toasting anyone before he or she has had a chance to do so first. A host, says Letitia Baldrige, "will not welcome a junior executive popping up in the middle of the meat course and prematurely toasting either the hosts or the guest of honor." A guest with a toast rising in his heart must *ask permission* of the host to give it, and then only if it looks as though no one else has previously arranged to do so.

Erasmus warns boys against being drawn into toasting, intentionally addressing himself, through his schoolmasterly persona, to adults who might be rough-necked enough to tempt boys to drink too much: "You should courteously acknowledge someone toasting you with his cup, and touching your own cup with your lips sip a little and pretend to drink: this will satisfy a polite man simply playing the buffoon. When someone boorishly presses you to drink, promise to reply when you have grown up." Women have rarely been expected to drink to other people; they are more usually commended for refusing to drink toasts, and even loving cups were supposed to pass them by with merely a kiss on the rim of the bowl. Women were not merely unequal to men, but altogether outside the drinking group and the wine it shared. They were often, however, the object of male competitive zeal, and as such the inspirers of toasts. Ancient Romans used to drink to absent women—a cup for every letter of a beauty's name being a favourite exploit, and one that has frequently been revived since. Drinking to absent women became common especially in Britain, where until very recently women have been expected to leave the men to themselves at the end of dinner.

A woman toasted in this manner became herself "the toast," after the piece of grilled bread which, as we have noted, once floated in British drinks. Lady Mary Wortley Montagu is said to have become the toast of the Kit-cat Club at the age of eight. A tradition reported in *The Tatler* (No. 24) has it that the transference in meaning took place at Bath in the reign of Charles II: a certain woman, standing in the water of the Cross Bath, was toasted by an admirer who used the water itself to drink her health. Another "gay fellow" offered to jump in, saying that "though he liked not the liquor he would have the toast." The story pleasantly makes the metaphor concrete—but toasting always does this to a certain extent. The formulae for toasting often turn the drink into the person or idea toasted ("Gentlemen, I give you—the Queen!"). When Humphrey Bogart raises his glass to Ingrid Bergman in *Casablanca* and says, "Here's looking at you, kid," the looking and the wine are equated, as the phrase says. When the supporters of Bonnie Prince Charlie responded to toasts giving each other "the King," they would hold their glasses over the water-bottle, secretly (or openly, depending on the company they were in) expressing their allegiance not to the usurper but to "the King who is over the water."

As long as toasting remained a matter of passionately maintained honour, as competitive in its way as duelling, and restricted to groups of men only, it was always blamed for causing excessive drinking. It has been frequently condemned or banned as a means of cutting down on drunkenness; the earliest known Temperance

Society was founded in 1517 with the express aim of abolishing toasting. The Dissenter William Prynne devoted his life to condemning drink, and especially toasting; he wrote a book against it called *Health's Sicknesse* (1628). Samuel Pepys went to a dinner in 1664 at which Prynne, ever faithful to his principles, "would not drink any health, no, not the King's, but sat down with his hat on all the while; but nobody took notice of it to him at all."

Competitive toasting died out, however, for social reasons which had little to do with moral wrath: the practice came simply to be seen as too demonstrative, and therefore embarrassing. Good manners increasingly required one to leave other people alone and not to show one's own hand too blatantly. Even the person toasted could feel annoyed at being singled out. "What could be more rude or ridiculous," demanded John Trusler in 1791, "than to interrupt persons at their meals with unnecessary compliments?" He explained in his *System of Etiquette* (1804) that toasting was "exploded," having become a proof of lower-class origins. The custom continued as a polite, slightly wooden gesture, or as an intimate sign of affection. *The Illustrated Manners Book* advises mid-nineteenth-century Americans not to toast at all—"it may however be done quietly and unobtrusively, as a familiar pleasantry." A woman to whom a glass was raised in company was taught to "catch the person's eye and bow with politeness. It is not necessary to say anything, but smile with an air of great kindness." By the end of the nineteenth century in England, it was thought "not the act of a gentleman" to mention a woman's name when the men met in the women's absence after dinner to drink port and smoke cigars.

Indeed, it could be felt as early as the seventeenth century that looking deeply into a person's eyes was sufficient; the drinking was merely metaphorical and could therefore be dispensed with. Ben Jonson was sensible of its poetic power, however, even as he dismissed it:

Drink to me only with thine eyes,
And I will pledge with mine;
Or leave a kiss but in the cup,
And I'll not look for wine.

Formal toasting, sternly exclusive of any rambunctious behaviour, is still a common custom—and perhaps, when done in private, as a "familiar pleasantry," toasting has regained a little of its power as a symbol of togetherness. In Germany, Scandinavia, and eastern European countries, it survives as a piece of etiquette important enough for foreigners to be warned, for example by Braganti and Devine, how to behave when encountering it. Their tradition is an ancient one, with powerful beginnings. It is believed that the bowl referred to in the Scandinavian toast "Skoal!" was originally made from the skull of a fallen enemy. Certainly *skoal* and *skull*, both meaning "a hollow thing," are etymologically related.

• *Table Talk* •

Few people become quite as disgusted as Europeans and North Americans do if diners eat with their mouths open. Chewing absolutely must be performed with the lips shut. Yet few also are the societies which insist, as we do, that at invited dinner parties everybody must talk during dinner. Among us it is rude to eat and not talk, unless the meal is a very intimate one where the rule is ignored or dropped. We need never think of our manners as weakening as long as this fiendishly difficult skill is demanded of us, that when we are in a convivial group we shall talk at all the correct moments, saying everything we should, and even everything we mean, but never be caught doing so with our mouths full.

Talking is of course one of the ways in which we "rise above food": we are not at table merely to eat, but in order to enjoy each other's company. "It isn't so much what's on the table that matters," said W. S. Gilbert, "as what's on the chairs." The ancient Greeks never tired of reiterating that "stomach" (*gaster*) was not enough, one needed "mind" (*psyche*) as well; that civilized people came together for each other and for philosophy, and not just to stuff themselves. A philosopher-host like Menedemus would provide a meal for only one or two of his guests; the others would have to dine before coming, bring their own cushions, and be content with a sip for everybody from one half-pint cup and nothing but a lupine or a bean for dessert. He offered a token dinner, but made it impossible for most guests to come to the party for anything but the conversation.

The Greeks turned discussion at a symposium into a literary genre in its own right: Plato's great dialogue, *Symposium*, Xenophon's *Symposium*, Plutarch's *Symposiacs* and *Banquet of the Seven Sages*, Macrobius' *Saturnalia* were the ancestors of collections of *Table Talk* or *Propos de table* which have continued as a minor tradition of European *belles lettres* down the centuries. Athenaeus wrote what must be one of the longest versions on record: fifteen volumes of chat, called *The Sophists at Dinner*. Books like these, as well as artistic representations, especially paintings of dinner parties on ancient Greek dinnerware, are the reason why so much information is available about ancient Greek and Roman attitudes towards eating and drinking together. (Their actual dining habits are more elusive. Like most people, the Greeks and Romans seldom described their table manners in detail because they considered them common knowledge.) Greeks in fact talked little during the meal itself. A few things were said, one of the tasks apparently being to decide, while dinner was being eaten, what the subject of conversation would be when talking did get under way.

The symposium or drinking party was the place and time for discussion, whether serious or trivial. Subjects at symposia ranged from "What is love?" to "Why meat spoils more readily in moonlight than in sunlight" and "Whether people of old did better with portions served to each, or people of today, who dine from a common supply"; subjects very often had something to do with food or drink. But the pangs of hunger had to be assuaged before conversation began. In Homeric times it was considered very rude to expect a stranger to speak at length to his hosts before he had eaten his fill; he was not even asked his name until he had been given dinner. But when speaking began, it was polite to contribute what one had to offer. People knew you by the way you behaved: it was only fair to give them material with which to make their judgement of your worth.

In some societies drinking and talk is done *before* dinner. A large Sherpa party begins with two, three, four, even five hours of discussion, quarrelling, joking, all facilitated by the drinking of beer. A large crowd assures people that they can work through grudges in safety, while at the same time assessing the opinion of neighbours and finding out who their friends are; the community can express either consensus or disapproval for the behaviour of various members, and ranking (symbolized by shifting seating arrangements) is adjusted among individuals. At a climactic moment, judged with finesse by the host, dinner will appear, to please, pacify, and relieve everybody. Silence falls, and everybody gratefully and happily eats. In the silence, any rough edges left by communal friction are smoothed over by the action of eating together. In China and Iran, the traditional rule is also "talk first, then eat."

Some people, among them the Newars of Katmandu, feel that silence when eating is formal behaviour, to be maintained in public; among friends and family one may talk, laugh, and dine at the same time. Other societies, including many people in our own culture, feel exactly the opposite on this point. The Japanese banquet begins in silence, that is, with formality and caution, and then "warms up," becoming louder and friendlier as it goes on. The "lubricating" effect of alcoholic drinks can help this transition to occur. In many African societies only the elders may speak, or else silence is maintained by everybody.

Our own culture's opting for conversation during meals is undoubtedly linked with our custom of dividing food into separate portions before eating begins. The "togetherness" of a meal in common requires boosting for us, and we intensify the sense of community by talking to each other; sharing a common dish as other people do entails a great deal of non-verbal cooperation and causes plenty of interpersonal relationship just in the course of eating. Indeed, sharing a common dish might need concentration on the matter in hand just to ensure that everyone gets a fair share. Westerners often remark on the speed with which foreigners seem to eat, and we have noted that food chopped in small pieces to be eaten with chopsticks will get cold if eating is too leisurely. Not talking saves time, and also stems from a different attitude towards mealtimes. Eating might be thought of as pleasurably and ceremonially sufficient; as needing all one's reverent concentration; or just as a quiet activity enjoyed in common with other people. Speaking can seem *de trop*, and even an unnecessary risk; the Babylonian Talmud (ca. A.D. 450) advises,

"When eating refrain from speaking, lest the windpipe open before the gullet, and life be in danger."

Often a compromise is sought between silence and speech: entertainment is laid on during the actual eating. (We have seen that elaborate theatrical interludes once took place in the *entremets* of a medieval banquet, that is, not during the serious eating but between courses.) People often like watching what they are doing when they eat, so the entertainment, unless most eating stops while it is going on, tends to be auditory; the guests keep silent and eat, while someone reads or speaks. The word "collation," which now means a small, intimate meal, comes from the *Conferences* ("Lectures," literally, "things brought together": "collation" is from the same Latin verb) of John Cassian, to which Benedictine monks listened during meals. There might be singing, as in the Saxon hall or at Homeric feasts. At ancient Greek symposia, guests would take turns singing; a myrtle branch was passed to each singer so that it was clear whose turn it was, and to make sure there were no rowdy interruptions.

Non-dining instrumentalists who play for the company have an ancient history; the tradition continues in some restaurants today. Where there is musical accompaniment, there have to be rules enjoining silence so that others can hear the music. Jesus, son of Sirach, writes in *Ecclesiasticus* (ca. 185 B.C.), "Speak, old men, it is proper that you should; but know what you are talking about, and do not interrupt the music." Madame de Sévigné complains in seventeenth-century France that the art of conversing at dinner is dying because music is increasingly played to the guests: "One assembles an excellent group of dinner-table companions, in order that they shall all be silenced." In countries where the host's role is not to participate in the meal but to bestow it upon his guests, he might be expected to give a speech, play an instrument, or sing to the group at dinner: they can eat undisturbed, and he is allowed to do all the giving while they remain completely passive receivers in his house.

It is increasingly remarked that North Americans watch more and more television during everyday meals at home. As many as 78 percent are thought to watch at least once or twice a week during dinner; about 24 percent of these always have the television on. The average length of an American dinner, with or without TV, is thirty minutes, which suggests that not a great deal of discussion is taking place. A British report shows that one distinguishing mark of a "proper" Sunday dinner, that is, a formal family meal, is "no TV." When people sorrowfully note the passing of dinner-time conversation, at least at family meals, we might recall that eating in silence is by far the most common human choice, and that entertainment has often replaced talk—unless food is turned into an art form, or the family gathering into an occasion for education or celebration. We have made silence informal partly because for us formal occasions require verbal communication. But where families spend less and less time together, removing dinner-time talk may well be a serious deprivation: it takes away what was scarce in the first place.

Our own culture has thought it worth while to work hard on polishing the art of conversation. Erving Goffman has pointed out that the family-sized dining-room table is a specially created "open region," where participants have the right "to engage anyone present." Talking at table is important for the information which is provided for others about any speaker who is not well known to them. The purpose of dinner-table conversation is partly to force people to go through their paces: to show that they have learned the rules and "polished" themselves, and will therefore, in the estimation of the company, "do." As we saw earlier, manners can constitute a cruel enforcement of class barriers; at table there is nowhere to hide, and the rule against silence means that there is no refuge from having to perform. "Taciturn people," says one nineteenth-century etiquette book firmly, "are not good for society, and should avoid it."

It is possible for rules to evolve which will help to keep everyone in order. In the French Navy during the 1920s, the conversation included (and may do so still) a series of silent aids to comprehension—the aids themselves proving, of course, that everyone was fully conversant with the code. There were miniature objects laid on the table, to be used especially when warnings were required: a tiny boat-hook, a *gaffe* in French and synonymous with an embarrassing faux pas, was placed before someone in danger of committing such an offence. A miniature ladder (the symbolism of which is unclear to me) was shown to a diner who became angry over anything; and a small model of a bronze wall was available for standing in front of one's own place to warn people that their talk was encroaching on private matters one did not wish to discuss.

People who converse in the context of dinner have always been warned not to talk about anything too important—not religion, not politics, or anything controversial. Arguments must certainly not break out, because manners have a primary mandate to prevent anything even resembling violence. A more avowable fear is that the gastric juices, and hence digestive processes, might be adversely affected by an unpleasant scene. One must not take advantage of the fact that everyone is pinned to his or her chair for the duration of the meal; one must not, for example, ask pointed questions, or questions requiring long replies. No one can or should hold forth for long periods at dinner: *everyone* must talk and therefore have a chance to do so, and everyone must have time to eat as well. No one should talk shop, or say anything so technical that the others cannot understand: everyone must be brought into the discussion, and anything which is done, even inadvertently, to exclude anyone is a sign of ill breeding. In his essay "On Experience," Montaigne becomes positively brutal about people who tried to be too intellectual during dinner: "What? Would they try to square the circle while mounting their wives?"

The art of dinner-table conversation, as it evolved from the seventeenth century onward, was that of interaction, almost for its own sake. Diners displayed their social awareness, their manners and tact, and showed respect for the rules they were all keeping. The young, for instance, had to defer to the old, keep silent most of the time, and yet demonstrate that they were listening and interested. They must not put anything into their mouths while they were being spoken to, and not hold on to a glass as though waiting for the interlocutor to stop talking in order to have a drink. They must never imitate—inadvertently of course, one would never do it on purpose—the expression on the face of anyone addressing them.

Manners were in part a moral code, forcing "good breeding" to include consideration for other people's rights and feelings. No one should show preferential treatment to any one guest over all the others, no two people should whisper together, and explanations were required if anyone laughed during a conversation that was not general, just in case someone thought they were being laughed at. No one must offend a guest by pronouncing a witticism at his or her expense. A host, in spite of or because of his power, ruined his reputation if he spoke too much, praised himself, served himself first, praised the dishes, or spoke about meals he had given before or dishes he had eaten and liked. *The Rules and Orders of the Coffee House* (1674) expressed most of the main constraints upon conversation:

> But let him forfeit Twelve-pence that shall Sweare:
> He that shall any Quarrel here begin,
> Shall give each Man a Dish t'atone the Sin . . .
> Let Noise of lewd Disputes be quite forborn,
> No Maudlin Lovers here in Corners Mourn,
> But all be Brisk, and Talk, but not too much.
> On Sacred things, Let none presume to touch,
> Nor Profane Scripture, or sawcily wrong
> Affairs of State with an Irreverent Tongue.
> Let Mirth be Innocent, and each man see
> That all his Jests without Reflection be.

It was during the seventeenth century, and increasingly during the eighteenth, that tables even at banquets became habitually surrounded by chairs. (At family meals they must always have been so.) Seating at large feasts, except at "high tables," was no longer arranged along one side only so that guests could be seen, and so that the tables could be approached more readily by processions of servants bearing dishes. From now on the ornaments and decorations were set mostly in the middle of the table, for the diners alone and not for an audience of people watching the show. The amount of silverware, however, and the number of dishes and ornaments meant that tables set for dinner *à la française* were so broad and encumbered that guests could scarcely talk to each other across the table—and it was expressly forbidden to shout. Gradually tables did become smaller. In the eighteenth century, "intimate suppers" for ten or fewer became the height of fashion. At these events servants were outlawed, food being set out in advance on side tables; the object, when women were invited, was often a projected seduction. The nineteenth-century dinner *à la russe* took away all need to choose from an array of dishes, and most of the obligation for guests to serve their neighbours; diners were more separated from each other than they had ever been, but the stage was left all the more free for conversation. People at dinner still tend to talk to those sitting beside them, but conversation across our much narrower, less laden tables is possible and encouraged.

In the mid-eighteenth century, Lord Chesterfield warned his son that gentlemen never laugh, they only smile; laughter makes a disagreeable noise and shockingly distorts the face. The rule is especially strict at table. One should take into account everything one knows about the guests—not "mentioning a rope in the house of a man who has been hanged." It is tedious to drag a subject willy-nilly into the conversation. Chesterfield knew a man "who had a story about a Gun, which he thought a good one and that he told it very well; he tryed all means in the world to turn the conversation upon Guns—but if he failed in his attempt, he started in his chair, and said he heard a Gun fired, but when the company assured him that they heard no such thing, he answered, perhaps then I was mistaken, but however, since we are talking of Guns,—and then told his story, to the great indignation of the company."

It was good manners, and openly acknowledged as such, not to draw attention to oneself, not to be loud, not to be embarrassing, not to be repetitious or boring. ("Bore" is an eighteenth-century word, first appearing in English in 1766.) One was expected, by our standards, to be deliberately artificial, thinking of subjects for conversation in advance, preparing witticisms, polishing paradoxes, seeking occasions to insert them—but all must be done with an air of complete naturalness and simplicity, with what the French were calling *je ne sais quoi*. Any signs of trying too hard, of not taking all the circumstances into account, not only spoiled the story being told but much more permanently ruined the reputation of the speaker. Ease constituted proof that one had had long practice in the social graces; one had "good breeding" and "a fine upbringing."

By the late nineteenth century, the rules—those expressed in the manners books, at any rate—were even more careful. People were supposed to memorize the names of everyone to whom they had an introduction (powerful and popular persons severely limited the number of people who could be introduced to them), and to talk correctly and without slang or vulgarisms such as "awfully pretty" and "immensely jolly." One listened even to the most boring talker: this was a person who had been deemed worthy of an invitation to dinner, and one owed it to one's host and to the whole company present to accept and encourage this interlocutor, at least for the time being. Even enmities were to be buried at the table—though an extremely experienced dinner-goer could save her hatred, her hostess's feelings, and the smooth operation of the whole gathering, all at the same time. Emily Post describes how "At dinner once, Mrs. Toplofty, finding herself next to a man she quite openly despised, said to him with apparent placidity, 'I shall not talk to you—because I don't care to. But for the sake of my hostess I shall say my multiplication tables. Twice one are two, twice two are four—' and she continued on through the tables, *making him alternate them with her* [my italics]. As soon as she politely could she turned again to her other companion." The man she disliked had shown that he was one of her sort: is it permissible to imagine Mrs. Toplofty unbending a little after this incident?

Nineteenth-century manners books, reflecting as they do the ideal of gentlemanly and lady-like behaviour, exhorted polite people to be sympathetic and animated but never flippant. Compliments must be sincere but flattery was vulgar, and scandal and gossip a disgrace. One must never interrupt, or allude to another person who is at the table ("How awkward to ask, 'Who is that vulgar, red-faced woman?' and receive the reply, 'My wife, Sir!'"). Private or indelicate matters must not be mentioned, or even given an opportunity to be thought of. Foreign languages, and even quotations from the classics, should be avoided, together with all ostentatious displays of knowledge, expatiation on one's hobbies, and dogmatic opinions: "Politeness is universal toleration." Impertinent questions, unsuccessful witticisms, and fault-finding were all social gaffes. Women had to realize that men had larger appetites than they, and should not ask questions which forced men to forego too much of their eating time. Women were now present at all dinners, and a gentleman should "Pay them the compliment of seeming to consider them capable of an equal understanding with gentlemen. . . . When you 'come down' to commonplace or small-talk with an intelligent lady, one of two things is the consequence; she either recognizes the condescension and despises you, or else she accepts it as the highest intellectual effort of which you are capable, and rates you accordingly" (1885). (It should be noted that many, if not most, of the etiquette books were now being written by women.)

No wonder it was so important to carry about a stock of small talk, and that successful hosts tried everything they could think of to keep the conversation flowing upon ego-soothing and probably safe subjects: "In order to prolong the time, and to enjoy the gentlemen's society as much as possible," wrote Alexis Soyer (1853), "I do not have the dessert placed on the table until ten or twenty minutes after the cloth is removed; this gives an opportunity for my guests to admire the beautiful Sèvres dessert plates, containing views of different French châteaux; this, of course, gives a subject of conversation to those who have visited them."

Dessert has remained a favourite locus for conversation, especially in those cultures where the table is still "de-served" or *desservie*, meaning that everything is removed and the cloth swept clean so that talking can continue, only raised to a higher intensity. In Hispanic countries the practice of conversation after dinner—the descendant of Greek and Roman symposia but without the copious drinking—is called *hacer la sobremesa*, "doing the tablecloth" or "doing dessert." Coffee is brought to the table (the sweet course itself usually counts as part of the dinner, and is removed for this ritual) and the guests linger, talking, sometimes for hours together. The Danes are similarly famous for conversation round the table. The table is felt actually to aid the conversation: moving away to the "withdrawing" room would mean a break in the togetherness achieved during dinner, and a moving apart from one another. The comfort of padded armchairs is not enough to tempt the group away. The table is something to lean on, to gesture over; it expresses what everyone has in common.

• *Feeding, Feasts, and Females* •

Because male and female sex roles are on a purely physical level complementary, gender has always been a primary metaphor for the allocation of roles in society. The image has allowed people to conceptualize such ideas as "Give and take," "Do what you can, and what you are most capable of doing," "Entrust yourself to other people when it becomes right to do so," and even "Take their wishes into account." The sexual model can be made to say other things also: "Protecting somebody proves the protector's superiority," "Might must prevail," or "Some are born to privilege and others to serve the lusts of the former." Poetic connections arise, as one would expect, from a metaphor: for example, production and reproduction may find themselves linked in thought, so that sexual behaviour is felt to influence the fruits of the harvest; if sexual behaviour is unsatisfactory, there will be nothing to eat. Men may decide that they too produce "babies," in the form of food; but men are needed for women to produce human babies, therefore women must help in the fields. The actual process of eating, which begins always with mother feeding and child being fed, is also "like sex," and the perceived similarity can influence such important social decisions as where and with whom people can be permitted to live. The provision of food and the serving of dinner are often organized on a sexual model, too. Men go, get food, and give it to their wives, while women stay, receive it, cook it, and serve it forth.

In order that all these perceptions and conventional distributions of power, and many others like them, might fit and operate without hitch, enormous care is taken to ensure that the sexual model translates smoothly into the social structure. Men and women differ sexually; everything must be done then to differentiate them (along the lines already perceived, of course) through the allocation and refusal of power and prestige, in kinds of employment, in clothing and socially approved physique, in carefully instilled outlook and expectation. Men and women must do different things, and doing different things will work better if they feel different things as well. If males and females are not constantly distinguished and kept separate, important features of the social structure, clear and comfortable features, might become blurred and shaky.

It has for most of history been common for men and women to eat apart, especially in public. Often taboos ensure that they eat different foods, women typically being forbidden various edible substances judged dangerous either to their morality or to their reproductive powers. Eating together in private often both entails and "means" marriage: it involves sharing the same house. Ceasing to eat together is tantamount to divorce—or ceasing to "sleep together," as we still put it. Our euphemism is not merely coy; it contains the suggestion of sharing the same private space. Cooking, like digesting, is a common metaphor for pregnancy. The woman offers cooking in exchange for sex; the man offers sex in exchange for cooking. It follows that women "receive" sex as men "are fed" food. Eating can be spoken of as synonymous with the sex act itself. In the languages of the Ghanaian LoDagaa and Gonja, the verb "to eat" is frequently used for sex, covering a semantic field very similar to that of the English word "enjoy."

The conjunction of the opposite poles of femaleness and maleness in the married couple is very commonly made to stand for socially and culturally vital oppositions, including one or more of the following: private and public, inside and outside, domesticity and "work," down and up, left and right, dark and light, cold and hot, back and front, curved and straight, soft and hard, still (female) and moving (male), and so forth. Being made to "stand for" these in turn enforces conformity with the expectations. If "a woman's place is in the home," her place implies all the "female" characteristics: interiority, quietness, a longing to nurture, unwillingness to stand forth, and renunciation of the "male" claims to authority, publicity, loudness, brightness, sharpness. These qualities have a multitude of practical applications; for example, they either make a woman altogether unfit and unwilling to attend feasts, or they influence the way she behaves while participating in them.

An ancient Greek wife would not have been seen dead at a symposium. She was thought—and considered herself to be—the embodiment of purity in the family. Her honour was, and had at all costs to remain, unassailable: the legitimacy of her offspring, and the honour of her menfolk, depended upon it. It was all right for *hetairai* (courtesans) to mix with revelling and orgiastic males; they were shameless women, outrageous in their freedom and lack of *tenue*. A dining room was called an *andron*, "a room for men": a woman eating there was a woman out of place, marginalized and unworthy of respect. Unphilosophically minded ancient Greeks apparently thought, as many people nowadays still do, that important ideas should never be discussed at table. Plutarch has one such symposiast put it like this: "Philosophy should no more have a part in conversation over wine than should the matron of the house." According to this view, the Persians got it right when they drank and danced with their mistresses, but never with their wives. Wives were serious, but *hetairai* and mistresses could be taken lightly. When men, therefore, were asked to a party, they left their wives at home. But a wedding feast was a crowded affair, Plutarch makes his sympotic conversationalists say elsewhere, because women were responsible for a lot of the activities at a wedding—and an invited woman must invariably come accompanied by her husband.

Formality at public events is almost invariably a male affair, because it involves social rank (which has often been denied to all but the very top women) and publicity. Formality has always been contrasted with relaxation and intimacy, which are enjoyed at home, where the women have their place. (Men inhabit both spheres, public and private, whereas women have rarely done so; this one-sided overlap is one of the important inconsistencies in the scheme.) It follows that at a banquet in many traditional societies, men observe rank and precedence at table, while women serve the diners, or sit and eat in a separate place where far less ceremony is observed; they might sit in a crowd in the middle of the room, for example, while the men are ranged in order round the walls. At a Winnebago Indian feast, the men sat observing strict precedence round the periphery of the meeting house, with plenty of room between them; the women and children crowded together in a tiny space behind a screen at the back. The women have generally cooked such feasts, though occasionally men will have insisted on handling the meat (a prestigious, "masculine" food) themselves. The women may even think of being permitted to serve the food as a tremendous, and jealously guarded, privilege. Women, say the Javanese who practise the *slametan* feast, are *mburi*, "behind" (that is, in the kitchen; during the feast they peep through the bamboo partitions at the men as they eat), whereas men are *ngarepan*, "in front," consuming the food prepared by the women.

In nineteenth-century Japan, women were seldom invited to dinner, but if they were they were expected to sit apart, in one corner of the room. In China, they feasted separately from the men, as women do in societies where there is a very strong division between the sexes. In the Ming period, the imperial women, dowagers, wives, daughters, and sisters of their men would host the wives of ministers and officials in the Inner Quarters of the Palace of Female Tranquillity. Their banquets were accompanied by female musicians. Hostesses were required, however, to offer fewer courses at dinner than the men, and to offer wine less often. It is assumed that in private, on ordinary occasions, male and female members of the imperial family ate together, as the commoners did. In the United Arab Emirates today, as in other Arab countries, women often meet and dine together, with complex and sophisticated civility.

It is with a great sense of superiority that a male host may "feed" his guests but not himself partake of the meal; and a woman who cooks and serves a dinner without eating much of it herself may do so with a real sense of the power conferred by the bestowal of food. (Guests always feel uncomfortable eating in front of an abstemious host.) But it is necessary for the giver to be present during the meal to enjoy this particular kind of ego enhancement, for prestige is personal: it is non-existent where there is no knowledge of the person being honoured. As late as the nineteenth century in French peasant households, the women would serve the men at table, but themselves eat standing, or draw up stools by the fire and hold their dishes on their laps; the old and the children might be expected to join them there. It is possible, but unlikely, that such an arrangement expressed appreciation and respect for women.

Young boys in strictly sex-segregated societies must one day make the transition from living as children with the women to joining the men. The initiation, whether accompanied or not by ceremonial rites, is effected in large part by the young male taking his predestined place in public life, among the men at dinner. Girls do not take this step; they remain, in this sense, children. (To "stay where you are," even metaphorically, is of course to cleave to the principle of stillness and centrality which has hitherto been so important in the symbolism of being female.) A man often prefers a woman to keep the status of dependent child: he may reward her for accepting this position by finding her sexually attractive if she does so.

A woman maintains her role as mother by feeding her family; some African societies are said to think of the wife as "mother of her husband" for this reason. Food is a female concern, and often one of the main sources of a woman's power in the household. Women gather food, shop, choose what is to be eaten, and cook it. Social anthropologists have long called women the "gatekeepers" of food supplies in the house. However, since they choose food which they know their husbands and children like and demand, the "gatekeeper" role is often merely executive. Women are reported to make their cooking expressive of their feelings: they "reward" men by producing a special dish, with particular care; they show disapproval by not having dinner ready on time, or by refusing to put effort into the meal. Gertrude Stein tells the story of her French cook Hélène, who disapproved of Matisse because a Frenchman "should not stay unexpectedly to a meal particularly if he asked the servant beforehand what there was for dinner." One could expect such behaviour from foreigners, but in a Frenchman it was unacceptable. When Matisse was invited to dinner she would, for example, serve him fried eggs, never an omelette. "It takes the same number of eggs," she coldly asserted, "and the same amount of butter, but it shows less respect." Monsieur Matisse would understand.

If an African wife refuses to cook at all, her husband cannot make her do it; men are often not only incapable of cooking but forbidden to cook. In some Nigerian tribes they are not allowed even to discuss food or express directly a desire to eat: a Jukun male will say, "I am going to eat," when he means he is thirsty, and use a phrase like "I shall go into my hut" (the *kunguni*, where Jukun males eat alone) for "I want some dinner." Eating, for him, requires the kind of euphemism which in our society is reserved for sex or excretion. This attitude towards eating is part of the allocation of roles, and again it goes back to the sexual model: "giving food" for women corresponds to "giving sex" for men; it would be extremely confusing to do things the other way round. It is fairly common for a man to refuse to eat what his wife has cooked, as a sign of his displeasure; he is protected, of course, from having to do without food altogether if he has several wives. A further connection between food and sex is suggested by the fact that a polygamous male usually eats food prepared by the wife he is currently sleeping with.

Brewing beer is an ancient female preserve; and where beer is central to the economy and nutrition of a society—as it often still is in Africa, among South American Indians, and elsewhere—control over it naturally becomes a source of female power. It may link up with another commonly traditional female skill and responsibility: that of making and controlling the use of clay pots. (The ancient Greek god Dionysus—feminine in so much of his nature—had power both over wine and over the area of Athens called Ceramicus, where pots were made.) We have seen how the Newar women of Nepal must personally serve the beer they have made, even at a public feast. Among the LoDagaa of Ghana, a woman's good beer can turn her home into a beer house, a place where people gather to exchange news and gossip. She sells her product, and pours it out for her clients, always setting aside a calabash of it for herself to show she has not poisoned the batch. She plays a role rather like that of European society hostesses who used to keep "open house" or a "salon" on certain days of the week where people could collect together and socialize. The hostess of a tea party, like the LoDagaa breweress, must pour the tea.

Because food and drink usually reach the family through the women's hands, fear of women frequently translates into suspicion that they are poisoners. Knives, in the traditional view, are "male" weapons. They are wielded aggressively, and they pertain to the masculine realm of fighting, war, and the hunt; they are essential for carving meat. From a symbolic point of view, knives are phallic. We have seen how in medieval Europe, men were supposed to cut for their womenfolk at table. Poison, on the other hand, is a secretive, sneaky way of killing anyone, in addition to which it is often liquid, and administered in food—all of which makes poison a peculiarly "female" weapon, certainly in the folklore and mythology of all races, and possibly in fact as well. Fear of poison can strengthen the pressure upon men not to rove, but stay with their families: they might eat only what is prepared for them by their wives or mothers, or by women otherwise in their control.

Alcoholic drinks, like knives, have always been thought especially dangerous in the hands of women, and men have taken great care to prevent their own partiality for alcohol from infecting "the fair sex." Their solicitude has, until recently, been effective: the percentage of female heavy drinkers has usually been comparatively very low. (It is now rising alarmingly, according to Noel and McCrady for example.) Women must take responsibility for their unborn children, and it is certain that heavy drinking during pregnancy can have ill effects. In any case, what was disgraceful behaviour in a man was always far worse if seen in a woman. During the nineteenth century in Europe, women at table were not to ask for wine; the men were expected to keep them supplied. A man would serve himself and his female partner simultaneously: he would bow, then drink with her. Women were expected not to accept wine every time they were offered it. In France it was correct for a man to offer a woman water at the same time as wine, for a woman, says the Baronne Staffe, never drinks wine neat except at the dessert: she always insists that it be *trempé*, mixed with water.

Women in the Mediterranean countries, from the sixteenth century until recent times, appear to have astonished visitors by their sobriety. In France, in particular, men "cut" their wine with water, but "honourable" French women, if they touched wine at all, "used it merely to redden their water slightly." Wine, these days, has become an object of awe and reverence; the only people who add water to it are those who can obtain it cheaply and drink it regularly, and who pay comparatively little regard to its quality. Women drink it at table as much as men do—but even the most recent of etiquette manuals cling to the idea that men should really serve women with the dangerous liquid, "regardless of the symbolism," as Miss Manners puts it. If the host (not the hostess) does not get up and refill glasses when necessary, then "each man should pour wine for the woman on his left."

"Young ladies do not eat cheese, nor game, nor savouries," states a late Victorian etiquette book. The reason was almost certainly the same as that occasionally suggested for women not drinking: their breath would cease to be pleasing to men. Women still conform to expectations about eating less than men do, and preferring lighter, paler foods—chicken and lettuce, for example, over beef and potatoes. In Japan, women were actually given smaller rice bowls and shorter, slimmer chopsticks. In the Kagoro tribe of northern Nigeria, men use spoons, but women are not allowed this privilege. Among the Pedi of South Africa, in the 1950s, women and children used the special men's porridge dishes, but only when they were cracked and "no longer sufficiently respectable" for male use. Cooking and serving food to the men as they do, women are accustomed all over the world to eating what is left over from dinner; they are often able, of course, to look out for themselves while preparing the meal. In Assam, where pollution rules mean that lower castes may accept food from higher castes but not the other way round, a woman eats from the same plates as her husband, after the men have finished their meal: nothing could make the pair more intimate, and nothing could more clearly demonstrate that she is lower than he.

In Europe, families have often eaten all together at home, though where several families lived in one dwelling and dinners fed a lot of people, it was probably most common for the men to be fed first, served by the women. It was the nobility who took part in most of the formal banquets, and among them women were sometimes admitted, sometimes allowed on sufferance, and sometimes excluded altogether. During the Middle Ages, women might sit in a gallery or balcony especially provided so that they could watch the men at dinner. But noblemen could at certain places and times sit each with a female partner beside him—"promiscuous seating," as the Victorians were to call this arrangement. Another possibility was for all the women to sit at one end of the table, apparently as meticulously ranked as were the men at their end. At very big banquets there might be ladies' tables, apart from the men's. We are told that Louis XIV would invite particular women whose company he fancied to join him at high table, or have the noblest and most beautiful women seated at his table for him; his wife the queen, who might be present, or obliged to preside over a separate, all-female dinner elsewhere, did not have the equivalent privilege.

From Elizabethan times women seem to have carved meat at British tables; this is a marked departure from the outlook which insisted that knives were the perquisites of males. In the early eighteenth century the hostess often did all the carving and serving of meat at table. Lady Mary Wortley Montagu as a young girl took carving lessons; on the days when she presided over her widowed father's table, "she ate her own dinner earlier in order to perform without distraction." As the century progressed, men would offer to help their wives or daughters in this task. But by the end of the eighteenth century, servants increasingly carved for the diners; and with the arrival of dinner *à la russe* in the mid-nineteenth century, carving at formal meals was invariably done by servants, away from the dining table itself. At family dinners, the tradition has survived in Britain of the chief male portioning out the roast before the assembled group.

At the end of dinner, wrote Emily Post in 1922, the hostess, having decided that the moment has come, "looks across the table, and catching the eye of one of the ladies, slowly stands up. The one who happens to be observing also stands up, and in a moment everybody is standing." The choreography is strict: the gentlemen give their partners their arms and conduct them out of the dining room into the drawing room. They bow slightly, then follow the host to the smoking room for coffee, cigars, and liqueurs. If there is no smoking room, the women leave the dining room alone. The host sits at his place at the table, and the men all move up towards his end.

Where port is served, the bottle on its coaster stands before the host, the tablecloth having been removed before the ritual begins. He pours for whoever is on his right—to save this person, seated in the honourable place, from having to wait until last to be served. Then the bottle is slid reverently along the polished wooden tabletop (originally so that the dregs might be disturbed as little as possible, though all good ports should be decanted before they are drunk); or it is rolled along in a wheeled silver chariot; or it is handed with special ceremonial gestures from male to male, as drinking cups were handed at ancient Greek symposia. But port is passed clockwise (to the left), not as drinks circulated in ancient Greece, to the right. "Beg your pardon, sir," says Jingle in *The Pickwick Papers*, after the waiter has left the men to themselves, "bottle stands—pass it round—way of the sun—through the button-hole [both these expressions are ways of saying "to the left": men's buttonholes are traditionally placed on the left]—no heeltaps [meaning "leave no wine at the bottom of the glass"]." At the British Factory House dinners in Oporto, the men move into a second dining room in order to enjoy vintage port, for fear of any smell of food interfering with the drink's aroma.

The men discuss politics, and sit with whomever they like; hierarchical seating is often suspended at this time. It is even correct for a man "to talk to any other who happens to be sitting near him, whether he knows him or not," wrote Emily Post in 1922: the men are at last among themselves, and rules can be relaxed. The women, meanwhile, are served coffee, cigarettes, and liqueurs in the library or the drawing room. The hostess sees to it that no one is left out of the conversations which take place. By the 1920s, all of this lasted no longer than fifteen to twenty minutes. The host "takes the opportunity of the first lull in the conversation" to shepherd the men to "join the ladies" in the drawing room. When the men arrive, they must cease talking to each other and find a woman with whom to converse.

This ritual performance was commonly carried out at formal dinner parties in Britain at least into the 1960s; it probably still occurs. Americans were told by Emily Post exactly how it was done into the middle of this century, even though at least one American etiquette book a hundred years earlier had professed disgust for the idea. Several foreign visitors to Britain in the eighteenth century had found the custom exotic and distasteful. On the Continent, the company and conversation of women had become essential to the makings of a good dinner party; there was no question of doing without them at any point in the proceedings. Men of polished manners were not supposed to hanker after the kind of behaviour, associated with male company, which could not stand the scrutiny of women.

For the point of the ceremony of women "leaving the table" and men being left alone until they "joined the ladies" was not only that men wanted to discuss matters which could not be expected to interest their wives or be understood by them. The origin of it lay in the heavy drinking and toasting, the coarse jokes and laughter among men which the presence of women might inhibit. The ladies would leave the men to it, and perhaps eventually have to go home alone, as drinking and roistering continued into the night. In eighteenth-century Scotland, according to Lord Cockburn's *Memorials*, "saving the ladies" meant that the men would take their womenfolk home, then return to the scene of the dinner party to drink competitive healths to them. They paired off to see who could imbibe more in honour of his true love, "each combatant persisting till one of the two fell upon the floor. . . . These drinking competitions were regarded with interest by gentlewomen, who next morning inquired as to the prowess of their champions."

Heavy toasting died out during the nineteenth century, but a new reason for the men staying on alone came in with the advent of smoking, which at first respectable women would not dream of trying. By the time the ceremony of the ladies' withdrawal was described by Emily Post, it had been firmly contained within constricted time limits. There had been significant changes: for example, it had previously been necessary for the women to send a servant in to call the men to them—in Thomas Love Peacock's novel *Headlong Hall* (1816), "the little butler now waddled in with a summons from the ladies to tea and coffee." At a later date, coffee would be sent in to the men to remind them soon to adjourn. Later still, the men were expected to curtail their own gathering and show at least ritual eagerness to rejoin the women. Both men and women, Post is careful to insist in 1922, now smoked; women must be supplied with cigarettes too, and the thought of anyone getting drunk does not even arise.

Another idea behind the ceremony was that when men and women were together, they felt constrained to behave very formally; only when the sexes were segregated could they relax and "be themselves." The dinner party, with its newly necessary "promiscuous" seating (men and women alternating at the table), had been an exhausting performance; it had actually been quite difficult, because of the seating, to speak to people of the same sex as oneself. The after-dinner time among men at the table or women in the drawing room was conceived as a relief from having too strictly to "behave." English nineteenth-century novelists often use the separation of the sexes after dinner as a chance to further the plot by means of free conversation, and a male character's arrival from the dining room, his choice of a female partner for conversation, became dramatic expressions of the women's interest in him, and of his preferences.

All through history, women have been segregated from men and from public power, and "shielded" from the public view; they have been put down, put upon, and put "in their place"—a place defined by males. Yet this is not the whole story; and in the long run it may not be the most important story. For women—and men have very often admitted it, in their behaviour if not always in words or in kindness—have been an enormous civilizing influence in the history of humankind. It is not only that the way women are treated in any specific society is an infallible test of the health of that society. Women have also played the role—and it has been with the connivance of men—of consciousness-raisers in the domain of manners, comfort, and consideration for others. And the more men prized civilized manners, the more they "behaved" in the presence of women. The ideal claimed by Americans in the nineteenth century, when the custom of the ladies leaving the men after dinner was found distasteful, was in fact a sign that grown men were ready to think it normal to behave decently even when there were no women present.

Women certainly felt more immediately the advantages of courtesy—"*la courtoisie généreuse*," the Baronne Staffe called it—and accepted the ceremonial artificiality which saw them as "weaker" than men, but also "finer." Women had to be bowed to, have hats lifted to them, doors opened for them, seats offered to them; they were served first at dinner. Theirs was, ritually speaking, the higher place, in spite of the underlying realities of their social and economic position. Women in "polite society" consequently became sticklers for etiquette—conservative perhaps, but also protective of the gains conquered. The etiquette manuals, many of them written by women in the nineteenth century, are filled with comments about male difficulties with correct behaviour, and bristling with advice about how men might improve themselves. They always assume that women find it far easier to manage all the skills and nuances required.

And in fact it has come to pass that in many important respects women have won. Men who succeed and are admired in our culture must demonstrate that they have opted for finesse, sympathetic awareness, and self-control. "Male" vices which men forbade in women, such as alcohol abuse and smoking, have become disreputable in men also—although many women are now claiming the "right" at last to indulge in them. Fighting, swaggering, overeating have all gone out of style; one result of the technological revolution has been to remove the requirement that "real men" should show themselves to be rough, tough, and overbearing: one does not need to be physically powerful in order to control the instruments of technology. The gap between the sexes has closed not only because women have increasingly entered what has until now been the men's public sphere of operations, but because men have gradually been made to feel that they should attain the level of behaviour which previously they expected only from the opposite sex. In short, they have become more like women.

• All Gone •

The last piece of food left, either on the serving dish or on one's own plate, is important. Either it must be eaten—it is offensive and irritating, lying there: someone must be encouraged to take it by being assured that the last piece brings prosperity; or it should be left—it is greedy to grab it, or to wipe one's plate too clean, and the one who does so will suffer misfortune later in life. Either the last piece is a "thrive bit" or a "force piece," promising future health and strength; or it is the "etiquette piece," which is there to be refused—the one who takes it will be an "old maid," remaining as single as that last piece on the plate. The host (or the mother of the family) wants the food eaten; diners at one's table are there to be given to, and an empty plate shows the host or the cook to be both generous and appreciated. But diners must not be greedy, must not be there merely for the food. Greedy people, especially greedy women (no one is called "an old bachelor" for taking the last piece), are not attractive to others.

The host, wishing to override the unwillingness of a polite guest, may force the issue by saying something like "Do take the last piece—or my daughter won't get married!" and the guest, who may or may not have wanted the last helping all along, will have to comply; it is an opportunity to show a desire to be obliging. A "last piece" from one's personal portion of food may be set aside because it is the most delicious morsel on the plate, as a "reward" to the eater, who has "saved the best for last," in the manner of dessert. A Chinese fortune cookie is a "last piece," rounding out the meal with a bland crunchy mouthful, and—now that dinner is over and we are ready to return to the fray—containing a message about the future.

It is extremely rude to take away a person's plate before he or she has finished eating. An ancient Roman would interpret this to mean sudden death to the person whose plate or "portion" it was: a meal, even a plateful, is symbolic of a life. Nowadays, a polite guest might be embarrassed to show too much interest in finishing the food: he or she might, in order to save face, swallow the resentment and let the error pass. Guests must, accordingly, have a means of letting it be known when they intend to eat no more. A Chinese guest will put down his chopsticks, often resting them across the top of his bowl, and tell all the other people to take their time eating. They ask him if he is full; he says he is, and by this means excuses himself from further helpings. He may leave the table at once without offence, or stay on until the others have finished. (The guest of honour is an exception; he, like the host, must stay till everyone has stopped eating.)

Users of knives and forks employ these implements to indicate whether they have finished eating or not. In Europe, every country has its own method, and foreign visitors are carefully instructed, in etiquette manuals for travellers, how to make this sign; it is one of the most obviously distinctive customs left, and not knowing what to do could have unfortunate consequences. In Greece, you cross your utensils on the plate, the knife safely *under* the fork, which must lie with the tines down. Alternatively, one may remove the napkin from one's lap and lay it beside the plate—an action which in other countries signifies a readiness to rise from the table. In eastern Germany or in Czechoslovakia, crossing the knife and fork would mean that you are *not* finished eating, just pausing for a break. (It must be a fairly long break, however, for it is rude to put the knife and fork down merely between bites; presumably people will receive a signal that something more important than mere chewing is about to occur.) The Belgians find it impolite to cross implements for whatever reason; when finished eating, they place their knives and forks (tines up) together across the top of the plate, *pointing left*. (Crossing things at table is often thought to be ill-omened: the Greek poet Hesiod, for instance, in the seventh century B.C., said a dreadful fate would attend the action of placing the ladle over the mixing bowl or crater.) If your fork is laid tines down in Denmark, it means you want more food: tines up expresses the end; but in Italy, forks are finally laid parallel to knives with tines *down*. If your knife and fork lie apart on the plate in Spain, you want more food. In Yugoslavia, both implements lying on the plate signify the end of the meal. Between courses, handles rest on the table, with tines and points on the edge of the plate—an arrangement from which Anglo-Saxons are severely discouraged from childhood. Americans are reminded by Emily Post never to push the plate away or to lean back and say, "I'm through"; they must lay down their knives and forks, tines up, usually parallel and either vertical or slantwise on the plate's surface, with the sharp edge of the blade facing in.

"When sitting by a person of rank," says the *Li Chi*, "if he began to yawn and stretch himself, to turn round his tablet, to play with the head of his sword, to move his shoes about, or to ask about the time of day, one might ask leave to retire." It is the host's duty at most parties to decide when the meal is over. At a Western meal, the serving of dessert and cheese, of course, alerts everyone that the last act of the drama is under way. At formal dinners until fifty years ago it used to be the custom to provide a dessert setting—dessert plate, doily, finger-bowl with flower petals floating in the water, dessert fork and spoon—which the diner had to set out on the table herself or himself. The finger-bowl was placed on its doily to the left of the place, the spoon and fork to the right and left of the plate. Dessert being over, fingers were dipped into the water (fingertips *only*) and dried on the napkin. The finger-bowl, as its restriction to formal occasions and fingertips shows, had become almost entirely ornamental.

We once rinsed out our mouths and spat the water back into this bowl—a custom which fell into disuse in the course of the nineteenth century. We once needed quite heavy washing, when we ate with our hands: finger-bowls were a faint echo of that ritual, surviving only because at dessert people peel fruit and eat smelly cheese. Polite diners—certainly if they were at a function formal enough to give rise to finger-bowls—never actually *touched* the cheese, however; they carried it to their mouths on pieces of bread. And at formal meals fruit requiring peeling should be attended to with knives and forks, not fingers. ("Never," advised a Victorian manners book, "embark on an orange.") Having achieved a uselessness sufficient to turn it almost entirely into a status symbol, the finger-bowl became the stuff of legends about ignorant foreigners and unaccustomed base-born guests who *drank* the contents of the finger-bowl; they had never seen a finger-bowl and took it for a sort of tumbler. Well-bred hosts had to put them at their ease by calmly following suit and drinking from their own finger-bowls, to save such guests from knowing how badly they had blundered and how much they had revealed of their unfortunate background.

In the Middle Ages, the final hand-washing was followed by a minstrel show. Some of these players were also experts in the art of making after-dinner wafers. In France, according to LeGrand d'Aussy, fruit, and presumably more hand-washing, came after the entertainment—but this changed in the fourteenth century, so that one last hand-washing, sensibly, followed the end of dinner. In England, the host or an honoured guest would say the end-grace; then the host stood and toasted the guests to finish off the meal. English royalty in the early seventeenth century had the high table dismantled so that it lay on the ground. They would then stand upon the "board" to wash their hands, a custom which the Constable of Castille, who witnessed it in 1604, called "very old"; he obviously thought it also quite exotic. In France, hot aromatized wine called hippocras was the *vin de congié*, the "parting wine"; it was accompanied by sweets, and taken standing. This was, LeGrand d'Aussy wrote in 1782, "the way we now drink our coffee."

We make a very heavy point of not permitting anyone to rise from the table before everyone has finished and agrees to leave. It is the host's responsibility to see that all have eaten their fill. He then puts his napkin on the table and rises to his feet, and all his guests follow suit: it would be extremely bad form, remarks Branchereau (1885), for a guest to make any sign of wishing to leave the table before this point. In Scandinavian countries, the end of the meal must include the formal thanks of the guests to the hostess, before leaving the table; this may be preceded by a tap on his glass from the male guest of honour, calling everyone to attention before he thanks the hostess on their behalf, and the female guest of honour then thanks the host. The *Li Chi* prescribes that polite guests, before leaving the dining space, should try to clear away the dishes; the host must, with forceful authority, prevent them from doing so. When processions into the dining room were important, processions left the room also—exactly the same precedence being observed.

In Assam, an orthodox Hindu diner must keep constant contact with his food, most often holding on to his plate with his left hand throughout the meal: to lose this connection is to turn his food into "left-overs," which are *cuva*—a pollution, capable of transmitting impurity. For this reason, all must finish their food and rise together. They then wash their hands, rinse their mouths, and chew betel nuts to purify them further. A Chinese host of a banquet asks his guests if they want any rice. They say they do, and this marks the end of the meal; no wine may be drunk with rice. When his small ritual serving of rice was completely finished, the extremely formal guest first placed his chopsticks on the bowl, then lifted it, bowed, and showed the company that all the rice in it had gone; it is still very bad manners to leave any rice uneaten. If the bowl was provided with a lid, he had then to cover it.

At the end of a European or American dinner, and perhaps again towards the end of an evening devoted to dinner and conversation, coffee is served. Where women left the men for the drawing room, they were there given coffee, and perhaps liqueurs; in the 1870s in

Britain, one way of summoning the men from their port, claret, and manly conversation was to send in coffee. Then, when the men had finished their coffee and returned to the womenfolk, everyone drank tea. The custom is a strange one, for caffeine prevents most people over the age of about forty from sleeping well that night. Part of the folklore of coffee and/or tea, however, is that it combats the effects of alcohol; it is served also because in our culture (in contradistinction to many others) we are expected to socialize after dinner, and not go to sleep.

In our own day, coffee plays an important role for us as a kind of initiation ritual, helping us to cross over boundaries which we have made increasingly strong, between work and leisure, home and "out." We take coffee "to wake us up in the morning" and to set us up for a day's work. Unless we have decided to treat coffee as an unhealthy and unworthy crutch which competent adults ought to do without, we drink it all day long in the office as well. (People trying to do without coffee provide themselves with sodas, juice, or water—often especially bought, purified water.) There may be a permanent coffee pot ready, full and hot, in one corner of the workspace. People often bring their own distinctive coffee mugs to work, a touching attempt to import some humanity and individuality into the office. Where tea is more popular, as it is in Britain, office workers listen for the jingle of the tea trolley arriving for the "break," or again have a set of teabags, sugar, milk, and permanent hot water on tap. Coffee and tea "keep us going" or "up to the mark." Coffee in North America is, mythically speaking, the opposite of alcohol: it is supposed to engender sobriety. When people have finished dinner, coffee "wakes them up" for conversation afterwards. Taken at the end of the evening it "gets them ready for driving," being felt to dispel any last lingering effects of alcohol. It ends the relaxation and pleasure of an evening out and marks the beginning of the return home. People afraid of not getting a good night's sleep if they drink coffee (they have to be ready for work in the morning) may be provided with coffee deprived of its caffeine: the taste, the colour, the social symbolism of the drink have become so important to them that they settle for coffee without what makes it (physically speaking) coffee.

Digestion, biologists and doctors tell us, is an exhausting business. Many cultures recognize this, and either end the evening immediately after dinner so that everyone can go home to bed, or they allow time for the guests to sleep off the meal before leaving. Lunch, in Hispanic countries, is followed by a siesta, as it is in traditional Iran. When H. Lichtenstein travelled in Bechuanaland in the first decade of the nineteenth century, he lunched with the African king, who sought out a quiet spot after the meal, lay down on the grass, and slept. The guests had to keep very quiet until he awoke; his councillors stood about meanwhile, waving ostrich feathers gently over him.

Since the women have often not participated in the meal, they feel less sleepy afterwards; indeed, even when they have taken part they need sleep less, and must clean up and do the dishes. Among the Newars of Nepal, a feast in honour of a tutelary divinity is a mixed male and female affair, eaten at a shrine in the country. A special clearing is made and a covering constructed beforehand. Lunch ceremonially ends with everyone being given a fraction of an areca nut to eat. Then the men smoke, chat, and sleep while the women wash the pots. (The convenient ceremonial dishes are leaves sewn together; they have become polluted by being left, and must be thrown away.) At about 4:00 p.m. the party feels sufficiently restored to return home to the village.

Dinner guests, especially if they have not been obliged to sit on chairs at a table, are often free to leave as soon as they have eaten their fill. After five minutes' eating at the *slametan* feast, an Indonesian guest in a low tone requests permission to "follow his will"; he gathers up the uneaten portion of his meal and leaves. In nineteenth-century Egypt, a guest needed only to say his end-grace aloud, and then he was free to go; and in Russia, where people used to eat a lot of food very quickly, they would soon go home to sleep it off. In such cases, the conversation takes place on arrival at the host's house; dinner itself is the climax and end of the occasion. A Chinese custom is for guests to attend several dinners in one night. They spend the evening coming, going, greeting, tasting, thanking, leave-taking; although they do try if possible to catch the "Four Heavies" (the Chinese version of the *pièce de résistance*), the four main dishes of the last course offered by the last host of the evening. (We should recall that Chinese banquets do not end with dessert.) This idea of moving from dinner to dinner, perhaps from restaurant to restaurant, one for each course, is enjoying some popularity in America today. It fits nicely into the mobility myth, and with the desire to cover as much territory, metaphorically as well as physically, as possible in the time allowed.

The hosts often decide when the guests should leave their house. One of the more spectacular exit rituals takes place in the United Arab Emirates. Aida Kanafani describes in detail an all-female dinner party, where the hostess announces the end of a visit by perfuming her guests in an elaborate ceremony designed to mark them with the honours of her house, so that when they return home their family will scent the difference, *her* difference, on their clothes. "Returning home, smelling nice, [the guest] is told: 'You must have been somewhere. You smell nice. Where were you? Who did you visit?'" Food is thought of as having nullified the aesthetic purity with which the guest, clean and perfumed, arrived at the hostess's house: she must have her purity renewed before she recrosses the threshold. When the food tray is removed, the end of the proceedings begins with the serving of coffee. The hostess then brings out her perfume box, and passes round several perfumes with bodkins for application. After all the guests have taken perfume, the incensing begins, with a lump of incense placed in the incense burner. Each guest first incenses her head, breathing the smoke in and passing the burner under her veil to let the scent impregnate her hair. At last she puts the burner under her robes and sits for a while with her dress and cloak tightly closed over the smoke; if any wisps of incense escape, she readjusts her clothes until it is all contained. After sitting like this for at least a minute, the guest hands the censer on to her neighbour. When all are done, the guests begin the ceremonial farewells that accompany their actual departure.

Deciding when to leave is often left up to the guests—but this does not mean that no rules apply. Guests must on no account leave too early, or stay too long. Formal dinner parties in western Europe and America used to last two and a half hours from arrival (on time) to departure, and a guest staying longer would not recommend him- or herself for another invitation. Leaving too early, on the other hand, can cause a whole party to break up; it is therefore very rude. "Never take out your watch to see the hour, as this would seem to remind others of the time," wrote John Trusler in 1804; one should rather "steal off as unnoticed as possible, for if you *chuse* to go, it is not necessary that you drag others with you." By this date, there was no longer the obligation to run the gamut of servants waiting for tips, then called "vails"; there was no need for an early leaver to feel suspected of skipping off without opening his wallet. Trusler actually says tipping is now impolite, because it looks as though you think your host is not giving good enough wages.

There are a few ways in which modern hosts can discreetly urge tardy guests to leave. In Germany, a guest must start being conscious of the time if the host ceases offering to fill the glasses; though if the hostess (as opposed to the host) pleads with one to stay, one should do so—but not for longer than thirty minutes. If a French host solicitously enquires "whether you would like something—*fruit juice perhaps?*," the cue has been given: either accept fruit juice or not, but leave in a short while. (Unfortunately, modern rules of this kind are usually unspoken and quite variable, so that one can never be absolutely sure, and must therefore opt for hypersensitivity.) A Romanian host is clearer: he quietly recorks the wine bottle.

In simpler, less time-constricted societies, feasts can last a very long time. Hosts may pressure guests, "prevailing upon" them, to stay for days, eating, sleeping, and talking, as in the terrible story of the Levite's concubine in the biblical *Book of Judges*, chapter 19. Or the guests, who might well have travelled some distance to make the visit, might simply refuse to depart. This clearly happens fairly often, because many societies have strategies in place for taking care of such an eventuality. The Pedi of South Africa take such abuses of hospitality very philosophically: they simply cease to consider the visitor to be a guest and turn him or her into a useful member of the family, with exactly the same work to do as everyone else, until the outsider gets tired and goes home. The Ainu of Japan actually have a feast they can give, called "the Feast of being Sent Back, the Mouth having been Cooked For." If the guest still refuses to take the hint, the host and hostess simply move out of the house and go to live with relatives; this apparently does the trick. The Elizabethan English used to play nasty practical jokes on guests who outstayed their welcome, such as inducing them to wipe their hands and faces with a wet napkin impregnated with powdered vitriol and gall—the effect of which was to stain their skin black.

In the past, getting home from a feast could be quite arduous, if visitors came from far away; and in any case the host wanted his banquet remembered as long as possible. It is therefore an ancient custom to give guests food to take home with them, or for eating on the journey back. Men whose womenfolk have had to be left behind might find an expectant family awaiting them at home: the unfortunate parasites of Greece and Rome must have used their dinner invitations in this way, to help support their kin. Ned Ward describes a banquet in seventeenth-century London:

When their Stomachs were Cloy'd, what their Bellies Denied,
Each clap'd in his Pocket to give to his Bride;
With a Cheese-cake and Custard for my little *Johnny*,
And a Handful of Sweet-Meats for poor Daughter *Nanny*.

The left-overs of a meal have often been a matter for concern—they should not be left lying around and wasted ("Gather up the fragments that remain, that nothing be lost," said Jesus after the multiplication of the loaves and fishes). The poor would gather about the gates of a house where a great feast had been held, expecting to be given what was left: hosts in the Arab world today cook far more than is required for the party, in order to display this largesse afterwards. Some restaurants now offer "doggy bags" in order that their patrons may take home the expensive food they have not been able to ingest at one sitting; Chinese restaurants have an old tradition of permitting this. Proust has a society hostess use this gesture of generosity to crush a guest, turning him into a kind of parasite: "'You shall have some galantine to take home,' said Madame Verdurin, making a cruel allusion to the penury into which Saniette had plunged himself by trying to rescue the family of a friend."

When everyone is dressed for the outdoors and ready to go, there follow the ceremonies of recrossing the host's threshold. This was a dangerpoint when important people used to need to restrict their acquaintance even further than the exclusivity of the party ensured, or when women had to exclude the possibility of recognizing merely interested, rather than interesting, males. The hostess rises, according to a nineteenth-century writer who calls him- or herself a "Member of the Aristocracy" (1881), and shakes the hand of everybody. Guests, he or she goes on, must on no account formally say goodbye to one another, but only to their host and hostess. They may salute other people only if they are nearby, or if they necessarily walk past them. Guests have come to honour their hosts; they must not seem to be openly using the occasion in order to rub shoulders with others. (The coarseness of the expression gives some idea of the danger: dinner brings people into close contact.)

In Japan, in the Arab world, and elsewhere, there follows the threshold business of putting on shoes. In many traditional societies the host would have to dress up as well and accompany his guests to the gates of his estate, or even take a guest of honour part of the way home. In Latin America, visitors—who are supposed to protest by saying *"No se moleste!"* ("Don't bother!")—must be accompanied without fail to the outside exit or to the street. A host will walk with them to the bus stop, and even wait there till the bus comes; or at the very least stand for a moment or two, watching the guests as they disappear down the street. A Tanga feast had not ended until, by means of a log-gong, all the villages in the vicinity had been informed about the details of the feast: how much food had been distributed, how long the party had lasted, how many people had graced it with their presence.

Later, there must be another feast. Sometimes the left-overs are kept especially for a smaller, more intimate party, or several of them, soon after. During the banquet, there has occasionally been time set aside for planning a future meal: who will give it, and at what date. When it does take place, the hosts of the present feast may be given special delicacies, to remind them and everybody else of their previous generosity. In our own culture, it has been the custom to call and leave visiting cards within a few days after a party; nowadays, thoughtful guests telephone, or better still send a card or letter with their thanks. They ought soon, of course, to plan a return invitation.

At a Tanga feast, guests who have finished eating simply gather up their food-baskets and leave without a word. They do not say goodbye, because feasting never ends, and to sound valedictory might be to insinuate that socializing—indeed, society itself—might conceivably grind to a halt.

5

No Offence

When Gargantua was a very young giant, he was "brought up and disciplined" as his father Grandgousier (Great Gullet) ordained. But the process took time, and Gargantua was not only "untamed" at first as ordinary infants are, but—such is the nature of giants—too big to control easily. Before he began his education under Ponocrates, and long before Rabelais's culminating utopian vision of the good life lived in communal harmony in the Abbey of Thélème, baby Gargantua's manners were abominable. His misbehaviour while eating, though joyful and natural, was especially hard for other people to take, and something would have to be done about it: "He was always rolling in the mud, dirtying his nose, scratching his face, and treading down his shoes. . . . He pissed in his shoes, shat in his shirt, wiped his nose on his sleeve, snivelled into his soup, paddled about everywhere, drank out of his slipper, and usually rubbed his belly on a basket. He sharpened his teeth on a shoe, washed his hands in the soup, combed his hair with his wine-bowl, sat between two stools with his arse on the ground . . . drank while eating his soup . . . bit as he laughed and laughed as he bit, often spat in the dish, blew a fat fart. . . ." He also threw up his food, picked his nose, ate his white bread before his brown, reckoned without his host, scraped his teeth with a pig's foot, and let his father's little dogs eat out of his dish, while he ate with them. He was rambunctiously dirty, grotesquely lacking in discrimination, ignorant of order and decorum, heedless of the squeamishness of others, and incapable of keeping his body under control for their sakes.

Claude Lévi-Strauss says that one difference between our own attitude and that of the "so-called primitive people," the American Indians he describes, is that good manners for us are a means of self-protection, whereas they seek to protect others from themselves. The etiquette of "pre-modern" people arises from an anxiety above all to spare others from their own impurity. We, on the other hand, "wear hats to protect *ourselves* from rain, cold, and heat; we use forks to eat with, and wear gloves when we go out, so as not to dirty *our* fingers; we drink through a straw in order to protect *ourselves* from the coldness of the beverage, and we eat preserved foods to make things easier for *ourselves* or to defend *ourselves* from the theoretical dangers associated with rawness or rottenness. Yet in other societies, today as in former times, hats, gloves, forks, drinking tubes and pre-served foods are meant as barriers against an infection emanating from the body of the user" [Lévi-Strauss's italics].

We are certainly more selfish than the Indian tribes as Lévi-Strauss describes them; but in fact we too are taught to consider the feelings of others, if only because we want to be accepted and approved by them. We learn as we grow up that behaviour like that of Gargantua makes people recoil from us in disgust—and unless we suffer from mental sickness we are all intensely aware of the reactions of others, and want to be favourably received. At table we are not only together but separate: we protect ourselves, but we also protect others from experiencing us as threatening, unpre-dictable, or disgusting. We know that we cannot commune unless "respect" (which entails social distance and physical propriety) is maintained. Our avoidance of disgusting behaviour when in com-pany (and even, if we are "socialized" enough, when we are alone) corresponds in part to the American Indians' "protection of others from their own impurity" which impressed Lévi-Strauss with its generosity of spirit.

Many breaches of table manners arouse disgust in the people obliged to witness them. "Gust" (French *goût*) is "taste," a culinary metaphor, and disgust is perhaps most primevally a reaction to dangerous or otherwise revolting food. It is actually bad manners openly to rejoice in gristle, spines, and cartilage (Athenaeus), or, like Dickens's villainous dwarf Quilp in *The Old Curiosity Shop*, to crunch eggs with their shells on and prawns complete with heads and tails. Disgust is also aroused by the improper *treatment* of food, by indelicate grabbing, slopping, splattering, and messing, by failures in bodily propriety while eating is performed. Inadequately controlled behaviour calls forth several gestures of avoidance from others. The face alone, apparently universally, evinces some or all of the following when disgust is aroused: lowered eyebrows, partially closed eyes, nostrils narrowed or shut by the nose being screwed up, upper lip raised, corners of the mouth turned down and back (the opposite of a welcoming smile), tongue moved forward or protruding (a metaphorical facial version of arms pushing something away). Expressions of disgust serve to warn other people, and to share the shock and disapproval with them. The human face does not produce all aspects of this expression, however, until its owner is between two and four years old—at the very age when children begin to learn how to be embarrassed. Before this stage, children know fear and shyness, but they never blush or cringe or react in other bodily ways to social faux pas.

Embarrassment, which often results from the disgust of others, is a mechanism that maintains awareness and teaches never-to-be-forgotten lessons in decorum. It is a painful experience of *social* pressure. We blush, fidget, go cold, or turn pale when we fail to live up to the expectations of others; embarrassment arises when one is revealed to be incompetent, in the presence of other people. Both factors are necessary: first wanting to look good, and second the audience to whose expectations one fails to measure up. It is immediately obvious that eating in a group sets the stage for possible misdemeanours of an embarrassing kind. There is at table a level of competency that everyone hopes for, a concerted determination to prevent the occurrence of disgust, and a circle of witnesses to every performance. Any kind of falling off—thinking spaghetti may be eaten in one's hands and proceeding to do so, letting custard drip down one's beard, a sudden involuntary noise—reveals incompetence, and gives rise to the possibility of disgust and therefore to embarrassment, not only in the perpetrator but in everyone else as well, for embarrassment is contagious. Embarrassment arises not from wickedness but from *impropriety*, from not "fitting in" or "measuring up," from letting everyone down and introducing into the company what everyone had hoped to avoid.

Both embarrassment and disgust are expressions of social pressure and exaction, yet they arise so intensely in the individual that they often produce involuntary physical reactions as well. They are symptoms of the power of interaction between the person and the group. The effects of both embarrassment and disgust are to halt and impede—disgust causing us to recoil when we encounter something offensive, and embarrassment freezing and inhibiting us when we have been caught out ourselves offending others and betraying the image we wish to present of ourselves to the world. Table manners, even nowadays, are underwritten by both sanctions; to know and practise them is to have nothing to fear, but to flout them is necessarily, sooner or later, to be required by others to pay.

• *Pollution* •

Human beings have always found it easy to believe that wickedness might have physical consequences, and conversely that visible and tangible things "out of place" can reflect something evil being done, or a past evil deed lying hidden and unrequited. Odysseus' men killed the forbidden cattle of the Sun, and the meat, cut up and skewered as shish-kebabs, wriggled and mooed at them, as a sign of the anger of Zeus. A prophet can see—they themselves cannot—that the outrageous Suitors, eating up the substance of Odysseus' fortune, are sitting down to a meal with the blood of their future deaths dabbled disgustingly over their food and dripping down the walls of the hall. Knocking over the salt cellar can be perceived as the sign of an evil fate: the gesture is a symptom of heedlessness and poor control, and probably reveals a psyche troubled. Blood—like salt—is to be kept where it belongs, in blood's case within the body, in salt's within the cellar. When it is spilled, it means violence: past viciousness and carelessness, and violent consequences. Modern people, who pride themselves on escaping such a primitive concept as a perceived connectedness between morality and physical symptoms, have found a new meaning for the word "pollution": black ooze covers golden sand beaches, the sky rains poison, plants and animals grow stunted and die—and we conclude that heedless human greed has come to haunt us in physical form. We ourselves are not only moral but physical beings—and we tend, often cruelly and irrationally, to accept the possibility of physical punishment resulting from moral corruption.

Pollution has always meant matter out of place, and rules broken. The *threat* of pollution has therefore been a powerful sanction for the rules and the categories by which a society organizes its life. Where there is a strong desire for clarity, for keeping people carefully in "their proper place," barriers are set up between societies and social classes, and the barriers are commonly "manned" by fears of pollution, which automatically infects anyone who tampers with the arrangements. Where pollution reigns, it is infectious, and no one can associate with a person polluted without receiving automatic contagion, until that person has been officially purified. Physical contact is an essential part of ideas about pollution: at their most direct, such laws achieve the desired avoidance and distance through the command, "Don't touch!" Eating food, cooking it, serving it, sharing it out, and passing it to others requires intensely intimate contact, both with the food and with the dinner companions. Pollution rules hedge food about, therefore, with particular fierceness.

The most famous and most complex examples of pollution-protected eating are to be found in India. There, social groups are set apart, as they often are elsewhere, by *what* they eat. If one society loves chicken, for instance, and another abominates it, an effective barrier has been erected between those groups: it is hard to draw close to someone with whom one never eats, and whose eating habits one finds unacceptable. On the other hand, the people who do eat chicken together identify themselves and one another thereby, and that symbol, interlocking with others, leads them on to discover how much more they have in common.

In India, where the caste system divides groups of people from other groups, prevents social mobility, and simultaneously fortifies the solidarity of those groups, eating rules sort people out and determine whether they are "high" or "low"—from the point of view of caste, and not necessarily of power—in relationship to one another. A person acceptable at one's table is also someone whose family might be eligible for alliance through marriage. Rejecting an offer of food is a sign of superiority towards the would-be giver—and it inevitably means that no daughter or son of the refuser could conceivably marry a child of the refused. It follows that weddings involve the powerful drama of families ceremonially and publicly eating together, with the bride and groom, and other members of their respective families, solemnly exchanging and eating pieces of food.

From the point of view of caste, the Brahman or priestly caste is the top of the heap, and the point of reference for classifying everybody else. Typically (and over-simply, for food rules are enormously complex and vary from group to group), castes are "higher" in the hierarchical order depending on whether or not Brahmans will accept food from them. To be able to give a Brahman water without his being polluted thereby is to be high-caste. If he will take fried food from you, your social level is higher still, and if he will allow you to give him boiled food, it is very high indeed. A low-caste person pollutes water on contact for those higher than himself; one lower still pollutes an earthenware receptacle by touching it; and if a brass receptacle cannot stay pure when you handle it, you are on the very bottom rung. (When someone becomes a holy ascetic, a *sannyasi*, he or she opts out of the caste system altogether. She, to take a female example, is much holier than a Brahman, who will bow to her and grasp her basest part, her foot—but will not eat with her, even if she was of a high caste before her religious conversion. The *sannyasi* scorns pollution rules, and is honoured for doing so; but Brahmans inhabit the world of human regulations, and the "indiscriminate" holy woman is therefore dangerous.)

In Bengal, Hindu society is divided as follows: first, Brahmans; second, those from whom Brahmans will accept water, that is, the royal or warrior Rajputs; then the nine branches of relatively pure serving castes; then those who can offer water but cannot have any but inferior Brahmans as priests. Below the water-givers come the groups who cannot offer water to a Brahman. The highest of these are the people who keep up their distinction from others lower than themselves by refusing to eat meat; then come people who will not eat beef, but permit themselves other kinds of meat and fowl. At the very bottom of the heap are people who stoop to eating beef, working leather, and other degrading—though entirely necessary—tasks. Because their pollution is so continuous and grave, other people cannot touch them. Contact itself has degrees of possible danger. In one village, touching is sorted into the following categories, in ascending order of gravity: touching your children, touching you, smoking your pipe (even without using the same mouthpiece, which would be horrendous behaviour), touching your brass utensils, serving you fried food, and (worst of all) serving you a boiled dish. People may in certain circumstances be considered so dangerous that they pollute by mere proximity, without any actual contact at all.

It is interesting to notice that, in India as elsewhere, purity is a state of being, and utterly passive—it can be lost, but not transferred, and it is powerless in the face of the impure. Pollution may be removed once it is incurred, and purity regained, by means of washings and other rituals. Also, the more intimate people habitually are, the less they pollute one another: they "belong together," and pollution is a *separating* mechanism. In India, the most ordinary everyday food is boiled rice—to which the most pollution danger attaches. Boiled, fatless, ordinary meals called *uta* are from this point of view *kacca*, or "imperfect"; you would tend to avoid eating these with strangers. Fried *tindi* or "snacks" are *pukka*, "perfect": they are purified by sacred butter (*ghee*), less liable to impurity, and therefore more "public" fare. Also, it matters desperately who cooks one's meal, for cooks touch pots, bowls, and the food itself. (They avoid tasting it, however, and learn to test doneness with their fingers and by smell.) When a Brahman gives a feast and wants as many people as possible to come, he chooses a menu of *pukka* food and cooks it himself, for his touch can pollute nobody.

For those who enjoy commensality, table manners decree that food should be passed to people higher than oneself with the right hand only. A woman may eat with her left hand and so symbolize her female, "left-handed" status; but she passes food with her right. Cups containing liquid may be correctly held in the left hand. Everyone must sit or squat on the ground; they must on no account stand, walk about, or lie down. (Modern custom, for example among the Jains, permits festal buffet dinners where people stand and eat; but this has become possible only within the past fifteen years.) Even the direction one faces is filled with symbolism relating to purity: looking east is purest, and most honourable, and no one whose parents are alive should be expected to face south. Washing, both before eating and afterwards, is meticulous; one's eating clothes must be absolutely clean, and bone dry. Dish washing is performed *before* the meal, not after: plates are most safely leaves, washed before use and discarded afterwards. It is dreadful to eat from a broken or impure vessel, or when one is suffering indigestion from a previous meal, or to eat too late, too early, or too much. People prefer not to eat in the open for this exposes food to unbounded social surroundings.

Walls round the dining space express purity as unviolated enclosure. Not only walls but the very outlines of one's body constitute a boundary to be kept unpenetrated and entire. Eating ineluctably crosses the boundary between "outside" and "inside," which is why one must be so careful when ingesting food. Saliva is extremely polluting—even if it is one's own; like excrement, it is a secretion from inside the body. One never presses one's lips to a cup's edge, because to keep doing so is to pollute one's own mouth: to a devout Hindu, our way of drinking out of cups and glasses is filthy and barbarous. In India, among Jains and others as well as Hindus, liquid is poured into the mouth from the cup, which does not touch the lips. One may be allowed to use the free hand to direct the flow of water, but without its touching the cup. Constant sipping is in any case discouraged by the custom of not drinking during a meal, but only afterwards. People may finally rinse their mouths with the water left over in their cups.

Eating boiled-rice-based meals with the hand is dangerous because fingertips and leaf plates are unavoidably touched and therefore defiled by saliva. The correct way to take food to the mouth is to grasp a small amount of it *from above*, pinching it with the fingertips. Food should never be scooped up, for then one would be eating—perhaps even licking—out of the hand, which is impermissibly defiling. Snacks, or *tindi* (fried morsels, dried fruits, sweets), can be—even though they often are not—tossed into the mouth so that there is no hand contact with the lips; this makes them safer than the relaxed, familial *uta*. If *tindi* items are too large to eat in one mouthful they should be broken, not bitten, because of the saliva. This is the reason why cooks cannot taste food, but must press and pinch it to see if it is done.

It is the porosity of clay bowls which makes them more dangerous than brassware at mealtimes; archaeological finds of huge numbers of clay sherds at Indus Valley sites suggest that in very early times the inhabitants of India were accustomed on occasion to employing clay vessels only once and ceremonially smashing them afterwards. Using a freshly cut, washed plantain leaf for a plate and throwing it away after the meal is both adequate and correct. Guests remove their own leaves, or hosts can do it for them out of courtesy and respect. A wife, as we have already seen, eats from her husband's leaf when he has finished his meal: it is a sign that she is "lower" than he. The husband must leave a little on his leaf as a sign of his affection, and so that she can honour him in this fashion. Children may similarly eat from their parents' "plates"; otherwise left-overs are extremely polluting, and diners should never end up with food remaining on their leaves.

Exotic as many of these rules might seem to Westerners, several of them are reflected in our own manners codes. We have looked briefly at how "good manners" have served in our own society to sort out the "refined" from the "gross," the "base-born" from the "well-bred." We call some of our reasoning "hygiene," but then dirt—matter "out of place"—is always a form of pollution. We are revolted, for example, by a fly in the soup; we are even likely, as one experiment demonstrated, to reject food that has been stirred with what we know to be a brand-new, unused fly-swatter. Alfred Hitchcock created a memorably nasty moment in *To Catch a Thief* (it is a film with many food-pollution devices) when Mrs. Stevens stubs out a cigarette in a fried egg. The audience invariably cringes with disgust.

Smoking used to be forbidden at table mostly because it offended against gourmet standards, ruining the "palate" of the smoker and the aroma of the food for everybody. Now, in North America, smoking commonly evokes what can only be called pollution reactions, including disgust and a fear of infection and contagion. Permission to smoke at the dinner table might be accorded only resentfully, or refused. People are often ejected from public buildings altogether if they insist on smoking, wherever the rule can be impersonally applied. (Pollution rules usually claim to be utterly impersonal.)

We are proud of expecting cleanliness at table, and love insisting that our standards in this regard have been raised considerably, and relatively recently; they are proofs, for us, of a typically Western concept, that of "progress." An eighteenth-century lady is said to have sat at dinner with filthy hands: we are given to understand that she had not adapted her old-fashioned aristocratic mores to the new standards of hygiene. When someone remarked on the grubbiness of her fingers, she is supposed to have coolly replied, "Madam, you should see my feet!" The story is memorable because awareness of our own comparative cleanliness "puts her down" in our estimation and shows how old-fashioned she was, even though we admire her unflustered confidence. We react to this, and to the shock, by smiling.

Bodily propriety with us includes consideration for others, and for the disgust they might easily (and rightly) feel: we agree with them, and would be similarly disgusted if they were the ones guilty of bad manners. Insisting on the rules protects the group, one and all. We raise the disgust threshold even higher by insisting that everyone should avoid not only doing anything likely to disgust others, but also *mentioning* anything disgusting. "As you would not bring upon the dinner or tea table anything which would affect the company unpleasantly," says the author of the anonymous American *Illustrated Manners Book* in 1855, "so you have no right to mention it." He or she goes on to list unmentionable subjects: details about diseases, operations one has undergone, battles and wounds, personal injuries, and deformities; these "wound the feelings, hurt the appetite, or impede digestion." Violence, once again, is too "close to the bone" at table. Less squeamish as we are in certain respects today, the stricture against lurid descriptions of gore and putrefaction still stands; we can expect listeners to such tales to be "put off their food." Accusatory and suggestive remarks about the food are also to be discouraged. The same nineteenth-century author gives as an example of tactlessness the story of a vegetarian lady who "characterized mince pie as 'chopped corpse and apples.'"

"You will do well," the writer goes on, "not to be talking of dogs when people are eating sausages," nor should one bring up the subject of cats when eating rabbit (presumably because sausages and cooked rabbit look as if they might be cooked dog and cat). We still hate having personally known an animal we are eating, and we even hate imagining that we might have known it. Dogs and cats are pets, and in a sense taboo: they are placed in a completely different category from animals we designate as to be "raised for" meat. We dislike thinking that we can have no idea what went into a sausage. Twentieth-century people feel so strongly about this that we have created unprecedentedly strict regulations governing such conglomerates as sausage meat; we prefer in any case not to speculate about what a sausage must once have been, especially while eating it. Finally, the author of the manners book humorously advises us "to skip this paragraph if you are reading aloud in company": laws have, unfortunately, to mention what it is that is forbidden. We do recognize a difference between polite "delicacy" and real danger, however—between fear and disgust. This is brought out in the advice of the comtesse de B., author of *Du savoir-vivre en France* (*On French Etiquette*, 1814): "Do not mention any caterpillars you may find in the salad, but do not hesitate to complain if there is glass or a pin in it."

The rule that diners should try not to offend means also that one should never behave oddly at table—not cut bread into strange shapes, show an excess of finickiness, wildly gesticulate, perform movements with too much elaboration. The idea is that one should not draw attention to oneself, and especially to one's manner of eating; it makes people feel insecure and distracts them from the conversation. If anything goes wrong, polite consideration enjoins that we should pretend it has not happened—for instance, if someone were suddenly to belch. It would even now be a singularly intimate gathering where jokes or other remarks could be exchanged about someone having belched.

The need for a polite facade is said sometimes to lead to a concerted covering up of faux pas, as when the host drank the finger-bowl water because the ignorant guest had done so, or when a visiting foreigner ate his asparagus tips and threw the ends over his shoulder: the Parisian *convives* all did the same in order to preserve him from the embarrassment of perceiving that his behaviour had been improper. Such events can never have been common, but they do form part of the mythology of etiquette; they are like small table dramas, complete with audience (us), hero, unpredictable visitor, chorus, and triumphant but civilized containment in a hilarious and satisfying climax. In fact, foreign guests have usually been expected to watch and follow the manners of their hosts, and it has always been possible and indeed courteous to explain one's customs to visitors. Occasionally we come across stories told about an impossibly arrogant guest, such as the Chinese warlord who was confronted for the first time with a banana, and ate it with its peel on. His host, to show him how it was done, conspicuously (but silently) peeled and ate his banana. The unregenerate guest grabbed another and said, "I always eat these things with the peel on," then proceeded to eat the second banana the same way he had the first.

Aspiring entrants to exclusive clubs are sometimes tested by being invited to dinner, to have their table manners scrutinized by the members who already belong: we cannot allow anyone into our solidary and frequently commensal group who does not "behave." (An especially disagreeable group might take pleasure in watching an ill-mannered guest, as when, in Buñuel's film *The Discreet Charm of the Bourgeoisie*, the chauffeur is invited into the company to display his ignorance of how to drink a martini.) It is said that at trial dinners like those for new Fellows at All Souls' College, Oxford, what examiners look for is not only knowledge of how to behave, but the correct ease and confidence of manner when unforeseen problems arise. A person on trial might, for instance, be given olives or cherries to eat but no plate for the stones. Approval is given not only for knowing that cherries and unsauced olives are correctly carried to the mouth with the fingers, but that pips (having been politely, that is, unobtrusively, ejected from the mouth into a covering right hand) can be laid on the table—provided that the action is performed calmly, with assurance, and without interrupting the flow of conversation.

• *The Rules and Regulations of the Mouth* •

One of the most powerful and paradoxical injunctions of modern Western table manners is that eating must be performed with the mouth closed. People who appear to have let their manners slide almost out of sight will, if they continue to eat in the presence of others at all, cling to this rule, partly out of habit (the majority of us are taught to eat like this from the beginning), but mostly because other people insist upon it. The rule is extraordinary because we are not expected to observe silence during meals. In many other cultures, people habitually eat in silence, and they have good reasons for doing so: requirements of speed, concentration, safety (gullets are for breathing as well as for swallowing; talking only adds a third complication), and a feeling that eating is sacred, with silence an expression of respect. We, on the contrary, consider it impolite, except in very intimate circumstances, *not* to talk—yet we are at the same time as strict as we are about anything that no one should be caught with an open mouth containing food.

In Europe, there were once regional variations on this point, and it could even be thought rather starchy to insist on keeping one's mouth shut when chewing. A sixteenth-century French text tells us that "Germans chew with their mouths closed, and find any other way of proceeding ugly. The French on the contrary half-open their mouths. . . . The Italians are very soft in the way they eat; the French, who behave more robustly, find the Italian manner too delicate and precious." The Italians appeared to be more relaxed than the tight-lipped Germans, though we are not told whether their mouths were open or shut: more probably open, since they are being compared directly with the French. Erasmus wrote, in a passage not referring specifically to table manners, as though closing one's mouth tightly were a rudeness: it "denotes someone afraid of inhaling some-one else's breath." On the other hand, he says that a mouth clamped shut, in paintings at least, gave the subject an air of probity. Germans seemed, perhaps, to be clean, controlled, and forthright about their preferences and fears when they chewed with their mouths closed. The French, in the passage quoted, appear to have been proud of their half-open mouths, and of suffering from neither Italian affecta-tion nor German strictness and standoffishness.

But gradually, in Europe and America, a consensus has been reached that we shall require everyone to eat with the mouth closed. Mouths are always, and in any case, to be guarded and treated with respect; they are bodily orifices, "weak points" in the body's defences. Through the orifices or "gates" in the wall of our body's outline, things foreign to it can enter, and substances which must be ejected issue forth. Excretions from the body emerge because they are unwanted, and we remove them and dispose of them as quickly and efficiently as we can. Faeces and urine are easy: they stink, and our reaction is direct. Tears, on the other hand, being salt and freely running, we separate off from the other excreta as belonging to the symbolism of water; they wash and purify, as we ceaselessly exclaim in poetry and song.

But other excreta are slimy or glutinous. Snot, for instance (which is usually produced, after all, when we weep), gives rise to something very different from the sympathy which tears evoke. It is nasty, vis-cous stuff, to be sniffed back, wiped away, or deliberately blown out and disposed of, as fast as possible. Such substances as phlegm, ear wax, vomit, and—most famously of all—menstrual blood have always aroused similar revulsion. Saliva, semen, and sweat (the last runs like tears but stinks as it ages) are sometimes easy to contemplate, some-times not: intimacy and affection are often required, and elaborate proofs of cleanliness and control, to make the difference. Effluvia and defluxions remind us of the symptoms of disease as well. Tears are striking but acceptable; a rheumy discharge from the eyes, on the other hand, is appalling—it is, for example, one of the attributes of the demons of pollution in Greek mythology, the Furies, whose pres-ence causes people to shudder with horror. (Shuddering, incidentally, is one of the primary reactions to pollution and disgust. Shuddering, shivering, or "goose-bumps" are the body's outline, its skin, reacting to threat. The word "horror" itself refers to the ultimate physical response to fear, which is the skin reacting so violently that tiny muscles in it contract and the hair stands erect—the basic meaning of *horror* in Latin is "hair standing on end.")

Negative physical reactions to body waste are common everywhere, though seldom experienced so strongly as by us; what is more unusual is our own extension of the category of stuffs arousing loathing to cover *anything* slimy. We hate whatever oozes, slithers, wobbles. Disgust at these physical properties may prevent us from liking, or even trying, to eat brains, lungs, eyes (the specificity of these animal parts—their reminding us of functions in living bodies—adds an extra dimension to our distaste). Some of us go so far as to refuse to eat okra, oysters, frogs, sticky rice or rice puddings, soft-boiled eggs, and the more glutinous porridges. The word "slime" is from *lime* or "glue," and is related to Greek *leimax* (French *limace*), a snail. Anglo-Saxons, more squeamish than the French, often find the idea of eating snails as abhorrent as eating frogs, merely because these creatures (when alive) are slimy and slippery; it is the *thought* of them, not the taste, which is offputting.

We feel happiest with what is *either* hard *or* soft, *either* solid *or* liquid: anything that is neither is "suspect," or too indeterminate to be safe. We prefer clear forms, firm outlines. One of the reasons why scuttling mice or cockroaches terrify otherwise sensible people is that they live in the cracks and joints of houses and furniture: they suggest that our lines, edges, and corners are not as secure as we rely upon them to be; they remind us how little we really are in control. Namelessness, shapelessness are liable to be associated in our minds with ooze, or "glug," a word that is currently receiving a new meaning: it originally imitated a swallowing sound, but is increasingly used to denote something gluey, a slimy mass which we would rather not investigate too closely. When we eat jelly or blancmange, we like to have it moulded first, and extremely clean-looking; moulded blancmange was actually called "shape" from the late eighteenth century to the early twentieth century in England.

When food is served to us on a dish, we like knowing what it is; Germans, British, Dutch, and North Americans particularly are liable to prefer it separated into clearly defined entities: meat, pota-toes, distinct vegetables. Sauced, jumbled dishes might be acceptable if thought of as "ethnic"; they are not clear and simple enough for "normal" eating. This is an attitude which is softening nowadays, as more and more "ethnic" food is becoming ordinary everywhere. But food in a dish is one thing—food in the mouth is something else. Do not open your mouth when you eat, wrote the author of *The Court of civill Courtesie* (1591), for people will see "the food rowle by—which is a foule sight and loathsome." Chewed food is on its way to being digested, mercifully out of sight. It is ground and thrashed about in saliva, mixed and mumbled in the mouth, and turned to slime. We are brought up, now as in the sixteenth century, to find the very idea of this—of something that has lost its characteristic shape and turned into a slimy mass—disgusting. No one must be allowed to show the contents of the mouth to others, or to remove food from the mouth once it has gone in.

An ancient Greek example of extreme laziness was the Mariandynian, Sagaris (not a Greek, of course), who "was fed until he was an old man at the lips of his nurse, not wishing to take the trouble to chew. . . ." The trouble with Sagaris was that he never grew up; weaning has usually been achieved by mothers pre-chew-ing food for their babies. This has long seemed distasteful in our own culture, the main reasons probably being the sliminess of the procedure and the taboo against adults removing chewed food from their mouths; the risk of germs spreading is, historically speaking, a secondary and late explanation. Yet we as parents are usually able to accept slimy sucked food from our toddlers without shock. One of the maturing rites of passage for new parents is learning to deal with slime, and with excreta generally. Babies reintroduce us to all of that. We learn to face what we had been taught was disgusting; we shall continue to be disgusted, but with more conscious awareness of the cultural dimensions of the taboo. And in any case our own babies are special: they are not to be separated from us, as other people are, by distancing reinforced with pollution avoidances. For somewhat comparable reasons, Indians hold saliva and left-overs to be horrible and polluting—yet men share food remains with their wives, and mothers with their children.

Where people eat with their hands from a common dish, it is etiquette that nothing bitten should be put back; it must be eaten entirely by the person who took it. In the days when it was good-natured to share food directly with others at table, people had to be reminded "not to offer a pear or some other fruit into which you have bitten." Such rules are made largely irrelevant by the modern custom of serving everybody separate portions, but we keep to the spirit of them by disliking teeth-marks left, for example, in bread. Bread is to be broken in pieces small enough to be consumed entire and not put back on the side plate: teeth-marks remind us of teeth, and anything bitten is "left-overs."

If a mouthful of meat proves too tough to chew, we are presented with a problem. In Erasmus's day it was polite to "turn away discreetly and toss it somewhere": the only area that counted, and had to be kept clean, was the table-top. However, bones and left-overs were on no account to be thrown on the floor in Erasmus's book, even though the dogs would have appreciated them. They were to be placed *neatly* at the side of one's trencher, or discarded in the dish called a voider. Special dishes for left-overs have officially returned to European dining-room tables in very recent years; the French call them *poubelles de table*, "table garbage containers." They are useful nowadays because they obviate some of the table-clearing. The disgust value of left-overs standing on the table is apparently reduced by carefully relegating them to their own particular, consciously provided dish.

Setting the table with knives and forks for everyone makes it possible for meat to be cut in small pieces before introducing it into the mouth, which is to be opened only just before the food reaches the lips. Gradually it has become improper for us to remove anything from one's mouth at all. "If food has been taken into your mouth," wrote Emily Post implacably in 1931, "no matter how you hate it, you have got to swallow it." "Only *dry* bones [my italics] and stones can come out again"—an example given is the tiny "second joint of a squab"—and those are to be taken "between finger and thumb and removed between compressed lips," or lowered discreetly onto a fork or into a cupped hand, and thence to the plate. They must first have been "made as clean and dry as possible in the mouth (with the tongue and teeth)." On no account must anything go directly from mouth to plate; a mediating, hiding, controlling hand or a deftly managed implement must always intervene.

Strictly speaking, what lifted the food to the mouth should also be used to remove bones or stones. But fish bones, having been lifted on a fork, may be removed with the fingers: fish bones are not only fine but frightening, and a special allowance is made for them. The special care demanded by fish enforces a delicate manner of eating it, and the myth of fish as "female" food—tender, pale, and not too copious—is underlined in consequence. Fish "tends to be regarded as an unsuitable food for men," writes Pierre Bourdieu of the French working class. It "has to be eaten in a way which totally contradicts the masculine way of eating—that is, with restraint, in small mouthfuls, chewed gently with the front of the mouth, on the tips of the teeth (because of bones)." The manner in which one must remove the bones with the fingers and deposit them on the plate is correspondingly fastidious. Fish makes one "nibble and pick," like a woman, and prevents "wholehearted male gulps."

Erasmus advised the boys to whom his essay on manners was addressed not to be first to take from the dish in case the food turns out to be too hot; one will be forced then "either to spit it out, or, if he swallows it, to scald his gullet—in either event appearing both foolish and pitiful." Knives, forks, and serving spoons, of course, made it less easy to judge whether a morsel was too hot. Seventeenth-century French etiquette demanded, if a scalding mouthful should inadvertently be taken, that one should lift the plate to one's mouth, spit out the food, and hand the plate to a servant; it was rude, in spite of the urgency of the situation, merely to let the food fall to the plate. Another method, mentioned in eighteenth-century French books of *civilité*, was to spit out the hot mouthful, but hold up one's napkin to hide the unpleasant sight. Again, it seems unlikely that someone in pain and shock would have the necessary presence of mind to carry this off. We are now much more used to hot food in the mouth—but probably far more cautious than we realize, sensing heat as the food approaches our lips. In any case the reappearance of the hot piece, since it would be unchewed, would not offend others too greatly, although the violence and the oddity of such an eventuality might.

Our dislike of seeing chewed food finds an echo in our distaste for people who squish and mash together the ingredients on their plates: everything should remain clean-cut and clear, even when it is speared or balanced on the fork, until it disappears neatly into the mouth. It was thought a "solecism to be avoided," in 1879, to carry two different things at once on a fork to one's mouth. Condiments were an exception—though smearing them with a knife onto food already impaled on a fork was fiddling too intently with the food and forcing one's morsel too insistently upon the attention of every-body present to be polite. Mashing food is a kind of chewing, per-formed on the open plate; such a view of mixing food is an impor-tant part of our own prejudice against many ingredients being amal-gamated into one mass.

When Roland Barthes wrote his eulogy of Japanese food (1982), he praised it for displaying qualities that are, in fact, not only Japanese but deeply ingrained modern European values. Even though he was himself French, he pooh-poohs what he calls "accu-mulation" and thickening, the blending and "enveloping" which are traditional in French but not Japanese culinary art. Barthes fore-shadows *nouvelle cuisine* in his praise for the "uncentredness" of the Japanese menu, and for the "raw, washed, fragmented" look of the food. (It is interesting to compare the fussiness of the Brahman, and his preference for the purely and safely raw.) Barthes writes ecstati-cally that *tempura* (which was, in fact, originally a Portuguese dish) is not only cooked before your very eyes and *not* glistening with oil as it would be in Mediterranean cuisine, but it is also "light, aerial, instantaneous, fragile, transparent, crisp," produced as it is by a cui-sine of "precision and purity." It is as different as it could be from how it will end up, chewed.

Eggs are problematic for us, because although we love eating them—what could be sounder or more innocent than a fresh egg?—they are, when less than hard-cooked, runny in the middle; when soft-boiled, the whites might even fail to coalesce, and turn out glau-cous and jelly-like, what we most wish to avoid. The result is that we are very fussy about how we eat soft-boiled eggs (indeed, many prefer not to risk them at all). Opening up the shell was once a miniature display, like carving. Louis XIV, according to Madame Campan, would slice the top off his boiled egg with a panache that excited admiration in the watching crowd. Erasmus had warned boys not to touch the egg's innards with their hands (special small spoons were rare): "It is ridiculous to clean out an eggshell with finger-nails or thumb; to do so by inserting one's tongue is even more ridiculous; the polite way is to use a small knife." It was also permissible to dip small bits of bread into a soft-boiled egg.

Even when special spoons became available, they were used for digging the egg out of the shell, and then half-drinking the yolk and white out of a glass or eating it off a plate. This habit itself came to be thought revolting in England during the late eighteenth century. The spread of egg-cups and the arrival of increasingly specialized cutlery seem to have been the reasons—and of course the distaste for any kind of mashing on the plate. Americans clung to the custom, however, and many nineteenth-century English-language etiquette books mention this disapprovingly. They generally (except for a few defiant American authors) advise taking the meat out of the egg in decorous, unmessy spoonfuls and eating them at once, so that the egg's flesh is scarcely visible to anyone. "Dipping" with bread became very informal behaviour. The *Illustrated Manners Book* advises Americans not to dig egg out and mash it, for fear of offending foreigners. "It may be, and probably is, the best way, notwithstanding, but not the fashionable method." Branchereau was still advising French priests against eating eggs in the old way in 1885; Newnham-Davis (1903) described, with an Anglo-Saxon *frisson*, the Italian institution of egg *da bere* ("to drink"): an egg with "the chill just taken off it" was drunk out of the shell, in front of everybody. It was, Davis complains, "not a pleasant operation either to see or to hear." In many places today mashing eggs with butter on the plate persists, on informal occasions. Italians still like drinking eggs, but they do it from a glass, and are not supposed to be noisy about it.

Since mouthfuls of food are so likely to cause offence, they are to be carefully limited as to size. Small mouthfuls have always been polite. Eubulus in *The Hunchback* (fourth century B.C.) describes a well-behaved ancient Greek courtesan, "not like other women, who stuff their jaws with leeks rolled up in balls, and greedily and disagreeably chomped great gobs of meat; no! from each item, as politely as a Milesian virgin, she popped in a tiny taste." One was never to fill both cheeks, of course, nor was even one cheek to bulge suggestively out; filled cheeks are constantly referred to in medieval manners books as reminding polite people of the behaviour of monkeys. Chewing was to be performed as noiselessly as possible, a requirement that reinforced the principle of the closed mouth. It was wrong to add food to an as-yet-unswallowed mouthful, and also to drink with food in the mouth. This was not only disgusting to watch, in case food might escape from a mouth strained to capacity, but it could also lead to choking. One should have only so much in the mouth at once that one could quickly swallow it if need be:

> If any man speak that time to thee
> And thou shalt answer, it will not be
> But wallowing [i.e., shifting the morsel about in the mouth],
>   and abide thou must—
> That is a shame for all the host.

In ancient China, respect for one's father was more important than any such decorum. The *Li Chi* ordains that if a father calls his son while he is eating, the son must immediately eject the food from his mouth and run.

During medieval times, tongues were tightly monitored: no licking *anything*—not even one's own plate if it looked dusty, said John Russell—or your own lips and chin; rather use a napkin, or the tablecloth. We ourselves are not allowed to lick our eating implements—not knives, it goes without saying, but not even forks or spoons. Tongues, of course, might be seen as themselves questionable objects—soft and versatile, slippery, and often very distasteful to behold. Tongues belong very definitely *inside* mouths, which is one reason why it is rude to stick them aggressively out at anyone.

Although it is difficult to prevent grease from spreading round the mouth, an attempt should nevertheless be made. It was holding and chewing bones that caused a good deal of the trouble. In the course of several centuries, lifting bones became very relaxed behaviour indeed, and frowned on in correct company; the knife and fork were supposed to remove the meat, even if a lot of it was sacrificed to the ideal of avoiding both the use of hands for eating, and grease. "There used once to be a rule," wrote Mrs. Humphry in 1897, "that a bone might be picked, if only the finger and thumb were used in holding it. But that was in the days when table cutlery was far from having been brought to its present condition of perfection. There is now no excuse . . ."—except in perhaps "the lowest grades of society."

The provision of special implements for moving food from serving dish to plate, as opposed to placing it in the mouth, came about slowly. European manners gradually changed—from several people taking it in turns to dip the one shared spoon into the pot and eating from it, to wiping a spoon carefully on a napkin before passing it on, to being provided with a spoon each for dipping and eating, to having to wipe even *that* spoon on a napkin before dipping it into the common dish just because one had sipped from it, to using a special spoon for serving and nothing else: one must never forget and use one's own spoon by mistake. More and more cutlery was required for all this purity—and of course owning a great deal of cutlery meant ensuring that it was all put to use. It is still a complicated business to remember, for example, not to take butter with one's own knife because jam and crumbs might disgustingly bespeckle the butter-pat, to use the special butter-knife (differentiated from the others in some way so as to remind people to leave it on the butter-dish), not to stir with the sugar spoon but with one's own teaspoon, and so on. Still, we are not as fussy as the ninth-century Abbasid gentleman who was flanked, as he ate, by servants whose job it was to hand him spoons from the right and take them away from the left. His standards were so high that he never used a spoon for more than a single mouthful.

Sharing cutlery at meals, like sharing plates, meant that people accepted great intimacy with those present at table. Norbert Elias has pointed out how table manners, in our own culture in recent times, have increasingly separated the diners physically from one another. Distaste for sharing cutlery came about not, to begin with, out of any fear of spreading disease: that is a modern discovery, which we now use to strengthen and rationalize an already existing taboo. Keeping our bodies clean and separate, and (therefore) safe from the disgust of others, seems in us to be a physical expression of a mental state, the positive aspects of which are self-sufficiency, self-control, and a partly self-interested consideration for feelings in others which are similar to our own. The negative aspects include unwillingness to share, to care, to touch, or to trust. The most persuasive example of Elias's thesis is the gradual choking off in our culture of the habit of spitting.

Spitting has carried since ancient times meanings that range from showing contempt to healing and good luck. It is an aversion signal, like sticking out the tongue (which is in some respects similar in meaning); ancient Roman women would spit down the fronts of their dresses to avert the evil eye, symbolically to protect themselves, and to show disapproval generally. Saliva is a kind of excrement, and as such was always potentially dangerous and suspect. Disgust at the thought of other people's saliva (unless they are our children or our lovers) is surely ancient and possibly universal. Take for example the horrid custom of saving a special morsel of food for oneself by spitting on it and so ensuring that nobody else will want it. This is recorded of the greedy ancient Greek Demylos, but it is a ruse doubtless older still; it has been used ever since, and is not unknown today. In the past it was often thought, in addition, that since saliva was excrement the body should occasionally get rid of it, no matter how revolting the process.

If one felt an urge to spit, one spat—it was unhealthy not to. The question was not whether or even when one did it, but where. It was rude while at dinner, in seventeenth-century Holland, for example, to spit on the table, or at the wall opposite one's seat. Polite people spat discreetly, on the floor beside them. They might even, with one foot, rub any conspicuous traces away. If you have to spit while standing and talking to someone (there being no table to permit one's spit to disappear from view), you should, Erasmus wrote, "turn away . . . to avoid spitting on or spraying someone. If any disgusting matter is spat onto the ground, it should, as I have said, be ground under foot lest it nauseate someone." An earlier manners book says one should not spit too enthusiastically or too far: it draws attention to the action, and makes it hard to find and tread on the result. When hand-washing is performed at table, one should resist the temptation, even though spit counts as "dirt," to expectorate into the wash-basin.

It seems that what came from the mouth and what came from the nose were treated similarly; both were called saliva. Rich people, who might be expected to own handkerchiefs, were exhorted in the sixteenth and seventeenth centuries to use them to spit into, just as they used handkerchiefs for blowing their noses, in the presence of people for whom they wished to express respect. In front of the lower orders, on the other hand, they could spit on the floor. Upper-class people have always tended to feel that they could treat the lower classes to very intimate views of their physical selves—after all, servants cleaned up after them, and did their laundry. Unless they were held back by puritanical attitudes, masters and mistresses might be unembarrassed to be naked in front of the servants, for instance, or to have them witness excretion or copulation; embarrassment, being a sign of consideration, regulated behaviour only before one's equals or betters. The need to inhibit spitting and other physical manifestations before *everybody* is in part an aspect of increasing egalitarianism.

There are many societies today where spitting is not viewed with the horror we feel. There, however, people are likely to be appalled by our custom of using a handkerchief—blowing into it, then rolling up one's snot and putting it carefully away in one's pocket. They might think it far less disgusting to dispose of it completely, as one ejects other excreta. We have now provided ourselves with disposable paper handkerchiefs, so we can partially meet this objection. And as for spitting, we have tabooed that so successfully that most of us never think we need to spit at all.

We were not the first to think of such total abstinence. Polite ancient Persians, as Xenophon and Herodotus tell us, were expected to refrain altogether from spitting. Greeks thought this an impressive, if "ethnic," display of self-control, as remarkable as the Persian insistence on always telling the truth. Giovanni della Casa, in his *Galateo* (1558), alludes to these finical Persians and asks, "Why, therefore, should not we too be able to refrain from it for a short time?"—that is, as long as it takes to eat a meal. Erasmus had complained about people who spat "after every third word, not through need but through force of habit."

Spitting is always regulated in some degree, and is unlikely ever to have been thought a particularly enjoyable sight; it was necessary to the body's cleanliness, and everyone therefore put up with occasions when other people spat, as a fact of life. Gradually, in the West, spitting was performed more guardedly, until a special piece of furniture was created, especially for spitting into. The provision of spittoons was an important proof of civilized forethought in Europe and America during the nineteenth century; they were common in public places until the mid-twentieth century in some Western countries, and still exist for example in modern China, where, although spitting in public is not really good manners, spittoons are often found in restaurants.

The spread of the smoking habit had increased the felt need to spit, especially in America where tobacco was often chewed. Visitors to the United States in the nineteenth century constantly bemoaned the necessity of witnessing tobacco-spitting in public. The nineteenth-century English gentleman spat only in private: his "smoking chair" often included a drawer underneath the seat, into which he could demurely spit from time to time. Spitting at the dinner table, however, was by this time out of the question; indeed, polite women *never* spat, and men "had to" do so only in certain circumstances. "If you must spit," the *Illustrated Manners Book* advises men in 1855, "then leave the room." By the early twentieth century, spitting had become officially unhealthy; the terrors of tuberculosis certainly contributed to society's categorizing spitting as a spreader of disease. This made the practice a mark of extreme disregard for the well-being even of people who were not present when one spat. Notices everywhere ordered pedestrians, restaurant customers, and train passengers not to spit; such signs were common in public places as late as the 1950s. Today, the signs are not posted because there is little need; most people rarely even think of spitting. If anyone does so, he or she gets a "filthy look" and other signs of disgust and avoidance from everyone near by. Die-hard spitters usually wait at least until they are out of the reach of direct obloquy. It may well be that people nowadays cough less and sniff less than they used to, because of changes in diet or control over the worst colds or for other physical reasons. But it remains true that there is a *social* taboo against spitting—one that has been increasingly enforced, with outstanding success.

Extra-fine sensibilities are put off by fellow diners who blow over their food to cool it. If the soup is too hot, what should I do? The polite Edwardian child was supposed to answer, "I should put my spoon down and wait a little while." Such restraint is part of the "proof," which is commonly required, that one is not actually longing to start eating: the ancient Chinese were told never to spread their rice out so as to cool it; it is better far to wait. Blowing is too busy, too much of a performance; it draws attention. Breath is also slightly disgusting. As Giovanni della Casa put it rather coarsely in the *Galateo* (1558): "There never was wind without rain." John Russell's *Boke of Nurture* says you should beware of "puffing and blowing," for it might "cast foul breath upon your lord." Antoine de Courtin warns in 1672 that one should not blow the ashes off truffles, "for the breath of the mouth sometimes disgusts persons." This is mentioned with the same pride in modern sensibility that he feels when explaining that spoons must be *wiped* after use, "because there are some so delicate that they would not wish to eat soup into which you have dipped the spoon after having brought it to your lips." Ancient Chinese servers were forbidden to breathe on the food or drink they were carrying to their superiors; if anyone chanced to speak to them while food was in their hands, they had to turn their heads to one side in order to answer.

Yawning is rude because it proclaims that you are tired, and perhaps bored. It involves opening the mouth wide, which is disconcerting, especially at dinner. People who try to speak while yawning are particularly trying. "Speak not in your Yawning, but put your handkerchief or Hand before your face and turn aside," said the *Rules of Civility* which George Washington copied out as a boy. But polite society fought hard to outlaw yawning, like spitting, altogether. De Courtin had written in 1672 that "time was when one was allowed to yawn, provided only that one did not speak while yawning: nowadays, a person of quality would be shocked [by any yawning at all]." Yawning is involuntary, and difficult to prevent; the battle on this point has not been nearly so successful as that against spitting.

Our manners decree that mouths must be kept calm, controlled, and *quiet*, except of course for the clear and clever conversation that must be carried on between (but not during) mouthfuls. There is to be no "squirting or spouting," says Russell's *Boke of Nurture*, no clacking of the tongue. All sounds, except those of well-modulated speech, are to be kept to a minimum—no scraping and clattering of plates and implements, no slamming down of glasses. Other cultures allow noise during eating, chiefly when the intention is to demonstrate delight, as when the Japanese slurp their noodles, the Chinese suck their bones, and lips are smacked for pleasure. None of these, be it noted, involves the baring of teeth; and chopsticks, like fingers, are much quieter than even well-controlled knives and forks. We are likely to eat as much as, and probably more than, the Chinese and Japanese, but we do not approve of dramatic expressions of enthusiasm about the food. We even forbid the universally enjoyable slurping of liquids, the sound of vigorous swallowing, the sigh of satisfaction at the end.

Chewing, above all, must be as silent as possible. A closed mouth helps achieve this, but even a closed mouth needs to be controlled for silence. We must never draw attention to the threat implicit in savagely grinding teeth: the specific fear of possible violence lurks behind all of our "civilized" fussiness. We certainly feel, at some level, like the Kwakiutl of British Columbia in Canada, who are extremely aware of the importance of table manners and regard fast eating and noticeable chewing as potentially disastrous: these will, the Kwakiutl say, "bring about the destruction of the world more quickly by increasing the aggressiveness" in it.

Picking one's teeth in public after a meal is disgusting for bringing to mind firstly teeth, and secondly what was chewed but not successfully swallowed. Relief for the very real discomforts of continuing to converse with particles of food wedged between one's teeth is offered by the ancient and convenient toothpick. This implement does discourage people from plunging their fingers into their mouths—a most improper crossing of boundaries, especially in a society which bans most eating with the fingers. But English and American sensibilities are so appalled by the thought of food stuck, unswallowed, in the mouth that we expect polite people to suffer and pretend they are perfectly at ease rather than admit the need for grooming of such humiliating directness. Yet tooth-picking is allowed in many societies today; it can very easily be regarded not only as common-sensical but hygienic. (The first toothbrushes, after all, were sticks chewed to a fur at one end. They were fastidiously discarded after use, unlike our own long-labouring brushes.) One is always expected, where toothpicks are offered, to use them with careful consideration, and a covering hand.

As early as the *Boke of Curtasye* (fifteenth century), polite English people were being exhorted:

> At meat cleanse not thy teeth nor pick
> With knife or straw or wand or stick.

By "cleansing the teeth," the author means rubbing them with his finger and a napkin, or even using the tablecloth; at that date most people in England never brushed their teeth, but polished and flossed them with cloth. Hugh Rhodes's *Boke of Nurture* has a more lenient attitude towards toothpicks:

> Pick not thy teeth with thy knife nor finger-end,
> But with a stick or some clean thing, then do ye not offend.

By the sixteenth and early seventeenth centuries in Europe, having one's own toothpick had become extremely chic. The clown in Shakespeare's *Winter's Tale* knows a nobleman "by the picking on's teeth"; jewelled gold or silver toothpicks were sometimes proudly pinned onto hats and jackets. Where disposable toothpicks were desired, people used feather quills, scented woods like mastic, or "small bones taken from the drumsticks of cocks or hens," as Erasmus suggested.

The permanent kind quite quickly came to be thought vulgar because they made people deduce that one was fixated on food. For della Casa in his *Galateo*, a toothpick is "a strange tool for a gentleman to be seen extracting from his shirt. . . . It also shows that person is well equipped and prepared for the service of his gluttony. And I cannot tell exactly why these men do not carry a spoon as well tied to a chain around their necks." But carrying a toothpick almost permanently in the mouth is to this day jaunty and macho in several Mediterranean societies. Like chewing gum, toothpicks can be categorized quite differently from chewed food, even when carried for long periods in the mouth; chewing gum and toothpicks held carefully between the teeth do not disintegrate, and they are often given cooling anise-related flavours, which symbolize to us cleanliness and hygiene. Besides providing a satisfaction of the infantile urge to chew and flex the tongue and mouth, they are signals that teeth and breath are pure.

Toothpicks, fairly successfully banished in England and America, have never been entirely rejected from the European Continent; it would be interesting to know just who uses them today, when, and what the strictures are. But another once-common hygienic measure has been abolished in Europe, though only very recently. This is the mouth-rinse after dinner. In 1885, Branchereau described how polite Frenchmen used the water supplied in finger-bowls at the end of the meal: you were not to swallow the water, but to swish it about in the mouth and spit it out into the deep saucer provided; a little was kept in the bowl, for dipping the fingers and wiping them on the *serviette*. It was important, Branchereau adds, to wash out one's mouth with as little noise as possible: no gargling. The rinsing habit had apparently gone out of fashion in France during the seventeenth and eighteenth centuries; it returned during the nineteenth. In Branchereau's day, one could rinse one's mouth or not, as one wished. Before the mid-nineteenth century, the British and the Americans seem to have dropped mouth-rinsing at table, its business and drama and its similarity to spitting, and did not take it up again. (North Americans remain, however—away from the dinner table— some of the most dedicated garglers and mouth-washers the world has ever seen.)

During the long period while mouth-rinsing after dinner was slowly being put down in Europe, there were shocked reports from travellers who saw foreigners doing it—it is often taken to be the proof of a superior sensibility to react with disgust. La Rochefoucauld-Liancourt considered that the mouth-rinsing he encountered among the upper classes in England in 1784 was "extremely unfortunate," and Louis Simond in 1810 described the English "all (women as well as men) stooping over" and washing out their mouths, "often more than once, with a spitting and washing sort of noise . . . the operation frequently assisted by a finger elegantly thrust into the mouth! This done, and the hands dipped also, the napkins, and sometimes the table-cloth, are used to wipe hand and mouth." Fifty years later Mrs. Beeton was just as horrified by the idea of putting one's refined and luxurious finger-bowls to such a use; she says it is a custom of "the French and other continentals."

• The Proprieties of Posture and Demeanour •

People photographed several decades ago often look strangely foreign to us. This is not only because of changing fashions in clothing, or in furnishings and photographic props, or the faded quality of the pictures. All these enter into it, of course, as does the technology of the time, which obliged people to "freeze" when their picture was taken. It is also their facial expression, their posture, their attitude towards the camera which are of another world.

Modern faces are far more self-conscious than faces used to be, and their expressions conform far more strictly to socially pre-set patterns; our posture too is stylized and conventional. Even our striving to look "natural" and "relaxed" is learned from such specifically modern experiences as a lifetime's acquaintance with photography. There have always been fashionable faces and expressions, as well as ways of moving and standing and sitting, which marked an epoch. There was for example in Europe a late seventeenth-century female face and gaze, which was *de rigueur* if a woman was to be considered desirable in fashionable circles; there was also an upper-class eighteenth-century stance, stiffly upright for women, deliberately nonchalant and carefully relaxed for men; there were nineteenth-century figures and a nineteenth-century walk; and so on. Today, there are new constraints (we prefer to call them "styles"; they change slightly every few years), imposed upon our demeanour by the ubiquity of images in our world.

We cannot live in a modern city without seeing ourselves constantly, in mirrors and panes of glass, in shop windows as we walk down the street, in photographs and moving pictures. We know what we are supposed to look like, from posters and television images of people whose shapes, faces, and expressions are admired, widely publicized, and imposed upon us as ideals to be emulated. In movies with historical subjects, although everything may be done to make costumes authentically of the period, postures—and particularly faces—are seldom convincing; modern actors have modern faces, especially if they are "stars," chosen for their value as trend-setting images.

One of the reasons why we frantically endeavour to reduce our weight is that the thinner the body, provided it is healthy, the better it seems to look *in a photograph*. Photographs are "framed" to select subject matter from a single point of view and to reject other things, other moments, other angles of vision. They are two-dimensional, incapable of change or response, and reflect visual signals only; they do not offer the total impression a living person makes. But their power as images, and the impression they give of capturing "reality," reflect social prejudices about body shape and stance; they then in turn manage those prejudices, and demand adherence to them. We learn how to stand, sit, turn our heads, smile when a photograph is taken. When we walk down the street or sit down in a restaurant, we compose our features and control our gestures to fit preconceived norms. We come to take up these poses and facial expressions habitually, and they then seem natural, to be taken for granted; people who fall away from the ideal look very strange to us, and are easily suspected of being mentally ill. As usual, eating together requires the utmost consideration for the expectations and sensitivities of others. It follows that, at table, faces and bodies should with especial strictness conform to the rules.

Manners books that survive from the past give us some idea of the iron control which we exercise over ourselves, for in advocating the norms we now almost automatically follow, they remind us that there are (or were) other possibilities. People are often told in such books, for instance, not to roll their eyes: do not roll them back when drinking, or stare up at the ceiling. "It is discourteous to look askance at others while you are drinking," Erasmus wrote, "just as it is impolite to turn your neck round like a stork lest a drop remain at the bottom of the cup"; it is preferable to confine your gaze by looking into the glass as you drink. Mouths must not pout or gape, twist, purse themselves up, or twitch, he went on; it is aggressive and threatening to bite the lower lip with the upper teeth, or the upper lip with the lower teeth. Facial expressions must not let feelings appear too obviously: an anonymous manners book advised, in 1701, that one should avoid frowning and glowering when one is not served with what is clearly a delicacy.

People needed in the seventeenth century to be told not to stare at what is on others' plates, not to look envious, or as though they were comparing amounts or keeping an account of how much every- one had eaten. One should even avoid the excessive piety which was suggested by rolling the eyes upward during grace. It was impolite, Erasmus had said, "to stare intently at one of the guests. It is even worse to look shiftily out of the corner of your eye at those on the same side of the table; and it is the worst possible form to turn your head right round to see what is happening at another table." He advises also against staring at someone with one eye open and one shut, and against arching the eyebrows arrogantly or lowering them fiercely; one should not have an irresolute brow like a hedgehog, or a menacing one, like a bull.

Modern faces are, comparatively speaking, exceedingly inexpres- sive: there is now, on this point, little need to warn people to "behave." We know that it is safest, most guarded, most "becoming" (and photogenic) to remain impassive and disengaged—what might today be called "cool." Other people are watching us, and we are extremely conscious of the way we look, of the narrow limits of facial expressiveness our culture permits, and of how they might therefore judge us. It would occur to few of us to single out some- one and stare at them with one eye shut. It has become habitual with us not to worry about getting enough to eat; and the excitement of noticing who gets the best piece of any dish has diminished, now that less meaning and status are attached to who gets what.

We probably smile more now than was customary in the past; in this respect we have become more expressive, rather than less. Until the end of the eighteenth century, the extent to which one should stretch one's mouth in a smile was subject to strictures. We have seen that baring the teeth for any reason could be startling at table; complaints about showing teeth used often to mention their black- ened state, and doubtless improvements in dental science and hygiene have contributed to our relaxation of rules about smiling and laughter. But in addition decorum, as so often, meant a tranquil demeanour, whereas laughter and even smiling mark emotional engagement and, if too vivid, a suggestion of loss of control. In the fifteenth century, grinning and "mowing," or making faces, at table is discouraged in *Stans puer ad mensam*. (It is certain that deliberately "pulling faces" to increase the expressivity of one's discourse was until very recently more common than it is now.) Portraits showing the sitter's teeth in a smile were always rare; laughing subjects appear usually in paintings where the decorum is deliberately low. Erasmus says that smiling so broadly that your cheeks wrinkled and your teeth were exposed was impolite, and reminded people of dogs. He suggests covering the face with a napkin if uncontrolled laughter should break out at table. (In the past, people appear to have covered their faces with cloths and kerchiefs on many occasions: for grief, for fear, for delicacy and shame.) A hand at least should cover a laughing mouth—a preference which still operates in modern manners, though we possibly do it more because of the risk of arousing disgust, especially when we have been eating, than because laughing is in itself indecorous.

The cause for any laughter is, of course, always to be out in the open: nobody is to be made to feel they might be the object of secret mirth. The distinction between laughing *at* somebody and laughing in sympathy or to show good-naturedness is very culture-specific, and still liable to cause misunderstandings in different parts of Europe. By the eighteenth century, any sudden bodily response to humour was frowned upon in genteel circles. William Pitt, in a letter to his nephew in the 1750s, said it was "rare to see in any one graceful laughter." Stooping, gesticulations, and "movements of the face" were similarly to be avoided. Colonel Forrester said in 1734 that passion is a "prodigious Enemy to Beauty." The rehabilitation of sentiment, and of the expression of strong feelings, was required before a cool classic pose could be broken, without embarrassment—but still within limits.

Stillness of feature, in the seventeenth and eighteenth centuries, corresponded to the immobility required by correct posture. At table, one was to sit bolt upright, in spite of the increasingly generous space allowed between diners. There were to be no leaning, either to left or to right, and no elbows on the table, for these encroached on the space of others and suggested a lack of total bodily control. "Stooping" forward was almost impossible for women and older men in corsets; and in any case the rule against any appearance of over-absorption in the food discouraged it. It was especially low—the mark of a peasant, over-attached to his dinner and solicitous for it—to embrace one's dish with one arm. Elbows on the table suggest familiarity, or the taking of liberty. "It is permissible for the elderly and convalescent to lean one or both elbows on the table," Erasmus had counselled, "but this, as practised by some affected courtiers who consider their every action elegant, is something to be avoided, not imitated." The idea that one might *very elegantly* place elbows on the table is clearly an old one; it is always essential, as we have seen, to do it only if all other signs indicate that one is controlled and securely mannerly. But the long insistence in our culture on showing bodily control and not trespassing upon the space of others has generally made elbow-leaning indecorous, in the manners books at least. In 1923, W. M. Handy says elbows on the table show that "one feels himself at home; and also, that at home he is apt to slouch!" Emily Post said one could lean on elbows only when "alone and ill." She wonders whether we should blame the reprehensible spread of the habit on noisy restaurants, where customers have to lean forward to hear properly.

Consideration for dinner companions means not interrupting the flow of eating, drinking, and conversation by drawing attention to oneself, not giving others cause for worry, not making them wonder what any of your movements might portend. A diner must show competence above all, and predictability: only these reassure the people present that they will eat in peace. Bodies are kept firmly under control in part because other people immediately imagine themselves suffering any physical misfortune they witness. There is sympathetic unease if one is seen pointing a knife at one's face, sweeping the soup spoon towards one's lap, swinging perilously on the chair, or sitting so far from the table as to be at risk of spilling food on its way to one's mouth—even if it never comes to that. Dirt that does not directly come into contact with others nonetheless disgusts their sensitive and sympathetic imaginations; seventeenth-century manners books insist, for example, that napkins should not become too soiled, because *other people* will feel sick if they see you wipe your mouth on a filthy napkin.

Overt greed is always banned at table. "Do not reach out for anything your host has his eye on," says the Old Testament book, *Ecclesiasticus*, "Do not jostle him at the dish." One must usually ask somebody close to the plate or to the condiment required to pass it; in this way, movements remain small, and diners are brought into relationship with one another. "Not reaching" is paying attention to the limitations of one's allotted space; it goes together, in this sense, with keeping one's elbows to one's sides and not putting them on the table. Reaching across the table is occasionally allowed, in Latin America, for instance—but only if manners are elaborated so that one can show that the reaching is done in order not to disturb others, and never just to snatch on one's own behalf. One may, for example, politely stand up in order to take something far away from one's place. Where talking is a necessary aspect of a meal together, *not* talking can be taken for a sign of greed, profiting from the conversation of others in order to get more eating done. Athenaeus gave an example at the turn of the second–third century A.D.

Anglo-Saxon table manners allow, even prefer, that a diner should eat, where only one hand need be used, with the left hand lying on his or her lap. It is a limitation upon one's ability to grasp things, like the decision to use only the right hand, or only three fingers. Emily Post, who is acerbic about the idea of using the right hand only ("That one should pretend to have a paralyzed left hand is not in accord either with traditional behavior or with good sense"), nevertheless suggests the practice as a good way of training children to hold unoccupied hands still, and not to prop their heads on one hand while eating: "By and by they can eat without thinking—after they have had enough of this training to check sloppiness instinctively. Do you see?" On the Continent of Europe, however, propriety enjoins diners to sit with both hands in full view of the company; most correctly, unused hands should rest on the table's edge, being visible only from the wrists. (Erasmus had commanded boys to "have both hands on the table, not clasped together, nor on the plate.") The

Anglo-Saxon custom of permitting guests to sit with one hand hidden seems, to Continentals, at best a sad sign of naïveté.

One reason for hands being kept in sight used to be that people had to learn not to scratch at table. Della Casa's *Galateo* says, for instance, that waiters were not to scratch their heads—or anything else—"nor place their hands on any part of the body which is kept covered, nor even appear to do so, as do some careless servants who hold them inside their shirt or keep them behind their backs hidden under their clothes. They must rather keep their hands in sight and out of suspicion. . . ." This rule holds even more strongly for diners, who are constantly warned not to stroke their beards, twiddle their moustaches, rub and pat themselves, or scratch their heads. Erasmus says it is unsightly to scratch, "especially if it is done through habit rather than necessity." John Russell's *Boke of Nurture* counsels against "clawing your back as if after a flea; or your head as if after a louse." Fleas, like gristle in the mouth or fibres wedged between the teeth, are to be ignored by polite people. The discomfort they cause must be heroically endured and not only hidden from view, but kept from the suspicions of others.

Gesticulation must be controlled, especially at dinner, for flapping arms might incommode one's neighbours and might even knock over objects standing on the table. Too much movement also sins against calmness of demeanour. It is clear that people untrained in upper-class immobility used to find gesticulations and fiddling at table a tremendous temptation. "Some people eat or drink without stopping," Erasmus tells us, "not because they are hungry or thirsty but because they cannot otherwise moderate their gestures, unless they scratch their head, or pick their teeth, or gesticulate with their hands, or play with their dinner knife, or cough, or clear their throat, or spit." He adds: "Such habits, even if originating in a sort of rustic shyness, have the appearance of insanity about them"—and the sociologist Erving Goffman has shown how, in our own day, these idiosyncrasies can still be judged as signs of idiocy.

The head must be held upright, not shaken or allowed to lean to one side. Bending one's head on one side suggested hypocrisy, according to *The Young Scholar's Paradise*; Erasmus says side inclinations of the head are the gestures of mimes. Hand movements must be precise and controlled ("With thy fingers mark thou not thy tale," says *Stans puer ad mensam*), and feet must be kept still. "Twist not your neck askew, like a jackdaw," entreats John Russell's *Boke of Nurture*. "Claw not at your codpiece. Let there be no picking or shrugging, as if ye would saw wood; do not wring and rub your hands, nor puff up your chest, nor pick your ears, nor be slow of hearing. . . . Beware of making faces . . . nor yet lick your lips or drivel. . . . Do not trample with your feet, or straddle your legs; *jetting* [thrusting the legs in and out or bouncing them up and down] is bad manners." It is rude to stuff your cheeks, not only because of the danger of arousing disgust but because, as the ancient Greeks had also insisted, a bulging cheek works too hard, and shows a lack of poise and balance. Erasmus adds that dinner guests should not sit with one shoulder up and the other down, or with one hand resting on the groin, even though some people think the latter gives a soldierly, macho air. He says crossing one leg over the other is "a sign of uneasiness," and sitting with the right foot resting on the left thigh used to be a posture customary in kings, but it has gone out of fashion. When people sat on benches and very close together, there were further temptations to misbehave, such as sliding a leg under a neighbour's thigh. "You are full lewd if you do it," says the first *Boke of Curtasye*; "lewd" then meant "ignorant" rather than "lascivious."

Noses must, of course, be kept clean and dry; no sniffing is allowed. We have seen why eating with a dripping nose is even worse than chewing with an open mouth. Blowing the nose, says Erasmus, is one of the attentions to the body that ought to be paid before the meal begins; others are urinating, defecating, and letting out the belt a few notches (it would be rude to do the latter at table because it looks greedy). One really should not blow the nose at table. If it is unavoidable, you must turn aside, use a handkerchief if you possess one, "nor look thereon," adds Hugh Rhodes; "to some it is loth." "If, in clearing the nose with two fingers, some matter falls on the ground," says Erasmus, "it should be immediately ground under foot." All noises, other than speech, are to be reduced to a minimum, and especially those that draw attention to the bodies of the diners. One must not sing unless everyone agrees to do so. "In the Presence of Others sing not to yourself with a humming Noise, nor Drum, with your Fingers or Feet" is the fourth rule of etiquette in the traditional collection written out by the young George Washington.

All the misdemeanours so far mentioned can be controlled with practice and forethought. There are others, however, most of them the result specifically of eating, which are involuntary. This does not mean that they are therefore condoned; on the contrary, the rules forbidding them are some of the strictest of all. A sneeze or a cough is nasty because it is a sudden sound and might spray the guests. We must handle a cough or a sneeze somewhat as we do a laugh, by muffling it; we must also turn away from the company while it is happening. In the ancient world, however, sneezing, like spitting, was slightly awesome behaviour. It was an omen, a message from what we would call the subconscious—people who say "God bless you" when someone sneezes, or who count sneezes and assign good or bad fortune to the number, do so in this tradition. Erasmus tells us that polite people in his day crossed their faces after sneezing, raised their caps and acknowledged the blessings of the company, and then begged pardon or gave thanks; it was very rude not to bless someone who sneezed, and polite boys raised their caps also when a high-ranking person sneezed and was blessed for it.

Hiccuping has tended to be blamed on eating or drinking a lot. It is therefore reprehensible in modern Europe and North America, where manners require one to eat or drink "an elegant sufficiency," but considered fortunate when repleteness is thought to be an especially pleasant state. Among the Tanga of Melanesia, for example, hiccuping is a sign that one has enjoyed the meal; and an especially strong attack of hiccups is a signal from the ghosts, who want a portion of food. Belching is always a more remarkable phenomenon than hiccuping, and not, like the latter, merely faintly ridiculous. (The most famous attack of hiccups in Western literature occurs in Plato's *Symposium*, where the remedies administered to the helpless, hiccuping Aristophanes include holding his breath, gargling, and tickling his nostrils to elicit a sneeze. The last method of the three is efficacious in his case. Eryximachus, the doctor who prescribes the cures, has a name which means "Belch-battler.")

Belches expel breath, while hiccups attempt to suck it in; and belches can be produced to order. In our own culture, burping is roundly disapproved of: polite people must struggle to repress it. If they fail, they are acutely embarrassed. With us it is purely the sound, the mouth opened neither to eat nor to speak, and the lack of ability to control a bodily lapse, which make everybody cringe; in the past it was really bad to belch near someone's face. In Hugh Rhodes's *Boke of Nurture* we read:

> Belch near no man's face with a corrupt fumosity;
> Turn from such occasion, it is a stinking ventosity.

John Russell puts belching in a group with various loud breathings: "Do not sigh with your breast, or cough, or breathe hard in the presence of your sovereign, or hiccough [his word is "yexe", otherwise known at this period as "to sobbe, or have the hicket"], or belch, or groan," and Erasmus warns that one can get into the habit of constantly belching and find it exceedingly hard to stop doing so. We are accustomed to ascribing extreme exoticism to cultures where a polite guest is expected to fetch up a belch in order to show appreciation; examples are traditional Chinese, Japanese, and Middle Easterners, or various African societies, such as the Pedi of South Africa, who have a charming onomatopoeic name for the happy belch: *pôtla*.

Coughing, sneezing, hiccuping, and belching were all to be muffled in sixteenth-century Italy, but the author of the *Court of civill Courtesie* warns against being too delicate and "nice" about such cover-ups. Erasmus had gone further: he firmly condemns people who, in the name of courtesy, demand that involuntary misdemeanours of the body should be stifled: "To suppress a sound which is brought on by nature is characteristic of silly people who set more store by good manners than good health." When he tells boys not to wriggle on their seats, the reason he gives is that shifting from side to side gives the appearance of farting, or "of trying to do so"; farting is to be avoided, to the extent that even the *appearance of trying to do so* is disconcerting to others. (John Russell had warned his readers to "beware of blasting from thy hinder part as from a gun.")

But it is wrong, Erasmus says elsewhere, to try to prevent wind attempting to get out by constricting the buttocks; he believes it is even more dangerous to do this than deliberately to constipate oneself. If you cannot withdraw and fart in private, he advises, "then, in the words of the old adage . . . cover the sound with a cough." (A similar trick, of making a sound with the foot against the end of the dining couch, had been recommended by Athenaeus fourteen centuries earlier.) The idea that stifling a fart was dangerous had a long history. The first-century emperor Claudius was said to have been so shocked by a man who had endangered his health by modestly restraining himself that Claudius wanted to pass an edict permitting diners to fart freely at table, quietly or noisily, as they wished; and Carl Ludwig, a nineteenth-century German physician, explained why so many women in his day suffered from chronic constipation. He thought it was because of the fear women had of accidentally farting after eating, and the consequent tensing of their buttocks.

In ancient Europe, people commonly cleared their stomachs by vomiting before an important meal; they would also throw up during the meal to make room for more, or simply because they felt over-extended. (An elegant Roman method was to tickle the gullet with a peacock feather.) The Old Testament book *Ecclesiasticus* recommends the practice. Roman banqueters took to it so enthusiastically that, the philosopher Seneca complained, "They vomit to eat and eat to vomit." Erasmus is again indulgent towards this bodily reaction, provided that morality is not being transgressed: "Withdraw when you are going to vomit; vomiting is not shameful, but to have vomited through gluttony is disgusting."

There were handsome bronze pans provided both for vomiting and for urinating at ancient Greek parties; they were thought to be so comforting that the luxurious Sybarites were credited with inventing them. People have been sorely tempted to keep chamberpots on hand at dinner parties ever since. The English were often censured by French and other travellers until the early nineteenth century, for keeping chamber pots in or just outside their dining rooms. "Drinking much and long leads to unavoidable consequences," writes Louis Simond in shocked tones, of British table manners. "Will it be credited that, in a corner of the very dining room, there is a certain convenient piece of furniture, to be used by anybody who wants it. The operation is performed very deliberately and undisguisedly, as a matter of course, and occasions no interruption of the conversation." It was always much more permissible for men than for women to relieve themselves publicly. Whereas women were often victimized by this prejudice, and men's drinking habits always made urinating a more pressing matter for them, it remains true that the modern insistence on the total privatization of excretion is part of the long-term victory of standards which previously applied only to women, while men were thought not only unwilling but unable to conform to them.

Postscript:
How Rude Are We?

Are we ruder than other societies are? Are we ruder than we were in the past? There is increasing concern for manners in the modern West: newspaper articles protest about the lack of them; the number of books telling people how to behave and their enormous sales attest to an anxiety on this score which rivals that experienced in the nineteenth century; and a new and expanding business is the etiquette industry, where people formally and for a fee teach protocol and the arts of the dinner table to ambitious business men and women. It is realized, in the commercial world at least, that bad manners might actually spoil a corporate image, hamper a deal, impede mobility; good manners might make a competitive difference. Since bad manners can be corrected, the demeanour of the staff is one of the things a careful company can try to polish and control.

The idea is to pinpoint trouble spots, moments where even we, with our insistence on informality, set up specific expectations which could trip up the unwary or the simply ignorant. We must know, for example, that at a formal meal served by waiters, serving dishes are likely to appear, silently and without warning, from the left; the serving spoon and fork must be used in a correct and unobtrusive manner to remove a portion of the food presented (do not take too long choosing your portion!); when eating is done, plates will be removed from the right. Most people are right-handed, and this rule is for their convenience. If plates should be presented already loaded with food, however, they are set down from the diner's right, and taken away from the left. The need to be prepared for such moments is heightened because formal meals are unusual, and important for reasons that go beyond eating for nourishment; and because etiquette involving the presence of servants is not everyday experience. We do eat out at restaurants, however, where practice in old-fashioned formality is available to us, as is the surveillance of our manners by people outside our families.

One of the guiding principles of modernity is mobility—the opportunity to move up the social scale, as well as to flee from any social "scene" we find uncomfortable and unaccepting. Physical movement facilitates social mobility; it is possible to live in an inexpensive neighbourhood, for instance, and still drive to a job in a smart area of the city. We have greatly reduced the likelihood that anyone need play a predetermined role on a "stage" dominated from the start by people born to power. Modern cities set out to offer many alternatives—a choice of "stages" upon one of which a person may hope someday to shine, and plenty of escape routes from unwanted constraints. None of us need tolerate surveillance and adverse judgements from people who have set themselves up as arbiters of elegance. We can move away if they disapprove or try to put us down. The metaphor behind the word "politeness" is "polish"—smoothness and gloss, brought about by continuous rubbing up against other people; the panoply of courtesies can subsequently be used to facilitate management of necessary relationships. Modern people try not to embark upon, or even preserve, unconditional relationships. They do have to survive, however, in a crowded, complex world. We all battle fiercely, in fact, to make each other knuckle down and behave in a civilized fashion.

Some things we can no longer ask from people; the range of formal politeness that is still appropriate has been greatly reduced. What is left of it, while only seldom sanctioned by powerful pressures like outrage and ostracism, has remained ornamental, becoming, image-enhancing. It is still very useful, in other words, to be polite. A polite demeanour is like fashionable clothing: it proves to people who are merely slight acquaintances that we have been schooled and "finished," that we can be counted on to behave predictably and in a manner calculated to be pleasing to others similarly schooled.

Universal rules governing modern manners usually take the form of unspoken, almost subconscious guidelines and constraints—a basic substratum or minimum standard which the majority of us carefully observes. Eating behaviour is still—and, I would argue, must always remain—guarded, enculturated, ritualized, and even taboo-laden. We can tell that taboos survive by the laughter that greets any suggestion that one of them might be broken. The tradition of Grobianus and of Juvenalian satire still rages, in the work for instance of P. J. O'Rourke, whose "advice" includes the following suggestions for making the most of a table napkin: "The best way to use a napkin is as a mantilla to imitate your grandmother in church while grace is being said or as a pretend matador's cape to wave at undercooked beef or as a bandanna to cover your face when you pull a stickup on your dinner partner with a lamb-chop pistol. . . ." This kind of humour relies on the extent to which it would never occur to well-behaved, "proper" people to do any of these things, even though we can all too vividly imagine them being done and the embarrassment they would afford us. There is still nothing like an uproar at table for arousing horror, hilarity, or fear; the chief purpose of table manners remains to prevent violence, usually by keeping it unthinkable.

Modern manners increasingly force us to be casual. We have no choice but to comply: the lowering of decorum and the flattening out of what the anthropologist Mary Douglas once called "intricacy" rule us as imperiously as protocol ever did. Politeness, whether formal or informal, has always involved manipulating social distance. The kind of politeness that we call formality deliberately keeps people apart. Its purpose is partly to prevent prying, and to slow down the process of familiarization in order to give each party time to appraise the other. But apartness creates distinction, so that formality also prevents or defers relationships between two people or two groups who want to be separate, or whose status is hierarchically differentiated. Informal manners, on the other hand, reduce distance; when they consciously impose themselves in opposition to formality, they express scorn for differentiation by status. Where informality reigns, there is less likelihood of either error or criticism. But rules there must be, otherwise there would be no means left of communicating with others or relating to them.

Informality has often been used as a contrast within a generally formal system of manners, to mark a stage in the progress of a relationship: one first encountered others with formal behaviour, for example, calling a person by a surname and title, with perhaps a plural pronoun like the Spanish *usted* (which is an abbreviation of *vuestra Merced*, "your Grace"). As friendship progressed, one gradually let the defences down, as it were, until a threshold was crossed beyond which informal manners were allowed; the day came when people were "on a first-names basis," and might use familiar pronouns like *tu* and *du*. (Advances towards the achievement of familiarity would almost certainly have been marked by one or more invitations to dinner.) Such polite rites of passage denoted acceptance on both sides, and proved to the world that tests had been applied and passed, time allowed to elapse, and agreements reached. Graduating from formality to intimacy, from the outer circle to the inner, was a performance both structured and demonstrative: it not only showed those concerned where they stood with respect to one another, but everybody else was expected to notice the new relationship as well.

Problems did arise; since respect was expressed through a distant manner, a denial of social distance could also mean lack of respect, so that servants, for instance, might be called *tu*. There could be uncertainty at dinner as to whether a waiter should be called *tu* because his rank was lower than that of the diners, or *vous* because he was socially distant and outside the dining group. Should children call their parents *vous* out of respect, or *tu* because of intimacy? Twentieth-century manners, where languages traditionally make *tu/vous* distinctions, have tended increasingly to stress solidarity to one's own group rather than differences in rank, so that children call their parents *tu*, and diners call waiters *vous*. The rising preference for ritual equality means that a waiter one knows and likes might, nowadays, also be called *tu*. The *tu* address is becoming more and more common. Informality is increasingly the normal tone to adopt; formality is now exceptional. The change represents a behavioural revolution.

With the exception of the rather rare occasions when we are asked to certain carefully orchestrated events, where people tend in any case to play at being formal—gala nights at the theatre, or dinner celebrations for visiting dignitaries—it has actually become rather rude to be formal. Rigid formality tends to be perceived these days (and politeness, now as ever, has everything to do with its perception by others) as an impolite and unkind expression of icy distance. It is very clear that separateness is no longer sought but regarded as an imposition, and guarding it by means of one's manner can be found offensive and even ludicrous. Official equality is what manners ritually express. Polite behaviour now demands constant assurances that one is in no way superior to other people—even if, and especially if, one is quite obviously in a position of power.

Modern society has more than enough devices for keeping people apart. We sleep in separate rooms, live and eat in separate quarters, move about behind the closed doors of metal vehicles. We form anonymous, hurrying crowds, and have to seek out opportunities to know or even meet other individuals as isolated as ourselves. When we meet, therefore, with the express purpose of socializing, we cannot afford to be distant. Modern egalitarianism at an interpersonal level is as much a recompense for the walls which separate each individual from everyone else as it is a political ideology and a purely moral ideal. Egalitarianism brings informality; and informality provides sorely needed access to other people. The word "casual" has two meanings, however. When defined simply in opposition to "formal," it means "relaxed": clothes are everyday, the number of eating rules is reduced, reserve is lowered. But "casual" derives from the same root as the word "accident" (compare "casualty"): it contains the idea of falling haphazardly, like dice. Casual behaviour leaves a good deal of the proceedings to chance: people "come as they are," sit anywhere, throw up no conscious barriers of demeanour between themselves and whoever else happens to be present.

A typically modern event is the "reception," "cocktail party," or "drinks," to which people are invited in order to make contact with one another. Drinks, and almost invariably food, are provided. Such a party is "casual" in the sense of productive of chance encounters; sufficient room is provided so that guests can both approach and escape from one another. Everybody present is free game; the only limiting factors are the aggressiveness required to gain the attention of the favoured on the one hand, and the lack of assertiveness that characterizes poor players in the game on the other. An injection of formal elements into a largely casual performance is administered to give everyone ritual distance and to prove that those invited in fact have the desired schooling and discipline. People dress up, the women in heels even though they have to stand, and in garments designed to draw attention, typically by means of up-to-the-minute fashion, glitter or brilliancy of colour, and sometimes dramatic plainness—there is not much time to make an impression, and one has to face a great deal of competition from everybody else. The first things to be discarded from the traditional sociable meal are the chairs and the table. Dining-room furniture limits numbers, prevents mobility, and promotes unwanted intimacy: people invited to "drinks" are not necessarily among those admitted to the closeness offered to guests for whom one cooks dinner. Receptions are outer-circle, not inner-circle events. The occasion usually takes place in the early evening, and is not meant to be the main event in anyone's day.

At receptions, people stand and move about, with a glass in one hand and the other free to gesture and to take something to eat. Food and extra drinks often circulate on waiter-borne trays. Considerable dexterity and bodily propriety are demanded and usually achieved. The food is reasonably various, formally decorative, and offered not only for its company-creating qualities but also for the purpose of giving people something to do. Choosing and eating it fills gaps in conversation; seeking it provides an excuse to break away from a talking group—the food might even on occasion give people something to talk about. Because it is hand-held, it must be dry and not crumbly, neither sticky nor too fatty, either cold or luke-warm, and divided in advance into small pieces, as food usually is wherever people eat with their hands. The noise helps keep talk small and inconsequential, profundity being entirely out of place, while the drink frees tongues and lowers inhibitions. Successful prac-titioners at such functions know how to break in upon conversations, and also how to extricate themselves readily from them. Because nobody is allowed to sit down, the whole thing is soon over, its pur-pose having been fulfilled—that of permitting multiple contacts, and many brief occasions both for sightings and for being seen.

Modern lives still find a place for out-of-the-ordinary, formally structured meals. Special occasions have always been celebrated by the eating of distinctive food, and plenty of it; here rules of behaviour are more intricate than usual, preparations tend to be lengthy, and occasions are provided for demonstrations of skill, social relationship, and generosity. Feasts, for special occasions or special people, are marked off from the quotidian and the normal. Indeed it has never been thought that feasting should be allowed to become ordinary, for then it turns into a meaningless expression of monotonous greed. The wicked Suitors in the *Odyssey* were guilty of endlessly and pointlessly stuffing themselves—"in vain," Homer says, "all to no purpose, effecting nothing." A feast should be excep-tional, and have a reason.

Day-to-day eating is regular, much less copious than feasting, and done with a few people whom we know more intimately than anyone else, largely because we often meet and eat with them. Everyday meals are not intended to surprise, impress, or challenge us. The expected is what we look for; we achieve it through custom-ary behaviour but low decorum, and through order. The basis of the word "ordinary" is "order." Daily meals in turn order our day, pro-viding occasions for meeting friends and family and for resting from work. There are fewer rules of politeness than we find at formal feasts, but rules exist and are observed.

An early precursor of the restaurant meal was dinner served to the public at fixed times and prices at an eating house or tavern. Such a meal was called, because of its predetermined aspects, an "ordinary," and the place where it was eaten came to be called an "ordinary," too. When a huge modern business conglomerate offers fast food to travellers on the highway, it knows that its customers are likely to desire No Surprises. They are hungry, tired, and not in a celebratory mood; they are happy to pay—provided that the price looks easily manageable—for the safely predictable, the convenient, the fast and ordinary.

Ornamental formalities are pruned away (tables and chairs are bolted to the floor, for instance, and "cutlery" is either non-existent or not worth stealing); but rituals, in the sense of behaviour and expectations that conform to pre-ordained rules, still inform the proceedings. People who stop for a hamburger—at a Wendy's, a Harvey's, a McDonald's, or a Burger King—know exactly what the building that houses the establishment should look like; architectural variations merely ring changes on rigidly imposed themes. People want, perhaps even need, to *recognize* their chain store, to feel that they know it and its food in advance. Such an outlet is designed to be a "home away from home," on the highway, or anywhere in the city, or for Americans abroad.

Words and actions are officially laid down, learned by the staff from handbooks and teaching sessions, and then picked up by customers in the course of regular visits. Things have to be called by their correct names ("Big Mac," "large fries"); the McDonald's rubric in 1978 required servers to ask, "Will that be with cheese, sir?" "Will there be any fries today, sir?," and to close the transaction with, "Have a nice day." The staff wear distinctive garments; menus are always the same, and even placed in the same spot in every outlet in the chain; prices are low and predictable; and the theme of cleanliness is proclaimed and tirelessly reiterated. The company attempts also to play the role of a lovable host, kind and concerned, even parental: it knows that blunt and direct confrontation with a huge faceless corporation makes us suspicious, and even badly behaved. So it stresses its love of children, its nostalgia for cosy warmth and for the past (cottage roofs, warm earth tones), or its clean, brisk modernity (glass walls, smooth surfaces, red trim). It responds to social concerns—when they are insistent enough, sufficiently widely held, and therefore "correct." McDonald's, for example, is at present busy showing how much it cares about the environment.

Fast-food chains know that they are ordinary. They *want* to be ordinary, and for people to think of them as almost inseparable from the idea of everyday food consumed outside the home. They are happy to allow their customers time off for feasts—on Thanksgiving, Christmas, and so on—to which they do not cater. Even those comparatively rare holiday times, however, are turned to a profit, because the companies know that their favourite customers—law-abiding families—are at home together then, watching television, where carefully placed commercials will spread the word concerning new fast-food products, and re-imprint the image of the various chain stores for later, when the long stretches of ordinary times return.

Families are the customers the fast-food chains want: solid citizens in groups of several at a time, the adults hovering over their children, teaching them the goodness of hamburgers, anxious to bring them up to behave typically and correctly. Customers usually maintain a clean, restrained, considerate, and competent demeanour as they swiftly, gratefully, and informally eat. Fast-food operators have recently faced the alarming realization that crack addicts, craving salt and fat, have spread the word among their number that French fries deliver these substances easily, ubiquitously, cheaply, and at all hours. Dope addicts at family "ordinaries"! The unacceptability of such a thought was neatly captured by a news story in *The Economist* (1990) that spelled out the words a fast-foods proprietor can least afford to hear from his faithful customers, the participants in his polite and practiced rituals: the title of the story was "Come on Mabel, let's leave." The plan to counter this threat included increasing the intensity of the lighting in fast-food establishments— drug addicts, apparently, prefer to eat in the dark.

The formality of eating at a restaurant belonging to a fast-food chain depends upon the fierce regularity of its product, its simple but carefully observed rituals, and its environment. Supplying a hamburger that adheres to perfect standards of shape, weight, temperature, and consistency, together with selections from a pre-set list of trimmings, to a customer with fiendishly precise expectations is an enormously complex feat. The technology involved in performing it has been learned through the expenditure of huge sums on research, and after decades of experience—not to mention the vast political and economic ramifications involved in maintaining the supplies of cheap beef and cheap buns. But these costs and complexities are, with tremendous care, hidden from view. We know of course that, say, a Big Mac is a cultural construct: the careful control expended upon it is one of the things we are buying. But McDonald's manages—it must do so if it is to succeed in being ordinary—to provide a "casual" eating experience. Convenient, innocent simplicity is what the technology, the ruthless politics, and the elaborate organization serve to the customer.

Many of "the proprieties" have, in our day, met their most implacable end in becoming merely inappropriate; they are perceived as being, at best, inconvenient complexities. "Proper" means "fitting": observing the proprieties means fitting in with the demands of other people for correct, predictable, smoothly acceptable behaviour. We might not share the experience of two American sociologists who claim—with approval—that nowadays "physical trespasses, such as slapping another on the back and relating sexual jokes that comment on one's intimate behavior, become recognized signs of friendship." But it would still be a brave man or woman who really did flout the convention that all of us must pretend to be relaxed when it comes to "the proprieties." A woman who will never leave the house, even on a bright warm day, without first finding and putting on a pair of gloves (a rule whose observance was a sign of excellent upbringing only thirty years ago) would now be thought obsessive; people who have never known the rule (anyone under thirty) might regard her with concern. A man who draws out a chair for a woman, then introduces it gently under her as she sits down, might well make her feel the object of rather unusual attention. Waiters can get away with this sort of thing, but then at smart restaurants we pay in part to experience elegance and formal manners, and to get away from low decorum. (In any case, it has often been customary for staff who have been hired to perform personal services to dress and behave as though they belonged to an era that has recently ended.)

But when instances of good manners—such as tipping hats or wearing kid gloves to dinner but taking them off before beginning to eat—vanish from the social scene, they always give way, in time, to new ones. Polite behaviour does not simply go away; it receives orders to fit in with different exigencies. Three such constraints, each of them influencing our attitude towards etiquette, are the disappearance of personal servants and of the constraint upon women to play a serving role in the modern world, our compulsion to race against time, and our obsession with being clean.

In 1922, Emily Post could write beneath a photograph of a table laid for a formal dinner the following caption: "The perfect example of a formal dinner table of wealth, luxury and taste, which involves no effort on the part of the hostess of a great house beyond deciding upon the date and the principal guests who are to form the nucleus of the party." The hostess would merely have her secretary bring her the guests' cards, we are told later, and she would place these round a plan of her table, "very much as though playing solitaire." Other than this task of deciding who would come and where they would sit, "she sends word to her cook that there will be twenty-four on the 10th; the menu will be submitted to her later, which she will probably glance at and send back. She never sees or thinks about her table, which is the butler's province." Invitations having been written out, her staff either sent them by mail or delivered them by hand. On the date of the dinner party they would lay the table with place cards correctly distributed, cook the food, serve the meal, clear the table, wash the dishes, and tidy the house when the guests had departed.

The hostess prided herself on the hard work that perfection represented; and we can only assume that Emily Post's readers—those who were not "hostesses of great houses"—were impressed. The silver, for instance, had to be handled with reverent care, never being picked up by a servant "except with a rouged chamois." "No piece of silver is ever allowed by the slightest chance to touch another piece. . . . The footman who gathers two or three forks in a bunch will never do it a second time, and keep his place. If the ring of a guest should happen to scratch a knife handle or a fork, the silver-polisher may have to spend an entire day using his thumb or a silver buffer, and rub and rub until no vestige of a scratch remains."

Service at table was swift and silent. There should be one footman for each lady at table, so that chairs may be held out for them and slid back in under them as they sat down. The butler stood throughout the meal behind the hostess, "except when ordering another servant or pouring wine. He never leaves the room or handles a dish." *Service à la russe* meant that servants carved all the dishes, handed them round, and returned them to the side table. Enormous care was taken not only of the cutlery but of the plates: "a smear or thumb-mark on the edge of a dish is like a spot on the front of a dress!"

But already the writing was on the wall. It was in the 1920s that the institution of live-in household servants began seriously to die out in North America; the process had begun earlier in Europe. The reasons for this social change are closely tied to industrialization and new opportunities for paid work, especially for women: as soon as household staff were given the choice, they left domestic service in droves. The disappearance of servants, in turn, finally secured the arrival in the home of technical aids to housework. In 1928, Emily Post added to her work a chapter called "On the Servantless House"; by 1931, platinum-finished silver cutlery had become a regrettable but understandable alternative to pure silver; its quality of not tarnishing "perhaps outweighs its handicap" where there are few or no servants. In 1945, Post found it necessary to emphasize to her readers that the maid or butler should not be introduced to the guests; to do so was "as out of place as introducing the bus driver to the passengers."

A good many of the opportunities for non-domestic employment which were siphoning off the supply of servants were in fact boring, stultifying, even dangerous jobs. The reasons why men and women preferred to work in factories, even where the pay was less than that offered to servants, have to do with personal relationships and social ranking—the very stuff of manners. Despite the advantages of domestic work (the possibility of good personal relations on the job and comfortable living quarters, and perhaps relative freedom from timetables and supervision), servants increasingly resented their social disabilities. They were dependent on the good will and courtesy of their employers, yet powerless to demand them; subject to a family not their own (they put up, in other words, with all the fear and insecurity of being a guest and received none of the power, the social rewards, or the honour); they worked long, ill-defined hours, and were allowed hardly any private life. Nowadays, most paid household work is done on an hourly or daily, live-out basis, where those who can afford it employ a "cleaning lady" to come in and do housework several times a month. None but the very rich keep maids, footmen, chefs, butlers—the servants who once waited at every middle-class table. We have, instead, lowered our normal expectations of dinner-time ceremony.

Women are no longer automatically expected to remain dedicated to the house and devoted to the maintenance of family polish. I have, of necessity, not addressed myself to the enormous implications of women's liberation from having to assume an exclusively housewifely role. This revolution's many consequences for manners in general are similar to those resulting from the disappearance of servants: the two changes are aspects of the same shift in the social system. The extent to which women are treated decently has been for many centuries one of the most telling tests of civility. This standard has now been raised higher than ever before; it has, moreover, come to be demanded and not merely hoped for. Constantly remembering to monitor our attitudes towards women, to weed preconceptions out of our own minds, is a difficult and attention-demanding exercise. The moral choice has been irrevocably made. We are for the most part still *parvenus*, however, in need of polishing our manners.

Behaving "properly" towards women in the modern world impinges, as "good manners" always do, upon our most personal behaviour. For instance, I myself have had to wage perpetual war on the prejudice of pronouns as I wrote this account. In my last book, published only a few years ago, I was far more "relaxed" on this point. It has become, in the interval, socially unacceptable to refer to people in general as "man," "men," or even "mankind": polite people say "humankind." Women host dinners as often as men do: do I call them "hostesses"? If I speak of hosts in the abstract, as performers of a role, do I then go on to speak of a host as "he," as "she," or as "he or she"? Do I dare to call him or her "them"? (I reject "s/he.") All writers will recognize the problems I have faced; it is a puzzlement none of us can avoid. Men wear hats much less commonly than they used to. I must forego, then, their lifting them on meeting me, forgive those who still wear hats for failing to do so, and perhaps positively wish they would not. But I can and must expect men not to refer to me as "he." Our table manners, apart from matters of seating and precedence, have in recent times concerned sexual discrimination comparatively rarely; but anyone who regrets a fall in levels of punctiliousness at table must take into account the very genuine and newly compulsory efforts being expended elsewhere.

Our society has worked hard to stop putting a whole class of people into the position of having personally to serve members of another class, whether the serving class be professional servants or women in general. This is not to say that modern Western society refrains from forcing people, more and more of them people living in countries other than our own, to work and produce goods cheaply so that we can maintain what we call "our standard of living." The fact remains, however, that the vast majority of us do have to shift for ourselves at home. We cannot get away with making other people devote their lives to servicing our personal needs continually and face to face. This means a reduction in levels of elegance and formality, certainly, but expecting nobody (including one's wife) to be one's servant requires formidable competence, as well as adherence to the intensely civilized ideal that we ought not to impose on other people. Doing without servants, in other words, like giving women a chance to pursue whatever career they like, is not only necessary because of the social system, but is also in itself a demanding form of civility.

"Manners" govern relationships with other people primarily in situations of close personal contact; they do not constitute virtue, but they do set out to imitate virtue's outward appearance; they are an admission of an ideal. It has become disgusting and ridiculous, proof positive that one has neither manners nor taste, openly to treat another human being as though she or he were intrinsically inferior; we cannot be caught doing so to any person's face, at any rate, and remain "respectable" ourselves. How we behave towards people we never actually meet—and the modern world places us in a complex symbiosis with people we never personally meet—is another story.

It is also said that the revolution in women's roles in our society is causing another shift in behaviour. Increasingly, North American and European householders—*young* people, in the affluent sectors of society—are hiring more and more personal servants. These are of course people poorer than themselves, imported, many of them, from other countries because few in our own society would want these jobs. Immigrants, on the other hand, might gratify us—even convince us that we are being civil—by feeling lucky that we consent to hire them.

Our perception that we have "no time" is one of the distinctive marks of modern Western culture. It cannot be attributed solely to our servantless state, or to the determination of large numbers of women to work outside the home. Our attitude towards time is as much a precondition of our social system as it is a result of it. Its effect upon manners is almost invariably to simplify them—except that it has, of course, become unprecedentedly rude to be perceived as wasting anybody's time. "No time" is used as an excuse and also as a spur: it both goads us and constrains us, as a concept such as "honour" did for the ancient Greeks. Abstract, quantitative, and amoral, unarguable, exerting pressure on each person as an individual, the feeling that we have no time escapes explanation and censure by claiming to be a condition created entirely out of our good fortune. We have "no time" apparently because modern life offers so many pleasures, so many choices, that we cannot resist trying enough of them to "use up" all the time we have been allotted.

"No time" is ingeniously bound up with our apparent conquest of space, by means of mobility. Never have things been done faster or been available from further away. (But then we *need* the speed, mostly because we have no time.) Travelling quickly, using machines to do the work, spending as little time as possible eating, or resting, or being otherwise unproductive—nothing seems to relieve the pressure. The freedom granted by speed is, in other words, more than balanced by the stress of being in a constant and unavoidable hurry. Powerful people love impressing upon those needing their services that they have trouble finding time "to fit them in": making others wait because one's own time is more precious than theirs is one of the great hallmarks of desirability and success.

Feeling rushed is also an important component of our economy; it causes people to buy more, pay more, try more things and more means to compensate for the stress, or at least to alleviate the anxiety. It also makes us work harder and longer—and therefore leave ourselves less time. It is not so much that we buy too many things and they use up our time, as that having no time forces us to buy more things. We eat out or buy ready-prepared food to eat at home in order to save time, but also—and more insidiously—because we feel we have no time to do otherwise. Many of us never really learn to cook, and therefore cooking remains not only time-consuming but unrewarding. We prefer to spend more money and less time on meals; we therefore tend obligingly to persuade ourselves that what we get for our money is pleasant eating.

Because casual manners are "relaxed," they are all we feel we can manage in our rushed and exhausted state. Eating a home-made meal with invited guests, or even with one's family, cannot be entirely "casual," at least in the accidental aspect of the word, because preparations and forethought are necessary, and all those present have had to turn down competing events and commit themselves in advance to appearing on a certain date. They have to sit down, face each other, and not get up and leave before everyone else is ready to do so. In comparison with acting out a sudden whim to consume a microwaved mug of soup within the next five minutes, eating together with friends can come to seem a formal, implacably structured and time-consuming event—even for those who do not have to cook. We are conditioned to think that even a low level of formality is a constraint just because it entails participation with other people, whereas being in one's own personal hurry must be free and preferable. It is an attitude that certainly suits the marketers of mass-produced individual portions of ready-prepared fast food.

Food is "fast" when it is immediately ready to be eaten, and can also be downed quickly. There must be either a puritanical renunciation of the pleasure to be found in savouring food, or a jadedness arising from too many competing calls for our attention—or both—for us to prefer eating fast; we have to *want* to settle for less. There was a time when having to eat food fast was considered to be a misfortune; the ideal state for a diner was that in which speed and food never had to coincide, except in the serving of it. Nowadays, "fast food" is a phrase that has become so common that a good deal of the disapproval it used to express has disappeared; another paradoxical expression, "junk food," was invented, but even it has acquired intimations of pleasurable naughtiness—of daring the unhealthy for the sake of speed and the assuaging of an addiction. An addiction is not a sharing matter; and speed is almost invariably impeded by the presence of other people. But the bodily proprieties observed while eating—no dribbles and smears, no loud chewing, no grabbing, staring, crumbling, slurping—are part of the socially enforced formalities of behaviour while consuming fast food, as they are for dining in any context. We may eat fast food anywhere—even while walking in the street—provided these basic manners are maintained. If they are not, no one is likely actually to complain; but the politest response we can hope to encounter if we let everyone down in this manner is to be ritually ignored.

One of the great modern demands is for cleanliness. Seldom in the history of the world have people washed as much as we do. We constantly wash ourselves, our clothes, our dishes, curtains, carpets, and cars. We have invented machinery to wash for us, and instead of resting on our laurels we have furiously raised our expectations about cleanliness higher and higher, so that home-makers work as hard now as they have ever done to keep their families "clean." The idea seems to be that if you can be even cleaner, then you must. Demonstrative cleanliness plays for us something of the role of pollution observances in India or in the ancient world: submission to purity rules becomes a precondition of acceptance in society. If we are not very careful, cleanliness rules can matter more to us than morality. In a social gathering such as the "cocktail party" described earlier, a known murderer or thief is likely to receive a warmer welcome from the host and guests than a filthy, smelly, but innocent tramp could hope for. Dirty people are by definition outsiders in our world: they offend sensibilities and give troubling intimations of the possibility of loss of control. The bodily proprieties, as we have seen, are extremely strict nowadays; they prove to other people that those who maintain them are exercising what others intensely desire of their fellow citizens: inoffensiveness, self-control, and obliging assurances that they need no help.

Where food is concerned, cleanliness is always so important that demands for it easily become obsessive. Cutlery, glasses, and plates must impeccably gleam before we can bear to begin eating. Modern design in tableware often stresses smooth forms and plain colours; glasses are clear, simple, and colourless. Such objects are easy to clean, but also encourage us to appreciate how clean they are—streamlined shapes, which modernity often claims as its hallmark, have what are called "clean lines." We like our fruit perfect (never a spot or a bruise), and our fast food is abundantly wrapped and cartoned (coverings suggest that everything is under control). It has taken a great deal of sophisticated reasoning to make the public realize that a perfect, spot-free apple is achieved with the help of pesticides, and that invisible, tasteless chemicals might actually be harmful. People understand the danger that chemical compounds can represent by thinking of them as pollution, a form of dirt. The discovery that detergents—cleansing agents!—can cause pollution was a fearful and paradoxical revelation in the 1960s.

At many periods in our history—often during the most stylized, elegant centuries of all—our own ancestors were freely and unconcernedly filthy. The recent and all but universal agreement to wash our bodies, our clothing, and our hair as much as we do expresses submission to a constraint massively underwritten by a very modern social consensus. Cleanliness is essential for good health; and smelly people repel others. These two axioms are sufficient to keep us all in line. For most of us, most of the time, it is the social sanction that is most decisive. We wash *for other people* and at their insistence, even though—and perhaps with the result that—feeling clean makes us personally "feel good." Keeping our houses clean has nothing like the same urgency that we feel for the washing of ourselves: glowing fresh bodies often issue from very dirty living quarters. The safe cleanliness promised by fast-food operators is one of their products' most powerful selling points, for people who cheerfully leave dirty dishes for a week in the kitchen—provided that nobody comes to visit.

The word "proper" in French is *propre*, meaning "one's own," the noun being *propriété* or "property"—something one takes possession of by "appropriating" it. At the end of the sixteenth century in France a new meaning was added to the original sense. *Propre*, "one's own; distinctive, characteristic, and intrinsic to oneself," now also signified "elegant" and "correct." Elegant people, literally "choosy" people, were fastidious and "naturally" graceful, with a *je ne sais quoi*. They stood out—but also fitted in; they were "proper." To do something *proprement* was to do it "appropriately," which now meant "fittingly," maintaining what we still call "the proprieties"—a word to which, in the seventeenth century, the English language gave a new sense to match the French meaning. Since then the concept has undergone another momentous and revealing revolution: *propre* in French is now the commonest word for "clean."

Since complying with the rule of cleanliness facilitates acceptance by others and breaking it means instant ostracism, washing constantly is essential for social mobility. A clean person is ready and acceptable at all times for meetings with old and new acquaintances. It is not all that easy to get to know people; it is therefore simply not worthwhile being dirty and risking our chances. In addition, being clean is a basic requirement that most people living in modern conditions can meet—which is one reason why it can be so implacably upheld; it provides an efficient means of sifting out the few diehards and giving the vast majority a chance to show that they like being thought proper. The trouble we go to in order to be always clean now takes up a good deal of the effort we are prepared to expend on mannerly behaviour. There are so many of us, we live and move in such proximity, and it is so difficult for us all to behave, that preserving bodily cleanliness has become a sort of charm or talisman, and a proof that at least we are trying.

References

Chapter One: *Behaving*

Introduction (pp.1–4)
For sharing behaviour among chimpanzees, and the evolution of human food sharing, see G. L. Isaac, and Teleki. Sahlins (1977) shows how culture is a "biological" necessity in human beings. "Women can be shared . . .": Firth (1973), 261.

The Artificial Cannibal (pp. 4–17)
Columbus is quoted in Knight, 16–17. Hulme disputes the accuracy of early European views of the Caribbean. Hankins looks at the roots of Caliban. Villa, *et al.*, describe the finds of bones at Fontbrégoua. The idea that cannibalism has a purely material basis was raised by Harner (1977) who describes what the Spanish saw and gives figures, and supported by Harris (1977). Díaz del Castillo: 181, 568–69; de Sahagun: 3–4, 48; and Staden: 155–63. Other sources on cannibalism include Sanday, Brown and Tuzin, Berndt, Strathern, Bloch and Parry, Glasse, Pouillon, Forsyth, P. Brown, and

Bucher. See also Montaigne, "Of the Cannibals," I.30, and Swift, "A Modest Proposal . . ." A Fijian fork made especially for cannibal eating is illustrated in Rudofsky (1980), 36. Ancient Maori cannibal practices are described and interpreted by Bowden; he quotes a comment by Tregear (1904), on the great courteousness of Maori society. See further on the Maoris, D. Lewis. "On the afternoon of the sixth day . . . ": Berndt, 272.

Ritual (pp. 17–27)

The newspaper article describing the boy eating spaghetti with his hands is by W. R. Greer for the *New York Times* (1985), and syndicated; an example of a picture showing how spaghetti was eaten in nineteenth-century Naples can be found in A. del Conte, *Portrait of Pasta* (London and New York: Paddington Press, 1976), 40. Goffman, esp. 1963, 1971, shows how important it is that we keep alert for small signs, and give assurances of competence at table and elsewhere; the broader uses of predictability on agreed occasions are stressed by Douglas and Gross. The story of the monkeys on Koshima Islet was reported by Kawai. Lange shows how we insist on enculturation in our food and eating habits. Other sources on ritual and its meaning include Turner, D'Aquili, Argyle, Brown and Levinson, Goffman, Laughlin and McManus, Lorenz, Bonner, Girard, Burkert (1983), Burkert Girard and Smith, Myerhoff, Scheff, J. Z. Smith, Strecker, and Tambiah. Jesus on hand–washing: Mark 7. 1–8; on ritual and on bad manners, see for example Matthew 3. 13–17; 5. 23–24; 6. 2–6, 16–18; 15. 10–11; 22. 11–14; 23. 5–8; Mark 2. 23–28; Luke 4. 16; 7. 44–47; 11. 37–43; 17. 11–19; 20. 45–47; 22. 7–8. On "bread alone": Matthew 4. 4, quoting *Deuteronomy* 8. 3.

Feasting and Sacrifice (pp. 27–37)

The *Fêtes* of Catherine de Médicis are described by Wheaton, 49–51, and Strong, 19–56; Bakhtin discusses the significance of Rabelaisian feasting in Chapter 4 of his book. Ashton quotes from the seventeenth-century "Trial of Fr. Christmas." For beer in the societies of the Kofyar, the Jívaro, and the Bemba, see Netting, Harner (1972), and Richards. Charsley investigates the history of the wedding cake. On the problem with meat feasts in Hong Kong earlier in this century, see Watson. Hieron of Syracuse on feasting: Athenaeus, 4.144d. The sacrifice of Eumaeus in the *Odyssey* (14. 414–56) is discussed by Petropoulou. Sources on sacrifice include Girard, Burkert (1983), Burkert Girard and Smith, Ashby, Bammel, Detienne and Vernant, Durand and Schnapp, Lissarrague and Schmitt-Pantel, Grottanelli and Parise, Harner (1977), Harris (1977), Hubert, Turner, and Van Baal. On the Seder and the Mass: Feeley-Harnik, Murphy, and several articles in *La Table et le partage* (Rencontres de l'Ecole du Louvre. Paris: La Documentation française, 1986). Murphy and J. Z. Smith between them cover the categories of ritual mentioned on page 36.

Chapter Two: *Learning to Behave*

Introduction (pp. 39–40)
The quotation about politeness being like the polishing of pebbles is from J. T. Trowbridge, *A Home Idyll* (1907). Mark Twain's idea that it is like the cauliflowering of cabbage is from *Pudd'nhead Wilson's Calendar*, 1893, Ch. 5.

Bringing Children Up (pp. 40–56)
Whiting and Child give a comparative study of nursing practices in the 1950s. Lowenberg explains why small children like packing their mouths. Food-related insults are discussed by Leach, and culturally imbued flavour preferences by E. Rozin. Wittgenstein's neophobia is mentioned by Malcolm, 69; the tendency of the modern Dutch to neophilia is described by van Otterloo. The encouragement of French children to "try a little of everything" is documented by Sjögren-de Beauchaîne; Mintz (Ch. 5) wonders why the French have withstood the onslaughts of sugar so well. Detienne shows how civilized people in ancient Greece were thought of as "between beasts and gods," and Syrkin looks at "fools for Christ's sake," who deliberately avoided "correct" behaviour. Chaga table manners in the 1930s are described by Raum, esp. 184, 127, 193–94; Read writes on those of the Ngoni of Nyasaland (now Malawi) in the

1950s (see 44–45, 79, 155); and Richards on those of the Bemba (see 1939, 76, 197; 1932, 68). On giving and sharing food as a means of socialization through the language required, among Kaluli children in Papua New Guinea, see now Schieffelin, esp. Ch. 6.

"Look thou be courteous standing at meat": Furnivall (1908), 123. Gloag, 59, looks at the seating of seventeenth-century British children. A. Hope has interesting information on Scottish table manners, today and in the past; I owe to her the quotation from Osgood Mackenzie (his pp. 95–97). The Malawian riddle is told by Chimombo. The Malayan children's initiation is from McArthur (1950), quoted by Yudkin and McKenzie, 54. Charles and Kerr report on the British "Sunday lunch," and on the importance of tables in the teaching of table manners to children, 184–85, 188, 190.

Inhibitions (pp. 56–68)

A whole school of sociology appears to be grouping behind the theories of Norbert Elias. Beside his works listed in the Bibliography, and others not relevant to table manners, see Mennell (1989), and the volume containing the article by Wouters. "Children have in the space of a few years . . ." : Elias, I.140; "Relaxation within the framework . . .": *ibid.* Aresty describes the old British custom of sending children to live with others as pages and maids; see further, the Introduction by Chambers to *A Generall Rule* . . . (Anon., fifteenth century). Early English manners books will be found in the two collections of Furnivall. The politicization of courtesy in seventeenth-century France is described by Ranum.

Aspirations (pp. 69–78)

"The barrier which society draws around itself . . . ": Anon.,1879. On *sprezzatura* in Castiglione: Saccone; on *je ne scais quoi* and "effortless simplicity" in seventeenth-century aristocratic French manners, see Magendie, Flandrin (1986), J. Revel; on "good taste" as a modern class barrier, see Bourdieu. "The expert removes the bones . . .": Chao. On nineteenth-century American manners, see the manners books listed, and also Schlesinger, Wecter, Kasson's book and articles, Mrs. Trollope, and Charles Dickens's *American Notes*. "A radical Protestant antipathy . . .": Kasson (1990), 63. "Their enterprise must be viewed . . . ": *ibid.*, 62. Elizabeth Post was quoted in an anonymous article in the Toronto *Star*, July 28, 1984. "Even polished brass . . .": Stanhope, *Son*, letter no. 118.

Chapter Three: *The Pleasure of Your Company*

Introduction (pp. 79–83)

The Wamirans of Papua New Guinea are the subject of Kahn's book; the PNG song is quoted from Bloch, 191. Assamese Hindu food customs are discussed by Cantlie. Men and women often eat separately in Africa: Goody (1982), 86, L-V. Thomas. See Okere, 193, for the dishing out of porridge in rural Igboland. The layout and the eating arrangements of the apartments of the Parisian bourgeoisie are described by Sjögren-de Beauchaîne. Emily Post's comment on cooking smells is to be found on page 301.

Company (pp. 84–89)

"Dinner-parties rank first . . ." : Anon.,1879. The Igbo song and proverb are from Okere, 196. The two kinds of feast in Wamira: Kahn, esp. Ch. 8. The Gogo ritual of reconciliation is described by Rigby. In Book 6 of the *Iliad*, Glaucus and Diomedes are about to do battle when they realize that their grandfathers had feasted together and exchanged gifts; this makes a fight between them impossible— although Diomedes cheats Glaucus in their own subsequent gift exchange. On Sherpa parties: Ortner, Ch. 4; on Sherpa "antirelationalism": 38–39. The remark about eating and drinking together is made by Hagias in Plutarch's *Symposiacs*, ii.10.643a. For a description of a host's problems at a large impersonal gathering, see Riesman. "To make those eat . . . ": L. Tendret, *La Table au pays de Brillat-Savarin*. Belley: Bailly-Fils, 1892. The power of *Geltungsbedürfnis* is brought out in Masters, 154, 157.

Hosts and Guests (pp. 90–99)

Emily Post's description of an embarrassingly inept dinner party is from the 1922 edition, 182 ff. On hospitality in Greece and Rome, see Gauthier, Grottanelli; for the rules in the modern Mediterranean region, Pitt-Rivers. The Ghost of Agamemnon's lament for his murder: *Odyssey*: 11. 409–20. Heal (1990, 1984) describes attitudes towards hospitality before and after the Reformation in England. The history of the Amphitryon myth is traced by Lindberger. For the establishment of the custom of making round-tipped dinner knives, see Pagé, and Gourarier (1985), 62. Gladiatorial combat during dinner among the Celts and Romans: Athenaeus, 4.153f–54c, and Gourarier (1985), 65; severed heads brought to the table: Athenaeus, 6.251a; hurling cups of wine: Athenaeus, 13.557d. Kottabos: Athenaeus, e.g., 15.666c–67b; Sparkes, Lissarrague, 75–82.

Invitations (pp. 99–109)

Clifford Geertz's *The Religion of Java* opens with a detailed description of the *slametan*. The subtleties and ingenious devices of Sherpa invitations are described by Ortner; the tactic of sending a child, and the quotation given, are on page 80. Bell explains how Tanga kin may claim their rights at a banquet. Louis XIV inviting his brother: Saint-Simon, quoted by Franklin (1908), II, 164. For invitations among the Chinese: Fitzgerald, Watson; among the Yao: Hubert. Hubert's book on the Yao of Thailand is an important recent contribution to culinary anthropology. The story of Gabba the parasite is related by Friedländer, 85. Southworth's book on medieval minstrels includes fascinating information about these important players in the drama of feasts; see specifically 47, 81. On comic parasites imitating the host's disabilities: Athenaeus, 6.249a, 249f, 10.435e; on Roman *umbrae*: Plutarch, *Symposiacs*, vii.6. The arrival of a crowd of inebriated uninvited guests at a drinking party is described by Plato in his *Symposium*, 212c–d. On Roman dinner-time superstitions, see Deonna and Renard. "Resistance was futile . . . ": Masters, 171-73. "Nothing but serious illness or death . . .": Emily Post (1922), 187–88. "Lame, branded, wizened with age . . .": Athenaeus, 3.125d. The legend of the Singing Bone is the subject of Mahler's cantata, *Das klagende Lied*. On Rembrandt's *Supper at Emmaus* in the Louvre, see de Mirimonde.

Coming Right In (pp. 109–121)

Braganti and Devine advise what gifts should be offered in which European countries. For manners in the United Arab Emirates, see Kanafani and Hawley; on the meaning attached to showing the soles of one's feet, see Hawley (1965), 67. On Socrates dressing for dinner: Plato, *Symposium* 174a; on the Roman *synthesis*: Suétonius, *Nero* 51.2, Martial, 5.79, Brewster, McDaniel. Post describes the problems of keeping gloves, bag, fan, and napkin from sliding off one's lap: (1922), 221, 717. On face veils: Post (1922), 246; and masks: Kanafani. The cover of the 1982 edition of Goody's book *Cooking, Cuisine and Class* reproduces an ancient Egyptian painting from a Theban tomb of the Eighteenth Dynasty, now in the British Museum, showing dinner guests with incense cones on their heads. The ceremony of the cola nut in Nigeria: Nzekwu; of the apéritif in France: Clarisse; of evening drinks in North America: Gusfield.

Taking Our Places (pp. 121–136)

"Hsiang Yu invited Liu Pang . . .": Ying-Shih Yü in Chang, 64. *The Rules and Orders of the Coffee-House* are published by Clair. Obey the host's seating arrangements: Branchereau, 210. Pitt-Rivers tells how a miffed diplomat could turn over his plate. On rank and seating during the French *ancien régime*, see Brocher. McCaffree and Innis have an introduction on protocol in general, and its history. For the custom of "turning the table," see Post (1945), 355. The rules of courtesy in different Latin American countries are laid out in Devine and Braganti. Ortner explains how ranking is expressed by seating among the Sherpa, 74–75. Seating and serving choreography is carefully described by Post (1937), 254–57; "The lady of highest rank . . .": Post (1928), 203–04; see also Miller. Fortes writes on the food manners of polygamous men among the Tallensi. Post speculates on "the great American rudeness" in edition after edition; see for example 1945, 361 ff. Hosts and hostesses sitting at table on stuffed easy chairs: Gloag, 170–71.

Chapter Four: *Dinner Is Served*

Introduction (pp. 137–138)

On Nero's banqueting hall: Suetonius, *Nero*,31.2; Lehmann. On death images at dinner: Herodotus, 2.78, Plutarch, *Sages*, 148.

The First Bite (pp. 138–146)

Medieval mealtime ceremony is described by Cosman, and Schiedlausky. For Ceaucescu and his taster, see Pick. Grace among the Abbasids: Ahsan, 102; the Igbo: Okere, 194; the Ainus: Batchelor, 9; the North Americans: Porter. Spanish formal offers to share the meal with strangers: Pitt-Rivers; Portuguese: Dias, 90. Starting the banquet in Melanesian New Ireland: Powdermaker. Grace at dinner with Ivan the Terrible: Smith and Christian, 112–13. Consciously consuming the first bite: Bennett.

Taking Note of Our Surroundings (pp. 146–155)

In the original, the quotation from Russell: "Pope, Emperowre, Kynge or Cardinalle . . ." includes "Duke" among them. Heal (1990) gives interesting plans of medieval halls, illustrating the hierarchical principles. On "banquets" after dinner: Girouard, Hughes. On tables in seventeenth-century Parisian apartments: Pardailhé-Galabrun. There are splendid illustrations of Baroque buffets in Bursche; Brett, 31, explains about the number of shelves. On Greek and Roman dinner tables, see Richter. On Japanese business lunches, Befu. Hewes enumerates and illustrates the sitting postures of humankind. On lying down to eat and drink, see Rudofsky, Dentzer, Murray (1983), Chuvin, and Boardman. The quotation from *The Book of Amos* is in 6. 4–7. "Cassander, at the age of thirty-five . . .": Athenaeus, 1.18a. Boardman suggests the reason why ancient Greek gods sit up at their meals. Plutarch on lying down at meals: *Symposiacs*, v.6.679e–80b. Horace, *Satires*, II.viii, describes a Roman dinner that ends in disaster; Petronius' Trimalchio's Feast is an important, if fanciful, source of information on Roman banqueting. Rudofsky (1980) reminds us of the oddity of St. John's behaviour in medieval and Renaissance depictions of the Last Supper.

The Prospect Before Us (pp. 156–167)
Friedländer documents the first mention of Roman tablecloths, 97. Belden, 17, explains the origin of place mats. For superstitions about salt, see Visser, Ch. 2. Oman gives an illustrated description and history of medieval salt nefs. Palmer's book is a scholarly and entertaining account of the times of day when meals have habitually been eaten in Britain, and how mealtimes have changed since the sixteenth century; he explains the history of lunch. The Veneerings' "caravan of camels": *Our Mutual Friend*, 10. Madame de Sévigné on the crashing pyramid: *Lettres* I.351. There is a picture of a *plateau* in Belden. General sources on the history of European and American table settings include Belden, Brüning, Lehne, G. R. Smith, Arminjon, Howe, and Wheaton. For *sableurs*, see Gruber, and Wheaton, 186–93. The information that eighteenth-century people often found real flowers not "cultured" enough comes from Belden; but Wheaton and Bursche show that real flowers were popular in France, Germany, and Italy. Staffe (1892), 221, gives an illustration of a huge nineteenth-century table loaded with a splendid flower display, round the edge of which the places are set.

Montaigne's words, "I would dine without a tablecloth . . ." are from his essay "On Experience." For the Flathead Indians of Montana, see Turney-High. Hot cloths for wiping faces in China: Lamb. Rolling tablecloths on tubes: Belden, 13–14. Folding table napkins in late sixteenth-century Italy, with illustrations: Giegher. The bread "usually fell on the floor": Post (1922), 197. Dogs tied to symposiasts' couches are depicted, for example, on a Corinthian crater (a large pot for mixing wine with water) now in the Louvre; see J. Charbonneaux, R. Martin, and F. Villard, *Archaic Greek Art* (New York: Braziller, 1971), 42. The illustration from the *Très Riches Heures du Duc de Berry* by the Limbourg brothers may be seen in C. Clifton, *The Art of Food* (London: Windward, 1988), 25. Deonna and Renard publish a photograph of an *asaroton* mosaic floor.

Fingers (pp. 167–178)
Ahsan's book on Abbasid social life is an invaluable source of information for ninth-century Arab manners; Lane's description of nineteenth-century Egyptian society is a classic in its genre; and

Kanafani's work on aesthetics in the United Arab Emirates is the kind of research of which modern ethnographers and historians of *mentalités* stand most in need. For the honest response of even broad-minded, well-travelled Westerners who come "up against reality" at a meal eaten with the hands, see Davidson. The greedy Greco-Roman banqueter: Athenaeus, 1.5e. Celts "clutch whole joints and bite": Athenaeus, 4.151e. The Chaucer quotation is in Nevill Coghill's translation, 20–21. For table manners in medieval Hungary, see Balassa and Ortutay, 157. On the hollowed table-top and dinner *à l'assiette*, R. Muchembled, 456; see also Gourarier (1985), 317.

Chopsticks (pp. 179–183)

Fr. Rodrigues on Japanese disgust at our table napkins: M. Cooper. Face-wiping with hot towels in China: Lamb, 15,18. "There is something maternal . . .": this quotation, and the others by Barthes in this section, 11–26. "The best mannered person . . .": Hsü and Hsü, in Chang, 304. Dixon gives the names for bad table manners in Japan. Hu Yaobang's opposition to chopsticks was reported by Burns. Twenty billion chopsticks in Japan: see the news story "'Nobel' Winner Silenced Over Rain Forests," *The Globe and Mail* (Toronto), December 3, 1988 (the figures are for "last year"). Lamb gives the proverb about rattling chopsticks.

Knives, Forks, Spoons (pp. 183–196)

For the uses of the Chinese cleaver: E. N. and M. L. Anderson, "Modern China: South," in Chang, 364. For more on folding knives carried habitually on the person and produced for use at dinner, see S. Moore. "Wrapping springy leaves around the tines . . .": Post (1945), 493. Pagé quotes Tallement on Richelieu's rule that dinner knives should have rounded ends. "When eating cheese . . .": quoted in Evans; "let the edge be turned downward . . .": Anon., 1845. The English eating peas from knife-blades: Le Grand d'Aussy, 3. 149. The Freudian slip with the cake: Freud, 201.

St. Peter Damian's horror of forks is alluded to by Henisch; Emery gives further details of the history of forks, esp. 39. On the pre-eminence of Italy and Spain in this history, see Franklin (1908) I, 287, and Lowie. The fresco with the flat metal plates standing on a buffet is in the Sala di Psiche of the Palazzo del Tè; see E. Verheyen, *The Palazzo del Tè in Mantua: Images of Love and Politics.* (Baltimore: Johns Hopkins University Press, 1977). Buhler and Graham stress the magnificence of French silver dinnerware in the seventeenth and eighteenth centuries. Eliza Ware Farrar's *The Young Lady's Friend* (published anonymously in 1837) appeared in 1880 with "Mrs H. O. Ward," as though she were the author, on the title page. This was a pseudonym of Mrs. C. S. Bloomfield-Moore. The quotation given is 1837, 346–47; the corresponding pages in 1880 are 297–98. Both knife and fork are to be held in the right hand, but the English way is easier: Branchereau, 188–89. The Freudian analysis of knife, fork, and spoon is by Hammel. Emery gives the history of the fig-shaped spoon bowl. "Never leave your coffee spoon . . .": Andréani, 156.

Sequence (pp. 196–210)

"A hundred soups . . .": Goudeau, 139–40. Aron on the "centre-piece" of a meal, *le rôt*: 161. "Dishes like hailstones": quoted by Belden, 34. The theory that a *pièce de résistance* meant a dish *for which* one resisted other dishes is suggested by Sokolov. C. A. Wilson describes a turtle dinner, 203–04. Entertainments at the Court of Burgundy at Bruges are described by de La Marche and Cartellieri. A description in 1868 of a *dîner à la russe* is given by Schuyler; the origin of the term is discussed by Wheaton in a note, 291; for a German dinner of a generally similar type, see Head. A description of a dinner setting for an *"ambigu" à la française* is quoted by Revel (1979), 231–33. The swift, carefully choreographed meal in 1680 is described by Wheaton, 142. The traditional three-fold structures of British meals are analysed by Douglas and Nicod (1974). Hudson and Pettifer include meals in their history of air travel. The Cantonese *sihk puhn* is described and analysed by Watson.

Helpings (pp. 210–227)

"A plate with food on it . . .": Post (1922), 203. On the Igbo famine, see Okere, 213. Post's suggestion that one should pretend to serve wine is on page 205. Musil describes the manners of the Rwala Bedouin. Crossed spoons on the table as a decoration: Belden. Mme de Rothschild's dinner service: Aron (1973), 233–34. The

Japanese care with cups at the Tea Ceremony, Cha No Yu, is described by Dixon; see also J. Young, and Kondo. The Chinese have "no rules," only "show appreciation": Chao. The problem of the French as to whether or not to praise the food is described by Burgaud. "Did you expect not to eat well in my house?": Pitt-Rivers. Quotations from the Baronne Staffe (1899): 210, 211. "To fill, or even to half fill, a soup plate . . .": Anon., 1879. "Smell not to thy Meat . . .": Anon., 1701. Polite Chinese guests eat warmed-up offerings as well: E. Cooper. Do not add salt and paprika before eating in Hungary: Braganti and Devine. Nigerian visitors do not say they have already eaten: Okere, 197. A Bedouin "enemy feast" is described by Seabrook. Displeased Pedi husband: Quin. Abbasid diners urge others to eat: Ahsan. The Canadian children's game is described by Shuman. Bringing one's own spoon and using it in the common dish, in seventeenth-century France: de La Salle. Lift food from the serving dish, do not slide it: Branchereau, 191. Taking "seconds" in various European countries: Braganti and Devine. It is rude to fill up on relish at ordinary meals in China: E. Cooper. Accepting only the third request: Anon., *Li Chi*; Hubert. The Sherpas fear "an empty mouth": Ortner, 81. Arab hosts entreat guests to eat: Hawley (1984). The version of the great fish being a salmon and the host Talleyrand: see Blond, 474; the version given here is from Dumas, 302. Taking away food from a Sherpa banquet: Ortner, 80. Seuthes flinging loaves: Xenophon, *Anabasis*; Athenaeus, 4.151a-b.

Carving (pp. 227–242)

T. E. White gives archaeological reports on the hunting, carrying, and sharing habits of early South Dakota Indians. A series of medieval and Renaissance *trousses* is to be seen in the Museum of the Tower of London. On modern American males enjoying cooking on special occasions, see T. A. Adler. Damas (1972) describes the sharing customs of the Canadian Copper Eskimo; those of other groups are explained by Zumwalt, Goody (1962), Boas, L. Marshall, and H. N. C. Stevenson. For the sharing of the kangaroo by Australian Aborigines, see Isaacs; of the camel by Touaregs: Gast. On meat-eating after sacrifice, see Burkert Girard and Smith, E. Isaac, and

Durand. For the possible origin of the word "hierarchy": Baudy. Heracles' rage when he was given too small a helping of meat: Athenaeus, 4.157f–58a. On medieval "great birds" eaten at dinner, and on swearing oaths over them: Witteveen, Whiting, de La Marche, Cartellieri, Baudrillart, Le Grand d'Aussy, and Blond. For the procession into the medieval hall of the Carver, the Taster, and other table dignitaries: Cosman. On medieval carving terms: de Worde, Hodgkin. Wooden models of joints for lessons in carving: Taylor (1664), 40, cf. Juvenal 11.138–41. "To do the honours of the table gracefully . . .": Stanhope, *Son*, letter no. 163; cf. *Son*, nos. 74, 243. Quotations from Mrs. Beeton: 502, 504, 506, 539–40. I have translated the story of Talleyrand's "beef lesson" from Branchereau, 238.

The Red, the White, and the Gold (pp. 242–262)
On ancient Greek libations: Tolles, Rudhardt. Beer parties among the Iteso of Kenya and Uganda: Karp. Bringing one's own cup, among the Igbo of Nigeria: Okere, 191. Claude Lévi-Strauss (1969) describes the ritual of pouring wine in popular Provençal restaurants. Sjögren-de Beauchaîne discusses modern bourgeois French habits of wine- and water-drinking at meals. "Three craters only do I mix for the temperate . . .": Athenaeus, 2.36b–c. On saké, at the Japanese business lunch: Befu. On the reason for covers on German beer steins: Newnham-Davis. The Illyrians used to tighten their belts: Athenaeus, 10.443b. Pouring beer, among the Newars of Katmandu: Toffin; for more on the Newars, see Löwdin. Asking for beer or wine in Tudor England: Burton (1976). The ancient Mongol anxiety that guests get drunk: Mote in Chang, 207. On tumblers: Brett, Price. A glass of Schnapps for every button: Price. Chinese finger-games: Lamb. Toasting ritual in seventeenth-century Ireland: Rich. On the "ring" of glass: Monson-Fitzjohn. Remembering names when drinking healths: Simond, 47. The quotation from *Little Dorrit*: 412. Ancient Roman toasting practices: Deonna and Renard. The earliest temperance society: Dickson. "Catch the person's eye and bow . . .": Crowen. Not mentioning a woman's name among the men: P. Mason, 79.

Table Talk (pp. 262–271)

On the philosopher Menedemus as host: Athenaeus, 10.419e–20c. On Sherpa dining: Ortner, 9, and Ch. 4. The Newars of Katmandu are among those who make silence formal and talking familiar: Toffin. A British "proper" Sunday dinner involves "no TV": Charles and Kerr, 184–85. See Goffman, esp. 1963, on dinner-table conversation. "Taciturn people are not good for society . . .": Anon., *Table Observances*, 36. The French Navy's tradition of table-top objects as aids and warnings for conversation is described by Arminjon and Blondel. Morel gives the rules for seventeenth-century dinner-time conversation in France; Clair publishes *The Rules and Orders of the Coffee House* (London, 1674). For the influence of table-top decorations on conversation, see Gourarier, and Burgaud. On the *souper intime*, see Wheaton, 156–59, with the illustration.

On Lord Chesterfield's attitude towards laughing: Heltzel; J. E. Mason, 297 ff. The quotations from Chesterfield are from Stanhope, *Son*, letter no. 259, and *Godson*, letter no. 141. There is a good selection of nineteenth-century conversation rules in *Australian Etiquette* (Anon., 1885). "At dinner once, Mrs. Toplofty . . .": Post (1922), 222. On the ideal of gentlemanly behaviour: P. Mason. "How awkward to ask . . .": Anon., *Table Observances*, 36. "Politeness is universal toleration": Anon., 1855. Women should not bother men, who have larger appetites: Anon., 1881. "Pay them the compliment of seeming . . .": Anon., 1885. Danes like conversing round the table after dinner: Braganti and Devine.

Feeding, Feasts, and Females (pp. 272–284)

Foodstuffs are men's "babies": Kahn, esp. Ch. 6. "To eat" is frequently used for sex: Goody (1982), 114. "Philosophy should no more have a part in conversation . . . ": Plutarch, *Symposiacs* 612f–13a. But a wedding feast was a crowded affair . . .: Plutarch, *Symposiacs* 667b. Sherpa men are ranked, but women sit in a crowd: Ortner, 75. On men and women at a Winnebago feast: Radin. Women considering it a privilege to serve at a feast: Powdermaker, H. N. C. Stevenson. The separation of men and women at a Javanese *slametan*: Geertz; in Japan: Dixon,1885; at the court in Imperial China: Mote in Chang, 220; in the United Arab Emirates:

Kanafani; in nineteenth-century French peasant households: Gourarier (1985), 348, and Gourarier (1986). Young boys take their place among the men: Gourarier (1986). Wife as "mother of her husband": L-V. Thomas. Women as "gatekeepers": Lewin. Women making cooking and serving expressive of their feelings: Okere, Appadurai. Men having nothing to do with food: Mcck, Okere. Men showing displeasure by refusing to eat: Okere, Quin. A polygamous male eats food prepared by the wife he is currently sleeping with: Goody (1982), 114.

Women's power over beer and clay pots: Quin; Dionysus ruling both wine and pots: Lissarrague, 22; women's power over beer: Toffin, Goody (1982), 73, 76. Fear of women as poisoners: Ortner, Bell; keeps men from roving: Quin. Nineteenth-century women neither asked for nor served themselves wine: Black; did not always accept it when offered: Anon., 1879; insisted, in France, that it be mixed with water: Staffe (1899), 208. On the Mediterranean custom of mixing water with wine: Flandrin (1983). Miss Manners on women not pouring wine: (1982), 653; a man should pour wine for the woman on his left: Bremner (1989). "Young ladies do not eat cheese . . .": Evans. Women's breath in danger of not pleasing men: Flandrin (1983). Slimmer chopsticks for Japanese women: Hirayama. The Kagoro tribe of Nigeria: Meek; the Pedi: Quin; the Assamese Hindus: Cantlie. Louis XIV and his queen: Wheaton, 132–33. Lady Mary Wortley Montagu's carving: Halsband; that of eighteenth-century servants: Stead. The hostess "looks across the table . . .": Post (1922), 223-24. Jingle in *The Pickwick Papers*, 85. British Factory House dinners in Oporto: Price, 26. On nineteenth-century American disapproval of the ladies leaving the gentlemen, see, for example, Anon., 1855. Lord Cockburn's *Memorials* are quoted in McNeill.

All Gone (pp. 284–295)
On the "thrive bit": Bringéus. Roman superstition about removing a portion before the diner has finished: Deonna and Renard. Chinese guest of honour must stay until the end: E. Cooper. Different ways of laying down knives and forks: Braganti and Devine. Medieval after-dinner waferers: Southworth. The medieval British custom of

toasting guests at the end: Black. The Constable of Castille at the English court in the seventeenth century: Rye. Marking the end of eating among Assamese Hindus: Cantlie; at a Chinese banquet: Fitzgerald. Drinking coffee, then tea, in nineteenth-century Britain: Anon., 1879. Coffee as an initiation ritual: Gusfield. A feast in the country among the Newars of Nepal: Toffin. Ending a meal in nineteenth-century Egypt: Lane; in nineteenth-century Russia: Schuyler. Catching the Chinese "Four Heavies": Chao. For the famous incensing ceremony in the United Arab Emirates, see Kanafani, 25–27. Various ways of ending the evening in Europe: Braganti and Devine. Strategies for making guests leave, among the Pedi: Quin; the Ainu: Batchelor, 88; the Elizabethan English: Burton (1958). Seeing guests off in Latin America: Townsend, 40. Ending a Tanga feast: Bell. A later party: Toffin, Dixon; special delicacies for the previous host: Powdermaker.

Chapter Five: *No Offence*

Introduction (pp. 297–300)
The Rabelais quotation is from Book I.11. The quotation from Lévi-Strauss: *The Origin of Table Manners*, 503–04. Rude to rejoice in gristle: Athenaeus 8. 347d–e. The facial muscles that express disgust: see Izard, 243. On expectations of competency at the dinner table, Goffman (1971).

Pollution (pp. 300–309)
The stories from Homer's *Odyssey*, of pollution expressed by the bending of natural laws, are in Books 12 and 20. Indian rules to protect eating from pollution are to be found, e.g., in Carstairs, Das, Dumont, Khare, Harper, Freed, and Sinclair-Stevenson; in Ceylon: Yalman; among the Jains: Mahias (who provides photographs), 77, 218, 231. Clay vessels smashed by ancient Indians: S. Wolpert, *A New History of India* (New York: Oxford University Press, 1977), 17. For the experiment with the fly-swatter, P. Rozin. See L. Wright, on the history of cleanliness in the cultures of western Europe and North America. The Parisian *convives* who flung asparagus ends over

their shoulders: Crapouillot. "I always eat these things with the peel on": Chang, 311.

The Rules and Regulations of the Mouth (pp. 309–326)

Eating is sacred, silence is respectful: see, e.g.,Walens, 88, 91, 95. "Germans chew with their mouths closed . . .": quoted by Bonnet, 100. On the symbolism of tears versus rheum, and for much else in this chapter, see Douglas (1966). "Ethnic" food is becoming more and more ordinary: van Otterloo. Sagaris the lazy: Athenaeus, 12.530c. "Not to offer a pear . . .": della Casa, 7. Opening the mouth only just before food enters it: see, e.g., Anon., 1879. Post on ejecting bones and stones from the mouth: (1931), 621-22; (1945), 489–90. On male versus female ways of eating: Bourdieu, 190–91. How to deal with a scalding mouthful, in seventeenth-century France: Bonnet, 100; in eighteenth-century France: Garrisson, 58. Barthes on Japanese food: 11–26. Branchereau on egg-mashing: 197–98; Newnham-Davis on egg-drinking: 233. The well-behaved Greek courtesan: Athenaeus, 13.571f–72a. On noiseless chewing: Erasmus, 284.

"If any man speak that time to thee . . .": Furnivall (1908), 179. Ejecting food and running when father calls: Anon., *Li Chi*, 24. Not licking a dusty plate: Russell (Furnivall, 1868), 19. Mrs. Humphry on picking bones, 69. The Abbasid gentleman and the spoons: Ahsan, 163. For saliva superstitions in ancient Rome, see F. W. Nicolson. Greedy Demylos: Athenaeus, 8.345c. On spitting rules in seventeenth-century Holland: Spierenburg, 12. The ancient Persians refused to spit: Xenophon, *Cyropaedia* I.ii.16, Herodotus, I.99, 138; neither would they vomit or urinate in front of others: Athenaeus, 4.144a. Spittoons in Chinese restaurants: E. Cooper, 181. On the English smoking (and spitting) chair: Gloag, 187–88. The ancient Chinese were taught not to cool rice by spreading it out: Chang, 39; Chinese servants must not breathe on food they are carrying: Anon., *Li Chi*, 80–81. The *Rules of Civility*, copied out by George Washington, are printed in Conway. The Chinese cover a toothpick in use, with one hand: E. Cooper, 181. The *Boke of Curtasye* and Rhodes's *Boke of Nurture* are in Furnivall (1868), 83 ff., and (1908), 136 ff. On Kwakiutl attitudes to aggressive behaviour at meals:

Walens, 95. Rinsing the mouth after dinner: Branchereau 192, de la Rochefoucauld-Liancourt, 29, Simond, 49, and Mrs Beeton, 13.

The Proprieties of Posture and Demeanour (pp. 326–337)

Norbert Elias uses manners books as evidence for increasing bodily self-control in our culture since the sixteenth century. Not rolling the eyes up during grace: Bonnet, 102. William Pitt and Colonel Forrester are quoted by J. E. Mason, 97, 271; cf. Heltzel. Handy, on slouching: 46; Post: (1931), 621. On seventeenth-century disgust at seeing a diner with a filthy napkin: Flandrin (1986), 272. Quotation from *Ecclesiasticus*: 31: 13–16. On modern Latin American manners: Townsend, 36. Athenaeus, on greedy people not talking in order to eat more: 10.421d. Post on training children to control hands and posture: (1931), 718. *The Young Scholar's Paradise* is in Furnivall (1908) (see p. 169); the first *Boke of Curtasye*: Furnivall (1868) (see p. 180). "Nor look thereon . . .": Rhodes, Furnivall (1908), 139. George Washington's rules of etiquette: Conway. Hiccuping, among the Tanga: Bell, 73; burping, among the Pedi: Quin, 142; in Hugh Rhodes: Furnivall (1908), 135. On the emperor Claudius' desire to permit farting: Suetonius, *Claudius*, 32. See further Franklin's Appendix, *Sur les flatuosités* (1908), II, 65–71. Carl Ludwig on the "green sickness" is quoted by Sennett, 182. *Ecclesiasticus* on vomiting: 31: 25. Chamber pots invented by the Sybarites: Athenaeus 12.519e. On the English and their chamber pots in the dining room, Simond, 49: see also Faujas de Saint Fond (1784); they were used by the toasting gentlemen after the ladies had left.

Postscript: How Rude Are We? (pp. 339–357)

"The best way to use a napkin . . .": O'Rourke, 45. Mary Douglas on intricacy: Douglas and Gross, 1981. On *tu/vous* pronouns: Brown and Gilman. On invitations to "drinks" not necessarily denoting intimacy: Douglas (1972), 65–66. Riesman *et al* describe the problems, for a modern host, of a large impersonal party. Homer on the Suitors' feasting in the *Odyssey*: 16. 108–10. The rituals at McDonald's are described by Kottak. "Physical trespasses, such as . . .": Annett and Collins, 164. "The perfect example of a formal dinner table . . .": Post (1922), 178, 198, 201, 235. On servants in North America, see Katzman. Platinum-finished silverware accepted: Post (1931), 701; not introducing servants to guests: (1945), 13. See Mintz, Ch. 5, on the pressures of No Time, and Cowan on Keeping Clean.

Bibliography

Abrahamson, H. *Victorians at Table*. Toronto: Ontario Ministry of Culture and Recreation, 1981.

Adler, E. M. "Creative Eating: The Oreo Syndrome," *Western Folklore*, 40 (1981), 4–10.

Adler, T. A. "Making Pancakes on Sunday: The Male Cook in Family Tradition," *Western Folklore*, 40 (1981), 445–54.

"Agogos." *Hints on Etiquette and the Usages of Society*. London: Longman, 1834.

Ahsan, M. M. *Social Life Under the Abbasids*. London: Longman, 1979.

Aimez, P. "Psychopathologie de l'alimentation quotidienne," *Communications*, 31 (1979), 93–107.

Alcouffe, D. "La naissance de la table à manger au XVIIIe siècle," in *La Table et le partage*. Rencontres de l'Ecole du Louvre. Paris: La Documentation française, 1986.

Alexander, C., *et al. A Pattern Language*. New York: Oxford University Press, 1977, Sections 139, 147, 182.

Ammar, H. *Growing Up in an Egyptian Village*. London: Routledge and Kegan Paul, 1954.

Anderson, E. N., Jr., and M. L. "Cantonese Ethnohoptology," *Ethnos*, 34 (1969), 107–17.

———. "Penang Hokkien Ethnohoptology," *Ethnos*. 37 (1972), 134–47.

———. "Modern China: South," in K. C. Chang, ed., *Food in Chinese Culture*. New Haven, Conn.: Yale University Press, 1977.

Anderson, E. N. *The Food of China*. New Haven, Conn.: Yale University Press, 1988.

Andréani, G. *Guide du nouveau savoir-vivre*. Paris: Hachette, 1988.

Annett, J. and R. Collins. "A Short History of Deference and Demeanor," in R. Collins, ed., *Conflict Sociology*. New York: Academic Press, 1975. Ch. 4.

Anon. (Compiled early first century B.C.). *Li Chi*. Trans. by J. Legge. 2 vols. New York: NYU Press, 1967.

Anon. (15th century). "A Generall Rule to teche every man that is willynge for to lerne, to serve a lorde or mayster in every thyng to his plesure," in R. W. Chambers, ed., *A Fifteenth-Century Courtesy Book*. London: Kegan Paul, Trench, Trübner, 1914.

Anon. *The Court of civill Courtesie* (trans. from Italian). London: Richard Jones, 1591.

Anon. *The School of Manners, or Rules for Children's Behaviour* (1701). Ed. J. I. Whalley, London: The Cockerill Press, 1983.

Anon. [Eliza Ware Farrar]. *The Young Lady's Friend, by a Lady*. Boston: American Stationers, 1837; by "Mrs. H. O. Ward," Philadelphia: Porter and Coates, 1880.

Anon. *The Art of Good Behaviour*. New York: C. P. Huestis, 1845.

Anon. *The Art of Pleasing; or, the American Lady and Gentleman's Book of Etiquette* (1852). Cincinnati: H. M. Rulison (1855 edition).

Anon. [R. de Valcourt]. *The Illustrated Manners Book. A Manual of Good Behavior and Polite Accomplishments*. New York: Leland, Clay, 1855.

Anon. *Table Observances*. London, n.d. (19th century).

Anon. *Etiquette for Ladies*. London: Knight and Son, 1857.

Anon. *Tipplers' Tales* (1869). London: Rosters, 1988.

Anon. "Table Customs," *Scribner's Monthly*, 8 (September 1874), 627.

Anon. *Manners and Tone of Good Society, or, Solecisms to be Avoided*. London: Warne, 1879.

Anon. *The Manners of the Aristocracy, by One of Themselves*. London: Ward, Lock and Co., 1881.

Anon. *Australian Etiquette*. Melbourne: People's Publishing, 1885. Repr. London: J. M. Dent, 1980.

Anon. Issue on "Les Bonnes Manières," *Crapouillot*, Paris (1952).

Anon. "Emily Post's Etiquette Bible Gets Updating and Revision," Toronto *Star*, July 28, 1984.

Anon. "Come on Mabel, let's leave," *The Economist* (February 17, 1990), p. 79.

Appadurai, A. "Gastro-Politics in Hindu South Asia," *American Ethnologist*, 8 (1981), 494–511.

D'Aquili, E. G., *et al. The Spectrum of Ritual: A Biogenetic Structural Analysis*. New York: Columbia University Press, 1979.

Arens, W. *The Man Eating Myth*. New York: Oxford University Press, 1979.

Aresty, E. B. *The Best Behavior*. New York: Simon and Schuster, 1970.

Argyle, M. *Bodily Communication*. London: Methuen, 1975.

Arminjon, C. and N. Blondel. "La table du commandant," in Z. Gourarier, ed., *Les Français et la table*. Paris: Musée national des arts et traditions populaires, 1985, pp. 407–18.

Arminjon, C. "L'utile et l'agréable: Le décor de la table du XVe au XIXe siècle," in *La Table et le partage*. Rencontres de l'Ecole du Louvre. Paris: La Documentation française, 1986.

d'Arms, J. H. "Control, Companionship and *Clientela*: Some Social Functions of the Roman Communal Meal," *Echos du Monde classique/Classical Views*, 3 (1984), 327–48.

Arnott, M. L., ed., *Gastronomy: The Anthropology of Food and Food Habits*. The Hague: Mouton, 1975.

Aron, J-P. "Essai sur la sensibilité alimentaire au XIXe siècle," *Cahiers des Annales*, 25 (1967).

———. *Le mangeur du XIXe siècle*. Paris: Editions Payot, 1989 (first published 1973).

Artus, Thomas, sieur d'Embry. *Description de l'Isle des Hermaphrodites . . . pour servir de supplément au journal de Henri III*. Cologne: 1605, pp. 105, 107.

Ashby, G. *Sacrifice: Its Nature and Purpose*. London: SCM Press, 1988.

Ashton, J. *A righte Merrie Christmasse!!!* New York: B. Blom, 1968.

Athenaeus (2nd–3rd century A.D.). *The Deipnosophists*. 15 vols. trans. by C. Gulick. Loeb Classical Library (7 vols.), London: Heinemann, 1927–1941.

Austin, G. A. *Alcohol in Western Society from Antiquity to 1800: A Chronological History*. Santa Barbara, Calif.: ABC-Clio Information Services, 1985.

Badham, C. D. *Prose Halieutics, or Ancient and Modern Fish Tattle*. London: Parker & Son, 1854.

Bailey, C. T. P. *Knives and Forks*. London: Medici Society, 1927.

Bakhtin, M. *Rabelais and His World*, trans. by H. Iswolsky. Cambridge, Mass.: MIT Press, 1965, Ch. 4 (first published 1936).

Balassa, I. and G. Ortutay. *Hungarian Ethnography and Folklore*. Budapest: Corvina Kiadó, 1979.

Baldrige, L. *Letitia Baldrige's Complete Guide to Executive Manners*, ed. by S. Gelles-Cole. New York: Rawson Associates, 1985.

Ball, J. D. *The Chinese at Home*. New York: Fleming H. Revell, 1912, Ch. 13.

Bammel, F. *Das heilige Mahl im Glauben der Völker*. Gütereich, Germany: Bertelsmann, 1950.

Barthes, R. *L'empire des signes*. Geneva: Skira, 1970, pp. 26–39. Tr. R. Howard, *The Empire of Signs*. London: Jonathan Cape, 1982, pp. 11–26.

Batchelor, J. *Ainu Life and Lore*. Tokyo: Kyobunkwan, 1927. Repr. New York: Johnson, 1971, Ch. 13.

Baudrillart, H. *Histoire du luxe*. Paris: Hachette, 1880–81. Vol. 3 pp. 453–509.

Baudy, G. J. "Hierarchie oder: Die Verteilung des Fleisches," in B. Gladigow and H. G. Kippenberg, eds., *Neue Ansätze in der Religionswissenschaft*. Munich: Kösel-Verlag, 1983, pp. 131–74.

Beeton, I. *The Book of Household Management*. London: S. O. Beeton, 1861. Repr. London: Jonathan Cape, 1986.

Befu, Harumi. "An Ethnography of Dinner Entertainment in Japan," *Arctic Anthropology*, 11 (Supplement, 1974), 196–203.

Belden, L. C. *The Festive Tradition. Table Decoration and Desserts in America, 1650–1900*. New York and London: W. W. Norton, 1983.

Bell, F. L. S. "The Place of Food in the Social Life of the Tanga," *Oceania*, 19 (1948), 51–74.

Benedict, St. (ca. A.D. 535). *The Rule of St. Benedict*, ed. by D. O. Hunter Blair. Fort Augustus: Abbey Press, 1886 (1948).

Bennett, J. G. *Food*. The Sherborne Theme Talks Series 4. Shaftesbury, Dorset: Coombe Springs Press, 1977.

Berndt, R. M. *Excess and Restraint. Social Control Among a New Guinea Mountain People*. Chicago: University of Chicago Press, 1962, Ch. 13.

Bierlaire, F. "Erasmus at School," in R. Le DeMolen, ed., *Essays on the Works of Erasmus*. New Haven, Conn.: Yale University Press, 1978.

———. "Erasme, la table et les manières de table," in *Pratiques et discours alimentaires à la Renaissance*. Paris: Maisonneuve et Larose, 1982.

Birdwhistell, R. *Kinesics and Context*. Philadelphia: University of Pennsylvania Press, 1970.

Black, M. *Food and Cooking in Medieval Britain; History and Recipes*. English Heritage: Historic Buildings and Monuments Commission for England, 1985.

———. *Food and Cooking in 19th Century Britain; History and Recipes*. English Heritage: Historic Buildings and Monuments Commission for England, 1985.

Bloch, M. *Political Language and Oratory in Traditional Society*. New York: Academic Press, 1975, p. 191.

——— and J. Parry, eds., *Death and the Regeneration of Life*. Cambridge: Cambridge University Press, 1982.

Blond, G. and G. *Histoire pittoresque de notre alimentation*. Paris: Fayard, 1960.

Blondel, N. "L'utilité des objets de la table," in *La table et le partage*. Rencontres de l'Ecole du Louvre. Paris: La Documentation française, 1986.

Boardman, J. "Symposion Furniture," in O. Murray, ed., *Sympotica*. Oxford: Clarendon Press, 1990, pp. 122–31.

Boas, F. *Ethnology of the Kwakiutl*. Annual Report of the Bureau of Ethnology. Washington, D.C.: Smithsonian Institution, 1913–14. Vol. 35, part 1, pp. 607, 750–76.

Boileau, N. Satire III, *Oeuvres* (1665). Geneva: Fabri et Barrillot, 1716.

Bois, C. du. "Attitudes Toward Food and Hunger in Alor," in D. Haring, ed., *Personal Character and Cultural Milieu*. Syracuse, N.Y.: Syracuse University Press, 1956 (first published 1941), pp. 241–53.

Bolchazy, L. J. *Hospitality in Early Rome*. Chicago: Ares, 1977.

Bonner, J. T. *The Evolution of Culture in Animals*. Princeton, N.J.: Princeton University Press, 1980.

Bonnet, J-C. "La Table dans les civilités," *Marseille*, 109 (1977), 99–104.

Bossard, J. H. "Family Table Talk—An Area for Sociological Study," *American Sociological Review*, 18 (1943), 295–301.

———— and E. S. Boll. *Ritual in Family Living*. Philadelphia: University of Pennsylvania Press, 1950.

————. *The Sociology of Child Development*. New York: Harper and Row, 1966, Ch. 7.

Bottéro, J. "Le plus vieux festin du monde," *L'Histoire*, 85 (1986), 58–65.

Bourdieu, P. *Distinction*. Trans. by R. Nice. Cambridge, Mass.: Harvard University Press, 1984 (first published 1982).

Bowden, R. "Maori Cannibalism: An Interpretation," *Oceania*, 55 (1984), 81–99.

Bowen, E. "Manners," in *Collected Impressions* (1937). New York: Knopf, 1950.

Braganti, N. L. and Devine, E. *The Travelers' Guide to European Customs and Manners*. Deephaven, Minn.: Meadowbrook, 1984.

Branchereau, L. *Politesse et convenances ecclésiastiques*. Paris: Vic, 1885.

Braudel, F. *La civilisation materielle. Economie et capitalisme. XVe–XVIIIe siècles. Les structures du quotidien*. Paris: Armand Colin, 1979, Ch. 3.

Brears, P. *Food and Cooking in 16th Century Britain; History and Recipes*. English Heritage: Historic Buildings and Monuments Commission for England, 1985.

————. *Food and Cooking in 17th Century Britain; History and Recipes*. English Heritage: Historic Buildings and Monuments Commission for England, 1985.

Bremner, M. *Enquire Within Upon Modern Etiquette and Successful Behaviour for Today*. London: Century, 1989.

Brett, G. *Dinner Is Served*. London: Hart-Davis, 1968.

Brewster, E. H. "The Synthesis of the Romans," *Transactions and Proceedings of the American Philological Association*, 49 (1918), 131–43.

Brillat-Savarin, A. *Physiologie du goût*. Belley: G. Adam (1948), 1826.

Bringéus, N-A. "The Thrive-Bit: A Study of Cultural Adaptation," in A. Fenton and T. M. Owen, eds., *Food in Perspective*. Edinburgh: John Donald, 1981.

Brocher, H. *Le rang et l'étiquette sous l'ancien régime*. Paris: Félix Alcan, 1934.

Brown, J. W. *Fictional Meals and Their Function in the French Novel 1789–1848*. Toronto: University of Toronto Press, 1984.

Brown, L. K. and Mussell, K., eds., *Ethnic and Regional Foodways in the United States: The Performance of Group Identity*. Knoxville, Tenn.: University of Tennessee Press, 1984.

Brown, P. "Cannibalism," in M. Eliade, ed., *The Encyclopedia of Religion*. New York: Macmillan, 1987.

―――― and S. C. Levinson *Politeness: Some Universals in Language Use*. Cambridge: Cambridge University Press, 1987.

―――― and D. Tuzin, eds., *The Ethnography of Cannibalism*. Washington, D.C.: Society for Psychological Anthropology, 1983.

Brown, R. and A. Gilman, "The Pronouns of Power and Solidarity," in J. A. Fishman, ed., *Readings in the Sociology of Language*. The Hague: Mouton, 1968, pp. 252–75.

Brüning, A. "Schau-Essen und Porzellanplastik," *Kunst und Kunsthandwerk*, 7 (1904), 130–51.

Bucher, B. *La sauvage aux seins pendants*. Paris: Hermann, 1977.

Buhler, K. C. and J. M. Graham. *The Campbell Museum Collection*. Camden, N. J.: 1972.

Bull, R., *Grobianus, or the Compleat Booby*, trans. of F. Dedekind, *Grobianus*. London: T. Cooper, 1739.

Burgaud, F. "Qu'en est-il aujourd'hui des convenances de table?" in *La Table et le partage*. Rencontres de l'Ecole du Louvre. Paris: La Documentation française, 1986.

Burke, P. "The Repudiation of Ritual in Early Modern Europe," in *The Historical Anthropology of Early Modern Italy*. Cambridge: Cambridge University Press, 1987, Ch. 16.

Burkert, W. *Homo necans*, trans. by P. Bing. Berkeley, Calif.: University of California Press, 1983.

———, R. Girard, and J. Z. Smith. *Violent Origins*. Stanford, Calif.: Stanford University Press, 1987.

Burns, J. F. "Peking Has Seen the Future—And It Lacks Chopsticks," *New York Times*, December 24, 1984, p. 1.

Bursche, S. *Tafelzier des Barock*. Munich: Schneider, 1974.

Burton, E. *The Elizabethans at Home*. London: Secker and Warburg, 1958, Ch. 5.

———. *The Early Tudors at Home, 1485–1558*. London: Allen Lane, 1976, Ch. 4.

Bynum, C. W. *Holy Feast and Holy Fast*. Berkeley, Calif.: University of California Press, 1987.

Cabous Onsor El Moali (11th century). *Le Cabous Namé*, trans. by A. Querry. Paris: Ernest Leroux, 1886.

Canetti, E. "On the Psychology of Eating," in *Crowds and Power*, trans. by C. Stewart. New York: Viking Press, 1960, pp. 219–24.

Cantlie, A. "The Moral Significance of Food Among Assamese Hindus," in A. C. Mayer, ed., *Culture and Morality: Essays in Honour of Christoph von Fürer-Haimendorf*. Delhi: Oxford University Press, 1981.

Carstairs, G. M. *The Twice-born: A Study of a Community of High-caste Hindus*. London: Hogarth Press, 1957.

Cartellieri, O. *The Court of Burgundy: Studies in the History of Civilization*. New York: Haskell House, 1970, Ch. 8 (first published 1925).

Cassel, J. "Social and Cultural Implications of Food and Food Habits," in E. G. Jaco, ed., *Patients, Physicians, and Illness*. Glencoe, Ill.: The Free Press, 1958, pp. 134–43.

Castiglione, B. *Il Libro del Cortegiano* (1514). Venice, 1528. Trans. by C. S. Singleton, *The Book of the Courtier*. Garden City, N.Y.: Doubleday Anchor, 1959.

Cervio, Vincenzo. *Il Trinciante*. Venice: Heredi di G. Varisco (1581; 1593).

Chang, K. C., ed., *Food in Chinese Culture*. New Haven, Conn.: Yale University Press, 1977.

Chao, B. Y. *How to Cook and Eat in Chinese*. London: Faber and Faber, 1956.

Charles, N. and M. Kerr. *Women, Food and Families*. Manchester: Manchester University Press, 1988.

Charsley, S. "The Wedding Cake: History and Meanings," *Folklore*, 99 (1988), 232–41.

Châtelet, N. *Le Corps à corps culinaire*. Paris: Seuil, 1977.

Chaucer, G. *The Canterbury Tales* (1387–1400). Trans. N. Coghill. Harmondsworth, Middx.: Penguin Books (1961).

Chimombo, S. "Riddles and the Representation of Reality," *Africa*, 57 (1987), 314–15.

Chuvin, P. "Manger assis, manger couché," *L'Histoire*, 85 (1986), 66–70.

Clair, C. *Kitchen and Table*. London: Abelard-Schuman, 1964.

Clarisse, R. "L'Apéritif: un rituel social," *Cahiers Internationaux de Sociologie*, 80 (1986), 53–61.

Clément, O. "Le repas et le partage dans la Pâque orthodoxe," *La Table et le partage*. Rencontres de l'Ecole du Louvre. Paris: La Documentation française, 1987.

Cohen, Y. A. "Food and Its Vicissitudes: A Cross-Cultural Study of Sharing and Non-sharing." In Y. A. Cohen, ed., *Social Structure and Personality: A Case Book*. New York: Holt, Rinehart, and Winston, 1961.

Conway, M. D. *George Washington's Rules of Civility Traced to Their Source and Restored*. London: Chatto and Windus, 1890.

Cooper, C. *The English Table in History and Literature*. London: Sampson Low, Marston, 1929.

Cooper, E. "Chinese Table Manners: You Are *How* You Eat," *Human Organization*, 45 (1986), 179–84.

Cooper, M., ed., *They Came to Japan*. Berkeley, Calif.: University of California Press, 1965, pp. 189–202.

Corson, J. *Practical American Cookery and Household Management*. New York: Dodd Mead, 1886.

Cortazzi, H. *Victorians in Japan*. London: Athlone Press, 1987.

Coryat, T. *Coryat's Crudities, hastily gobled up in five moneths travells*, (1611). Glasgow: J. Maclehose, 1905.

Cosman, M. P. *Fabulous Feasts: Medieval Cookery and Ceremony*. New York: Braziller, 1976.

Counihan, C. M. "Female Identity, Food and Power in Contemporary Florence," *Anthropologica Quarterly*, 61 (1988), 51–62.

Courtin, A. de. *Nouveau traité de la civilité qui se pratique en France parmi les honnestes gens*. Paris: Hélie Josset, 1672.

Cowan, R. B. *More Work for Mother: The Ironies of Household Technology from the Open Hearth to the Microwave*. New York: Basic Books, 1983.

Crawley, E. *The Mystic Rose*. Vol. 2. New York: Boni and Liveright, 1927.

Crowen, T. J. *The American Lady's System of Cookery*. New York: Auburn, Derby and Miller, 1852.

Cuisenier, J., "Le goût et la manière," in *La Table et le partage*. Rencontres de l'Ecole du Louvre. Paris: La Documentation française, 1986.

Cussler, M. and M. L. DeGive. *'Twixt the Cup and the Lip*. Washington, D.C.: Consortium, 1952.

Damas, D. "Central Eskimo Systems of Food Sharing," *Ethnology*, 11 (1972), 220–40.

Damianus, P., St. (11th century). *Institutio Monialis*. Ch. 11, in J. P. Migne, ed., *Patrologiae cursus completus*, Vol. 145. Paris: Migne, 1853.

D'Aquili, E. G., *et al.*, eds., *The Spectrum of Ritual: A Biogenetic Structural Analysis*. New York: Columbia University Press, 1979.

Dart, R. "The Predatory Transition from Ape to Man," *International Anthropological and Linguistic Review*, 1 (1953), 201–19.

Das, V. *Structure and Cognition: Aspects of Hindu Caste and Ritual*. Delhi: Oxford University Press, 1977.

Daumas, J-M. "La cène dans la conception de l'Eglise réformée," *La Table et le partage*. Rencontres de l'Ecole du Louvre. Paris: La Documentation française, 1986.

Davidoff, L. *The Best Circles*. London: Croom Helm, 1973, Ch. 3.

Davidson, A. "Attacking a Lamb with Our Fingers," in *A Kipper with My Tea*. London: Macmillan, 1988, pp. 24–26.

De Quincey, T. "The Casuistry of Roman Meals," in D. Masson, ed., *The Collected Writings*, Vol. 7. London: A. and C. Black, 1897.

Dedekind, F. *Grobianus* (1549–52). Darmstadt: Wissenschaftliche Buchgesellschaft, 1979. See Bull, R.

Deetz, J. *In Small Things Forgotten: The Archaeology of Early American Life*. Garden City, N.Y.: Anchor Books, 1977.

Della Casa, G. *Galateo* (1558). Trans. by K. Eisenbichler and K. R. Bartlett. Toronto: University of Toronto Press: Centre for Reformation and Renaissance Studies, 1986.

Delphy, C. "Sharing the Same Table: Consumption and the Family," trans. by D. Leonard, in *The Sociology of the Family: New Directions for Britain*. Keele, Staffs: University of Keele Press, 1979, pp. 214–31.

Dentzer, J-M. *Le motif du banquet couché dans le Proche-Orient et le monde grec, du VIIe au IVe siècle avant Jésus-Christ*. Paris: de Boccard, 1982.

Deonna, W. and M. Renard. *Croyances et superstitions de table dans la Rome antique*. Brussels: Latomus, 1961.

Detienne, M. "Between Beasts and Gods," in R. L. Gordon, ed., *Myth, Religion and Society*. New York: Cambridge University Press, 1981, pp. 215–28.

——— and J-P. Vernant. *La Cuisine du sacrifice en pays grec*. Paris: Gallimard, 1979.

Devine, E. and N. L. Braganti. *The Travelers' Guide to Latin American Customs and Manners*. New York: St. Martin's Press, 1981.

Dias, E. M., T. A. Lathrop, and J. G. Rosa. *Portugal: Lingua e Cultura*. Newark, Del.: Cabrilho Press, 1978.

Díaz del Castillo, B. *The Discovery and Conquest of Mexico 1517–1521*. Trans. by A. Maudslay. London: Routledge, 1939.

Dickens, Charles, *The Pickwick Papers* (1836–37). Harmondsworth, Middx.: Penguin Books, 1972.

———. *American Notes, and Pictures from Italy* (1842). London and Toronto: Dent and Dutton, 1908.

———. *A Christmas Carol* (1843). New York: Harper, 1844.

———. *Little Dorrit* (1857). Harmondsworth, Middx.: Penguin Books, 1985.

———. *Great Expectations* (1861). Edinburgh: R. and R. Clark, 1937, Ch. 22.

Dickson, P. *Toasts*. New York: Delacorte Press, 1981.

Divonne, M. de la F. and I. Maillard, *Festins de France*. Paris: Herscher, 1987.

Dixon, J. M. "Japanese Etiquette," *Transactions of the Asiatic Society of Japan*, 13 (1885), 1–21.

Dolgoy, R. "Development of Dining Etiquette Indoors and Outdoors," in *Consuming Passions. Eating and Drinking Traditions in Ontario*. Willowdale, Ont.: The Ontario Historical Society, 1990, 211–25.

Doran, J. *Table Traits*. New York: Redfield, 1855.

Dosi, A. and F. Schnell. *Vita e Costumi dei Romani antichi. 1. Le abitudini alimentari dei Romani. 2. Pasti e vasellame da tavola. 3. I Romani in cucina*. Rome: Museo della Civiltà Romana, Quasar, 1986.

Douglas, M., ed., *Food in the Social Order: Studies of Food and Festivities in Three American Communities*. New York: Russell Sage Foundation, 1984.

———, ed., *Constructive Drinking*. Cambridge: Cambridge University Press, 1987.

———. *Purity and Danger: An Analysis of Concepts of Pollution and Taboo*. London: ARK, 1989 (first published 1966).

———. *Natural Symbols*. New York: Vintage Books, 1973.

———. *Implicit Meanings*. London: Routledge and Kegan Paul, 1975.

———. "Food as an Art Form," *Studio International*, 188 (1974), 83–88.

———. "Deciphering a Meal," *Daedalus* 101 (1972), 61–81.

——— and J. Gross, "Food and Culture: Measuring the Intricacy of Rule Systems," *Social Science Information*, 20 (1981), 1–35.

——— and M. Nicod, "Taking the Biscuit: The Structure of British Meals," *New Society*, 30 (1974), 744–47.

Dreyer, C. A. and A. S. "Family Dinner Time as a Unique Behavior Habitat," *Family Process*, 12 (1973), 291–301.

Dumas, A. *Le grand dictionnaire de cuisine* (1873). Paris: Pierre Grobel, 1958.

Dumézil, G. *Le Festin d'immortalité*. Paris: Geuthner, Annales du Musée Guimet, 1924.

Dumont, L. *Homo Hierarchicus*, trans. by M. Sainsbury, L. Dumont, and B. Gulati. Chicago: University of Chicago Press, 1970, esp. Ch. 6 (first published 1966).

Dupuy, B. "L'eucharistie et le seder pascal juif," *La Table et le partage*. Rencontres de l'Ecole du Louvre. Paris: La Documentation française, 1986.

Durand, J-L. "Bêtes grecques," in *La cuisine du sacrifice en pays grec*, ed. by M. Detienne and J-P. Vernant. Paris: Gallimard, 1979, pp. 133–65.

———— and A. Schnapp. "Boucherie sacrificielle et chasses initiatiques," in C. Bérard, *et al.*, eds., *La cité des images*. Paris: Fernand Nathan, 1984, pp. 49–54.

Dyson-Hudson, R. and R. Van Dusen. "Food Sharing Among Young Children," *Ecology of Food and Nutrition*, 1 (1972), 319–24.

Earle, A. M. *Child Life in Colonial Days*. New York: Macmillan, 1915.

Eckstein, E. F. *Food, People and Nutrition*. Westport, Conn.: AVI, 1980.

Edwardes, M. *Everyday Life in Early India*. London: Batsford, 1969.

Elias, N. *The Civilizing Process*. Vol 1: *The Development of Manners*, (1939). Trans. by E. Jephcott. New York: Urizen, 1978.

————. *The Civilizing Process*. Vol. 2: *Power and Civility* (1939). Trans. by E. Jephcott. Oxford: Basil Blackwell, 1982.

————. *The Court Society* (1969). Trans. by E. Jephcott. Oxford: Basil Blackwell, 1983.

Emerson, R. W. *Works*. "Manners," Vol. iii, pp. 115–50; "Behavior," Vol. vi, pp. 161–89. Boston and New York: Houghton Mifflin, 1860.

Emery, J. *European Spoons Before 1700*. Edinburgh: John Donald, 1976.

Encyclopédie ou Dictionnaire raisonné des sciences, des arts et des métiers. Articles: "Civilité, politesse, affabilité," Vol. 3, and "Politesse," Vol. 12. Paris, 1753, 1768.

Erasmus, Desiderius. *De civilitate morum puerilium libellus*. Froben, Bâle, 1530. Trans. by B. McGregor, in *Literary and Educational Writings*, Vol. 25 of *Collected Works of Erasmus*, ed. by J. K. Sowards. Toronto: University of Toronto Press, 1985.

Evans, H. and M. *The Party That Lasted 100 Days. The Late Victorian Season: A Social Study*. London: Macdonald and Janes, 1976, pp. 69–75.

Farb, P. and G. Armelagos. *Consuming Passions*. Boston: Houghton Mifflin, 1980.

Faujas de Saint Fond, B. *Voyage en Angleterre, en Ecosse et aux Iles Hébrides*. 2 vols.. Paris: H. J. Hansen, 1797 (The voyage was made in 1784).

Feeley-Harnik, G. *The Lord's Table*. Englewood Cliffs, N.J.: Prentice-Hall, 1981.

Feild, R. *Irons in the Fire*. Marlborough, Wilts: Crowood, 1984, Ch. 7.

Fenton, A. and E. Kisbán, eds., *Food in Change*. Edinburgh: John Donald, 1986.

—— and Owen, T. M., eds., *Food in Perspective*. Edinburgh: John Donald, 1981.

Février, P-A. "A propos du repas funéraire: culte et sociabilité," *Cahiers archéologiques*, 26 (1977), 29–45.

Fielding, H. "An Essay on Conversation" (1743). *The Complete Works of Henry Fielding*. Vol. XIV. New York: Frank Cass, 1967, pp. 245–77.

Finkelstein, J. *Dining Out*. Oxford: Polity Press, 1989.

Firth, R. W. *We, the Tikopia*. London: Allen and Unwin, 1936.

——. *Symbols Public and Private*. London: Allen and Unwin, 1973.

Fischler, C. "Gastro-nomie et gastro-anomie," *Communications*, 31 (1979), 189–210.

——. "Food Habits, Social Change and the Nature/Culture Dilemma," *Social Science Information*, 19 (1980), 937–53.

Fisher, M. F. K. *Here Let Us Feast. A Book of Banquets*. San Francisco: North Point, 1986 (first published 1946).

——. *The Art of Eating*. New York: Macmillan, 1990 (first published 1937–54).

Fitzgerald, C. P. *The Tower of Five Glories*. London: Crescent Books, 1941, Ch. 9.

Flacelière, R. *Daily Life in Greece at the Time of Pericles*. Trans. by P. Green. London: Weidenfeld and Nicolson, 1965.

Flandrin, J-L. "La diversité des goûts et des pratiques alimentaires en Europe du XVIe au XVIIe siècle." *Revue d'histoire moderne et contemporaine*, 30 (1983), 66–83.

——. "Boissons et manières de boire en Europe du XVIe au XVIIIe siècle," in M. Milner and M. Châtelain, eds., *L'Imaginaire du vin*. Marseilles: Jeanne Laffitte, 1983.

————. "La Distinction par le goût," in P. Ariès and G. Duby, eds., *Histoire de la vie privée*. Vol. 3. Paris: Seuil, 1986, pp. 266–309.

————. "Pour une histoire du goût," *L'Histoire*, 85 (1986), 12–19.

Forsyth, D. W., "The Beginnings of Brazilian Anthropology: Jesuits and Tupinamba Cannibalism," *Journal of Anthropological Research*, 39 (1983), 147–78.

Fortes, M. and S. L. "Food in the Domestic Economy of the Tallensi," *Africa*, 9 (1936), 237–76.

Frake, C. O. "How to Ask for a Drink in Subanun," in *Language and Cultural Description*. Stanford, Calif.: Stanford University Press, 1980.

Franklin, A. *La Cuisine. La Vie privée d'autrefois*. Vol. V. Paris: Plon, 1888.

————. *Les Repas. La Vie privée d'autrefois*. Vol. VI. Paris: Plon, 1889.

————. *Variétés gastronomiques. La Vie privée d'autrefois*. Vol. XI. Paris: Plon, 1891.

————. *La Civilité, l'étiquette, la mode, le bon ton du XIIIe au XIXe siècle*. 2 vols. Paris: Emile-Paul, 1908, Chs. 3, 5.

Freed, S. A. "Caste Ranking and the Exchange of Food and Water in a North Indian Village," *Anthropological Quarterly*, 43 (1970), 1–13.

Freud, S. *The Psychopathology of Everyday Life* (1901). Trans. by A. Tyson. New York: W. W. Norton, 1965.

Furnivall, F. J. *Early English Meals and Manners*. London: N. Trübner, 1868. Repr. Detroit: Singing Tree, 1969.

————. *The Babees' Book*. London: Chatto and Windus, 1908.

Garine, I. de. "The Sociocultural Aspects of Nutrition," *Ecology of Food and Nutrition*, 1 (1972), 143–63.

————. "Food, Tradition, and Prestige," in D. Walchner, N. Kretchmer, and H. L. Barnett, eds., *Food, Man and Society*. New York: Plenum Press, 1976.

Garrisson, J. "D'où viennent nos manières de table?" *L'Histoire*, 71 (1984), 54–59.

Gasperini, B. *Il galateo di Brunella Gasperini*. Milan: Sonzogno, 1975.

Gast, M. "Partage de la viande à Idélès," *Libyca*, 11 (1963), 235–44.

Gaster, T. H. *Customs and Folk-ways of Jewish Life*. New York: W. Sloane, 1955.

Gauthier, P. "Notes sur l'étranger et l'hospitalité en Grèce et à Rome," *Ancient Society*, 4 (1973), 1–21.

Geertz, C. *The Religion of Java*. London: The Free Press of Glencoe, 1960.

Giegher, M. *Li tre trattati*. Padua: Paolo Frambotto, 1639.

Gille, B. *Comment vivre chez les anglais*. Paris: Gigord, 1981.

Gillet, P. *Par mets et par vins. Voyages et gastronomie en Europe, XVIe–XVIIIe siècle*. Paris: Payot, 1985.

Girard, R. *La Violence et le sacré*. Paris: Grasset, 1972.

Girouard, M. *Life in the English Country House*. New Haven, Conn.: Yale University Press, 1978.

Glasse, R. "Cannibalism in the Kuru Region of New Guinea," *Transactions of the New York Academy of Sciences*, 29 (1967), 748–54.

Glixelli, S. "Les Contenances de Table," *Romania*, 47 (1921), 1–40.

Gloag, J. *The Chair*. South Brunswick, N. J. and New York: A. S. Barnes, 1964.

Goffman, E. *The Presentation of Self in Everyday Life*. Garden City, N.Y.: Doubleday, 1959.

———. *Behavior in Public Places*. New York: Free Press, 1963.

———. *Interaction Ritual*. New York: Anchor Books, 1967.

———. *Relations in Public*. New York: Basic Books, 1971.

Gofton, L. "The Rules of the Table: Sociological Factors Influencing Food Choice," Ch. 7 in C. Ritson, L. Gofton, and J. McKenzie, eds., *The Food Consumer*. Chichester, W. Sussex: John Wiley, 1986.

Goody, J. *Death, Property and the Ancestors*. Stanford, Calif.: Stanford University Press, 1962.

———. *Cooking, Cuisine and Class*. Cambridge: Cambridge University Press, 1982.

Gottschalk, A. *Histoire de l'alimentation et de la gastronomie depuis la préhistoire jusqu'à nos jours*. (2 vols.) Paris: Hippocrate, 1948.

Goudeau, E. *Paris qui consomme*. Paris: Henri Béraldi, 1893.

Gould, J. "HIKETEIA," *The Journal of Hellenic Studies*, 93 (1973), 74–103.

Gourarier, Z., et al. *Les Français et la table*. Paris: Musée national des arts et traditions populaires. Editions de la Réunion des musées nationaux, 1985.

Gourarier, Z. "Convivialité et civilité," in *La Table et le partage*. Rencontres de l'Ecole du Louvre. Paris: La Documentation française, 1986.

Greenewalt, C. H. Jr. *Ritual Dinners in Early Historic Sardis*. Berkeley, Calif.: University of California Press, 1978, esp. Part IV.

Greer, W. R. "Table Manners: A Casualty of Changing Times," *New York Times*, October 16, 1985, C 1, 10.

Grimod de la Reynière, A. B. L. *Le Manuel des Amphitryons* (1808). Paris: Métailié, 1983.

Grottanelli, C. "Notes on Mediterranean Hospitality," in *Dialoghi di Archeologia*, 9–10 (1976-77), 186–94.

———— and N. R. Parise, eds., *Sacrificio e società nel Mondo Antico*. Bari, Italy: Laterza, 1988.

Grover, K., ed., *Dining in America 1850–1900*. Amherst, Mass.: University of Massachusetts Press, 1987.

Gruber, A-C. "Les décors éphémères de la table aux XVIIe et XVIIIe siècles," *Gazette des Beaux-Arts*, June 1974, 285–98.

Guazzo S. *La civil conversazione* (1574). Trans. by G. Pettie and B. Young, 1581, 1586: *The Civile Conversation of M. Steeven Guazzo*. London: Constable, 1925 (2 vols.), esp. Book 4.

Gullestad, M. "Meals," in *Kitchen-Table Society*. Oslo: Universitetsforlaget 1984, 109–113.

Gusfield, J. R. "Passage to Play: Rituals of Drinking Time in American Society," in M. Douglas, ed. *Constructive Drinking*. Cambridge: Cambridge University Press, 1987.

Hackwood, F. W. *Inns, Ales, and Drinking Customs of Old England*. London: Fisher Unwin, 1909.

————. *Good Cheer: The Romance of Food and Feasting*. London: Fisher Unwin, 1911. Repr. Detroit: Singing Tree, 1968.

Hall, E. T. "The Anthropology of Manners," *Scientific American*, 192 (April 1955), 84–90.

————. *The Silent Language*. Garden City, N.Y.: Doubleday, 1959.

Halsband, R. *The Life of Lady Mary Wortley Montagu*. Oxford: Clarendon Press, 1956.

Hammel, E. A. "Sexual Symbolism in Flatware," *Kroeber Anthropological Society Papers*, 37 (1967), 23–29.

Hampson, J. *The English at Table*. London: Collins, 1944.

Handy, W. M. *The Science of Culture*. Garden City, New York: Doubleday, 1923.

Hankins, J. E. "Caliban, the Bestial Man," *Publications of the Modern Language Association of America*, 62 (1947), 793-801.

Harner, M. *The Jívaro, People of the Sacred Waterfalls*. Garden City, New York: American Museum of Natural History, Doubleday/ Natural History Press, 1972.

———. "The Ecological Basis for Aztec Sacrifice," *American Ethnologist*, 4 (1977), 117–35.

Harper, E. B. "Ritual Pollution as an Integrator of Caste and Religion," *Journal of Asian Studies*, 23 (1964), 151–97.

Harris, M. *Cannibals and Kings: The Origins of Cultures*. New York: Random House, 1977.

———. *Good to Eat*. New York: Simon and Schuster, 1985.

Hawley, D. *Courtesies in the Trucial States*. Beirut: Khayats, 1965.

———, ed. *Debrett's Manners and Correct Form in the Middle East*. London: Debrett's Peerage, 1984.

Head, F. B. "The Dinner," in *Bubbles from the Brunnens of Nassau*. London: John Murray, 1835, pp. 68–80.

Headland, I. T. *Home Life in China*. London: Methuen, 1914, pp. 178–80.

Heal, F. "The Idea of Hospitality in Early Modern England," *Past and Present*, 102 (1984), 66–93.

———. *Hospitality in Early Modern England*. Oxford: Clarendon Press, 1990.

Hellmann, E. "Urban Native Food in Johannesburg," *Africa*, 9 (1936), 277–90.

Heltzel, V. B. "Chesterfield and the Anti-Laughter Tradition," *Modern Philology*, 26 (1928), 73–90.

Henisch, B. A. *Fast and Feast: Food in Medieval Society*. University Park, Pa.: Pennsylvania State University Press, 1976.

Herodotus (5th century B.C.). *The Histories*. Trans. by A. de Sélincourt. Harmondsworth, Middx.: Penguin Books, 1954.

Hewes, G. W. "World Distribution of Certain Postural Habits," *American Anthropologist*, 57 (1955), 231–44.

Hing L. M., G. M. Caotorta, and S. T. Hsi. *Step by Step Chinese Cooking*. London: Century, 1983, pp. 313–14.

Hoban, R. *Dinner at Alberta's*. New York: Crowell, 1975.

Hodgkin, J. "Tearmes of a Keruer," *Transactions of the Philological Society* (1911), 52–94, 123–37.

Hodous, L. *Folkways in China*. London: A. Probsthain, 1929, Ch. 13.

Hoffmann, H. *Strüwwelpeter, or Merry Stories and Funny Pictures* (1876). London: Blackie and Son, 1922.

Homer (8th century B.C.). *The Iliad*. Trans. by R. Fagles. New York: Viking/Penguin, 1990.

———. *The Odyssey*. Trans. by R. Fitzgerald. New York: Anchor Books, 1963.

Honigmann, J. J. *Foodways in a Muskeg Community: An Anthropological Report on the Attawapiskat Indians*. Ottawa: Northern Co-ordination Research Centre, 1961.

Hope, A. *A Caledonian Feast*. London and Glasgow: Grafton, Collins, 1987.

Horatius Flaccus (1st century B.C.). *Satires*, II. viii. Trans by H. R. Fairclough, Loeb Classical Library. Cambridge, Mass.: Harvard University Press, 1966.

Howe, B. "Decorating the Victorian Dinner Table," *Country Life*, January 7, 1960, 1–11.

Hubert, A. *L'Alimentation dans un village Yao de Thailande du nord: "de l'au-delà à la cuisine."* Paris: C.N.R.S., 1985.

Hudson, K. and J. Pettifer. *Diamonds in the Sky: A Social History of Air Travel*. London: Bodley Head, 1979.

Hughes, G. B. "The Old English Banquet," *Country Life*, 117, February 17, 1955, 473–75.

Hulme, P. *Colonial Encounters: Europe and the Native Caribbean*. London and New York: Methuen, 1987.

Humphrey, T. and L. T. *"We Gather Together": Food and Festival in American Life*. Ann Arbor, Mich.: University Microfilms Inc. Research Press, 1988.

Humphry, Mrs. *Manners for Men*. Exeter: Webb and Bower, 1897.

———. *Manners for Women*. London: James Bowden, 1897.

Isaac, E. "Myths, Cults and Livestock Breeding," *Diogenes*, 41 (1963), 70–93.

Isaac, G. L. "Food Sharing and Human Evolution," *Journal of Anthropological Research*, 34 (1978), 311–25.

————. "The Food-Sharing Behavior of Protohuman Hominids," *Scientific American*, 238 (April 1978), 90–108.

Isaacs, J. *Bush Food: Aboriginal Food and Herbal Medicine*. Sydney: Weldons, 1987.

Izard, C. E. *The Face of Emotion*. New York: Appleton-Century-Crofts, 1971.

Jackson, A. V. W. *Persia Past and Present*. New York: Macmillan, 1906.

James, E. O. *Christian Myth and Ritual. A Historical Study*. Gloucester, Mass.: Peter Smith, 1973 (first published 1937).

Japanese National Commission for UNESCO. *Japan: Its Land, People and Culture*. Tokyo: Ministry of Finance, 1958, pp. 911–19.

Jastrzebowska, E. "Les scènes de banquet dans les peintures et les sculptures chrétiennes des IIIe et IVe siècles," *Recherches augustiniennes*, 14 (1979), 3–90.

Jeaffreson, J. C. *A Book About the Table*. 2 vols. London: Hurst and Blackett, 1875.

Jeanneret, M. *Des mets et des mots*. Paris: José Corti, 1987.

Jefferson, T. "Etiquette" (1803) in H. A. Washington, ed., *The Writings of Thomas Jefferson*. New York: Derby 1861, Vol. 9, pp. 454–55.

Johnsson, M. *Food and Culture Among Bolivian Aymara. Symbolic Expressions of Social Relations*. Stockholm: Almqvist and Wiksell, 1986.

Juvenal (1st–2nd century A.D.). *The Satires*, in *Juvenal and Persius*, trans. by G. G. Ramsay, Loeb Classical Library. London: Heinemann, 1950.

Kahn, M. *Always Hungry, Never Greedy: Food and the Expression of Gender in a Melanesian Society*. Cambridge: Cambridge University Press, 1986.

Kanafani, A. S. *Aesthetics and Ritual in the United Arab Emirates*. Beirut: American University of Beirut, 1983.

Karp, I. "Beer Drinking and Social Experience in an African Society," in I. Karp and C. S. Bird, eds., *Explorations in African Systems of Thought*. Bloomington, Ind.: Indiana University Press, 1980.

Kasson, J. F. "Civility and Rudeness: Urban Etiquette and the Bourgeois Social Order in Nineteenth-Century America," *Prospects*, 9 (1984), 143–67.

———. "Rituals of Dining: Table Manners in Victorian America," in K. Grover, ed., *Dining in America 1850–1900*.

———. *Rudeness and Civility: Manners in Nineteenth-Century Urban America*. New York: Hill and Wang, 1990.

Katzman, D. M. *Seven Days a Week*. New York: Oxford University Press, 1978, esp. Ch. 7.

Kawai, M. "Newly Acquired Precultural Behavior of the Natural Troop of Japanese Monkeys on Koshima Islet," *Primates*, 6 (1965), 1–30.

Kearney, M. "The Social Meaning of Food Sharing in Mexico," *Kroeber Anthropological Society Papers*, 43 (1970), 32–41.

Khare, R. S. *Culture and Reality*. Simla: Indian Institute of Advanced Study, 1976.

King, H. "Food as Symbol in Classical Greece," *History Today* (September 1986), 35–39.

Kirkwood, K. P. *The Diplomat at Table*. Metuchen, N.J.: The Scarecrow Press, 1978.

Kirwan, A. V. *Host and Guest*. London: Bell and Daldy, 1864.

Knight, F. W. *The Caribbean*. Oxford: Oxford University Press, 1978.

Knutson, A. L. "The Meaning of Food," in A. L. Knutson, ed., *The Individual, Society, and Health Behavior*. New York: Russell Sage Foundation, 1965.

Koenig, J. *New Testament Hospitality*. Philadelphia: Fortress, 1985.

Kondo, D. "The Way of Tea: A Symbolic Analysis," *Man*, 20 (1985), 287–306.

Kottak, C. P. "Ritual at McDonald's" in M. Fishwick, ed., *Ronald Revisited: The World of Ronald McDonald*. Bowling Green, Ohio: Popular Culture Press, 1983 (first published 1978).

Krumrey, H-V. *Entwicklungsstrukturen von Verhaltensstandarden (1870–1970)*. Frankfurt: Suhrkamp, 1984.

Labat, J-B. *Voyage aux îles de l'Amérique* (1693–1705). Paris: Séghers, 1979.

La Bruyère, J. de. "De l'Homme" (1688), in *Oeuvres complètes*, ed. A. Chassang. Vol. I. Paris: Garnier, 1876.

Lair, M. *A la fortune du pot*. Paris: Acropole, 1989.

La Marche, O. de. *Mémoires d'Olivier de La Marche, maître d'hôtel et capitaine des gardes de Charles le Téméraire*. 4 vols. Ed. by H. Beaune and J. d'Arbaumont. Paris: Renouard, 1885, Vol. 3.

Lamb, C. *The Chinese Festive Board*. Hong Kong: Vetch and Lee, 1935. Third edition, 1970.

Lane, E. W. *An Account of the Manners and Customs of the Modern Egyptians*. London: John Murray, 1871.

Lange, F. *Manger, ou les jeux et les creux du plat*. Paris: Seuil, 1975.

La Salle, J-B de. *Les règles de la bienséance et de la civilité chrétienne* (1713, 1729). Rouen, 1782.

Lasne, S. and A. P. Gaultier. *A Dictionary of Superstitions*, trans. by A. Reynolds. Englewood Cliffs, N.J.: Prentice-Hall, 1984.

Latham, J. *The Pleasure of Your Company*. London: A. and C. Black, 1972.

Lattimore, O. *High Tartary*. Boston: Little, Brown, 1930.

Laughlin, C. D., Jr., and J. McManus. "Mammalian Ritual," in E. G. D'Aquili, *et al.*, eds., *The Spectrum of Ritual*.

Laurioux, B. "Le Mangeur de l'an Mil," *L'Histoire*, 73 (1984), 90–91.

Lautman, F. "Pas de fête sans repas!" in *La Table et le partage*. Rencontres de l'Ecole du Louvre. Paris: La Documentation française, 1986.

Laver, J. *The Age of Optimism: Manners and Morals 1848–1914*. London: Weidenfeld and Nicolson, 1966, Ch. 6.

Leach, E. "Animal Categories and Verbal Abuse," in *New Directions in the Study of Language*, ed. by E. H. Lenneberg. Cambridge, Mass.: MIT Press, 1964.

Lebault, A. *La Table et le repas à travers les siècles*. Paris: Lucien Laveur, 1910.

Lebra, T. S. *Japanese Patterns of Behavior*. Honolulu: East-West Center Press, 1976.

Le Grand d'Aussy, P. J. B. *Histoire de la vie privée des français depuis l'origine de la nation jusqu'à nos jours*. 3 vols. Paris: Pierres, 1782.

Lehmann, K. "The Dome of Heaven," *The Art Bulletin*, 27 (1945), 22.

Lehne, B. *Süddeutsche Tafelaufsätze vom Ende des 15. bis Anfang des 17. Jahrhunderts*. Munich: Tuduv, 1985.

Leininger, M. "Some Cross-Cultural and Non-Universal Functions, Beliefs, and Practices of Food," in J. Dupont, ed., *Dimensions of Nutrition*. Fort Collins, Colo.: Proceedings of the Colorado Dietetic Conference, 1970, pp. 153–79.

Leslie, E. *Miss Leslie's Behaviour Book* (1853). Philadelphia: T. B. Peterson and Brothers (1859 edition). Repr. New York: Arno, 1972.

Levenstein, H. A. *Revolution at the Table*. New York: Oxford University Press, 1988.

Lévi-Strauss, C. "The Culinary Triangle," *Partisan Review*, 33 (1966), 586–95.

———. *The Origin of Table Manners*, trans. by J. and D. Weightman. New York: Harper and Row, 1978 (first published 1968).

———. "The Principle of Reciprocity," in L. A. Coser and B. Rosenberg, eds., *Sociological Theory*. London: Macmillan, 1969.

Lewin, K. "Forces Behind Food Habits and Methods of Change," in *The Problem of Changing Food Habits*. Bulletin no. 108. Washington, D.C.: National Academy of Science, National Research Council, 1943, pp. 35–65.

Lewis, D. *The Maori*. London: Orbis, 1982.

Lewis, W. H. *The Splendid Century: Life in the France of Louis XIV*. Garden City, N.Y.: Doubleday Anchor, 1957.

Lichtenstein, H. *Travels in Southern Africa in the Years 1803, 4, 5, and 6*, trans. by A. Plumptre. 2 vols. London: H. Colburn, 1812.

Lindberger, Ö. *The Transformations of Amphitryon*. Stockholm: Almqvist and Wiksell, 1956.

Liselotte. *Le Guide des convenances*. Paris: "Petit écho de la mode," 1915.

Lissarrague, F. *Un flôt d'images: Une esthétique du banquet grec*. Paris: Adam Biro, 1987.

——— and P. Schmitt-Pantel. "Partage et communauté dans les banquets grecs," *La Table et le partage*. Rencontres de l'Ecole du Louvre. Paris: La Documentation française, 1986.

Lorenz, K. Z. "Evolution of Ritualization in the Biological and Cultural Spheres," *Philosophical Transactions of the Royal Society of London*, ser. B.: Biological Sciences, 1966, 278–84.

Lorey, E. de and D. Sladen. *Queer Things About Persia*. London: Nash, 1907, pp. 78–85.

Loveday, L. and S. Chiba. "Partaking with the Divine and Symbolizing the Societal: The Semiotics of Japanese Food and Drink," *Semiotica*, 56 (1985), 115–31.

Lovejoy, A. *Primitivism and Related Ideas in Antiquity*. Baltimore: Johns Hopkins University Press, 1934.

Löwdin, P. *Food Ritual and Society Among the Newars*. Uppsala, Sweden: Research Report in Cultural Anthropology, 4, 1985.

Lowenberg, M. E. *Food for the Young Child*. Ames, Iowa: Collegiate Press, 1934, Ch. 4.

————, E. N. Todhunter, and E. D. Wilson. *Food and Man*. New York: John Wiley, 1968, Ch. 3.

Lowie, R. H. *Are We Civilized?* London: George Routledge, 1930, Ch. 6.

Lucian (2nd century A.D.). *Symposium, or The Lapiths*. Trans. by A. M. Harmon. Vol. 1, Loeb Classical Library. London: Heinemann, 1979.

MacCauley, C. "Seminole Indians of Florida," *Annual Report of the Bureau of Ethnology*. Washington, D.C.: Smithsonian Institution, 1883–84, pp. 504–06.

MacDonogh, G. *A Palate in Revolution: Grimod de La Reynière and the Almanach des Gourmands*. London and New York: Robin Clark, 1987.

Mackenzie, O. H. *A Hundred Years in the Highlands*. London: Edward Arnold, 1921.

Macrobius (5th century A.D.). *Saturnalia*. Trans. by P. V. Davies. New York: Columbia University Press, 1969.

Magendie, M. *La Politesse mondaine. Les Théories de l'honnêteté en France au XVIIe siècle, de 1600 à 1650*. 2 vols. Paris: Félix Alcan, 1925.

Mahias, M-C. *Délivrance et convivialité: Le système culinaire des Jaina*. Paris: La Maison des sciences de l'homme, 1985.

Malcolm, N. *Ludwig Wittgenstein, a Memoir*. London: Oxford University Press, 1958.

Malinowsky, B. *The Sexual Life of Savages*. London: Routledge and Kegan Paul, 1982 (first published 1929).

Mallery, G. "Manners and Meals," *The American Anthropologist*, 1 (1888), 193–207.

Manger et boire au moyen age. (Actes du Colloque, October 15–17, 1982), no. 27, 2 vols. Nice: Centre d'Etudes médiévales, 1984.

Marchi, C. *Quando siamo a tavola*. Milan: Rizzoli, 1990.

Marett, R. R. "Food Rites," in E. E. Evans-Pritchard, *et al.*, eds., *Essays Presented to C. G. Seligman*. London: Paul, Trench, Trübner, 1934.

Mars, G. and M. Nicod. *The World of Waiters*. London: Allen and Unwin, 1984.

Marshall, L. "Sharing, Talking, and Giving: Relief of Social Tensions Among !Kung Bushmen," *Africa*, 31 (1961), 231–49.

Marshall, M., ed., *Beliefs, Behaviors, and Alcoholic Beverages*. Ann Arbor, Mich.: University of Michigan Press, 1979.

Martial (1st century A.D.). *Epigrammata*. Trans. by W. C. A. Ker. 2 vols., Loeb Classical Library. London: Heinemann, 1919–20.

Martin, J. *Miss Manners' Guide to Excruciatingly Correct Behavior*. New York: Warner Books, 1982.

———. *Miss Manners' Guide for the Turn-of-the-Millennium*. New York: Pharos, 1989.

Martínez Llopis, M. M. *Historia de la gastronomía española*. Madrid: Alianza, 1989.

Mason, J. E. *Gentlefolk in the Making*. Philadelphia: University of Pennsylvania Press, 1934.

Mason, P. *The English Gentleman: The Rise and Fall of an Ideal*. London: André Deutsch, 1982.

Masters, B. *Great Hostesses*. London: Constable, 1982.

Mauss, M. *The Gift: Forms and Functions of Exchange in Archaic Societies* (1923–24). London: Cohen and West, 1954.

———. "Body Techniques," in *Sociology and Psychology: Essays* (1935). Trans. by B. Brewster. London: Routledge and Kegan Paul, 1979, pp. 95–123.

McAllister, P. A. *Umsindleko: A Gcaleka Ritual of Incorporation*. Grahamstown, South Africa: Institute of Social and Economic Research, 1981.

McCaffree, M. J. and P. Innis. *Protocol: The Complete Handbook of Diplomatic, Official and Social Usage*. Englewood Cliffs, N.J.: Prentice-Hall, 1977.

McCarthy, M. "The Genial Host," in *The Company She Keeps*. New York: Simon and Schuster, 1942.

McDaniel, W. B. "Roman Dinner Garments," *Classical Philology*, 20 (1925), 268–70.

McNeill, F. M. *The Scots Cellar, Its Traditions and Lore*. Edinburgh: Macdonald, 1956.

Meakin, B. *Life in Morocco and Glimpses Beyond*. London: Chatto and Windus, 1905, Ch. 11.

Meek, C. K. *The Northern Tribes of Nigeria*. Vol 1. London: Oxford University Press, 1925.

Meigs, A. *Food, Sex, and Pollution*. New Brunswick, N.J.: Rutgers University Press, 1984.

Mennell, S. *All Manners of Food*. Oxford: Basil Blackwell, 1985.

———. *Norbert Elias*. Oxford: Basil Blackwell, 1989.

Miller, L. *The Encyclopedia of Etiquette*. New York: Crown, 1967.

Mintz, S. W. *Sweetness and Power: The Place of Sugar in Modern History*. New York: Viking Press, 1985.

Mirimonde, A. P. de. *Le langage secret de certains tableaux du musée du Louvre*. Paris: Editions de la Réunion des musées nationaux, 1984.

Monson-Fitzjohn, G. J. *Drinking Vessels of Bygone Days*. London: Herbert Jenkins, 1927.

Montaigne, M. (1533–1592). *The Complete Works of Montaigne: Essays: Travel Journal: Letters*. Trans. by D. M. Frame. Stanford, Calif.: Stanford University Press, 1958.

Moore, H. B. "The Meaning of Food," *American Journal of Clinical Nutrition*, 5 (1957), 77–82.

Moore, S. "Pocket Knives at Table? Whatever Next," *Petits Propos Culinaires*, 16 (1984), 35–41.

Morel, J. "La politesse à table au XVIIe siècle," *Marseille*, 109 (1977), 93–98.

Morris, H. *Portrait of a Chef: The Life of Alexis Soyer*. New York: Macmillan, 1938.

Mowat, F. *The People of the Deer*. Toronto: McClelland and Stewart, 1965, Ch. 7.

Muchembled, R. *L'invention de l'homme moderne*. Paris: Fayard, 1988.

Murcott, A. "On the Social Significance of the 'Cooked Dinner' in South Wales," *Social Science Information*, 21 (1982), 677–95.

———, ed. *The Sociology of Food and Eating*. Aldershot, Hants: Gower, 1983.

Murphy, G. R. "A Ceremonial Ritual: the Mass," in D'Aquili, E. G., et al., eds., *The Spectrum of Ritual*.

Murray, O. "The Symposion as Social Organisation," in *The Greek Renaissance of the Eighth Century B.C.: Tradition and Innovation*, ed. by R. Hägg. Lund: Paul Aströms Förlag, 1983.

————, ed. *Sympotica: A Symposium on the Symposion*. Oxford: Clarendon Press, 1990.

Musil, A. *The Manners and Customs of the Rwala Bedouin*. New York: American Geographical Society, 1928.

Myerhoff, B. *Number Our Days*. New York: Dutton, 1978.

Needham, R., ed. *Right and Left*. Chicago: University of Chicago Press, 1973.

Nenci, G. "Pratiche alimentari e forme di definizione e distinzione sociale nella Grecia arcaica," *Annali della Scuola Normale Superiore di Pisa*, 18 (1988), 1–10.

Netting, R. "Beer as Locus of Value Among the West African Kofyar," *American Anthropologist*, 66 (1964), 375–85.

Newnham-Davis, N. *The Gourmet's Guide to Europe*. London: Grant Richards, 1903.

Nicolson, F. W. "The Saliva Superstition in Classical Literature," *Harvard Studies in Classical Philology*, 8 (1897), 23–40.

Nicolson, H. *Good Behaviour*. London: Constable, 1955.

Noel, N. E. and B. S. McCrady. "Target Populations for Alcohol Abuse Prevention," in P. M. Miller and T. D. Nirenberg, eds., *Prevention of Alcohol Abuse*. New York and London: Plenum, 1984.

Norbeck, E. "A Sanction for Authority: Etiquette," in R. D. Fogelson and R. N. Adams, eds., *The Anthropology of Power*. New York: Academic Press, 1977.

Norman, H. *The Real Japan*. London: T. F. Unwin, 1908.

Nzekwu, O. "Kola Nut," *Nigeria Magazine*, 71 (1961), 298–305.

Okere, L. C. *Anthropology of Food in Rural Igboland, Nigeria*. Lanham, Md.: University Press of America, 1983.

Oman, C. *Medieval Silver Nefs*. Victoria and Albert Museum Monograph no. 15. London: Her Majesty's Stationery Office, 1963.

O'Rourke, P. J. *Modern Manners: An Etiquette Book for Rude People*. New York: Atlantic Monthly Press, 1983.

Ortner, S. B. *Sherpas Through Their Rituals*. New York: Cambridge University Press, 1978.

Orton, A. *Tudor Food and Cookery*. Published privately, 1985.

Pagé, C. *La Coutellerie*. 6 vols. Châtellerault, France: Rivière, 1896–1904.

Palmer, A. *Moveable Feasts*. Oxford: Oxford University Press, 1984 (first published 1952).

Pardailhé-Galabrun, A. *La naissance de l'intime*. Paris: Presses Universitaires de France, 1988, pp. 302–09.

Parnatella, T. B. "Sumptuary Laws and Social Etiquette of the Kandyans," *Journal of the Ceylon Branch of the Royal Asiatic Society*, 61 (1908), 119–28.

Pepys, S. *The Diary of Samuel Pepys* (1660–69). Ed. by R. Latham and W. Matthews, 11 vols. London: G. Bell and Sons, 1970–83.

Petronius Arbiter (1st century A.D.). *Satyricon*. Ed. by K. Müller, Munich: Ernst Heimeran, 1961. (Trans. by W. Arrowsmith, New York: Mentor Books, 1959, pp. 38–84.)

Petropoulou, A. "The Sacrifice of Eumaeus Reconsidered," *Greek, Roman and Byzantine Studies*, 28 (1987), 135–49.

Pick, H. "My Joust with the Lay God," *Manchester Guardian Weekly*, January 7, 1990.

Pin, E. J. and J. Turndorf. *The Pleasure of Your Company*. New York: Praeger, 1985.

Pitt-Rivers, J. "The Law of Hospitality," in *The Fate of Shechem*. Cambridge: Cambridge University Press, 1977.

Plato (4th century B.C.). *Symposium. Platonis Opera*. Vol. 2. Oxford: Clarendon Press. Trans. by M. Joyce in *The Collected Dialogues of Plato*, ed. by E. Hamilton and H. Cairns. New York: Bollingen Foundation, 1961.

Plutarch (1st–2nd century A.D.). *Symposiacs*. Loeb Classical Library: *Moralia*. Vols. 8, 9. Trans. by P. A. Clement and H. B. Hoffleit, Cambridge, Mass.: Harvard University Press, 1936.

———. *Banquet of the Seven Sages*. Loeb Classical Library: *Moralia*. Vol. 2. Trans. by F. C. Babbitt. Cambridge, Mass.: Harvard University Press, 1921.

Porter, K. W. "Humor, Blasphemy and Criticism in the Grace Before Meat," *New York Folklore Quarterly*, 21 (1965), 3–18.

Post, Emily. *Etiquette*. New York: Funk and Wagnall, 1922, then numerous editions to 1975.

Post, Elizabeth. *Emily Post's Etiquette*. New York: Funk and Wagnall, 1984.

Pouillon, J. "Manières de table, manières de lit, manières de langage," in *Fétiches sans fétichisme*. Paris: Maspéro, 1975.

Powdermaker, H. "Feasts in New Ireland: The Social Function of Eating," *American Anthropologist*, 34 (1932), 236–47.

Price, P. V. *Wine: Lore, Legends and Traditions*. Twickenham, Middx.: Hamlyn, 1985.

Pringle, G. *Etiquette in Canada*. Toronto: McClelland and Stewart, 1932.

Proust, M. *A la recherche du temps perdu* (1908–22). 3 vols. Paris: Pleiade. Trans. by C. K. Scott Moncrieff and T. Kilmartin, *Remembrance of Things Past*. London: Chatto and Windus, 1981.

Pückler-Muskau, Prince H. L. H. *Pückler's Progress* (1826–29). Trans. by F. Brennan. London: Collins, 1987.

Pullar, P. *Consuming Passions*. London: Hamish Hamilton, 1970.

Pyke, M. *Technological Eating or Where Does the Fish-Finger Point?* London: John Murray, 1972, esp. Ch. 7.

Quercize, F. de. *Guide des bons usages dans la vie moderne*. Paris: Larousse, 1952.

Quin, P. J. *Foods and Feeding Habits of the Pedi*. Johannesburg: Witwatersrand University Press, 1959.

Rabelais, F. *The Histories of Gargantua and Pantagruel* (1532–64). Trans. by J. M. Cohen, Harmondsworth, Middx.: Penguin Books, 1955.

Radin, P. "The Winnebago Tribe," *Annual Report of the Bureau of Ethnology*. Washington, D.C.: Smithsonian Institution, 1915–16, pp. 318–28, 427–550.

Ranum, O. "Courtesy, Absolutism and the Rise of the French State, 1630–1660," *Journal of Modern History*, 52 (1980), 426–51.

Rasmussen, K. *The Netsilik Eskimos*. Report of the Fifth Thule Expedition, 8 (1931), 1–548.

Rathje, A. "The Homeric Banquet in Central Italy," in O. Murray, ed., *Sympotica*. Oxford: Clarendon Press, 1990, pp. 279–88.

Raum, O. F. *Chaga Childhood*. London: Oxford University Press, 1940.

Read, M. *Children of Their Fathers: Growing Up Among the Ngoni of Nyasaland*. London: Methuen, 1959.

Renfrew, J. *Food and Cooking in Prehistoric Britain: History and Recipes.* English Heritage: Historic Building and Monuments Commission for England, 1985.

———. *Food and Cooking in Roman Britain: History and Recipes.* English Heritage: Historic Buildings and Monuments Commission for England, 1985.

Renner, H. D. *The Origin of Food Habits.* London: Faber and Faber, 1944.

Revel, J. "Les usages de la civilité," in P. Ariès and G. Duby, eds., *Histoire de la vie privée.* Paris: Seuil, 1985, Vol. 3, pp. 168–209.

Revel, J-F. *Un festin en paroles.* Paris: Pauvert, 1979.

Rhodes, H. *Book of Nurture and School of Good Manners* (1550), in F. J. Furnivall, *The Babees' Book*, pp. 126–41.

Rich, Barnabe. *The Irish Hubbub, or the English Hue and Crie* (1617). London: John Marriott, 1619.

Richards, A. I. *Hunger and Work in a Savage Tribe.* London: Routledge, 1932.

———. *Land, Labour and Diet in Northern Rhodesia.* London: Oxford University Press, 1939.

Richter, G. M. A. *The Furniture of the Greeks, Etruscans and Romans.* London: Phaidon Press, 1966.

Riesman, D., R. J. Potter, and J. Watson. "The Vanishing Host," *Human Organization*, 19 (1960), 17–27.

Rigby, P. "Gogo Rituals of Purification," in E. Leach, ed., *Dialectic in Practical Religion.* Cambridge: Cambridge University Press, 1968.

Rochefoucauld-Liancourt, F. de la. *Mélanges sur l'Angleterre* (1784). Ed. by J. Marchand and trans. by S. C. Roberts as *A Frenchman in England 1784.* Cambridge: Cambridge University Press, 1933, pp. 29–34, 240–41.

Root, W. and R. De Rochemont. *Eating in America.* New York: Morrow, 1976.

Rose, G. *A Perfect School of Instruction for the Officers of the Mouth.* London: Bentley and Magnes, 1682.

Rouche, M. "Le banquet des moines au moyen–age," *L'Histoire*, 85 (1986), 71–73.

Rozin, E. *The Flavor-Principle Cookbook.* New York: Hawthorn, 1973.

Rozin, P. "The Selection of Foods by Rats, Humans, and Other Animals," in *Advances in the Study of Behavior*, Vol. 6 (1976), pp. 21 ff., esp. pp. 62–67.

Rubel, P. G. and A. Rosman. *Your Own Pigs You May Not Eat*. Chicago: University of Chicago Press, 1978.

Rudhardt, J. *Notions fondamentales de la pensée religieuse et actes constitutifs du culte dans la Grèce classique*. Geneva: Droz, 1958, pp. 240–48.

Rudofsky, B. *The Kimono Mind*. London: Gollancz, 1965.

———. *Now I Lay Me Down to Eat*. Garden City, N.Y.: Anchor Books, 1980.

Rudskoger, A. *Fair, Foul, Nice, Proper*. Stockholm: Almqvist and Wiksells, 1952.

Rühl, E. *Grobianus in England*. Berlin: Mayer und Müller, 1904.

Russell, J. *The Boke of Nurture, followyng Englondis gise* (1460), in F. J. Furnivall, *Early English Meals and Manners*, and in Furnivall, *The Babees' Book* (modernized English).

Russell, J. G. *The Field of Cloth of Gold: Men and Manners in 1520*. London: Routledge and Kegan Paul, 1969, Ch. 6.

Rye, W. B. *England as Seen by Foreigners*. London: John Russell Smith, 1865.

Saccone, E. "*Grazia, Sprezzatura, Affettazione* in the *Courtier*," in R. W. Hanning and D. Rosand, eds., *Castiglione: The Ideal and the Real in Renaissance Culture*. New Haven, Conn.: Yale University Press, 1983.

Sahagun, B. de. *Florentine Codex: General History of the Things of New Spain. Book 2. The Ceremonies*. Trans. by A. J. O. Anderson and C. E. Dibble. Santa Fe, N.M.: The School of American Research and the University of Utah, 1981.

Sahlins, M. *Stone Age Economics*. Chicago: Aldine-Atherton, 1972, Ch. 5.

———. *The Use and Abuse of Biology*. London: Tavistock Press, 1977.

———. "Raw Women, Cooked Men, and Other 'Great Things' of the Fiji Islands," in P. Brown and D. Tuzin, eds., *The Ethnography of Cannibalism* (1983).

Sanday, P. R. *Divine Hunger*. Cambridge: Cambridge University Press, 1986.

Scappi, B. *Opera*. Venice: Alessandro de' Vecchi, 1622 (1st edition, 1570).

Scheff, T. J. "The Distancing of Emotion in Ritual," *Current Anthropology*, 18 (1977), 483–90.

Schiedlausky, G. *Essen und Trinken. Tafelsitten bis zum Ausgang des Mittelalters*. Munich: Prestel, 1956.

Schieffelin, B. B. *The Give and Take of Everyday Life: Language Socialization of Kaluli Children*. Cambridge: Cambridge University Press, 1990.

Schlesinger, A. M. *Learning How to Behave: A Historical Study of American Etiquette Books*. New York: Cooper Square, 1968 (first published 1946).

Schneider, C. D. *Shame, Exposure and Privacy*. Boston: Beacon Press, 1977.

Schopenhauer, J. *A Lady Travels: Journeys in England and Scotland* (1816). Trans. by R. Michaelis-Jena and W. Merson. London: Routledge, 1988, pp. 153–61.

Schuyler, E. *"Dîner à la Russe 1868,"* *Petits Propos Culinaires*, 28 (1988), 22–27.

Schweinfurth, G. *The Heart of Africa*, trans. by E. E. Frewer. 2 vols. London: Sampson, Low, Marston, Searle and Rivington, 1878.

Schwimmer, E. G. "Feasting and Tourism: A Comparison," *Semiotica*, 27 (1979), 221–35.

Scully, T. "The Mediaeval French *Entremets*," *Petits Propos Culinaires*, 17 (1984), 44–56.

Seabrook, W. B. *Adventures in Arabia*. London: Harrap, 1928.

Sedgwick, C. M. *Letters from Abroad to Kindred at Home*. 2 vols. London: Moxon, 1841.

Sennett, R. *The Fall of Public Man*. New York: Knopf, 1977.

Sévigné, Madame M. de. *Lettres*. Ed. by Gérard-Gailly, 3 vols. Paris: Gallimard, Pleiade, 1953–57.

Shankman, P. "Le Rôti et Le Bouilli: Lévi-Strauss' Theory of Cannibalism," *American Anthropologist*, 71 (1969), 54–69.

Sherwood, M. E. W. *Manners and Social Usages*. New York: Harper, 1897. Repr. New York: Arno, 1975.

Shuman, A. "The Rhetoric of Portions," *Western Folklore*, 40 (1981), 72–80.

Simmel, G. "Soziologie der Mahlzeit," in *Brücke und Tür*. Stuttgart: Koehler, 1957, pp. 243–50.

Simond, L. *Journal of a Tour and Residence in Great Britain (1810–11)*. Edinburgh: George Ramsay, 1815. Vol. 1, pp. 43–50.

Simoons, F. J. *Eat Not This Flesh*. Madison, Wis.: University of Wisconsin Press, 1961.

Sinclair-Stevenson, M. *The Rites of the Twice-Born*. London: Oxford University Press, 1920, pp. 240–47.

Siverts, H., ed. *Drinking Patterns in Highland Chiapas*. Bergen, Norway: Universitetsforlaget, 1973.

Sjögren-de Beauchaîne, A. *The Bourgeoisie in the Dining Room*. Stockholm: Institutet för folklivsforskning, 1988.

Smith, G. R. *Table Decoration Yesterday, Today, and Tomorrow*. Rutland, Vt.: Charles E. Tuttle, 1968.

Smith, J. Z. *Imagining Religion: From Babylon to Jonestown*. Chicago: Chicago University Press, 1982.

Smith, R. E. F. and D. Christian. *Bread and Salt*. Cambridge: Cambridge University Press, 1984.

Smollett, T. *Travels through France and Italy*. 1766. London: Oxford University Press, 1907.

Sokolov, R. "From Platter to Plate," *Natural History*, 6 (1987), 62–63.

Southworth, J. *The English Medieval Minstrel*. Woodbridge, Suffolk: Boydell, 1989.

Sparkes, B. A. "Kottabos: An Athenian After-Dinner Game," *Archaeology*, 13 (1960), 202–07.

Spierenburg, P. *Elites and Etiquette*. Rotterdam: Erasmus Universiteit, 1981.

Staden, H. *The True History of His Captivity 1557*. Trans. and ed. by M. Letts. London: Routledge, 1928.

Staffe, Baronne. *Usages du Monde* (1899). Paris: Flammarion, n.d.

———. *La Maîtresse de maison*. Paris: Victor-Havard, 1892.

Stanhope, P. D., Fourth Earl of Chesterfield. *The Letters of Philip Dormer Stanhope, Fourth Earl of Chesterfield* (1777). Ed. by Bonamy Dobrée. 6 vols. London: Eyre and Spottiswoode, 1932.

Stead, J. *Food and Cooking in 18th Century Britain: History and Recipes*. English Heritage: Historic Buildings and Monuments Commission for England, 1985.

Stein, G. *The Autobiography of Alice B. Toklas*. New York: Vintage Books, 1960 (first published 1933).

Stevenson, H. N. C. "Feasting and Meat Division Among the Zahau Chins of Burma," *Journal of the Royal Anthropological Institution of Great Britain and Ireland*, 67 (1937), 15–32.

Stevenson, M. C. "The Zuñi Indians," *Annual Report of the Bureau of Ethnology*. Washington, D.C.: Smithsonian Institution, 1901–02, p. 369.

Strathern, A. J. "Witchcraft, Greed, Cannibalism and Death: Some Related Themes from the New Guinea Highlands," in M. Bloch and J. Parry, eds., *Death and the Regeneration of Life*.

Strecker, I. *The Social Practice of Symbolization*. London: Athlone Press, 1988.

Strodtbeck, F. L. "The Latent Intellective Factor in the Food Cycle," in N. S. Scrimshaw and J. E. Gordon, eds., *Malnutrition, Learning, and Behavior*. Cambridge, Mass.: MIT Press, 1968, pp. 363–85.

Strong, R. *Splendor at Court*. Boston: Houghton Mifflin, 1973.

Suetonius (1st–2nd centuries A.D.). *De vita Caesarum*. Trans. by J. C. Rolfe, 2 vols. Loeb Classical Library. London: Heinemann, 1935.

Sumner, W. G. *Folkways and Mores*. New York: Schocken Books, 1979.

Swift, Jonathan. "A Modest Proposal . . ." (1729); "A Complete Collection of Genteel or Ingenious Conversation" (1738); "Directions to Servants" (1745), in T. Scott, ed., *The Prose Works of Jonathan Swift, D. D.* 12 vols. London: George Bell, 1908.

Sykes, E. C. *Persia and Its People*. London: Methuen, 1910.

Syrkin, A. Y. "On the Behavior of the 'Fool for Christ's Sake,' " *History of Religions*, 22 (1982), 150–71.

Tambiah, J. "A Performative Approach to Ritual," in *Culture, Thought, and Social Action*. Cambridge, Mass.: Harvard University Press, 1985, pp. 123–66.

Taylor, R. *The Court and Kitchen of Elizabeth Cromwell* (1664). Ed. by M. Liquorice, as *Mrs. Cromwell's Cookery Book*. Peterborough, Hants.: Cambridge Libraries, 1983.

Teleki, G. "The Omnivorous Chimpanzee," *Scientific American*, 228 (January 1973), 32–42.

Thackeray, W. M. *The Book of Snobs*, Chs. 19, 20, in *Miscellanies*. Vol. 4. London: Smith, Elder, 1877.

Thomas, K. *Man and the Natural World: Changing Attitudes in England 1500–1800*. London: Allen Lane, 1983.

Thomas, L-V. "Essai sur la conduite négro-africaine du repas," *Bulletin de l'Institut français de l'Afrique noire*, 2 (1965), 573–635.

Thornton, T. P. *Grobianische Tischzuchten*. Berlin: E. Schmidt, 1957.

——. *Hofische Tischzuchten*. Berlin: E. Schmidt, 1957.

Toffin, G. *Pyangaon, communauté newar de la vallée de Kathmandou: la vie materielle*. Paris: C.N.R.S., 1977, Ch. 4.

Tolles, D. *The Banquet-Libations of the Greeks*. Ann Arbor, Mich.: Edwards, 1943.

Townsend, E. M. *Latin American Courtesy*. Mexico City: Summer Institute of Linguistics, 1961.

Trollope, F. *Domestic Manners of the Americans* (1832). Repr. New York: Vintage Books, 1960.

Trusler, J. *The Honours of the Table . . . with the Whole Art of Carving* (1791). Cork: Daly and Croker, 1804.

——. *A System of Etiquette*. Bath: W. Meyler, 1804.

Turnaturi, G. *Gente Perbene: Cent'anni di Buone Maniere*. Milan: SugarCo., 1988.

Turner, V. *The Forest of Symbols: Aspects of Ndembu Ritual*. Ithaca, N.Y.: Cornell University Press, 1967.

——. *The Ritual Process*. Chicago: Aldine, 1969.

Turney-High, H. H. "The Flathead Indians of Montana," *Memoirs of the American Anthropological Association*, 48 (1937), 129.

——. "The Ethnography of the Kutenai," *Memoirs of the American Anthropological Association*, 56 (1941), 122–25.

Van Baal, J. "Offering, Sacrifice and Gift," *Numen*, 23 (1976), 161–78.

Vanderbilt, A. *Amy Vanderbilt's New Complete Book of Etiquette*. New York: Doubleday, 1967.

Van Otterloo, A. H. "Foreign Immigrants and the Dutch at Table, 1945–1985. Bridging or Widening the Gap?" *Netherlands Journal of Sociology*, 23 (1987), 126–43.

Vennum, T., Jr. *Wild Rice and the Ojibway People*. St. Paul: Minnesota Historical Society Press, 1988.

Verdier, Y. *Façons de dire, façons de faire*. Paris: Gallimard, 1979.

Vergil (1st century B.C.). *Aeneid*, Books 3 and 7. Trans. by H. R. Fairclough, Loeb Classical Library. 2 vols. Cambridge, Mass.: Harvard University Press, 1947.

Vigée, C. "Le partage de la nuit pascale," *La Table et le partage*. Rencontres de L'Ecole du Louvre. Paris: La Documentation française, 1986.

Villa, P., C. Bouville, *et al.* "Cannibalism in the Neolithic," *Science*, 233 (1986), 431–33.

Visser, M. *Much Depends on Dinner*. Toronto: McClelland and Stewart, 1986.

Wagner, P. M. "Food as Ritual," in S. M. Farber, N. L. Wilson, and R. H. L. Wilson, eds., *Food and Civilization*. Springfield, Ill.: Charles C. Thomas, 1966, pp. 60–82.

Walens, S. *Feasting with Cannibals: An Essay on Kwakiutl Cosmology*. Princeton, N.J.: Princeton University Press, 1981.

Walker, T. *Aristology, or the Art of Dining*. London: George Bell, 1835.

Ward, E. *O Raree Show, O Pretty Show, or the City Feast, by the author of The London Spy* (1704). Quoted by J. C. Drummond and A. Wilbraham in *The Englishman's Food*. London: Jonathan Cape, 1939.

Waring, P. *A Dictionary of Omens and Superstitions*. London: Souvenir Press, 1978.

Watson, J. L. "From the Common Pot: Feasting with Equals in Chinese Society," *Anthropos*, 82 (1988), 389–401.

Wecter, D. *The Saga of American Society*. New York: Scribners, 1937, Ch. 5.

Westman, H. O. *The Spoon*. New York: Harper, 1844.

Wheaton, B. K. *Savoring the Past*. Philadelphia: University of Pennsylvania Press, 1983.

Whiffen, T. *The North-West Amazons*. London: Constable, 1915.

White, L. A. "Etiquette," in *The Evolution of Culture*. New York: McGraw-Hill, 1959, pp. 225–31.

White, T. E. "Observations on the Butchering Technique of Some Aboriginal Peoples," *American Antiquity*, 17 (1952), 337–38; 19 (1953), 160–64; 19 (1954), 254–64; 21 (1955), 170–78.

Whiting, B. J. "The Vows of the Heron," *Speculum*, 20 (1945), 261–78.

Whiting, J. W. M. and I. L. Child. *Child Training and Personality: A Cross-Cultural Study*. New Haven, Conn.: Yale University Press, 1953, esp. pp. 69–73.

Widdowson, J. D. A. "Food and Traditional Verbal Modes in the Social Control of Children," in A. Fenton and T. M. Owen, eds., *Food in Perspective*. 1981, pp. 377–89.

Wildeblood, J. *The Polite World*. London: Oxford University Press, 1965.

Wilkinson, J. G. *Manners and Customs of the Ancient Egyptians*. 2 vols. London: Murray, 1978.

Williams, S. *Savory Suppers and Fashionable Feasts*. New York: Pantheon, 1985.

Wilson, C. A. *Food and Drink in Britain from the Stone Age to Recent Times*. London: Constable, 1973.

Wilson, F. M., ed. *Strange Island: Britain Through Foreign Eyes 1395–1940*. London: Longmans, 1955.

Witteveen, J. "The Great Birds," *Petits Propos Culinaires*, 24, 25, 26, 32, 36 (1986–90).

Worde, Wynkyn de. *The Boke of Kervynge* (1508), in F. J. Furnivall, ed., *Early English Meals and Manners*.

Wouters, C. "Informalisation and the Civilising Process," in P. R. Gleichman, *et al.*, eds., *Human Figurations: Essays for Norbert Elias*. Amsterdam: Sociologisch Tijdschrift, 1977.

Wright, L. *Clean and Decent*. London: Routledge and Kegan Paul, 1960.

Wright, T. *A History of Domestic Manners and Sentiments in England During the Middle Ages*. London: Chapman and Hall, 1862.

Xenophon (4th century B.C.). *Symposium*. Trans. by E. C. Marchant, Loeb Classical Library, *Xenophon*, Vol. 4. Cambridge, Mass.: Harvard University Press, 1968.

Yalman, N. "On the Meaning of Food Offerings in Ceylon," in R. F. Spencer, ed., *Forms of Symbolic Action*. Proceedings of the American Ethnological Society Meeting. Seattle: University of Washington Press, 1969, pp. 81–96.

Yanagida, K. *Japanese Manners and Customs in the Meiji Era*. Tokyo: Toyo Bunko, 1969.

Ying-Shih Yü. "Han," in K. C. Chang, ed., *Food in Chinese Culture*.

Young, J. "Chanoyu for the West," *Chanoyu Quarterly*, 1 (1970), 28–38.

Young, M. W. *Fighting with Food*. Cambridge: Cambridge University Press, 1971.

Yudkin, J. and J. C. McKenzie. *Changing Food Habits*. London: MacGibbon and Kee, 1964.

Zumwalt, R. L. "The Return of the Whale," in A. Falassi, ed., *Time Out of Time: Essays on the Festival*. Albuquerque, N.M.: University of New Mexico Press, 1987.

Index

E

I

J